The brief pontificate of John XXIII caused extraordinary changes in both the Catholic Church and the modern world. Without understanding the remarkable man whose long life and complex personality so powerfully shaped both the epochal Council he convened and the *aggiornamento* it effected, neither the current ecumenical dialogue nor the future course the Catholic Church is likely to take can be understood. In this detailed biography, Meriol Trevor places Pope John in the context of his time, dramatizing each important event in his life, and demonstrating how he affected —and was affected by—the history of the last half century.

At the moment of his election in 1958, few people outside the Church knew Angelo Roncalli as anything more than a kindly, unobtrusive man with a country priest's patience and a Bergamese peasant's hardy constitution. Few recognized that "Papa Roncalli" had spent a long, intent, and sometimes painful life deeply involved in the major events of his church, his country, and his age. As a youthful seminarian, he had struggled to overcome the narrow moral and intellectual confinement of the nineteenth-century seminary system; as a young priest, he had embraced the teachings of Leo XIII and had firmly engaged himself in social movements that later developed into the Christian Democratic Party; as a diplomat, he had traveled extensively in Bulgaria, in Turkey, in Greece, in France, gaining experience in international politics; and as Patriarch of Venice, he had devoted himself to a pastoral ministry promoting peace and unity. Long before he became Pope, Angelo Roncalli was profoundly aware of the world around him—aware that it needed to be changed.

In POPE JOHN, Meriol Trevor renders fully both the visionary faith and the deeply felt commitment to social justice that made this extraordinary man one of the central figures of the modern age.

D1108742

POPE JOHN

By Meriol Trevor

IMAGE BOOKS
A Division of Doubleday & Company, Inc.
Garden City, New York

Image Books edition 1968
by special arrangement with Doubleday & Company, Inc.

Image Books edition published October 1968

Nihil Obstat
JOHN M. T. BARTON, S.T.D., C.S.S.

✠ *Imprimatur*
PATRICIUS J. CASEY, *Vic. Gen.*
Westmonasterii, Die 22 December 1966

CONTENTS

On Writing the Life of Pope John

The idea that I should write a Life of Pope John was not my own; but once it had been suggested I could not put it aside. Some months of reading convinced me that though the time had not yet come for an authoritative biography, which could only be based on material not yet available, there was room for a book which would gather together memories of eyewitnesses and much that is scattered through many publications, some of which have only appeared in Italy, and which needs a certain amount of interpretation to readers of other nations.

My aim has been to elucidate the character of Angelo Roncalli through the events of his life and to present him in the context of his time, and especially in relation to the history of the Church in the last sixty or seventy years. Without knowing something of the internal and external conflicts of the Church in this modern world, Pope John cannot be known either. His short pontificate made extraordinary changes in these complex relationships, changes extended by the Council he called; this was no accident. Since Papa Roncalli was an historian by predilection, I hope he would approve this historical approach.

Simplicity was one of the great aims of his life and so I hope he would also approve the attempt to write straightforwardly about him. For at least a century books written about Popes seem to have been a cross between royal biography and fairy-tale hagiography, often told in aggrieved tones by apologists for the Roman See, martyred by the modern world. As a Catholic I believe that the successor of St. Peter is the divinely appointed center of unity for Christ's Church on earth, but this does not commit me to believing that the historical expression of this function has ever been perfect, any more than that the men have been perfect who have sat in the Apostle's seat. Criticism of the policy of past

Popes, and of the instrument of papal policy, the Roman
Curia, so far from implying disbelief in the apostolic office,
is directed by the desire that its true nature should be ever
more clearly understood and find means of exercise better
adapted to the standards of the Gospel and the needs of our
time.

John XXIII was that rare phenomenon: a charismatic
Christian in an hierarchical position. What he did was what
he was; so it is the man we want to know, not the ecclesiastical
functionary. We are lucky in that until he was sixty-three
Roncalli was not a top-ranking Vatican diplomat and even
after he had proved himself a successful Nuncio in postwar
France, he was not a member of the ruling group in Rome.
Consequently his life is more accessible than that of most
Roman prelates and more interesting to the ordinary person.
It may be too soon to present a complete picture: the most
I hope to do is to draw a true outline. Material has been
contributed from several sources, for which I am most grate-
ful, but I alone am responsible for the use made of it. This
book is in no sense official.

One of a crowd of thousands I saw Pope John in St. Peter's
on two April Wednesdays at Easter 1963, only a few weeks
before he died. The sight of his face, so pale it was almost
white, immediately suggested that he was a dying man, yet
his voice interpreted a spirit magnificently alive. He told us,
on the eve of St. Mark, that peace must be made by every one
of us, in our homes, in our work, in the world. This book is an
attempt to tell the story and understand the meaning of the
life of a true peacemaker.

ACKNOWLEDGMENTS

First of all I would like to thank Monsignor Loris Capovilla, Pope John's literary executor, for his encouragement when I visited him at the Vatican and his kindness in answering queries, allowing me to quote from his writings and for sending books I found it difficult to get from England. I would like to thank too Father Henry ten Kortenaar of the Roman Oratory who assisted me so courteously in Rome and in correspondence.

I am extremely grateful to H.E. the Most Reverend Archbishop Igino Cardinale, Apostolic Delegate in England who, as Pope John's Chief of Protocol, worked closely with him during the pontificate. To him I owe the story behind Archbishop Slipyi's release and the Cuba appeal for peace. He gave me details of some of the early incidents of Pope John's reign. Archbishop Cardinale has not read my book and must not be regarded as responsible for any views expressed in it, but it was a privilege and a pleasure to hear about Pope John from someone for whom he is so truly "of happy memory."

Monsignor Thomas Ryan, now Bishop of Clonfert but once secretary to the Apostolic Delegation in Istanbul, who also worked with Pope John in his pontificate, is another to whom I owe the pleasure of listening to personal reminiscence. Bishop Ryan kindly clarified for me the complicated system of ecclesiastical jurisdiction in Istanbul and it was through him I was able to meet the Reverend Austin Oakley, who knew Pope John for nine years while he was in Turkey, as chaplain to the British Embassy and the Archbishop of Canterbury's representative to the Ecumenical Patriarch of Constantinople. I am most grateful to Father Oakley, who wrote a memorandum for me and later added details in conversation and showed me photographs and personal mementos.

Special thanks to Père Louis Bouyer of the French Oratory, who gave me some introductions in France and to Canon E. Berrar of St. Germain des Prés, who wrote me a most interesting letter on Roncalli as Nuncio in Paris; and also to H.E. the Most Reverend Archbishop Bruno Heim, now Apostolic Delegate in Copenhagen, but once secretary to the Nunciature in Paris.

Many, many thanks to all who have helped with advice and assistance of various kinds: to Monsignor Hugh Montgomery, Mrs. Dorothy White, Father Charles Stephen Dessain of the Birmingham Oratory, John Coulson, Madeleine Charles (and William), Mr. Edward Hales and the Most Reverend Archbishop Thomas Roberts S.J.

1 *Sotto il Monte*

Pope John liked to proclaim, even in St. Peter's, that he came from Sotto il Monte—because it was such an insignificant place. When he was Patriarch of Venice he said to a fellow countryman of Bergamo province, "I know where you come from, but you won't know where I come from!" He did not expect anyone to have heard of the hamlet, for it could hardly be called a village, "just two or three handfuls of cottages scattered about," as he said himself. Now, because he was born there, signposts at every corner direct the traveler.

Sotto il Monte really does lie "under the mountain," on the lower slopes of the first steep ridge of hills rising out of the great Lombard plain, the outposts of the Alps. The village is one of the smallest of many clustering on the Isola d'Adda, the triangle of ground islanded between the hills and the rivers of the Adda and the Brembo. The river Adda, which runs down from Lake Como, is the boundary between Bergamo and Milan. Although so close to the ancient and powerful duchy of Milan, Bergamo, which was a free commune in the early middle ages, became the westernmost province of Venice in 1428. Its fortunes remained linked with those of Venice until the unification of Italy. Ecclesiastically it is still linked and when Angelo Roncalli became Patriarch of Venice in 1953, and metropolitan of nine dioceses, he felt that in a true sense he was coming home.

Pope John often quoted from *I Promessi Sposi* (*The Betrothed*), the famous historical novel by Alessandro Manzoni, which is set in seventeenth-century Milan and the country round Lake Como and Bergamo. Manzoni was amused by the local patriotism of the Bergamese; when his hero, the young peasant Renzo, fleeing from injustice, crosses the Adda into the territory of Bergamo, he finds to his disgust that the local people call everyone from Milan fools. Manzoni's tale has a strong nineteenth-century flavor, but it reflects the fact that he, a deeply religious Catholic (reconverted as an adult), was also a liberal whose views were not altogether popular in the Rome of his day. This kind of Christian liberalism, independent of the reactionary trend in Rome under Pius IX, was typical of North Italy and especially of Bergamo, and strongly influenced Angelo Roncalli from his boyhood.

But for his first years even Bergamo, eight kilometers away, was virtually unknown. Sotto il Monte was the whole of his world. Now it is growing, like all the villages, new houses dotted about everywhere, tarred roads and not far away a big cement works with buckets sailing up and down an overhead cable across the hills. But in 1881, when Angelo Roncalli was born, it was a place of dusty lanes and peasants' cottages, solidly walled and tiled but with a ramshackle look owing to the rough beams and lattices of the loggias, or balconies, that ran along at first-floor level, providing extra living space. The few handfuls of houses were gathered in two main groups, at Camaitino on the higher ground, above which stood the old parish church of San Giovanni Battista, and at Brusico on the lower level, where a newer church had been built in the eighteenth century and dedicated to the Madonna: Santa Maria in Brusico.

San Giovanni, the original parish church, built in Romanesque style in the fourteenth century and rebuilt in the early eighteenth, stood so high up on the steep hill that only fifty years after its restoration Santa Maria began to take its place because it was more convenient. The old font was brought down and it was in this font, at Santa Maria in Brusico, that Angelo Roncalli was baptized. As the countryside began to prosper again toward the end of the nineteenth century it was decided to demolish San Giovanni and build a new church at Camaitino. There it stands now, a large pale gray building with a tall campanile and a carillon of loud bells. It was consecrated in 1929 by Archbishop Roncalli, on holiday from his post as Apostolic Visitor in Bulgaria. Of the old church of San Giovanni that Pope John knew as a child, there is left only the tower, which he could see from the window of his little bedroom in the house at Camaitino, rented as a holiday home for many years, where two of his sisters lived till they died in the 1950s. Pope John chose his papal name partly in memory of his father, who was Giovanni Battista, and partly in honor of St. John the Baptist, the patron of the original church of the village where he was born and where, for many years, he had hoped to be buried.

Roncalli was always interested in history, especially local history, and he discovered something about the origins of his own family. They came from the Valle Imagna in the mountain country and he conjectured that the name derived from the *ronchi—roncai* in local dialect—the ridges cut in the hillsides for the culture of vines. The first Roncalli to come to Sotto il Monte, in about 1500, was Martino, known as Maitino, who built himself a house called ever after Ca' Maitino, Casa Martino, Martin's house. When renovations were being made for Angelo Roncalli in the 1920s, frescoes were discovered on what must once have been the exterior wall: of the Madonna and Child, St. Anthony the Abbot and St. Bernardino of Siena. They were carefully preserved and can still be seen inside the house. A coat of arms—a tower on a field of red and white bars—was also discovered and as it seemed likely to have been Martino's, Angelo Roncalli, when he was made a bishop, adopted it as his own; for according to the still-existing medieval custom, bishops bear arms.

In spite of this (doubtful) title to a crest, Pope John was proud of his simple farming ancestry. The word "peasant" has misleading associations in English. The Roncallis were not laborers but tenant-farmers, *mezzadri*, well-established though not well-off. When Angelo Roncalli was Patriarch of Venice a certain Count Roncalli called on him and suggested that they must belong to the same family. "I doubt it," said the Patriarch, "for while your ancestors have always been *conti*, mine have always been *contadini!*" (Counts-countrymen: a typical punning repartee.) On another occasion he remarked that to be a *mezzadro* was one of the best-known ways of staying poor. "There are three ways of ruining yourself: wine, women, and agriculture! My father chose the dullest."

The Roncalli were in fact very poor in Angelo's infancy, but after they moved to La Colombéra in 1891 their industry began to reap a reward and eventually, in 1919, the father and sons bought the land they worked and the house from the owners, the Counts Morlani. Count Morlani had been a good landlord and his brother, a Canon and Prior of Santa Maria Maggiore in Bergamo, assisted Angelo through the seminary.

The head of the Roncalli family, known among the Bergamese as the *Barba* (the Beard), was Zaverio, the elder brother of Angelo's grandfather. He never married but took the lead in all family affairs till he died in 1912 at the age of eighty-eight. Curiously enough, his brother Angelo (Pope John's grandfather) lived exactly the same span: two years younger than Zaverio, he died two years later, in 1914. It was a long-lived clan. Pope John's father, Giovanni Battista, was born in 1854 and lived to be eighty-one; his mother, Maria Mazzola, born the same year as her husband, died four years after him, in 1939. Her widowhood was spent in her son's house, Camaitino, and she died there, but she asked to be buried from La Colombéra, a gesture which Angelo Roncalli, then in Istanbul, understood perfectly. It was the *casa paterna*, the family home.

Pope John was devoted to his parents and kept pictures of them in his bedroom. Old when their portraits were taken, they too have solid, smiling faces. They had thirteen children, of whom ten survived infancy. One who died young was the eldest child, Maria Caterina; born in 1877, she died in 1883. The next two children were also girls, Teresa and Ancilla.

Angelo, the first boy, was born on the morning of November 25, 1881. At that time his parents were living in part of an old house built round a courtyard. It was awkwardly arranged and has been a good deal altered since then. The ground floor, as was usual in the houses of the *contadini*, was partly used for animals and farm gear, but the kitchen was there too. The parents' room, however, was reached by an external flight of nineteen stone steps, outside the gateway to the courtyard. It is now replaced by a wooden stair, still external to the house, but in the courtyard, and under the loggia. This rustic balcony was a useful shelter from sun and rain. Next to the matrimonial bedroom was a little room once used for storing grain, where the girls slept. The rooms had tiled floors and whitewashed walls. There was the solid wooden *letto matrimoniale* (marriage bed), always a prized possession in these country households, but little else.

When Uncle Zaverio heard that the baby was a boy, the family heir, he hurried across to the church of Santa Maria to arrange for the child to be baptized at once. But the parish priest, Don Rebuzzini, was out. Zaverio, who was very devout, knelt down and said all fifteen decades of the rosary and the litany of the Blessed Virgin, ending by promising the Madonna that the baby should be dedicated to her. At that moment, Don Rebuzzini returned. Zaverio went home to fetch the baby, to whom he stood godfather. The sturdy mother got up and came too, with her husband who, during the time of waiting, had proudly gone to register his son and heir. When Angelo Giuseppe was duly baptized in the name of the Father, the Son and the Holy Spirit, Uncle Zaverio carried out his pledge and dedicated him before the statue of the Blessed Virgin Mary. The only other thing that everybody always remembered about that November day was that it was very cold and stormy.

Angelo did not remain the only boy for long. About eighteen months later his brother Zaverio was born, displacing Angelino (as he was called in childhood) from the *letto matrimoniale*. Uncle Zaverio took the little boy into his room, which faced the street in front of the house. Such was the poverty of the family at that time that there was no cradle for the child; he slept in a makeshift bed made out of two benches placed upside down along the wall. What did he care? He was loved and cared for, growing up in this big family. He used to look out of the bedroom window and watch the swallows flying. He trotted about in the yard, looked after by his sister Maria Caterina till she fell ill and died when he was two years old. He used to sit on a low wall and wave a wooden spoon at the passers-by. His mother worked in the fields.

She had many other children. After Zaverio came two more girls, Maria Elisa and Assunta; then two boys, Alfredo and Giovanni Francesco—the latter was just ten years younger than Angelo and was born the year they moved to the new house. Enrica came next; she was to die, unmarried, at the age of twenty-five. Then there was Giuseppe and finally the youngest, Luigi, who was born in 1896 and lived barely two years. In the same house there lived Battista's cousin Luigi with his wife and their children, also eventually ten in number. It was the impossibility of bringing up all these young creatures in such cramped quarters which finally made a removal necessary. The two families separated and Battista's children, with great-uncle, grandfather, and various aunts, moved to La Colombéra. But this was not till November 1891, when Angelino was nearly ten.

His real childhood, then, was lived in the old house round the courtyard, among the brood of cousins. They were very poor, but they had enough to eat, though it was simple fare. Pope John himself said: "There was never any bread on our table, only *polenta*; no wine for the children and young people, and seldom meat; only at Christmas and Easter did we have a slice of homemade cake . . . And yet when a beggar appeared at the door of our kitchen, where the children— twenty of them—were waiting impatiently for their bowl of *minestra* [vegetable soup], there was always room for him, and my mother would hasten to seat that unknown person beside us." He was exaggerating a little the numbers of hungry children, since while the cousins lived together neither family was complete. *Polenta* was a local dish, made of maize flour. At eleven o'clock in the morning the bell of the little friary down the road at Boccanello sounded. "Listen! The Frati's bell!" Marianna Roncalli would say. "Time to put on the water for the *polenta!*" She had no clock. She roused the family at the Angelus bell, saying to her husband: *"Su, dunque, Battista: Angelus Domini nunxiavit Mariae . . ."* ("Come on, Battista: The angel of the Lord declared unto Mary . . .") *Nunxiavit* was her version of *nuntiavit*.

The Franciscans often came into the Roncallis' house on their way to and from Boccanello. The family was faithful to the long tradition of the Church. Years later, on July 15, 1945, the Mayor of Fleury-sur-Loire apologized to the Papal Nuncio for his simple speech, referring to his peasant origins. Angelo Roncalli was delighted to reveal that he too was "a son of the soil" and the fact that the local church was dedicated to St. Benedict prompted him to recall how his father used to tell him and his little brothers that it was the sons of St. Benedict who had come over the mountains a thousand

years ago and taught their forefathers to cultivate the fertile
plains. He was referring to the priory of Sant' Egidio (St.
Giles) founded by the Benedictines of Cluny at Fontanella
del Monte, which lasted from 1080 to 1473. The ancient
church was visible from Sotto il Monte and is now included
in the same municipal district.

Almost the earliest memory in Angelo's mind was of the
little local shrine of the Madonna of Caneve in the woods
near Sotto il Monte. On November 21, the Feast of the
Presentation of the Virgin, the tiny sanctuary was crammed
and children could see nothing. It was the only day it was
open. Angelo's mother picked him up in her arms and standing outside, held him up to a window. Through it, for one
glorious moment, he saw above the altar the picture of the
Virgin. The impression remained deep in his mind and he
always used to go back to pray at the sanctuary of Caneve
whenever he returned to Sotto il Monte. The ancient feast
celebrates the legend that in her youth Mary lived in the
Temple at Jerusalem. Although it has no historical foundation, the legend illustrates the way in which the minds of our
ancestors transformed symbols into events. Mary was to become the temple where the Son of God dwelt and so it seemed
fitting that she should dwell in the temple of God in Jerusalem.

Great-uncle Zaverio was exceptionally devout; he led the
family in reciting the rosary in the kitchen every evening.
(Prayers said with the aid of beads, commemorating mysteries
connected with the events of the Incarnation, Passion, and
Resurrection of Christ.) He read to them from the Meditations of a saintly Spanish Jesuit, Luis da Ponte, translated
into Italian and published in a six-volume edition in 1853.
Zaverio Roncalli also took in the *Salesian Bulletin* and the
Catholic newspapers started in Bergamo just before his great-
nephew was born. It was he who taught Angelino his prayers
and used to take him with him to pray at the local shrines.
The old man's special devotion was to the Sacred Heart of
Jesus and the child learned from him this love for the human
loving-kindness of the Saviour. When, in 1889, Zaverio went
on pilgrimage to Rome, Angelino wanted to go too. It was
much too far, but his father took him instead to a gathering

of Catholic Action contingents at Ponte San Pietro, the nearest small town in the opposite direction from Bergamo. It seemed vast to the child and he thought the church, all gilded and full of people singing, was the great St. Peter's of Rome! So that he could see the procession his father hoisted him on his shoulders. A lifetime away and the small boy, grown old, was lifted up in the *sedia gestatoria* of St. Peter's itself. Afterward, Pope John told an audience of people from Bergamo and Venice, that it had reminded him of that time, long ago, when he had been lifted up on the shoulders of his father, as he now was on the shoulders of his sons. "We must let ourselves be carried by the Lord," he said then.

By the time he was five Angelino was going to Mass not only on Sundays but often on weekdays as well, with the adults of the family. Shoes and best clothes for Sunday churchgoing had to last for years and years. Angelino was soon an altar server and whenever there was a baptism he wanted to hold the salt and the candle for the priest. The church was only a little way down the road; the child could see it from the window of the room he shared with Uncle Zaverio. Years later, asked about his vocation to the priesthood, he said that perhaps it had come to him as he watched the village women respectfully saluting Don Rebuzzini as he went into the church. Pope John may have had his tongue in his cheek when he suggested that he wanted to be a priest because it was so obviously the most revered position in his little world. As Pope, in March 1963, the last year of his life, he presided at the beatification of a holy priest of the diocese of Bergamo, Luigi Palazzolo, who had died when he was only four years old. But he could remember Don Rebuzzini announcing it from the pulpit: "Don Luigi Palazzolo is dead. He was a saint . . ." To be a priest was evidently the way to be a saint.

Pope John used to say that he only told two lies in his childhood, and one was to Don Rebuzzini. He had been sent off to Boccanello to hear the preacher at "the pardon of Assisi"—the Franciscan indulgence, to be gained on August 2. But Angelino never got there; he played in the country instead. When he came back the parish priest asked him if the Frate had preached and he said yes. "Was he wearing a cotta?" asked Don Rebuzzini. "Yes," said Angelino, giving himself away, since friars do not wear cotta or surplice to preach. Pope John told this story to his nephew, Giovanni Battista Roncalli, now a Canon of Bergamo cathedral, and he ended it with a phrase in dialect: *"Chèla còta del Frà la m'à imbroiàt."* ("That Friar's cotta got me into trouble.")

His other lie was self-betrayed too. One day his mother heard the bell for Mass and hastily pushed a basket of dried figs under the bed. While she was out Angelino found them and took one, and then another . . . and when he was stuffed, covered them up again. His mother came back. "Angelino, have you been eating the figs?" *"Io, no!"* he said innocently. "Me? No!" Two hours later he had such dreadful pains in the stomach that he never afterward cared for dried figs.

Angelo's favorite playmate was a little girl cousin. They were always up to something. One day, for a joke, they went into a house and ran upstairs and peeped into a room. There on a bed was an old woman lying dead with her mouth open and one fang of a tooth showing. Horror-struck the two children turned tail and ran helter-skelter down the stairs again.

Angelo told this little cousin that he wanted to be a priest. It was his own idea. No one in the family had suggested it to him. Indeed, the idea of a penniless country boy going to a seminary was as unlikely as his going to a secondary school. Besides, Angelo was the eldest boy and would be wanted on the farm. Pope John asserted that neither his parents nor great-uncle Zaverio ever spoke of such a thing. But Don Rebuzzini did not rebuff the little boy. He allowed him to make his first holy communion at the age of six, very young for the custom of those days. This great event took place on a cold morning in the Lent of 1888; there was nobody in the church but the priest, the curate, and the boys and girls. Afterward Don Rebuzzini chose Angelo to write down their names as they enrolled in the Apostolate of Prayer. It was the first writing exercise he remembered doing; he never forgot it because he was so proud to do it.

By this time he had been at school for over a year. He first went when he was nearly six, in October 1887. The school was then in a little house in the district of Camaitino. There were four rows of benches and the children learned their ABCs. The next year they all moved to the new school, built in the district of Bercio. The schoolroom was on the ground floor and the teacher lived above it. Battista Agazzi, known as Battistèl, a boy a little older than Angelino, sat by him at school and remembered long afterward the look of him in his little fustian breeches and braces, with his school pinafore and clogs. Battistèl told Davide Cugini, who has recorded it in his book on Pope John's childhood at Sotto il Monte, that the other boys teased Angelo; they jeered at him, called him *chierichetto* (little cleric) and thought him a fool. At that period the teachers in the state schools were appointed by the government and were often anticlerical. The teacher at Bercio was one of these, and did not stop his tougher pupils teasing little Roncalli.

One day an inspector came and asked the children: "Which weighs the most, a quintal of hay or a quintal of iron?" "A quintal of iron!" they all chanted. But Angelo Roncalli said, laughing, "They weigh the same!" Of course when they got out of school the other boys set on him and he had to run home with Battistèl—the "liberal" teacher looking on, through his monocle, with a mocking stare.

Don Rebuzzini obviously had hopes of Angelo's intelligence. When the boy was seven he sent him to be confirmed, on February 13, 1889, by Bishop Guindani of Bergamo, at Carvico, the next village to Sotto il Monte and a bigger and more coherent place. Later, he asked Don Bolis, the parish priest at Carvico, if he would give Angelo Roncalli lessons in Latin. It was the first test; if he could not learn Latin, Angelo could not be a priest.

Don Bolis was enough to scare most boys off both Latin and the priesthood. He was a big strong man with hands "like the giant Polyphemus" and he used them freely. Every time his pupil made a mistake Don Bolis boxed his ears or slapped his head. Sometimes he made him go and kneel down outside the house. So they studied Caesar's *De Bello Gallico*, blow by blow.

Pope John used to recall the thunderous slaps of his first steps in Latin, with a smile, but he did not approve the method. In the lightly punning style so difficult to translate he said: "If a schoolboy is hit, he must . . . fall (fail). *Si deve spiegare e non . . . spregiare:* one should explain, not condemn; and explain *con l'arte e non con . . . l'artiglio,* with skill, not with claws. *Non ogni colpa merita di essere colpita*—not every fault deserves a flogging. These are the phrases he used to make his point when he was an old man, Patriarch in Venice.

In view of his painful initiation it is surprising that Angelo Roncalli ever came to enjoy Latin, but he did; to the end of his life he was always quoting Cicero, whose humane pre-Christian good sense suited his temperament. Nor did he stop wanting to be a priest, although the thought of dressing in a long cassock and wearing such a tight collar alarmed him. In summer, he used to watch the sweating priests run their fingers round the constricting band of starched linen. Don Rebuzzini, no doubt catching that wide-eyed gaze, used to tease him: "Don't you be a priest, Angelino! Look at our hard collars, how they cut into our necks and hurt us!" But after closer observation the little boy decided that it was not such a torture that he could not get used to it.

A year of Don Bolis's direct method sufficed to gain an entrance for Angelo at the diocesan college at Celana, about five miles away on the other side of the hills. It was too far for the boy to walk both ways every day and so it was arranged that he should board during the week with some relatives of his mother's who lived at Ca' de Rizzi, only about three kilometers from the college. On Mondays he went all the way, and came home to Sotto il Monte on Saturday evenings, carrying his washing for the week. He climbed over the steep hills, going up the path past the old church of San Giovanni, then still standing, where he always stopped to say a prayer. On the way to the college from Ca' de Rizzi he used to meet Pietro Donizetti, whose father was manager of a brickworks, and they went on to school together. Donizetti became a professor in later life.

Angelo started at the college on October 15, 1891, when he was about a month short of ten years old. Celana, which had been founded in the sixteenth century by St. Charles Borromeo, as one of the first seminaries recommended by the Council of Trent, had later become a diocesan college where boys who were going into lay professions, as well as those destined for the priesthood, got their secondary education together in a Catholic foundation. This was an excellent arrangement and in later years Roncalli never spoke of the college with anything but respect and admiration. But as a boy, he was not at all happy there. He was one of the youngest and the others were all from a higher social class. It was the first time he had felt this difference and ten years old is very young to face the pressures of being odd one out in a social group.

To complete his bewilderment he could not grasp the teaching methods, which were not those of Don Bolis. When he was Patriarch of Venice, Roncalli said, "I was no hero at Celana! The professor made me forget what little I had learned already. May he rest in peace! He knew much less about teaching than about Latin."

On top of all the strangeness and difficulties of this new world Angelo had at least six kilometers to walk every day, even to Ca' de Rizzi, and he was not happy there because these relatives were in the midst of a heated litigation over an inheritance. Because of this, his mother finally took him away. He was only two terms at Celana.

As a matter of fact, he was very nearly expelled. He was caught in school with some apples. No food was allowed into class. Angelo said he had bought the apples for some boarders. The master did not believe him, the culprits dared not confess and Angelo would not give them away. Because of this episode and because he had low marks in the half-termly tests, he was to be sent away. The rector wrote a letter to Don Carlo Marinelli, parish priest of San Gregorio and a distant relative who had interested himself in Angelo's vocation, and he gave it to Angelo to deliver. But, guessing what was in it, the boy tore it up on the way. Don Marinelli discovered this but he believed Angelo when he said it had contained an unjust accusation and only gave him a light slap on the head as punishment. He must have explained the situation to the rector, as Angelo did not have to leave in disgrace. But he felt the injustice deeply. As Patriarch of Venice he might joke about apples having been a temptation to man ever since Eve, but he was serious even then when he maintained, "It was an unjust accusation." The two lies of his childhood were long past. Once, as he walked over the hill he saw a pumpkin in a field and thought of the Gospel which told of God's feeding the birds. God had evidently provided the pumpkin for hungry Roncalli boys. So he carried it home. But when Uncle Zaverio met him and sternly demanded, "Who gave you that pumpkin?" he answered truthfully, "Nobody; I picked it myself." The old man, unaware that the boy had thought he was following the teaching of the Gospel, considered it stealing and told him he must take it straight back, but presently relented so far as to allow him to wait till next morning, when he had to take the pumpkin to the farmer who owned the field. "Well, only a pumpkin—you might have kept that," the man said kindly. "But your uncle, he's a wonderful man. He's right to teach you not to take things which are not yours. Give him my regards."

In spite of his unhappy career at Celana, Don Rebuzzini still had confidence in Angelo's vocation and succeeded in getting him into the junior seminary in the town of Bergamo. He was to start in the autumn of 1892.

Meanwhile the great family move to La Colombéra had taken place, in November of the year in which he went to Celana. The house was only about a hundred yards from the other but it was bigger, with eighteen rooms altogether. It needed to be large to accommodate the Roncalli family, who still live there, numerous as ever. Some of Pope John's sturdy little great-nephews must look very much as he did. The house faces into its own yard, walled, with a high iron gate. In Angelo's boyhood it looked less solid than it does now, for the beams of the loggia, then of wood, are now concrete. The renovations were done after the First World War. On the ground floor were the usual farm sheds and the kitchen; later the animals were moved away. There are two stories up above, each with its loggia; from the top there is a view out over the country. Hay was kept on the first floor and grain above; people fitted in as best they could. But Angelo, because he was going to be a priest, had a little room assigned to him as bedroom and study. Up there he used to sing—and not always hymns. He had a good strong musical voice. His family remembered him singing as he came downstairs:

> *"Sul mare luccica*
> *L'astro d'argento . . ."*
>
> (On the glittering sea,
> the silver star . . .)

The vicissitudes of Angelo Roncalli's education in its first stages show two things clearly: the difficulties in the way of a boy from such a simple background ever, at that time, coming out of it; and his determination to be a priest, even when he did not fully understand what priesthood was. A priest was—Don Rebuzzini, the respected father of the village, saying Mass, hearing confessions, teaching the children catechism, always concerned with the things of God, with prayer and holiness. That was what Angelo Roncalli wanted to be and to do. In order to become a priest he had to learn Latin and so he did, in spite of Don Bolis's resounding slaps and the professor at Celana, and the "rich" boys there who, he felt, despised him and yet would not own up when they got him into a scrape. And to be a priest he had to go to a seminary to be trained. And so, aged just eleven, he went.

2 Bergamo: The Seminary

Bergamo is really two towns, almost three, rising one above the other on the spurs of the steep hills, the beginning of the mountain country. The lowest layer is the so-called new town, much of it pleasantly nineteenth-century, with a wide tree-lined central street, though houses, hospitals, and factories are still spreading out into the plain. Arriving on a gloomy evening in torrents of rain, it was a surprise to look out of the window in the night and see, floating floodlit in the darkness above, ancient square towers and the domes of churches.

This was the Città Alta, the ancient walled town, a city indeed so high that the easiest way up is by the funicula.

The narrow streets and cobbled squares of the Città Alta are full of life, by no means drained by the humming modern city below. Bergamo is a true provincial capital and the university, schools of art and music and other centers of cultural activity are suitably situated in the old town. So are the cathedral, the seminary, and the splendid church of Santa Maria Maggiore. There are shops and cafes; in spite of some motorcars the atmosphere is that of an old European town before human intercourse was drowned by mechanical noise. Both towns are attractive but in the Città Alta there is no difficulty in imagining what it was like in the 1890s when Pope John was a boy.

An even steeper funicula climbs to San Vigilio, the highest hump of hill, which is an old-fashioned country suburb, with villas and gardens and places where visitors can eat out of doors, looking on a landscape of valleys and mountains. To one of these, poised above a deep ravine, Toscanini used to take his friends—which shows how close Bergamo is to the world of Milan, for all its Venetian past.

Bergamo's incorporation into the territory of the Most Serene Republic was peaceful and it gave to Venice the services of one of the most famous of the *condottieri*, Bartolommeo Colleoni, whose equestrian statue (one of the first in Europe) still stands near the church of Sts. John and Paul, known to the Venetians as San Zanipolo. But Colleoni was buried in Bergamo; his beautiful, intricately decorated renaissance mortuary chapel is built on to the external wall of Santa Maria Maggiore, contrasting with the ancient little separate baptistry nearby. The Lion of St. Mark is everywhere evident in Bergamo; there are even sturdy little stone lions round the fountain in the central piazza. In 1797, after a brief Napoleonic interlude in the Cisalpine Republic, Bergamo came with all Venetia under the rule of Austria and so remained until this hated yoke was thrown off in 1859, during the campaign for national independence and unity known as the Risorgimento.

A foreign visitor gains an insight into local history and character by looking round the Museum of the Risorgimento,

housed in the medieval castle on the Rocca, the fortress of
the old city. There is a unique relic kept there: the red flag
that followed Garibaldi from Bergamo—with the papal arms in
the center! Bergamo provided Garibaldi with his largest contingent of volunteers; yet the province was staunchly Catholic: *cattolicissima città* was the town's proud nickname, most
Catholic of cities. Garibaldi himself was a tough unbeliever
and Mazzini an intellectual anticlerical, but in the north at
least there were many Catholics who were both patriots and
radicals. This tradition was bred in Angelo Roncalli's bones.

In another part of the museum are tragic memorials of the
partisans of the Second World War, seeking by guerrilla
methods to redeem the fatal error by which Mussolini had
linked Italy's fate with Hitler's National Socialist regime in
Germany. Between these two patriotic campaigns of the community are the records of a local hero of the First World War
and the twenties: the poet-aviator Locatelli. In England at
that time the poets became soldiers, but in Italy they seem to
have taken to the air. Not all poet-airmen were compromised
with the Fascist movement, as was the most famous of them,
Gabriele D'Annunzio. One has only to remember the tragic
fate of Lauro de Bosis, shot down after scattering anti-Fascist
pamphlets over Rome in 1931.

Bergamo, an ancient center of the silk-weaving industry,
has always been renowned for the arts. It was the original
home of the *Bergamasque,* the *Commedia dell'Arte,* our old
friends Harlequin and Colombine, Pantaloon and the rest.
This musical dramatic and humorous tradition is typical of
the people, who love singing and dry wit. Pope John shared
both these characteristics; the quick wordplay, the shrewd
repartee, the pungent aphorism have become famous and no
one who ever heard his fine deep resonant voice will soon
forget it. Humor, especially humor that is kind, has an immediate appeal but Pope John's voice expressed the strength
and depth of personality behind the genial manner that attracted so many.

Bergamo's most famous composer was Gaetano Donizetti,
who was buried in Santa Maria. The city is also known for its
artists and craftsmen; perhaps the most famous today is the
sculptor Manzù, who designed the new door for St. Peter's, on

which there is a fine relief portrait of Pope John. Manzù made other portraits, medals, and a head of the Bergamasque Pope, all wonderfully simple and powerful.

The cathedral of Bergamo and the church of Santa Maria Maggiore stand at right angles to each other and above the porch at Santa Maria is the statue of the city's patron saint, Alexander, mounted on his horse. He was a Roman martyr, about whom little is known. The church, redesigned in the baroque period, is hung with Florentine tapestries and the base of the screen by the choir stalls is ornamented with marvelous panels of marquetry, representing Biblical scenes. On one wall a large medieval fresco of the Last Supper has been uncovered.

The cathedral is less interesting, but a fine church in its way. Originally Romanesque it was rebuilt in the seventeenth century and finally restored in 1886, with some later additions. It is highly decorated in white and gilt and probably looks its best during great ceremonies. There is a side chapel which houses a treasured crucifix. In this cathedral, aged fourteen, Angelo Roncalli watched the consecration of a missionary bishop and was fired anew to dedicate his whole life to God. Later, in the decade before the First World War, he was often in the cathedral with the bishop, Radini-Tedeschi, as his secretary.

The major seminary stands high up in the Città Alta in a corner of the walls, commanding a wide view over the great plain. It is the biggest building in the place and is now being completely rebuilt. Angelo Roncalli went first to the junior seminary, in November 1892. At first he found the lessons very difficult; this was hardly surprising considering the hazards of his earlier education. But he was happy in the atmosphere of a religious school, settled down and began to make progress. On June 24, 1895, when he was still only thirteen, he received the tonsure, the first step to the priesthood, and the clerical habit which he would wear when he went to the major seminary the next November. By then he was considered a promising pupil and had been admitted to the Sodality of the Annunciation of Mary Immaculate, which only the best students were allowed to join. He was given their Little Rules, which he copied into the first of the notebooks which he entitled *Giornale dell' Anima,* spiritual journal, published in English as *Journal of a Soul.*

Some people, opening this book with the shrewd and smiling image of the old Pope in mind, have been alienated by the piety of the seminarian of the 1890s and have wondered how the one could grow out of the other. The Little Rules, of course, were not composed by him. They were designed to train boys in habits of prayer and self-examination and though overloaded with pious practices they contain no severities, no undue emphasis on obedience to superiors or morbid aspirations for expiatory suffering—faults that can be found in other systems of the period. The teaching on "purity," reinforced by the retreat notes that follow, seems entirely negative—not to look at suggestive pictures, or at women, not to listen to improper conversation. But it must be remembered that this attitude was common to most forms of education at that time. The human psyche is remarkably tough and most of that generation, like Pope John himself, seem to have taken in their stride all the taboos and inhibitions and to have survived some sixty years of chaotic change with sanity and humor.

Nevertheless the atmosphere that breathes through the first part of the journal, largely a reflection of the piety of Roncalli's teachers, the fidgetings of conscience over trivial misdemeanors and the emasculated image of sanctity hold up for imitation, may give the impression that the seminary was an ivory tower remote from all reality. In the case of Bergamo this would be misleading, for however old-fashioned about moral training, the clergy were often involved in the new movements of Catholic social action which were the beginning of Christian Democracy in Italy. The seminarians were not directly concerned but they were not unaware of the issues. Bishop Guindani held conferences in the seminary building and even founded a chair of social studies there, an extremely unusual step in those days.

The movement had started after the stalemate between the Pope and the new government of Italy in 1870, when Rome itself followed the fate of the Papal States, seized by Piedmont without the consent of Pius IX, who regarded his temporal possessions as a trust and as a necessity of his office. It was not an article of faith that the Pope's sovereignty must be secured by the ownership of an independent state, but to Pius IX it seemed almost a divine decree. In consequence he forbade Catholics to vote in the new government's elections. To politically conscious Catholics, especially in the north, it seemed impossible that such a situation could last and they decided to organize themselves to prepare for future activity. The first national congress was held at Venice in 1874, the next at Florence the following year, when it was decided to set up a permanent committee. Thus was born *L'Opera dei Congressi*, the nucleus of Christian Democracy in Italy, since from the first it was orientated towards a program of social welfare and an elective system of government.

When Pius IX died in 1878 the directors of the movement hoped that the ban on the elections would be raised, but Leo XIII, so open to liberal ideas in most fields, confirmed it. He maintained that the Italian government had no right to make a unilateral settlement and for this reason refused to accept the Law of Guarantees, which offered a special position, with indemnities, to the papacy as a supranational institution. Leo XIII may have thought the new government would not long survive; he had seen many revolutions come and go during his long life, and he had started his career as a clerical administrator in the Papal States. But United Italy did survive and the working governments, partly in reaction to the papal attitude, became increasingly anticlerical, attacking Church property and religious teaching in schools by means of a series of laws which the Catholics were powerless to oppose.

But Leo did not ban the municipal elections and so it came about that many important local positions were held by Catholics; in Bergamo, almost all. Bergamo was the native province of one of the organizers of *L'Opera dei Congressi*, Count Medolago-Albani, and it became the home of Nicolo Rezzara, a professor of economics who devoted his life to the movement. It was in Bergamo that he started two of the first papers to reflect its aims: the daily newspaper *L'Eco di Bergamo* in 1880, and five years later the weekly *Il Campanone*, which he edited himself. These were the papers old Zaverio Roncalli read to the family. At the seminary the students were forbidden to read newspapers, even the *Eco*, and this caused

Angelo some crises of conscience in the vacation, since Don
Rebuzzini wanted to discuss its contents with him. Angelo
Roncalli remained ever faithful to *L'Eco di Bergamo* and
had it sent to him in Turkey, though more for the local news
than for political comment at that period, when Fascism was
in power.

Guindani was made bishop of Bergamo by Leo XIII and
supported the aims of *L'Opera dei Congressi*. Under his
guidance clergy and laity worked together on social projects.
Rural banks, communal kitchens and dairies, winegrowers'
societies and insurance schemes were started; by 1895 there
were fifty-four associations for assistance and forty-four for
credit, production and insurance. There were already 42,000
members in the province. This co-operative welfare network
assisted families like the Roncalli to rise above the subsistence
level at which they had been living during Angelo's childhood, to the modest, hard-working prosperity of later years.
The organization annoyed the anticlerical liberals since they
thought it reinforced clerical power. But in fact the Christian
Democratic movement was to provide a way out of the impasse between clerical and anticlerical, though it was long
enough before either side recognized this.

So the diocese of Bergamo was not a backwater but a center
of social and political activity, even though this was not reflected in Angelo Roncalli's spiritual journal. There is almost
nothing in it concerning the development of his general ideas,
his interest in history or his opinions on Church and State—
he had them, because he continually accused himself of airing
them too frequently! But for the year 1898, when he was
sixteen, the entries are sufficiently numerous to provide some
kind of picture of his feelings, almost in the manner of an
ordinary journal. Canon Luigi Isacchi, his spiritual director,
encouraged this introspective habit.

The year's notes do not begin very promisingly for the
modern reader. "February 27, 1898. Considering that it is only
a week since I finished the Spiritual Exercises I must admit
that I have spent the time very badly, because of my continual distractions during prayers . . . The worst of it is that,
instead of making an act of humility when I became aware
of wandering thoughts, I grieved over them and became anx-

ious. Enough of this and may God forgive me! Evidently he wants to disillusion me; he has put me to the test and shown me how worthless I am . . . God knows that in the midst of my miseries I love him and want everyone to love him. May he bless me and not despise me, although I am a sinner. 'Lord, you know that I love you.'" He was often to quote this protestation of St. Peter's, from St. John's Gospel.

The excessive preoccupation with small failings and distress at their recurrence reflects the narrow perfectionism so common in all Christian circles of the period, often dangerously egocentric in tendency. Luckily the next entry, though it worried the boy, is a relief to us. "I will be less of a chatterbox during recreation and will not let myself become too merry." As numerous other entries show, Angelo Roncalli did not succeed in this pious resolution. He tried hard to be solemn but cheerfulness would keep breaking through. By the winter, although still bewailing "excessive mirth" he could remark: "But after all, it is always better to be merry than to be melancholy. And remember: 'Be glad in the Lord.'"

After Easter he had a week or two at home; it was not altogether a happy holiday. The family was still finding it difficult to make both ends meet but worry was not the only cause of Angelo's dissatisfaction. He wrote: "There is one matter in which I have been most at fault, because this is a natural failing with me: wanting to be a Solomon, to sit in judgment, to lay down the law left and right! Alas! what presumption, what pride! it is my old self-love making itself felt again. This will make me more careful during the next vacation. Well, it's over now. I do not think I disgraced myself during these holidays, thanks to Jesus Christ. Tomorrow I begin another term. What a joy!"

Unfortunately other people thought he *had* disgraced himself. He was reported to his superiors, it seems by one of the Friars at Boccanello. Angelo had become a Franciscan tertiary at the age of fourteen, as he liked to tell the sons of St. Francis whom he met in later life. "My superiors have received an account, I think exaggerated, of my having behaved arrogantly during the vacation," he wrote in the journal on June 3, "and I have been duly rebuked. So I have had to humble myself against my will. But as a matter of fact there is a grain

of truth in this. Ah well, if I am now to be out of favor with
my Superiors, what am I to do about it? I shall let the matter
rest, leave it alone; time will show how much was true and
how much false in these accusations against me. In any case
it has been a nasty blow, and has given me food for thought
and for tears. Perhaps I have thought too much about it. And
the reason for all this is that although, thanks be to God, I
was never guilty of those excesses imputed to me, nonetheless
pride is always present, and it is this pride which gave rise
to the accusations. Now at last my eyes have been opened
and I have begun to learn . . .

"This is the month of the Sacred Heart, and my own
month, and so I must make some progress in humility, which
means also in love, and in this way I shall prepare myself for
those tiresome holidays and give certain people no further
excuse for making up stories about me."

It is clear enough that Angelo was happy at the seminary
and not so happy at home. His self-accusations in each place
were different. At home he was tempted to show off his knowledge; at the seminary he "yielded to the desire to play the
wit," as he wrote on June 12. He was no prig and had more
common sense than some adolescents inspired with religious
ideals. "One of my failings is that I am never orderly, not even
in spiritual matters, and yet I am always recommending order-
liness to others. I really must make sure that I never tell
others to do what I do not practice myself, because until now
I have been doing just the contrary." He grasped very early
the idea, expressed in July, that the priesthood must be "a
service of love." By that time he was at home again. It is from
these long trying months of vacation in the summer of 1898
that the clearest picture of the boy emerges. The spiritual
notebook became almost a diary, in which he could find relief
for his feelings.

"July 19, Tuesday. 'Save us, Lord, we are perishing.' I have
had three days of my vacation and already I am tired of it.
At the sight of such poverty, in the midst of such suspicions,
weighed down by so many anxieties, I often sigh and sometimes I am driven to tears. So many humiliations for me! I
only try to do what is right, to love sincerely even those who
do not seem to have much affection for me, and perhaps think

me a worthless fellow. At times I think that even those who
have taken an interest in me, those to whom I have confided
all, now look at me askance and are afraid to touch certain
chords, certain subjects. Ah, how sad this makes me feel! Perhaps I am only imagining this. I hope so, I would like to be
sure this was so, but meanwhile I must suffer; I am suffering
when I thought I would be rejoicing."

Then he wrote a long exhortation to himself on humility
and love and on confidence in Jesus. In the evening of the
same day he added a note which refers to his reported
arrogance.

"As for my familiar friend"—i.e. self-love—"I must confess
he made his presence felt a little while I was coming back
from Boccanello, where I had called on that excellent person
who, I thought, received me coldly. He made himself felt
when I thought of what had happened at Pentecost, and the
part played, as I think, by that person in that affair."

Angelo thought he had been misrepresented by this person
and he had been made very unhappy about it; now, when he
swallowed his pride and called, he was received with coldness.
Injustice and misunderstanding are felt so painfully in youth.
"But enough of this," Angelo concluded, "—these occasions
must serve to humble me more and more, and the next time
anything of the sort happens I shall at once try to humble
my self-esteem, saying: it serves you right!"

Things continued to be difficult at home. By Saturday he
was writing: "Well, there it is, today I have fallen again, chat-
tering here and there, like the greatest speechifier in the
world. No sooner have I erred in this way than I notice it and
am sorry, but I must think before I speak. I do not think I
spoke ill of anyone, but vigilance is always needed. It is all
self-love making itself heard: it is the desire to cut a good
figure." On Sunday, July 24, he wrote: "I will beware of utter-
ing the slightest word of reproach to my family, however much
they may hurt me. O Jesus, do see to this!" The next day:
"This evening I have wept, in the presbytery and when I was
with Jesus. O Jesus, accept my suffering and my tears. Use
them to wash away my sins, and grant humility to me and to
my family too. Mary, help me!"

The next day was his monthly day of recollection; he was

full of good resolutions and hopeful that Jesus would help him "to fulfill that mission of peace among the members of my too deeply troubled family." But soon a new hazard emerged, the temptation to chatter not only in the kitchen at La Colombéra, but in the presbytery with the curate, Ignazio Valsecchi. "Oh dear!—will I never get it into my head that I must keep silence with that blessed curate when matters of no concern to me crop up in conversation? Even if I say nothing wrong, it is obvious that I have a natural inclination to pronounce judgment like a Solomon. In any case, when I stop talking even when I think I have been caution itself, I am always aware I have talked too much. And this is pride."

The subjects of conversation in the presbytery were probably not the same as at the farm. On August 4 Angelo was again reminding himself: "I must still be careful not to argue with the curate, as sometimes I have done rather too much, in order to defend certain persons or actions which are really blameworthy, or others which seem to me not to be so. Although everyone may know that I speak like this just for fun, or turn the matter into a jest even when I take it seriously, nevertheless it is always wrong to go too far on certain things and even the smallest trifle may be used to build a whole fabrication on."

Talking about things "which are no concern of seminarists" occurred again when he was invited to dinner at the presbytery, with some visiting clergy, the day after the Feast of the Assumption. The curate broached some subject about which Angelo had meant to keep silent, and asked his opinion. He thought he had been circumspect but worried that his superiors might disapprove his making any comment at all. "O Jesus, when shall I begin to be a real source of satisfaction to you?"

What these topics were is suggested by an entry for August 31, his next monthly day of recollection. "I will never, never meddle in matters concerning newspapers, Bishops, topics of the day, nor take up the cudgels in defense of anything which I think is being unjustly attacked and which I think fit to champion, but if I were urged by others to do so I would do all I could to champion it with success, while showing charity at all times."

Although Bishop Guindani was himself a forward-looking man, he had to contend with some of his clergy who had entrenched themselves in the outlook of Pius IX. Among them, according to Leone Algisi, was the archdeacon of the cathedral, Canon Cossali. The opposition came to a climax when an action against the bishop was brought to the Vatican, supported in the great Catholic daily newspaper of Milan. Naturally this scandalous dissension was discussed by the clergy and it was probably in connection with this that the impulsive Angelo found it difficult not to take sides. It shows that his ideas and feelings were strong; the art of *not* sitting in judgment, which later he practiced so well, did not come naturally. Typical is his readiness to act the champion if others requested it, and otherwise to control his impulse to take the initiative. It was this attitude, which became a guiding principle in his life, which made his pontificate such a surprise to the Catholic world.

"I waste too much time in the kitchen, in idle chatter," he wrote at the end of July. "I must also learn to control my curiosity about things which are nothing to do with me. I shall also take care not to doze during meditation, as I did this morning . . ." Drowsiness during meditations beset him often in the hot summer weather. He thought he was sleeping too long in the afternoon siesta and set his alarm clock, giving himself three-quarters of an hour. He was still not orderly. "Never again, even absent-mindedly, must I go out of the village and as far as Carvico without wearing a hat, as I did today." Did he meet some disapproving face on the road, which reminded him of the prim rules about clerical dress which he had dutifully copied down?

On August 5 he recorded: "I neglected one of my most important duties, that of hearing my little brothers say their prayers . . ." The next trouble was bad toothache. Then there was a gap in the entries. "The other evening I had no candle, last night I had no ink, and so for two evenings running I have written nothing." On August 13 he noted: "I must also be careful with certain people not to touch on certain subjects which irritate them, because by doing so one only provokes irritability over matters which after all have nothing to do with virtue."

Things did not improve in September. He wrote on 6: "It seems quite impossible. The more I make resolves, the less I keep them. This is all I am good for: gossiping away, promising the earth, and then? Nothing! If only I knew how to be humble. Sometimes I spend far too much time talking with the curate and it might be said of me 'when words abound, sin is found.' Then there is another thing—I am really very greedy about fruit." This trouble about fruit was to come up again, and after he was grown up.

The next day he wrote: "I need still more invocations, especially when I am studying. They will help me out in the difficulties I often come up against because of my lack of brains—and they will give me more energy. I must take note also that I tend to linger too long in the kitchen after supper, talking things over with my family. They always talk about their worries and this depresses me. Indeed it would not be surprising if at times they led me to forget the great law of charity. So, as soon as the rosary is over, I will say a few words and then go to my room. They certainly have their worries and many of them! But my own worries are of a different kind. Theirs are about their bodies and material things; mine are about souls. This is what is hardest for me to bear, to think that in the case of my dear ones suffering seems to serve no good purpose, but rather to do them harm.

"O God, you who have lived through all this, you know how heart-rending it is! O Mary, give my dear ones true charity through which they may forgive with all their hearts and bear with resignation the crosses laid upon them by those they believe to be their enemies. Enough—let us pray."

About two years later Angelo wrote from Rome to his family a letter so pious, almost a sermon on patience, that we may well feel that there were two sides to those depressing evenings in the kitchen and that it was not easy for the elders, discussing their affairs, to listen to the conventional piety of their sixteen-year-old seminarist. After all, they may have thought, thanks to Canon Morlani and others, he was on the way to a profession which would at least secure him a safe livelihood. As he grew older Angelo Roncalli realized so fully the solid goodness of the older generation that he seems to have forgotten these painful tensions of adolescence. Some were no doubt due to the situation, in which a son was being educated beyond the rest of the family.

On September 20 he noted: "In everything I do I must behave like a boy, the boy I really am, and not try to pass myself off as a serious philosopher and a man of importance." It was wise advice, but in the circumstances it was difficult for him to behave like a boy. With all this tension at home, the restraint he tried to impose on his impulsive communicative nature and his nagging dissatisfaction with himself, it is hardly surprising that he had to record: "Although I generally manage to keep him at arm's length, the 'natural man' still makes himself felt in certain hellish dreams in which I find myself entangled unawares." He does not seem to have been oppressed with guilt about these dreams, as some boys might have been, given the stringent negative standard of "purity" impressed on the seminarists.

But now two real troubles came upon him. The first was an illness of his little brother Giovanni, aged seven, serious enough to give them all great anxiety. On September 24 Angelo wrote: "This morning everything was a bit disordered; afterward, this evening to be more precise, I was perhaps a little ill-mannered with those present when we were talking about the best way to cure my beloved brother. I ought to have been more calm. I see that if at times I keep silent even for the best of reasons, I must suffer for it, and I have to bottle everything up and feel stifled, but I will offer up all this to Jesus and Mary for the greater good of my soul and that of my little Giovanni. When I feel so troubled I seem to cast myself with more confidence into the arms of God, and I rejoice at this. Oh, how blessed, a thousand times blessed, are those religious who live in God alone, far removed from the cares of this world. I long too much to be as they are. But no, Jesus wants me in this state; he sends me the cross for me to bear it. May he be blessed ten thousand times!" For him, to join a religious order would have been an escape from reality, an evasion of God's will.

The next day, Sunday, September 25, Angelo suffered a fearful shock. He found his parish priest, Don Rebuzzini, dead on the floor. "I did not weep—but inside I turned to stone. To see him there on the ground, in that state, with his mouth open and red with blood, with his eyes closed, I thought he looked to me—oh, I shall always remember that sight—he looked to me like a statue of the dead Jesus, taken down from the Cross. And he spoke no more, looked at me no more.

"Last night he said to me 'Arrivederci!' O Father, when will that be? When shall we see each other again? In paradise. Yes, I turn my gaze to paradise and there he is, I see him, he smiles at me from there, he looks at me and blesses me.

"Oh how fortunate I am to have been taught by so great a master! Death took him unawares, but he had been preparing for it for the last seventy-three years. He died when he was trying to pull himself together, to master the malady that had seized him—and he was doing this to try to get to the celebration of Holy Mass. So it was, after all, a noble and enviable way to die! If only my own death could be like that! As I said, the position in which I found him showed that he had knelt down and fallen backward, unable to rise again."

So he meditated on the sudden loss of one who had watched over him so long—"for I believe I was his Benjamin." After the funeral on Tuesday Angelo wrote: "But I am left an orphan, to my immense loss. How painful it was for me today to have continually to hide those tears which nonetheless at times burst from my eyes. This is my greatest sorrow, the greatest I have ever felt! I am bewildered. I do not know how to behave, how to do any good, how to do any good to others also; I no longer know how to live in a world which has become strange to me."

He took heart in the Heart of Jesus and was happy to be given Don Rebuzzini's copy of *The Imitation of Christ*, which the priest had used since his seminary days. "To think he became holy, poring over this little book!"

About this time, when he got back to the seminary, Angelo lost his "kind director" Canon Luigi Isacchi. Though he did not feel this loss as intensely as that of his parish priest, yet it was another break with the past. Of his new director, Canon Quirino Spampatti, he wrote in January 1899: "I am certainly not so well-known to my new director as I was to Isacchi, and so I do not yet feel that sense of familiarity which I had before; but I must just be patient and these things will adjust themselves. As for my habit of making these jottings, as I had done from last year until this month, the new director does not seem to think so highly of this as the other did. In short, one thinks in one way, one in another. That is why there is such a gap between the last entry and today's." He noted that his "beloved Rector" had also died. He seems to have liked and respected all his teachers and superiors.

As a result of the change of spiritual directors Angelo's notes became less like a diary and more strictly confined to retreat resolutions. There were only seven entries in the whole of the next year. During the course of it he received minor orders and was made prefect of rhetoric, having under his charge boys older than himself. He had evidently regained the confidence of his superiors and was becoming one of the best students, intelligent and hard-working, if not brilliant.

In 1900, when Angelo was eighteen, there are some long retreat notes extant and a few holiday jottings. In August, trying to study at home, he wrote: "I felt out of sorts with everything, bored stiff with sermons and reading, with everything in fact. What was I to do? Praise be to God all the same. We are always in his hands, come what may. It gave me a good chance to mortify my excessive desire to study, to get on well, etc." He was still dissatisfied with himself for talking too much, still finding it difficult not to eat too much fruit. And he remarked: "As regards purity, it is true that, thanks to my Immaculate Lady, I do not have any strong temptations contrary to this virtue—yet I must confess that I have two eyes in my head which want to look at more than they should, and sometimes, I think unconsciously, they get the better of my soul." But pride and self-love continued to worry him more than these occasional straying glances.

This summer occurred one of the most painful episodes in his relations with his family. On August 29 he wrote: "This evening to disturb my peace of mind, there was an incident which, though insignificant in itself, has made a profound and painful impression on me. My mother was rather hurt by something I said (which, I confess, might have been put more gently) rebuking her curiosity about a certain matter. She was deeply offended and said things to me which I would never have expected to hear from my mother, for whom, after

God, Mary, and the saints, I bear the greatest love of which my heart is capable. To hear her tell me that I am always uncivil to her, without gentleness or good manners, when I feel that I can say with all sincerity that this is not true, has hurt me too deeply; she was distressed because of me, but I was very much more distressed to see her grieving and, to put it frankly, giving way like this. After so much tender love to be told by my mother that I dislike her, and other things I have not the heart to remember any longer—oh this was too much for the heart of a son, and of a son who feels the most profound natural affections. This gave me the most bitter sorrow, wounded the most intimate and sensitive fibers of my heart. How could I help giving way to tears? O mother, if only you knew how much I love you, and how I long to see you happy, you would not be able to contain your joy!"

It was perhaps inevitable that there should be such misunderstandings. The son was nearly nineteen, a young man, not a boy, and he was living a life quite different from the farming round his family followed. His education alone had taken him into another dimension. The mother felt the difference and blamed Angelo rather than the choice he had made; she felt the gap between them as a lack of affection, whereas it was mostly due to his preoccupation with things she could not share. In any case the affection of a young man for his mother is a different thing both from her love for him and from his own earlier, almost unconscious love for her. But the realization need not have been so painful had Marianna Roncalli understood that Angelo's manner did not mean that he despised his parents but was the awkwardness of a young man who was discovering his own powers and finding a student's difficulty in submitting an active mind to the simple affairs of farm and home.

After this trouble with his mother Angelo had to visit Bergamo, eight kilometers there and back; he returned tired out with his long walk. Then he had to go to Carvico for a ceremony of blessing the bells. On September 1 he wrote: "Sometimes with the reverend priests I allow myself to hold forth as an authority about politics, airing my opinions about this and that, one question after another—in short, flinging myself into the discussion in a way unsuitable for a seminarist

in my condition . . . Some things must wait till I am a priest
. . . For the rest I must be content to listen, even feigning
ignorance about these matters, especially when the conversation turns on more important questions than are usually
discussed in my homely talks with the parish priest and the
curate. How would St. Francis de Sales behave in this case?"

St. Francis de Sales, the Catholic bishop of Geneva after
Calvin had made it the organized center of the Reformed
Church, had already become one of Angelo Roncalli's favorite
heavenly patrons. His picture, and that of St. Charles Borromeo, were to accompany him everywhere. Though he had a
great admiration for St. Charles, Roncalli's own spirit was
nearer to that of St. Francis, who understood so well people
living "in the world" and based all he did on a wise and loving
common sense.

However doubtful Angelo Roncalli felt of the propriety of
expressing his opinions on politics, social and ecclesiastical,
the fact that he had them shows his alert intelligence and an
independence typical of his native province. It was not surprising that at the end of this year he was chosen, as one of
the three best students, to complete his studies in Rome.

3   Military Service and Roman Seminary

From the seventeenth century Bergamo diocese had a small
college in Rome, maintained from a charitable foundation
made in 1640 by Canon Flaminio Cerasola, but this had
been gradually absorbed into the major Roman seminary,
known as the Apollinare. During the last decade of the nineteenth century protracted negotiations were going on which
finally resulted in a restoration of the Cerasola scholarships
for Bergamesque students from the diocesan seminary. Angelo Roncalli, Guglielmo Carozzi, and Achille Ballini were the
first three students admitted under this new arrangement.

They arrived at half-past six in the morning of January 4, 1901.

It was not Angelo's first visit to Rome, for he had come there the previous September with a party from the Bergamo Seminary for the Holy Year pilgrimage. But now he came to work. He had already done a year's theology but on account of his youth he was put back to the beginning of the course. Yet in the examinations the following June, as well as passing in theology, he won a prize for Hebrew. Anyone who reads the *Journal* or his Allocutions will notice how frequently he quoted the Bible, including the Old Testament, and this love of Scripture was with him from the beginning. Hebrew was bound to interest him.

Late in April he made a retreat and recorded in his notes "longing, perhaps even excessive, and not always free from considerations of vanity, to study, to learn a great deal, to acquire a wealth of knowledge so as to be able to use this means, which has now become one of the most important, of winning souls for Christ." Because Pope John delighted to recall his humble origins many people are unaware that he valued intellectual work and made the most of his own opportunities. In France, in his sixties, he was still enlarging the area of his knowledge and had to watch lest he took too much time for his private reading. That he so early recognized the importance of learning for the Christian apostolate in the modern world is vital to an understanding of his character; the way in which this developed was due to the circumstances of the time, crucial in the intellectual life of the Church.

Angelo Roncalli, in these first retreat notes made in Rome refers to "certain rebuffs to my pride" but does not specify what they were. Probably it was humiliating to be sent back to the start in theology. Possibly he felt more conscious of his social origin in this new milieu. There is no social, as there is no racial discrimination in the choice of candidates for the Catholic priesthood; suitability is based on moral qualities and intelligence. Nevertheless social status is not thereby eliminated and European society in 1900 was more firmly stratified than it is now. In the Apollinare were gathered the best students from many Italian dioceses, though young men of noble rank (a definite class) were generally sent to the *military life*

Accademia dei Nobili Ecclesiastici, training ground for future Vatican diplomats. Even without intending it the other students might make a working-class boy feel some embarrassment. Angelo Roncalli knew his home and his poverty were nothing to be ashamed of, but he had to reassure himself by recalling that Christ was a carpenter, and a poor man. His later insistence on his humble origins may be partly the consequence of the time when it cost him something to admit them.

His first spell in the Roman Seminary was a short one; in November 1901, when he reached the age of twenty, he was due to begin a year's military service. By Canon Law priests are not allowed to bear arms and it was regarded as an anticlerical imposition that seminarists (in France as well as in Italy) were included in the military call-up. However, there was nothing to be done but to accept the situation and after a holiday at Sotto il Monte he duly presented himself at the barracks in Bergamo at the end of November.

In later years Roncalli considered that his time in the army had been good for him, widening his experience of men, and at the beginning of his service he wrote with stoical good sense to Monsignor Bugarini, the Rector of the Roman Seminary, in spite of a little preliminary dramatizing. "My life here is one of great suffering, a real purgatory." But he went on to say that the commanding officers treated him with consideration and allowed him every opportunity for religious practice; that his fellow soldiers, from Bergamo and Brescia, showed him respect and affection; and that every evening he was allowed to go and visit his old superior, the Rector of the Bergamo Seminary. The fact that it all took place in Bergamo must have made it much easier to endure.

Nevertheless, psychologically it proved a painful initiation into the immorality of the ordinary world. After his return to Rome he called it "the Babylonian Captivity" and in a ten-day retreat, made in December 1902, filled pages with meditations and resolutions. Several passages reveal his feelings.

"I know what life in a barracks is like—I shudder at the very thought of it. What blasphemies there were in that place, and what filth! . . . O the world is so ugly and filthy and loathsome! In my year of military service I have learned all about it. The army is a running fountain of pollution, enough to submerge whole cities. Who can hope to escape the flood of slime, unless God comes to his aid?

"I did not think that a reasonable man could fall so low. Yet it is a fact. Today, after my brief experience, I think it is true to say that more than half of all mankind, at some time in their lives, become animals, without shame. And the priests? O God, I tremble when I think that not a few, even among these, betray their sacred calling.

"Now nothing surprises me any more: certain stories make no impression on me. Everything is explained. What cannot be explained, is how it is that you, O most pure Jesus, of whom it was said 'he pastures his flock among the lilies' can put up with such infamous conduct, even from your own ministers, and yet deign to come down into their hands and dwell in their hearts, without inflicting on them instant punishment.

"Lord Jesus, I tremble for myself too. If 'the stars of the sky fell to earth' what hope have I, who am made out of dust?

"From now on I intend to be even more scrupulous about this matter, even if I become the laughingstock of the whole world. In order not to touch upon impure subjects, I think it better to say very little, or hardly anything at all about purity. 'We have this treasure in earthen vessels.' I have reason to tremble. 'Is my flesh bronze?' "

The only anxiety he had expressed about himself, before military service, occurs in the first retreat notes made in Rome, April 1901: "Most of all, a careful watch over my eyes during our walks, especially in certain districts." But when the opportunity came for more than accidental glances at girls, Angelo Roncalli seems to have been more disgusted than tempted; the very crudity of the barracks may have helped him. But he came back thankfully to the seminary and for all his revulsion from army life, in his resolutions to serve the Lord better he used a lot of military metaphors. After all, he had been quite an efficient soldier. He was promoted corporal in May 1902 and sergeant before he completed his year in November.

Angelo's first retreat on his return to the Roman Seminary

was made under the direction of Francesco Pitocchi, a Re-demptorist father appointed as a confessor to the students by Leo XIII, in 1899. When Angelo Roncalli came under his care Pitocchi was fifty and curiously enough suffered from the same muscular disease as the founder of his order, the eighteenth-century lawyer and missioner, St. Alphonso Li-guori: neither could lift his head, which was sunk on his chest. It was Father Pitocchi's health which confined him to Rome and often to his monastery, so that the students used to visit him in his own bare and simple cell. When he died in 1922 Angelo Roncalli wrote a memorial of him, full of affectionate reminiscence.

Pitocchi was kind and—essential quality in those who deal with the young—a sympathetic listener. He listened much and said little, but seemed to understand their difficulties at once. His example did more than his words to help them. Devoted to his order, which he had chosen after a spell as a parish priest, Pitocchi illustrated his spiritual teaching with anec-dotes of his founder and other holy Redemptorists. He was austere but mild, detached from worldly affairs. The motto he gave Angelo Roncalli at their first meeting was: "God is all—I am nothing." This the young man adopted with en-thusiasm, feeling that it gave him a new view of his life, and from then on Father Pitocchi became his guide and con-fidant, a real father to him while he was at the seminary, and someone he afterward visited and consulted until he died.

In his memorial Angelo Roncalli expressly mentions the influence of Father Pitocchi in counteracting certain opinions then circulating, later to be lumped together and character-ized as Modernism and to be condemned as such in 1907 by Pope Pius X. Pitocchi did not influence the students by argu-ment so much as by his dislike of extremes and his un-worldliness. His kindness too, Roncalli recorded, "enabled him to win our good will even before his thoughts had con-vinced our minds, thus leaving us no opportunity for any resistance." Roncalli was early convinced that in the discus-sion of ideas, moderation was essential. A few years later the violence of the defenders of orthodoxy distressed him more than the dangers of heresy. Coming from the most progres-sive diocese in Italy, where modernization in the social field was already under way, young Roncalli was predisposed to listen to new ideas. But he disliked anything like secrecy; he would not read things that were passed round in a clandestine way.

Writing in the changed climate of 1922, at the age of forty, Roncalli said: "The Superiors of the Seminary were very strict with us, and at times did not hesitate to impose stern restrictions which made us believe and say that they were too much opposed to anything modern in study or ways of thinking, and overconfident that the future would justify their deeds. In fact, after a short time the turn of events proved them quite right, and showed the timeliness, foresight, wisdom, and practical good sense of their attitude . . . The spirit of modernity, liberty, and criticism is like good wine, bad for weak heads."

To the formation of "good sound heads" Father Pitocchi made a notable contribution. "He used to say, and repeated even in recent times, that it is better for a young cleric to be somewhat strait-laced than inclined to broad-mindedness. This was not because he was concerned with questions of rigorism or laxism, but because he rightly considered that this youthful austerity, aided by later experience, was the best way of finding the exact middle point where truth, justice and charity meet."

This method may have worked for Angelo Roncalli but it may not have been equally effective with men who were less open-hearted, less practical and less willing to learn from experience than he. Strait-lacing did not make him narrow and rigid, but it can have that effect on the timid and introspective, just as it can encourage the insensitive to adopt a domineering and intolerant attitude, or provoke the high-spirited and clever to open rebellion. Without questioning the holiness of Father Pitocchi or the good intentions of the superiors of the Roman Seminary, one may doubt the wisdom of the system which they operated.

Seminaries were founded as an essential part of the renewal of the Church in the second half of the sixteenth century, after the Council of Trent. They were intended to provide a moral and intellectual training necessary for men whose ministry was to be exercised in that period of moral corruption and theological confusion. At the time of their institution and for the whole of the seventeenth century seminaries were fully integrated into the social and intellectual pattern of Europe. Even in Protestant circles there was a considerable period during which universities remained under clerical control; Oxford was almost wholly the preserve of Anglican clergymen until well into the nineteenth century. Latin remained the *lingua franca* of scholars whatever their religious allegiance. This situation ensured that priests were among the best educated men in Europe. Lesser clergy might forget much they had learned but they were certainly more literate than their flocks.

The trouble began in the eighteenth century when religion and learning drifted apart and many scholars, ridiculing or rejecting the institutions of Christianity as they knew them, became either Deists or occasionally complete skeptics. Christian attempts to meet this intellectual challenge were not radical enough to be effective and politics remained the chief preoccupation of highly placed clerics. After the traumatic events in France at the end of the century, fears of revolution tied the politically minded to conservative regimes, sometimes oppressive and reactionary. The rationalizing tendencies of German Protestant theologians drove most Catholics into a fundamentalist traditionalism—but a tradition which had received its shape at the time of Trent, with its Reformation conflicts and preoccupation with the preservation of medieval structures. Consequently society in Europe tended to split between Catholics and skeptical liberals, with a preponderance of intellectuals on the side of skepticism. It was no accident that education became the principal bone of contention between the Church and the increasingly anticlerical governments. Seminaries were gradually cut off from secular education and the teaching in them took on the psychological flavor of a battle course.

Unfortunately this battle course was gravely deficient just where it needed to be strongest, on the intellectual side. Catholic theology had become divorced from philosophy, tied to the system of late-medieval scholasticism; it had scarcely come into contact with the new sciences of historical scholarship and criticism. As taught to seminarians it was a closed system which gave an illusion of completeness and was elaborated down to the last detail. There was little life in it and it generally only attracted methodical academic minds.

Roncalli's own notes show how little connection there was between theology and devotional life, which at that time was also cut off from a real liturgical expression by the petrifaction of the Mass in its late medieval form. Devotion proliferated instead in a riot of a-liturgical ceremonies. Catholics, of course, continued to live by loving Christ and finding unity with him through the sacraments, but the means through which they understood and expressed their faith became less and less adequate to adult minds. As a result the Church seemed to favor the intellectually and emotionally immature and Christianity appeared to many educated people a meaningless tradition of myth and magic, a ritual habit. This situation was already a trouble to a writer such as Manzoni, who succeeded in transcending it in his novel by emphasizing the essentials of Christianity while not despising or rejecting the popular expressions of it. It is well to remember how much Angelo Roncalli loved this book. He, in his different way, found out in his youth how to follow the Gospel clue through the thickets of devotions.

The entries in the *Journal*, less naïve than in his boyhood and consequently less attractive, reflect the devotional style of the period, which today only obscures his robust faith and trust in God's providence. The baroque discovery of the personal adventures of the soul on its individual journey through the world had, in the course of three centuries, become gradually standardized and sentimentalized, elaborated into a network of pious practices and impoverished by endless introspection of motive. The danger of such spirituality is to focus attention on the self, rather than on Christ. Besides this, the ideal setup for the seminarian to copy was originally monastic and so quite unsuitable for priests who were to work in the world. The school discipline and routine of the seminary, the lack of responsibility and the isolation from the world, suggested an imitation monastery. The exemplars presented to the students were three aristocratic novices of the Society of Jesus who had never lived to attain adulthood: St. Aloysius (Luigi) Gonzaga, St. John Berchmans, and St. Stanislas Kostka. In the corrupt sixteenth century they had set an example, forsaking luxury and power for a life of poverty and obedience in the new order founded by St. Ignatius of Loyola; but by the nineteenth century they had been etherealized into three sexless wonders who never did anything wrong and went to heaven just at the age when the seminarian was thrown out into the world to work.

For this was the tragedy of the seminary system, as it had evolved by the end of the nineteenth century. The boys who had put on cassocks at twelve or fourteen lived in these pious boarding schools until they were ordained priests—usually at the minimum canonical age of twenty-three. They had been kept under strict supervision for years, never mixed with laymen of their own age, or with skeptics of any age, had been prevented from acquiring any real knowledge of politics— even at Bergamo newspapers were forbidden. As for women, apart from mothers and sisters they were an unknown race, scarcely more than sources of temptation. Yet at twenty-three the products of this intensively sheltered life were turned out into the ordinary world to minister to the needs of all kinds of people in all sorts of situations. The wonder was, not that some broke down, but that so many became reasonably sane and faithful priests. Because of the rule of celibacy people tend to equate priestly failure with some sexual or emotional entanglement, but there have been some who lost the faith they had never learned to relate to the world and others who have suffered nervous breakdown, sometimes not till middle age. And while women may be an attraction to the Latins, northerners are as likely to take to the bottle.

Segregation was the real trouble; if students had mixed with others of their kind, either at universities or on social courses, it would have been a better preparation for the life they actually had to lead. The seminary system prolonged the immaturity of young men destined for the priesthood, trained them in the pattern of an enfeebled monasticism without a sufficiently modernized intellectual formation, and then, at the crucial moment, abandoned them to their own resources. Nor was the psychological damage to the priests the only bad result of the system; it also ensured that the gap between priest and layman grew wider and deeper as time went on, as the priest's education became more and more remote from that of his lay comtemporary. The secular situation had entirely changed from that of the sixteenth century, but such changes as had been made in the seminaries tended away from reality—as in the sentimentalized images of the saints.

Luckily for himself and (later) for the Church, Angelo Roncalli was not seriously inhibited by the moral and intellectual constriction of his prolonged incarceration in seminaries. Intellectually he was saved by his interest in history, later encouraged by the exceptional bishop who took him into his household. Morally, his common sense got the better of the introspective spirituality impressed on him.

For instance, on January 16, 1903, he wrote in his *Journal:* "Practical experience has now convinced me of this: the concept of holiness which I had formed and applied to myself was mistaken. In every one of my actions, and in the little failings of which I was immediately aware, I used to call to mind the image of some saint whom I had set myself to imitate down to the smallest particular, as a painter makes an exact copy of a picture by Raphael. I used to say to myself: in this case St. Aloysius would have done so and so: or he would not do this or that. However, it turned out that I was never able to achieve what I thought I would do and this worried me. The method was wrong. From the saints I must take the substance, not the accidents of their virtues. I am not St. Aloysius, nor must I seek holiness in his particular way, but according to the requirements of my own nature, my own character, and the different conditions of my life. I must not be the dry, bloodless reproduction of a model, however perfect. God desires us to follow the examples of the saints by absorbing the vital sap of their virtues and turning it into our own lifeblood, adapting it to our own individual capacities and particular circumstances. If St. Aloysius had been as I am, he would have become holy in a different way."

"*I am not St. Aloysius!*" This discovery of the difference between imitating and following the saints (and Christ himself) was a typical piece of realism, of the kind people later found so attractive in Roncalli. It serves to show that his was not the unconscious simplicity of a child or a primitive but of a maturity won the hard way, through persistent honesty and singlemindedness. They were wrong, who thought him "just an old parish priest" and his pontificate, with all its new departures, a kind of accident, misinterpreted by progressives with their own axes to grind.

The young Roncalli did not blame his superiors for setting up an impossible model—to think of that thickset country boy trying to copy the emasculated image of the angelic novice! He was always loyal to his teachers and early learned to make the best of unpromising situations and people without adverting to the fact. Some twenty years later, living and working in Rome, he took the ex-rector to live in his house, though Bugarini must have been one of those whose strictness about modern views irked the eager students. The difficulties Roncalli had to meet are often obscured by his habit of praising the good qualities of those who opposed or snubbed him; he was still doing this as Pope. His own words can mislead one to suppose he never had to cope with personal conflicts.

Of course this loyalty to superiors meant that Roncalli accepted uncritically the current ecclesiastical attitudes. In 1903 the *Journal* is full of comments which read ironically in the light of his open-minded old age. It was the year in which Leo XIII, aged ninety-three, celebrated his papal jubilee —twenty-five years in the See of St. Peter. As the student Roncalli triumphantly noted, the old Pope had outlived many of his enemies. Then, in the spring, first Edward VII of England and then Kaiser Wilhelm II of Germany came to Rome and called on the Pope at the Vatican. Roncalli, having cheered Leo to the echo, moralized over the pomps and vanities of worldly monarchs as he watched the state processions, but rejoiced to think that the visits of these powerful sovereigns must portend the return of their heretical nations to the fold. This typically Roman view of the event was just what the Protestant subjects of the two monarchs feared. At that time Roncalli had probably not met a Protestant outside a textbook. The next year, just before his ordination, he was asked to look after a young convert, but only heard from him of the prejudice in which he had been brought up.

Although somewhat triumphalist (if innocently) in his attitude to foreign kings, Roncalli had already assimilated the social tradition of Bergamo. The day after he realized that he was not St. Aloysius he attended the funeral of Lucido Cardinal Parocchi, Leo XIII's Vicar General since 1884 and the promoter of *L'Opera dei Congressi*. Roncalli was impressed by the Cardinal's learning, acknowledged even by "unbelievers." In 1892 Professor Toniolo, one of the originators of the Christian Democratic movement in Italy, had called him "a man of exceptionally liberal views." Naturally such a man had enemies. Roncalli noted in his *Journal* on January 18, 1903: "Opinions may differ about Cardinal Parocchi's political views—I know that some malicious insinuations have been made—but no one will ever question his enthusiastic loyalty to Church and Pope, even when, as always happens to generous souls, his fortitude has been severely tried. Oh, if only I had his learning and his fortitude, I should be well content."

He might well mourn the death of this liberal Cardinal; things were soon to take another turn. On July 20 that year Leo XIII died and in the ensuing conclave the College of Cardinals elected, on August 4, Giuseppe Sarto, saintly Patriarch of Venice, once an even poorer country boy than Angelo Roncalli, walking to school barefoot to save his shoeleather. Sarto took the name of Pius in memory of Pius IX— the Pope associated in the minds of all with the struggle to keep the temporal sovereignty, the Pope of the antiliberal Syllabus of Errors. Giuseppe Sarto, Pius X, was crowned on August 10, 1903.

4 Becoming a Priest

On the first anniversary of the coronation of Pius X, August 10, 1904, Angelo Roncalli was ordained priest. He was three months short of the canonical age of twenty-three. But the irrevocable step had really been taken in April 1903 when, at twenty-one, he had been ordained subdeacon.

In the first centuries deacons and priests performed different functions in the Church and a man did not necessarily proceed from one order to the other. The deacons, though closely involved in liturgical action, were principally the bishop's assistants in his social and administrative duties; whereas the priests were associated with him in the teaching and sacramental ministry. The restoration by the Second Vatican Council of the diaconate as a separate order, which can be conferred on married men, should hasten the time when its functions, urgently necessary in our times, will be performed by men (and women) specially trained for the purpose. Overburdened priests would then have more time and energy for their own true function and the Christian community would benefit by the team work involved.

No doubt we shall look back with surprise to the time when the diaconate was regarded simply as a step to the priesthood, but such it was when Angelo Roncalli was ordained. The apparently unimportant order of the subdiaconate had become the moment when a young man bound himself to the obligations of the priesthood, including celibacy. This gave to the first ordination a deep emotional significance; it was by no means a formality but constituted the ordinand's gift of himself to God and to the Church. The later ordination to the priesthood was the occasion of his final acceptance and commissioning in the Church by Christ, its Lord and head.

Roncalli's notes for his retreat in April 1903, which ended with his ordination as subdeacon on Easter Day, reveal his thoughts and feelings when he took this irrevocable decision. Not that he had the smallest doubt of his vocation; he had never wanted to be anything but a priest and no real difficulties had come up during his long training. The interest lies not in uncertainties, but in his assessment of himself and in his aims.

He began by addressing the Lord: "I long to consecrate myself with all solemnity to you, once and for all. The Church has called me, you invite me: 'Lo, I come.' I have no pretensions, I have no preconceived plans, I am trying to strip myself of all that is self, I am no longer my own."

In the first days of the retreat he felt dry and arid; during them he examined his personal failings. It is interesting that the first thing he noted was a lack of detachment about his poverty. "At times dire necessity obliges me to contract small debts with the bursar, and I dislike very much having to do this; it makes me feel wretched. But this is not right: God permits this to happen, and that is enough." Yet though he could not entirely banish anxiety or an occasional wish to be better dressed, poverty did not really worry him, since he knew it was better for Christians to be poor than rich.

What did worry him was his continually reviving desire to do well in his examinations. In this he saw a worldly ambition for the praise of others and for a successful (priestly) career. "Mind and memory are gifts from God," he reminded himself. "Why should I lose heart if others have more of these gifts than I? Might I not have received even less than God has given me? Examination results and successes are things which, whether I will or no, mean a great deal to me. Very well, when I have done all that God has required of me, what does the good or bad result of my studies matter?"

He returned again to the thought of Jesus, living his obscure life as a carpenter at Nazareth: "Before such a shining example the judgements and way of thinking not only of this world but also of the overwhelming majority of ecclesiastics lose all value and seem in direct contradiction to it." But he was honest enough to admit that "it is only with the greatest effort that I can resign myself to the thought of real obscurity such as Jesus experienced and such as he taught men to desire."

A few months later, when he was making a retreat in December before receiving the diaconate he returned to the same problem. "Golden dreams of working one way rather than another, highly colored plans of what I hope to be able to do tomorrow or next year or later: away with all these! I shall be what the Lord wants me to be. It is hard for me to think of a hidden life, neglected, perhaps despised by all, known to God alone; this is repugnant to my pride. And yet, until I succeed in doing such violence to my own likes and dislikes that this obscurity becomes not only indifferent but welcome and enjoyable, I shall never do what God wants of me." Again: "Why do I feel all this anxiety and trepidation about the results and success of my studies? At rock bottom, it all springs from caring what public opinion may say about me, for I am a slave to the judgments of man. What idiocy!"

The next year, in retreat before his ordination to the priesthood, the same question recurred. "What will become of me in the future? Shall I be a good theologian or a famous jurist, or shall I have a country parish and be just a simple priest? What does all this matter to me? I must be prepared to be none of all these, or even more than all these, as God wills. 'My God and my all.' After all, it is easy for Jesus to scatter to the four winds my dream of cutting a brilliant figure in the eyes of the world. I must get it into my head that, just because God loves me, there will be no plan for me in which ambition plays a part; so it is useless for me to rack my brains about it."

In another note made in the same retreat he wrote: "I come back to the subject of detachment because, when all is said and done, this is the hardest pill for me to swallow . . . First of all, that craze for study, which was really with a view to cutting a dash in the examinations, before the worldly eyes of ecclesiastics; then the sheer intellectual effort prompted by pride, fearful and alarmed by the threat of being recalled from Rome, which would have meant the ruin of all those rosy hopes conceived in happier days. All this work was excellent in itself but not without its weak side, at least as regards the way I went about it. God saw my heart becoming divided and agitated and let me go on like this for a little while, and then, well, we know what happened." What happened was that he did not do so well as he had hoped in the examinations, though he was not recalled from Rome and succeeded in gaining his doctorate in theology.

He ended: "My studies! What a great many preconceived ideas I have about these! I have ended by judging them as the world does. Learning is always a fine thing, a secondary ingredient of a useful priestly life and also a secondary means of saving souls in these modern times. God preserve me from underestimating study, but I must beware of attaching to it an exaggerated and absolute value. Study is one eye, the left eye; if the right one is missing, what is the use of a single eye, of study by itself? After all, what am I now that I have secured my degree? Nothing, a poor ignorant fellow. What use am I to the Church with that alone? . . . In future I shall study with even more enthusiasm than before, but I shall call things by their right names; I shall be studying not so much for the examinations as for life itself, so that what I learn will become an integral part of me."

Reading these confessions of ambition one after the other, it may be easy to make too much of them. As soon as he was at work in the world Roncalli was able to take his own advice as far as study was concerned; as a student, there was no other outlet for his energy and will power. Yet education has always been the poor man's way to power. Coming from his country farm, without any worldly advantages, learning was the only available means of self-realization for Roncalli. He had no intellectual facility but he was intelligent and industrious and this made for greater satisfaction when he did well. People who find tests easy, or scholars absorbed in their subjects, cannot know the drama with which hard workers invest the *results* of examinations.

It must also be remembered that in Italy a clerical career could (and still can) be very much more powerful than anywhere else. Although the Popes were no longer the rulers of territories in Italy, they retained the civil service of sovereignty along with the royal mentality. The Roman Curia is the old papal court and when the administration of the Papal States was forcibly removed from its care, its composition and methods did not change overnight. In fact, as the Italian government was for so long regarded as an usurper, the Curia was run for years by men with the outlook of political exiles. This attitude affected ecclesiastical affairs, national and universal. The Church in Italy formed a sort of nation within the nation, an organization in which men in the top ranks of the central administration exercised a considerable, if hidden, power. There was nothing to stop a priest rising in the executive machine till he became Cardinal, or even Pope. Outside Italy no priest is likely to imagine he might be Pope; until recently very few entered the Curia. But for Italian clerics ecclesiastical power is a reality and ambition not a temptation to be dismissed with a smile.

Roncalli's ambition was not an imaginary danger, nor did it leave him when his examination days were over, as the *Journal* notes of his middle age show. This is interesting, because one of his strongest attractions as Pope was his open determination not to exercise a dictatorial authority but to allow others freedom to operate. Roncalli had to learn how to sit light to human power; by nature his energy and strong will kept leading him toward action and the exercise of influence on other people. The whole of his life was to be a curious interweaving of success and obscurity. His steady promotion in the service of the Church looks like a simple success story; yet when each period is examined it becomes clear that, as a career, it was full of frustration and unexpected difficulties and not without humiliations.

Roncalli's unpredictable future lends interest to his youthful struggles with the demons of personal ambition. Because he never had the type of cleverness which makes people call a man "brilliant" his natural qualities, intellectual and imaginative, have often gone unnoticed. He was more sensitive and self-conscious than some people have realized. In his retreat of April 1903 he wrote: "A careful examination of myself and the motives of my self-love has enabled me to perceive that within me, besides the imagination, always the crazy inmate of the house, are two reasoning minds, as it were, both of which do their utmost to make themselves heard. They are the reasonable reasoning mind, my own real mind, and the other reasoning mind, which is my inveterate foe. When I am meditating seriously, and considering goodness in general and in practice, this other mind always discovers a lot of ifs and buts, makes fun of all my resolutions and always finds some objections or some soothing arguments in its own favor." In those pre-Freudian days there was no difficulty in ascribing this "other reasoning mind" to the devil's suggestions, and he determined to take the advice of St. Francis de Sales, to "let the devil bang and scream at the door of the heart" but not to open it to him by taking any notice of what he said.

In the retreat before the diaconate, in December 1903, thinking about detachment, he remarked that in theory he succeeded well but in practice often failed. "When something happens here which even indirectly affects me personally, my imagination and my pride torment me to an extraordinary degree." He was honest enough to admit that he did not really want the humiliations which piety taught him to welcome in theory. "O loving Jesus, I kneel at your feet sure as I am that you will know how to bring about what I cannot even imagine. I want to serve you wherever you wish, at any cost, at any sacrifice. There is nothing I can do; I do not even know how to humble myself. But I will say this to you, and say it very firmly: I want to be humble, I want to love humiliations and being treated with indifference by my fellows. I shut my eyes and hurl myself with a sort of voluptuous delight, into the flood of scorn, suffering and shame which you may be pleased to send me. I feel a great unwillingness to say this to you, it tears my heart, but I give you my promise; I want to suffer, I want to be despised for you. I do not know what I shall do—indeed I do not really believe myself—but I will not give up wanting this with all my heart and soul: 'To suffer and be despised for you.' "

This passage illustrates one aspect of the popular piety of the period which is otherwise not often evident in Roncalli's notes—a desire for suffering and humiliation which too easily became morbid, as the lives of saintly novices who died young and pious nuns frequently demonstrate. Roncalli's imaginary plunge into the flood of scorn is much less convincing than his bewildered recognition that he was hurt and disturbed when he met the real thing. It upset the view of Christian perfection which he had dutifully assimilated: that holiness was achieved by the elimination of natural feeling, or even its reversal. Hurt feelings were regarded solely as a sign of pride and to enjoy other people's opposition and dislike was "supernatural." People, especially young people, certainly have to learn to accept opposition without sinking into self-pity, but to try to force themselves to love being unloved seems a poor preparation for loving. That Roncalli was sensitive to rebuff shows that his was an affectionate nature. All his "faults"—talking too much, trying to be (and being) funny, forgetting to make those endless self-examinations, being upset by other people's indifference to his efforts to help them—all indicate an outgoing temperament, someone to whom sympathy and companionship means much. He seems to have abandoned the attempt to make himself enjoy suffering, and settled for the more sensible principle of trying to bear patiently whatever happened to him.

On January 24, 1904, he made a few hasty notes in the *Journal* which reveal both his youthfulness and the generous practical nature which was not in the end warped or cramped by this narrow "supernaturalism." He wrote: "My pride in particular has given me a good deal of trouble because of my unsatisfactory examination results. This, I must admit, was a real humiliation; I have yet to learn my ABC in the practice of true humility and scorn of self. I feel a restless longing for I know not what—it is as if I were trying to fill a bottomless bag." Anyone who has a true memory of youth will remember this restless unformulated longing—it is part of youth itself, of the incompleteness of being young.

"I pray rather hurriedly in fits and starts," he continued, "without composure or serenity of mind. I have become more remiss in the practice of self-denial, and self-indulgent when faced with little opportunities for it. Although I mean to make the most of every scrap of time, I waste hours without achieving anything. I am less reserved in my speech and more effusive, and also a little less cautious in my criticism . . . I must beware of speaking ill of anyone, even indirectly. I must always preserve a natural, not an affected dignity. Above all, I must be extremely careful when I am talking about our Superiors. It would also be very wise to avoid effusions about my own affairs: I must not pour out my feelings about everything, to everyone."

In August, preparing for the priesthood, he noted: "I profess to aim at perfection but in practice I like the way of perfection to be mapped out by me and not by God." This is a common failing, not so commonly recognized. Every Christian has to learn his own lesson over and over again; the pattern of these self-examinations is repeated all through Roncalli's life, though with deepening understanding and increasing serenity. To learn how to curb the self-indulgent and self-glorifying elements in his open and outgoing nature, while retaining the capacity for love and broadening its deployment without becoming shallow: this was the personal task set before him. His temptations were those of an active man, chiefly the danger of converting a life of service into a means of self-satisfaction, by trying to dominate circumstances instead of accepting as the will of God what was determined for him by others. He recognized this early and for the rest of his life showed all the dogged patience of his farming forebears, tilling the same patch every year, never surprised by the recurring weeds but always rooting them out, and remaining hopeful that next season would bring a better harvest.

But entrance into the holy orders was not all a matter of penitence and self-discipline; on each occasion Angelo Roncalli was carried forward by an impetus of love which overflowed in joy and happiness. The retreat for the subdiaconate in Holy Week 1903, which had begun with days of dryness, ended in a spontaneous outburst of rejoicing. "The joy of my ordination was too great for me to describe it. 'How lovely is thy dwelling place, O Lord of Hosts! My soul longs, yea, faints for the courts of the Lord! Truly my heart and my flesh sing for joy to the living God.' This morning's ceremony in St. John Lateran was solemn in itself, more solemn for me, and never to be forgotten. Now I am really a new man: the decision has been taken. His Eminence the Cardinal Vicar, in the name of the supreme Pontiff and the Church, has received blessed and consecrated my renunciation of all the things of this world, my whole-hearted, absolute, irrevocable dedication to Jesus Christ."

The Cardinal Vicar was Pietro Cardinal Respighi, Vicar General of the Pope and the ceremony took place in the Lateran basilica, the cathedral of Rome, on April 11, 1903, Holy Saturday.

"When, after the solemn prostration, I approached the altar, and the Cardinal, accepting my vow, robed me in my new and glorious habit, it seemed to me that the Popes, confessors, and martyrs who sleep in their silent tombs in the great basilica arose and embraced me like brothers, rejoicing with me and joining in the chorus of the Resurrection angels to praise Jesus who in all his glory has deigned to raise such an unworthy creature to so great a height. O the tongue cannot describe all the emotion of that moment, but its memory will last for ever in my heart and I shall never cease to extol the love of my God, his greatness, his glories.

"The only words my stammering tongue can utter are those of St. Paul: 'It is no longer I who live, but Christ who lives in me.' Now I am no longer my own, I am Christ's. This I have said so many times, but today I repeat it from my heart. I am Christ's."

On Easter Day, April 12, he recorded a few more thoughts. "Today as a newly ordained subdeacon, officially consecrated to his (God's) cause as a minister of Jesus, in the sight of the whole heavenly court and the whole Church, I was quite overcome by the feeling of confidence that comes from freedom, that holy freedom which he procured for us by his glorious death and Resurrection. Now I am free from all earthly ties and made more vigorous and more ready to rise to the heights of sacrifice, with him and for him." And he went on to pour out a long prayer of praise and thanksgiving. Of course the emotion did not last, but it left a memory of joy in his heart which echoed into old age, so that as Pope, he expressed the wish that he could be buried in St. John Lateran.

The priesthood was conferred on Angelo Roncalli not in that ancient basilica but in the Church of Santa Maria in Monte Santo, one of the twin seventeenth-century churches where the Corso enters the Piazza del Popolo. He was ordained by Archbishop Giuseppe Ceppetelli, Vicegerent of Rome and titular Patriarch of Constantinople. (This title, dating from the Crusades, has now been allowed to lapse.) It was curious that there should have been this connection with Constantinople, where Roncalli was later to spend so many years and lay the foundations of a better understanding with the Orthodox Patriarch.

Before ordination, Roncalli, along with nine other ordinands, made a retreat with the Passionist Fathers at Sts. John and Paul on the Caelian Hill. "I still remember," he wrote in a private note of 1912, quoted in *Journal of a Soul*, "the impression made on me every night, when they rose for Matins, and I heard the sound of their footsteps and the trailing of their long black habits along the dark corridors." The order had been founded in the eighteenth century by the ascetic Paul Danei, canonized as St. Paul of the Cross; the Fathers, devoted to the Passion of Christ, are well-known for the type of parish mission so successful in the nineteenth century for rousing the lapsed to fervent penitence. Roncalli was impressed by the humble brother who swept his room. Every day he visited their church, built over the house of the Roman martyrs, the brothers John and Paul. From his window he could see the Colosseum, site of so many martyrdoms, the Lateran and the Appian Way. In the afternoons the ordinands practiced saying Mass in the room where St. Paul of the Cross had died.

On the eve of the appointed day the Father in charge granted Roncalli's wish to visit some special shrines and accompanied him to St. John Lateran, where he renewed his act of faith, to the Scala Santa, which of course they climbed on their knees, and to St. Paul's-without-the-Walls. "What did I tell the good Lord that evening, over the tomb of the Apostle of the Gentiles? It is locked in my heart." It was to be in this basilica, built over the tomb of St. Paul according to tradition, that Pope John announced his intention of calling an Ecumenical Council of the Church.

The day of his ordination, August 10, 1904, was the Feast of St. Laurence. He did not write of the ceremony at the time, but recalled some memories in 1912 which are included in *Journal of a Soul*. "When all was over and I raised my eyes, having sworn the oath of eternal fidelity to my Superior, the Bishop, I saw the blessed image of our Lady, to which I confess I had paid no attention before. She seemed to smile at me from the altar and her look gave me a feeling of sweet peace in my soul and a generous and confident spirit, as if she were telling me that she was pleased, and that she would always watch over me."

The Vice Rector of the Roman Seminary, Father Domenico Spolverini, who had fetched him from Sts. John and Paul that morning, now took him back to the Seminary—deserted, since the students were on holiday at Roccantica. First Roncalli wrote to Bishop Guindani of Bergamo, renewing the vow he had made that morning to the ordaining prelate. "Then I wrote to my parents, so that they and all the family should share in the joy of my heart, begging them to thank the Lord with me and to implore him to keep me faithful. In the afternoon I was alone, alone with my God, who had raised me so high, alone with my thoughts, my resolves, the joys of my priesthood. I went out. Utterly absorbed in my Lord, as if there were no one else in Rome, I visited the churches to which I was most devoted, the altars of my most familiar saints, the images of our Lady. They were very short visits. It seemed that evening as if I had something to say to all those holy ones and as if everyone of them had something to say to me. And indeed it was so."

Among those he visited was St. Philip Neri at the Chiesa Nuova. He had written with love of this saint on his feast day, May 26, 1903, when he had visited the little rooms where he had lived and died, nearly eighty years old, in 1595, a Florentine who came to be called "Apostle of Rome" and whose humor, kindness, and gaiety had an affinity with his own.

The next morning Father Spolverini accompanied Angelo Roncalli to St. Peter's where he said his first Mass at one of the altars in the crypt above the Apostle's tomb—near where his own tomb stands today. He said the votive mass of Sts. Peter and Paul. "I remember that among the feelings with which my heart was overflowing," he wrote in 1912 (when he was thirty), "the most powerful of all was a great love for the Church, for the cause of Christ, for the Pope, and a sense of total dedication to the service of Jesus and of the Church . . . I said to the Lord over the tomb of St. Peter: 'Lord, you know everything; you know that I love you.' " This phrase of St. Peter's, so often on Roncalli's lips, sometimes seems almost a premonition.

"I came out from the church as if in a dream. On that day the marble and bronze Popes aligned along the walls of the basilica seemed to look at me from their sepulchers with a new expression, as if to give me courage and great confidence."

At midday he was again in the Vatican, at an audience arranged for him by the Vice Rector, who presented him to Pope Pius X. "The Pope smiled and bent down his head to hear what I said to him. I was kneeling before him, telling him that I was glad to be at his feet repeating to him the intentions which I had offered during my first Mass over the tomb of St. Peter, and I told him of these briefly, as well as I could.

"The Pope then, still bending down, placed his hand on my head, and speaking almost into my ear said, 'Well done, well done, my boy . . . this is what I like to hear, and I will ask the good Lord to grant a special blessing on these good intentions of yours, so that you may really be a priest after his own heart. I bless all your other intentions too, and all the people who are rejoicing at this time for your sake.' He blessed me and gave me his hand to kiss. He passed on and spoke to someone else, a Pole I believe; but all at once, as if following his own train of thought, he turned back to me and asked when I should be back at my home. I told him: 'For the Feast of the Assumption.' 'Ah, what a feast that will be,' he said, 'up there in your little hamlet (he had earlier asked me where I came from) and how those fine Bergamasque bells will peal out on that day!' and he continued his round smiling."

Pope Pius X came from just such another hamlet in Venetia, from Riese in the plains. Thus one Pope blessed his successor, both unaware of it.

In the evening Roncalli went out to Roccantica; the villa was all lit up, the students met him on the bridge and in the chapel they sang *Tu es sacerdos*—Thou art a priest forever, according to the order of Melchisedech. (In Christian tradition Melchisedech, the good pagan priest-king who worshiped the Most High God and offered Abraham gifts of bread and wine, became the type of Christian priesthood because his being "without father" suggested the new distinction from the tribal priesthood of Aaron.) The next morning the new priest said Mass and gave communion to all the students. The Gospel homily was preached by Father Francesco Pitocchi, Roncalli's Redemptorist director. "That Father was too kind in what he said about me: his affection blinded him a little," Roncalli noted in 1912. If we are not careful, the earnest self-examination of the *Journal* may blind us to the fact that the young Roncalli was not only a very good student but a very popular one.

Then he went north; Mass in Florence on August 13 at the Santissima Annunziata; Mass in Milan next day, at the tomb of St. Charles Borromeo—"How much I had to tell him! And from then on the veneration and love which bind me to me to him have grown stronger," he wrote eight years later. At last, "On 15th, the Feast of the Assumption, I was at Sotto il Monte. I count that day among the happiest of my life, for me, for my relations and benefactors, for everyone."

In his memoir on Father Pitocchi, written in 1922 when his kind director died and he himself was forty, Roncalli once more recalled the happy rejoicings at Roccantica. In order to illustrate Father Pitocchi's kindness he told then the story of his own first sermon, to be preached in honor of Mary, during the celebrations for the fiftieth anniversary of the proclamation of the dogma of her immaculate conception—the doctrine that God preserved the Mother of the Saviour from the otherwise universal implication of the human race in original sin, the basic disobedience to the divine will of love. Father Pitocchi arranged for his protégé to deliver this sermon to the Children of Mary, an association for girls and women, in the chapel of the Madonna at San Gioacchino (St. Joachim, the traditional name of the Virgin's father), a church built in the country near Roccantica to celebrate the jubilee of Leo XIII.

"Naturally I wrote everything down: I did my best to weave a flowery garland of praise for our dear heavenly Mother," Roncalli wrote eighteen years later. "At the time I was quite pleased with it, but now that I am more mature I would take care not to prepare it in that way: it was too studied, too flowery, too poetical. On the preceding evening I recited it all to my Father, on my knees, after confession. He listened to me, smiling kindly and encouraging me.

"The next day, complete failure! . . . I was at once put off by the general atmosphere which to me, a countryman, seemed too aristocratic. I lost my presence of mind, my fluency, my fervor; I even lost my way in my own manuscript: I confused the New Testament with the Old, the witness of the Doctors of the Church with the imagery of the prophets, St. Alphoneus with St. Bernard, the middle with the beginning and the beginning with the end: in short, a disaster! When I had finished and tore myself away from the altar, I was like a shipwrecked man cast up on the shore, completely lost.

"But I found myself in the arms of Father Francesco, in his

little room near the sacristy, and he was doing all he could to encourage me, even more than on the evening before, and with such kindness in his bearing and words, words of such persevering kindness, that in the end I was content to have suffered that mortification, which he made me offer to our Lady, with a resolve to attempt another public sermon as soon as possible."

Oh those aristocratic young ladies, sitting so decorously with their pious and elegant mammas! Did any of them live to listen again to that young priest, who mixed up his flowery sentences so ludicrously, when he came to speak, as Pope, so fluently and naturally, in St. Peter's?

5　*Papal Politics*

At the beginning of the new academic year in November 1904 Angelo Roncalli enrolled in a course of Canon Law which should have added another doctorate to the one he already held in theology. But that October Bishop Guindani of Bergamo had died and his successor, Giacomo Radini-Tedeschi, who was appointed soon after, wanted a secretary from the diocese. He made inquiries at the Roman Seminary and his choice fell on Roncalli. So the young priest's course was set, for his nine years with Radini-Tedeschi formed his adult character. He found the new bishop a leader after his own heart.

Radini-Tedeschi was known in Italy as "the orator of *L'Opera dei Congressi.*" He had traveled the country promoting the movement for social action and his apartments in Rome became the center where people interested in it gathered. Leo XIII himself had encouraged Radini to take up this work, after an interview in which the young priest had frankly declared that he did not want to be a diplomat. Radini, who came from a noble family of Piacenza, had attended the Accademia dei Nobili Ecclesiastici and after a spell of teaching in his diocesan seminary had been summoned to the Secretariat of State in Rome. Tall and upright, with an almost military bearing, he was endowed with those gifts of charm and eloquence which open so many doors, especially in Italy. He was not, all the same, an ecclesiastical politician. His work for social justice was for him part of his religious vocation; he was consulted by nuns as well as by Catholic Actionists, led pilgrimages to Lourdes and the Holy Land and liked to fulfill pastoral duties when he could, preaching and hearing confessions. In 1904 he was forty-seven, at the height of his powers. Then the organization which he had helped to build was destroyed overnight by the new Pope, Pius X.

In order to understand the development of Angelo Roncalli's mind and character and the motives behind his actions as Pope in the middle of the twentieth century, it is necessary to get some idea of the political and intellectual tensions within the Church at the beginning of it. In every European country there was great unrest, though it did not always appear on the surface, and while the open conflicts were between the anticlerical liberals and conservative Catholics, a new struggle was already being prepared between revolutionary socialism and various political reactions to it. In Italy Benito Mussolini was still an extreme anticlerical socialist but the type of patriotic authoritarian movement which he later adopted and called Fascism was already burgeoning in France as *L'Action Française* under the inspiration of Charles Maurras, the editor of its influential newspaper. Maurras did not believe in God but saw the Church as a bastion against the new international revolutionary creed. So many French Catholics who hated and feared this creed were drawn into this nationalist movement, with its romantic royalism and suspicion of democracy. Because Mussolini became master of Italy Fascism is much better known in the world; yet Maurras' related movement is important for the history of the Church as well as of France.

Pius X inherited a delicate relationship with France. In the years after 1890 Leo XIII had shocked the monarchists by directing French Catholics toward a policy of *ralliement* with the Republic. There was a very poor response, and when the moderate liberals then in power gave place to violent anticlericals, the attacks on religious orders and on the teaching of religion in state schools made cooperation from Catholics virtually impossible. In 1902 Emile Combes headed a government determined to bring about the official separation of Church and State. The existing relationship dated from the concordat made between the Holy See and Napoleon in 1801; after all the constitutional changes of the century the Church still kept its status and priests received salaries, in lieu of the property confiscated during the Revolution. The State had the right to nominate bishops. Under the Combes regime two unsuitable appointments which Pius X was unable to confirm became the occasion for a clash between the Holy See and the French government which led to the breaking off of diplomatic relations and the passing of the Law of Separation in 1905.

The Separation could have been of advantage to both parties, since it would free the bishops from secular control and the law included a measure to allow property to be held by Church associations. The French bishops were not unwilling to set these up. Time and opportunity for negotiation were not lacking but in the event the separation became a national drama on a grand scale. For two reasons: the fanatical anticlericalism of Combes, who had reacted against his seminary education into violent anti-Christianity and was engaged in expelling the teaching orders from France; and the equally fanatical intransigence of the Vatican, which acted over the heads of the French bishops and condemned the proposed Church associations on the ground that they might be run by laymen insufficiently under episcopal control. The French Church was thus forced into a position of masochistic noncooperation, or, as the romantic preferred to call it, martyrdom. The Roman diplomats who controlled this situation were advised by the French superiors of the exiled orders and were led by the young Cardinal Secretary of State, Rafael Merry del Val.

Merry del Val was a key figure in that crucial decade. Half Spanish, half English, he had started a thoroughly Roman career when Leo XIII insisted on his being transferred from the Scots College to the Accademia dei Nobili Ecclesiastici, the nursery of papal diplomats. His religious intransigence has sometimes been put down to his Spanish ancestry, but his English seminary training probably had a good deal to do with it. At that period English Catholics, a tightly knit minority, were belligerently Roman and, in the upper ranks, strongly tied to the old European order. Merry del Val kept his English friends all his life and has been greatly admired by English Catholics. He was athletic, a good swimmer, a good shot, and considered a very handsome man. He was also a wonderful linguist and born to the life of courts—his father was a diplomatic representative for Spain, first in London where the Cardinal was born and then in Rome.

Merry del Val was only thirty-eight when Pius X made him his Secretary of State, trusting him to deal with the daunting political duties of the papacy, unfamiliar to the saintly prelate who had rarely been outside Venetia and knew no language but Italian. There was a strong mutual affection between the Pope and his Secreatry of State; Pius valued in the younger man not only his ability but his real piety, for under his cosmopolitan culture Merry del Val hid an ascetic self-discipline and deep, even passionate religious feeling. Merry del Val, in his turn, loved Pius for his personal holiness, simplicity and mild humor; he also felt for him that intense veneration for the Vicar of Christ which at that period was such an important part of the devotional life of loyal Catholics.

Had the shrewd Mariano Cardinal Rampolla del Tindaro still been in charge of the Secretariat of State it seems unlikely that the French Separation Laws would have been carried out so drastically as they were under the guidance of Merry del Val. When Rampolla's pupil, Giacomo della Chiesa, became Pope Benedict XV in 1914 he did in fact negotiate a settlement, on the basis of the Church associations, slightly modified, which was completed under Pius XI. Ironically, the later Popes had to deal with intransigent French bishops appointed directly by Pius X. For a significant factor in the crisis had been the centralizing and autocratic tendency in the Vatican, which reached its peak under Pius X. It was useless in 1905 for the French bishops, appointed by the Republic

and approved by Leo XIII, to discuss national policy in conference; the Pope and his Secretary bypassed them, dealing
with the government through the Papal Nuncio and sending
orders to the episcopate. The Pope's powers were then unde-
fined by the consideration of episcopal collegiality as the
Second Vatican Council has elucidated it. It now appears that
papal authority sometimes exceeded its proper limits and to
a large extent this was due to the continuing belief in temporal, that is, political papal sovereignty. At the very beginning of his reign Pius X felt himself to be "insulted" by the
French President's visit to the King of Italy. Victor Emmanuel improved the occasion by driving President Emile
Loubet under the very walls of the Vatican.

Catholic writers have often presented the acts of Pius X
and Merry del Val toward France as the unworldly stand of
high-principled saints, concerned only with the freedom of
the Church from state interference. At this distance of time
it looks as if authoritarian ideas of papal supremacy played
as much part as unworldliness, especially when we find that
Maurras' reactionary *Action Française* was increasingly favored as "a defense of the Church" while the Christian Democratic movement was censured and circumscribed. This becomes clearer when the policy of the pontificate is seen as a
whole.

In Italy the situation was complicated by the Roman
Question. For thirty years the *Non Expedit* had been in
force; no Catholics were supposed to vote in the national
elections. It must be remembered that during the whole of
this period Italy had only a restricted franchise; most voters
were middle or upper class and women had no vote. The
majority were liberals but this did not mean they were an
organized body like the Liberal Party in England at that
time. Politicians were individualists and there were many
parties; several had to combine to form a government. Liberalism implied disbelief in Christianity, and a hostile policy to
Church organizations, incuding schools. People in English-
speaking countries find it hard to realize what it meant to have
a militantly anti-Christian middle class, since (perhaps as a
legacy of Protestantism) the English and American middle
classes remained committed to religion and at the very least

it was respectable to go to church. Leading Liberals in England, like Gladstone, were often strong churchmen and the party's strength lay among non-conformists. Such an attitude was inconceivable in Italy, though militant anticlericals often had wives and daughters who attended Mass. It had to be overlooked as feminine weakness—and they had no vote.

As time went on patriotism among Italian Catholics made the papal isolation policy harder to maintain. Leo XIII, perhaps because of his extreme age, never raised the electoral ban but Pius X, so much more conservative in outlook, did begin to allow exceptions. It was Bergamo which first won permission to vote. A deputation from that city convinced Pius X in 1904 that if Catholics were not allowed to vote a socialist would be elected. After deep and anguished thought the Pope said: "You must act according to your conscience." Hardly able to believe it the deputies went away to elect the first two Catholic members of the Italian parliament. It was the fear of Socialism that had done the trick.

Socialism had established itself in Italy during the '90s in a strongly Marxist and revolutionary form, but about 1900 a more moderate party, favoring cooperation with the liberals, began to advocate *riformismo*, a gradualist reformism rather than revolution. From then onward these two tendencies were always at work within socialism; the Russian revolution divided the party into Communists and social democrats and the latter split again after the Second World War. All were anticlerical and atheist; it was one of the few principles they shared with the liberals, otherwise despised for their bourgeois individualism.

L'Opera dei Congressi had started long before the organized socialist parties but inevitably their appearance altered the political balance. Till then it was the Catholics, rather than the liberals, who had organized labor and social welfare, even if it was sometimes done in a paternalist manner, from above. But a strong antireligious proletarian political movement caused alarm among those Catholics who had never cared for the democratic inspiration of the Congresses. Even Leo XIII, in his last years, published the encyclical *Graves de Commune* in 1901 to check the exuberance of the Christian Democrats, who had just published a declaration which began *Noi vogliamo*—we want: universal suffrage for men and women, workers' unions, proportional representation, agrarian reform, freedom for religious teaching in schools and a scaled income tax. A moving spirit behind this manifesto was Don Luigi Sturzo, a Sicilian priest with an active career in municipal government behind him, who was later to found the *Partito Popolare* and clash with Mussolini. But in 1901 the program seemed too revolutionary to the old Pope; still more so, of course, to those conservative Catholics who regarded Leo himself as a liberal.

Noi vogliamo reflected the tension within the *Opera dei Congressi* which was not resolved by *Graves de Commune*. The movement had become divided and the democratic progressives were increasingly impatient of papal restrictions. There were changes of leadership in the attempt to keep people together. At a meeting of the central committee at Bologna in July 1904 Count Giovanni Grosoli, the head of the *Società Editrice Romana* (the Catholic Press Trust), and the new president of the Congresses, thought he had reconciled the conflicting elements: those who counseled caution and those who advocated direct political action. He read out a letter of approval from the Secretary of State, Cardinal Merry del Val. Shortly afterward a circular was sent out to the regional committees in which the Roman Question was (indirectly) referred to as a dead letter. This circular was confiscated by the Holy See and Grosoli was forced to resign. Without further warning a letter signed by Merry del Val was sent out on July 28 to all the bishops of Italy announcing the dissolution of *L'Opera dei Congressi*. The only central (national) committee allowed to continue was that of social action, under the Bergamasque Count Medolago-Albani, a personal friend of Pius X's and politically a conservative. All other activities from now on were to be conducted by diocesan committees under the direct control of the bishops.

This drastic action against a national movement of thirty years standing, the only movement which allowed Catholics to act in and on the society in which they lived, illustrates the policy of the new pontificate, which can only be described as reactionary and authoritarian. By dissolving the central committees and making the regional branches dependent on the bishops the political power of the movement was virtually annihilated. Catholic laymen were not to be allowed to act on a national scale; the ecclesiastical authorities must retain control of politics. Catholic Action inevitably became parochial and clerical, and Christian Democracy lost its organized national basis. Had Pius X and his advisers dealt less stringently with *L'Opera dei Congressi* in 1904 there would have been a solid, national, Christian, lay, democratic movement on which to build a political party which could have withstood the Fascist movement after the First World War. Even as it was, Don Sturzo's *Partito Popolare,* founded with the encouragement of Benedict XV in 1919, commanded more popular support than the Blackshirts and more seats in Parliament. It seems improbable that Mussolini could ever have gained power if the Christian Democratic movement had been allowed to develop naturally without papal and clerical interference.

The destruction of *L'Opera dei Congressi* was a catastrophic blow to Giacomo Radini-Tedeschi, who for years had given his best energies to it. He was loyal to the Pope, for whom he had a personal veneration, and just as loyal to the papal *idea* as Merry del Val himself, treating the Vicar of Christ almost as if he represented Christ's person rather than his authority within a particular situation. Radini used to quote St. Catherine of Siena's phrase "sweet Christ on earth"—addressed by that determined woman to a papal politician about whose personal qualities she had few illusions, because she wanted him to return to his see of Rome. But during the nineteenth century the habit had grown of regarding the Pope all too literally as Christ on earth. Nobody identified the Pope with Christ, nor was he a Christ-substitute; the very men who cultivated a devotion to the Pope were those who expressed their personal love of Christ in frequent communion, Eucharistic adoration and the cult of the Sacred Heart—the human love of the Saviour for mankind. Yet the reverential obedience with which every utterance of the Pope was treated came too close to that absolute submission which can only be given to Christ himself.

Pius X was the last Pope to receive this type of adulation, distilled from the Ultramontane papalism of the nineteenth century; the upheavals which began in 1914 and the all-too-similar adoration offered to un-Christian dictators have helped to destroy its power. Pius himself, a simple and humble man, did not encourage flattery but he accepted the current exalted view of his office and acted in accordance with its almost superhuman image. His personal goodness and, let it be said, his beautiful and dignified presence, played a part in the religious devotion which surrounded him. It was not he, but the devotees who risked corruption. As everyone knows, papal acts are often in effect the acts of the leaders of the Roman Curia; by an exaggerated deference to the Pope's policy (as distinct from the acceptance of his spiritual authority) Catholics risk allowing their social conscience to be directed by a group of religious civil servants. Failing to make the necessary distinctions between the various functions of the Pope has long been all too common in the Church. It is specially difficult for Italians since he is also primate of Italy.

Bishop Guindani of Bergamo died conveniently for the advisers of Pius X, who had already suggested several bishoprics for Monsignor Radini-Tedeschi, in the hope of getting him removed from the center of operations in Rome. Pius himself told Radini: "They proposed that you should be Archbishop of Palermo; I said no; they proposed you for Ravenna; I said no. Then, here's Bergamo: I said yes." Bergamo, the center of Catholic social action, was the obvious solution. Radini would have a diocese sympathetic to him and he would be just the man to keep frustrated Christian democrats loyal. Pius X continued: "Go there, then. Bergamo, in all that can rejoice a bishop, is the first diocese of Italy." He meant this kindly and it was so taken by Radini-Tedeschi, who liked to recall these words. Pius also reserved to himself the right to consecrate the new bishop.

Nevertheless, in the English Parliamentary phrase, Radini was being "kicked upstairs"—promoted, but to a position of less real influence. His friends in Rome were disconsolate. He was leaving a national field for a merely diocesan one. Nor was Bergamo, unlike Milan or Venice (or Palermo!) the see to carry an automatic Cardinalate. That a monsignor in Rome could be more powerful than a bishop outside it was typical of the topheavy centralization of the Church's governmental structure as it had developed from the late middle ages.

One of Radini-Tedeschi's best friends was Giacomo della Chiesa, another of Cardinal Rampolla's pupils. Della Chiesa came of a noble family of Genoa; like his friend he had attended the Accademia dei Nobili Ecclesiastici and, after a similar spell teaching in his diocesan seminary, had been summoned to Rome to work in the curia. He became a *minutante* in the Secretariat of State, preparing in précis the world's news for his chief, Rampolla. Della Chiesa had nothing of his friend Radini's presence; he was not only unusually small but slightly deformed; he walked with a limp and one eye was higher than the other, giving his face an odd, quizzical expression. He was shy and reserved, silent, with a dry humor, extremely orderly and industrious; but he had both feeling and courage, as the events of his life show.

Della Chiesa's turn to be kicked upstairs came in 1907, just after the condemnation of Modernism in the encyclical *Pascendi Gregis:* nor were the two events unrelated. He had remained loyal to Cardinal Rampolla who, superseded as Secretary of State by Merry del Val, was so much out of favor that people said della Chiesa's frequent visits to him were "bad diplomacy." Della Chiesa, who suspected he would be removed from Rome, expected to be sent as Nuncio to Spain, where he had started his career as Rampolla's assistant. Instead, Pius X, in a personal interview, told him he had appointed him Archbishop of Bologna. This was an alarming appointment for a shy bureaucrat, for Bologna, like most of the cities in the ex-Papal States, was strongly anticlerical. When he took his anxieties to his old chief, Rampolla encouraged him brusquely: "Well, you just go to Bologna and behave like an Archbishop." But it must have taken courage to face, not only the anticlericals but the Bolognese Catholics, who did not hide their disappointment at their new Archbishop's insignificant appearance. Nor were his reforming activities wholeheartedly welcomed, nor his tireless visitations which, in the mountainous districts, he accomplished on horseback.

The Archbishop of Bologna was traditionally a Cardinal, ever since the days when it was the greatest city of the Papal

States, but years went by and no Red Hat was given to della Chiesa. The Catholic Bolognese took this as a slur and rumor went that a deputation was sent to ask the Pope either to make their present Archbishop a Cardinal or to send them another. In fact it was not till the spring of 1914, seven years after his appointment to the see, that della Chiesa was made a Cardinal. It was the Pope himself who inserted his name on the list prepared by Merry del Val. It was well known that Merry del Val had little use for Giacomo della Chiesa. Yet only a few months later, on September 3, it was not the celebrated Secretary of State who was elected Pope but the rusticated Cardinal Archbishop of Bologna.

Benedict XV's career illustrates the methods used in Rome to cope with opponents. Like Radini-Tedeschi he was consecrated by the Pope himself; like him he was determined to prove his loyalty by becoming a model bishop. While both were in mitered exile they remained close friends, corresponding and visiting each other and if Radini had not died two days after Pius X it is likely that Benedict would have made him a Cardinal. As it was, Benedict was to summon his friend's secreatry, Angelo Roncalli, to Rome and set him on the path that would lead to the papacy.

Della Chiesa had less personal affection for Pius X than had Radini-Tedeschi. It was Rampolla who had won his friendship and admiration. Sometimes the Archbishop of Bologna would go to meet the long-distance train carrying Rampolla to a transalpine holiday and talk to him during the scheduled wait. After Rampolla's death della Chiesa kept a photograph of him on his desk and when he became Pope he told a visitor that he was still a pupil of Leo XIII—"and of him" with a nod to the picture. Rampolla had been one of the few highly placed prelates in Rome to protest against the excessive zeal of the anti-Modernists and it was Benedict, in his first encyclical *Ad Beatissimi*, who put an end to the official encouragement these heresy hunters had enjoyed in the previous pontificate.

Benedict's new policy came too late to save a famous movement in France, of Christian Democrat inspiration, known as *Le Sillon* (The Furrow) after its lively paper, which was censured by the Holy See in 1911. Its leader, Marc

Sangnier, a layman, submitted to the Pope's will, just as had the leaders of *L'Opera dei Congressi* seven years earlier. *Le Sillon* was essentially a youth movement and Sangnier is said to have been less successful with his adult colleagues, but the circles he started were centers for educating the social conscience and many Christian Democrats, later well-known, had their first political schooling with Marc Sangnier. *Le Sillon* made a great contribution to the *Semaines Sociales*, the itinerant summer schools of social action which continue to this day in France.

As if to emphasize that "the Church" supported quite another social and political outlook, it was during these years that Charles Maurras and the Catholic leaders of *L'Action Française*—also a paper as well as a movement—received so much favor at the Vatican. Young Catholics in France, including seminarians, were encouraged to join; the paper was widely read by bishops and priests, in spite of the fact that Maurras himself did not believe in Christianity and advocated actions hardly compatible with Christian ethics. The banner of his paper read: *Politique d'abord* (politics first). Catholics who had refused to follow Leo XIII's policy of *ralliement* with the Republic, who had been fanatically committed against the unjustly condemned Alfred Dreyfus, listened eagerly to Maurras' glorification of the destiny of France, a Catholic France, dedicated to an authoritarian "order" and crusading under a Catholic King. Because of this patriotic vision they swallowed much else of dubious quality.

Even at the time the Holy Office was forced to examine the morality of the *Action Française* and after long delays reported to the Pope that the movement's moral principles were not compatible with the Catholic Faith. In spite of this, Pius X decided not to publish the condemnation. Marc Sangnier, the faithful Catholic democrat, was disowned, but Charles Maurras, the avowed atheist, was allowed immunity. Seldom has political sympathy influenced more clearly a papal act, or refusal to act.

Benedict XV, caught up in the European War, did not live long enough to deal with *Action Française*, though he took care to let Marc Sangnier know of his esteem and his hope that he would become the leader of a new party formed on

Christian Democrat principles. It was not to be; for various reasons Sangnier was unsuccessful in politics after the First World War. When he died, in 1950, Angelo Roncalli was Nuncio in France and sent a message of sympathy to his widow, with a sincere tribute to his work and influence.

It was Pius XI who eventually condemned *Action Française* in 1926. The original papers on the subject in the Holy Office had been "lost" but when, after a new inquiry, the same conclusion was reached, they appeared again. The censure raised an unprecedented uproar in France. A large number of Catholics did not break off relations with *Action Française* preferring to live without the sacraments rather than desert the cause of Maurras. After endless representations to the Vatican Pius XII eased the restrictions in 1939. While the condemnation may have been applied too severely (Italians were surprised, as usual, that other nations actually obeyed the Pope) it is interesting that conservative and reactionary Catholics were not as obedient as the democrats they had labeled social modernists. When it comes to the pinch, Catholic authoritarians find it almost impossible to believe they can be wrong.

All this has a direct bearing on Angelo Roncalli's life, since he was formed in the school of the Christian Democratic movements and attended the French *Semaines Sociales* with his bishop; the bound volumes are still on the shelves of his house in Sotto il Monte. He was one of the first supporters of Don Sturzo's *Partito Popolare* in 1919 and was sent to France in 1944 partly because he was thought to be acceptable to the *Mouvement Republicaine Populaire* which sprang up at the Liberation. His own social encyclical in the Leonine tradition, *Mater et Magistra,* and his allowance of an "opening to the left" in Italian and world politics, rise from his experience of the vicissitudes of Christian Democracy.

6 Modernists and Anti-Modernists

When he became Pope in 1958 at the age of seventy-seven, Angelo Roncalli was virtually unknown to the world; he was not a Church statesman, nor a writer. His lovable personality soon caught the attention of everybody, but his actions were put down to the impulses of an open heart and not to any convictions he might have about the needs of the Church. People believed him too readily when he said he was not a *savant*, not a theologian; they assumed that he had no ideas beyond the Italian clerical party-line, familiar even to outsiders from the columns of the Vatican newspaper, *L'Osservatore Romano*. As to his past life, everyone heard about his pastoral training in Bergamo but nothing was said about Modernism although it was the burning question (almost literally) of his youth. This silence is not surprising, for in Rome any connection with Modernism is still regarded with suspicion. Pope John is said to have remarked once that the Holy Office still held a postcard he had written long ago to a friend with Modernist leanings.

Yet as Pope, Roncalli took the extraordinary step of calling a Council to modernize the Church—what else does his much quoted word *aggiornamento* mean? The immediate explanations issued to modify its impact show how dangerous a word it appeared to officialdom. Modernization is a different thing from Modernism, a heresy condemned by Pius X in 1907. Yet if the Modernists were doing anything they were trying to modernize the Church, to bring it up to date, to make contact with the modern world. When they were condemned, so was this "modern world." Yet Pope John made it clear that he found much good in the modern world and wanted the Council to find ways for the Church to work for and with the world, wholeheartedly and fraternally. Was he a Modernist?

To some people the phrase "modern world" means no more than "technological society." They expected the Council to be a Catholic version of the assembly of the United Nations and were disappointed when, instead of proposing instant solutions to current problems, the Fathers began to discuss the nature of the Church, the collegial authority of bishops, the reform of the liturgy and the relationship between Scripture and Tradition in the interpretation of Divine Revelation. What did this have to do with the modern world?

But a Council is a deliberative and legislative body whose sphere of direct action is precisely the Church. Yet its decisions will influence Christians in the world. In order to modernize the Church it is first necessary to know what the Church is and what its situation in the world. The conciliar decisions only seem remote from the modern world if their implications are left unexamined. In discussing the collegial responsibility of the bishops the Council was reviving the fraternal element in the Church, long submerged by the paternalism of a papal monarchy. The synodal, elective tradition preserved, though not without defects, in the eastern and Orthodox churches, is once more in active development in the west, and with it a whole constellation of related ideas—the responsibility of laymen, dialogue within and without the Church, liberty of conscience, Christian democracy. The ideas outlined in the context of the Church have a tremendous potential for action in the world. They integrate the structure of the Christian society with the highest communal and fraternal ideals of the human society—not by identifying them, but by looking at both with new eyes.

Pope John was not only in sympathy with these developments but pointed the way to them. In his magnificent speech at the opening of the first session of the Council on October 11, 1962, when nobody quite knew what was going to happen, he said: "In the daily exercise of our pastoral office we sometimes have to listen, much to our regret, to voices of persons who, though burning with zeal, are not endowed with too much sense of discretion or measure. In these modern times they can see nothing but prevarication and ruin. They say that our era, in comparison with past eras, is getting worse and they behave as though they had learned nothing from history, which is, nonetheless, the teacher of life. They behave as though at the time of former Councils everything was full of triumph for the Christian idea and life and for proper religious liberty.

"We feel we must disagree with these prophets of doom who are always forecasting disaster, as though the end of the world were at hand.

"In the present order of things Divine Providence is leading us to a new order of human relations which, by men's own efforts and even beyond their expectations, are directed toward the fulfillment of God's superior and inscrutable designs. And everything, even human differences, leads to the greater good of the Church."

Simple as it sounds, this was a new outlook for Rome. In another key passage John XXIII dealt with the errors of the modern world, so often denounced by these prophets of doom. Recent Popes have reiterated condemnations of them. But John said: "Often errors vanish as quickly as they arise, like fog before the sun. The Church has always opposed these errors. Frequently she has condemned them with the greatest severity. Nowadays however the Spouse of Christ prefers to make use of the medicine of mercy rather than that of severity. She considers that she meets the needs of the present day by demonstrating the validity of her teaching rather than by condemnation."

He pointed out, moreover, that men of today could judge the falsity of certain opinions by their consequences. And he was not speaking only of Christians but of men in general when he said: "Men are ever more deeply convinced of the paramount dignity of the human person and of his perfecting, as well as of the duties which that implies. Even more important, experience has taught men that violence inflicted on others, the might of arms and political domination, are of no help at all in finding a happy solution to the grave problems which afflict them."

Pope John put on his spectacles to read this speech, flipping over its pages in a businesslike way, completely and unself-consciously devoted to the real needs of an occasion which others had tried to turn into a pageant. In his own person he had already transformed the autocratic papacy into a ministry of fraternal love, and now he gave the impetus to those who were out to do the same in the many fields of action covered by the program of the Council. But to understand what was being done we must examine, however briefly, the historical situation which had enthroned the prophets of doom in the Vatican and made denunciation of the modern world seem almost an article of the creed.

Advanced technology does not worry the prophets of doom, who are willing to use typewriters and radio to proclaim the wickedness of the modern world. To them, the modern world is the world which has emerged from the triple revolution, political, industrial and scientific, of the last two hundred years. All these movements originated outside the Church and often in opposition to it. Most Catholic leaders reacted to all three with denunciation and lamentation, while nourishing the hope that all would be well if "the right people" returned to power and the Church regained command of society. Consequently, all through the nineteenth century the mind of the Church, so far as authority represented it, was turned toward the past; the past was idealized, the present rejected, the future feared. This attitude contrasted with the cult of progress then current in the secular world, which was equally unbalanced. Extremes feed each other by their violent antagonism.

Of course it was not only the Catholic Church in Europe but Christianity as a whole which endured this prolonged crisis. Regarded from one point of view it dated from the advent of the first denial of God's existence, of an eternal reality beyond this present world. Initially confined to circles of clever men this type of disbelief has spread till it has now reached large masses of people. It is not to be confused with the religious ignorance of the poor in nineteenth-century cities, who knew little of God but scarcely knew they did not believe. Conscious disbelief, even if more imaginative than intellectual, is quite different from religious ignorance. The progress of this disbelief was linked with the progress of science, partly because of the inability of Christians to face new ideas. The situation was most acute in France, where until the end of the century the learned world was virtually composed of atheists. Because it was the largest and most coherent Christian body in Europe the Catholic Church exemplifies the position, but others besides Catholics tried to escape the challenge of the present by a retreat into the past, or into a private world. This was the "emigration to the interior" of the nineteenth century, a concentration on personal devotion and a rejection of current political and intellectual developments. The Church was almost totally divorced from the world.

In this situation of siege, criticisms from without could be denounced as the malice of the enemies of God, but when criticism came from within, then panic set in. Hence the frenzied reaction to Modernism: "the modern world" had somehow got inside the Church itself. The liberal, social, and scientific ideas of the world were being applied to the Church by men who professed to be Catholics. Social ideals had already got a footing under Leo XIII—the prophets of doom now realized that it had been the thin end of the wedge. So L'Opera dei Congressi was disbanded in Italy and later Le Sillon in France. But the directing force of this invasion of the Church by the modern world was ideological rather than political, a hideous theory or complex of theories; an insidious heresy. Someone had the bright idea of calling it Modernism.

Maurice Blondel, the French Catholic philosopher, meditating on the crisis at the turn of the century, thought its real cause was what he called Veterism—the system of those who made the past the measure of the present. The standard was not the whole past of the Church, but that part of tradition codified in the post-Reformation centuries. Recently this type of Catholicism has been described as nonhistorical orthodoxy, because it was worked out before the modern idea of history had revolutionized the whole world of learning. In the time of Pius X its exponents called it Integral Catholicism—Catholicism uncontaminated by any idea from the world outside the Church. In France this gained these intransigents the nickname of intégristes, and in that country they were usually associated with the reactionary movement of L'Action Française and often with the revival of scholastic theology. Integrism was proudly self-sufficient. It had no need of that modern world which had arisen outside the Church.

The integrists did not realize that their system was in fact enclosed by the forms of European society. At a time when

Europe dominated the world this passed unnoticed and even after the events of 1914–18 (which included the Communist revolution in Russia) it was possible for many to close their eyes to the shifts of power. The Second World War completed the break-up of the old Europe and its national colonial empires. In this new world Christianity was suddenly to find itself in a situation where the norms of its European past were almost meaningless. The process of rethinking which had begun long since was now accelerated and the survivors of Integral Catholicism, entrenched in the curial congregations of the Vatican, found themselves faced in the Council with a landslide toward that other tradition which for so long they had tried to suppress.

For there has always been another tradition in the Church, though for over a century its exponents have suffered from the misunderstandings of the men in power at Rome. The greatest prophet of this submerged tradition in the nineteenth century was John Henry Newman, who was born in 1801 and died in 1890, when Angelo Roncalli was a little boy in Sotto il Monte. Newman was a prophet with a mission to the Church in the modern age; he was one of the first to perceive history as a process of development and apply this to Christianity. His knowledge of the Bible and of the Fathers of the first centuries gave him a base sufficiently broad for a restatement of Christian doctrine to meet the challenge of conscious disbelief. To use Pope John's terms, he saw the uselessness of denouncing errors without demonstrating (in modern terms) the validity of the true teaching. Not for nothing has Newman been called the invisible father at the Second Vatican Council. At the First he was suspected of crypto-heresy because he supported the minority who opposed the extreme papalists and succeeded in modifying their original proposals for the decree on the Pope's infallibility. At the time of the Modernist crisis some tried to trace the new heresy to Newman's works; they failed and he was not condemned. Indeed, had he been better understood, some false starts might have been avoided. Just because the tradition Newman represented had been squeezed almost out of existence, too many men based their attempts at modernization merely on current philosophical and scientific theories. In consequence Modernist writers like George Tyrrell now seem dated to the early twentieth century, and appear much less modern than Newman, whose last great work appeared in 1875.

Many Catholics are shocked at talk of parties within the Church. Indeed it has been part of the anti-modernist mystique that there could be no differences of opinion of any importance. Unity was equated with uniformity. There was only one theology, only one philosophy, just as there was only one Church; anyone who failed in any way to conform to the dominant system was suspect. Yet we have only to read history to realize that there have always been differences within the Church; without them the understanding of Christian doctrine could not have developed. Newman was right to deplore the lack of differing theological schools in his own time, and in his first encyclical Pope John quoted Newman's favorite aphorism, inherited from the Fathers: *"in necessariis unitas, in dubiis libertas, in omnibus caritas"* ("in what is necessary, unity; in what is uncertain, liberty; in all things, charity"). Yet differences have always led to violent clashes of feeling. The conflict between Modernist and Veterist was no exception; people were afraid because no one doctrine was at stake but the approach to all doctrine, to Christianity itself. Fear breeds violence. The repercussions were still echoing fifty years and more after the condemnation of 1907.

Pope John's remarks, at the opening of the Council, on how to deal with errors, arose out of a passage in which he suggested "how much is expected of the Council in regard to doctrine." He said: "Our duty is not only to guard this precious treasure, as if we were concerned only with the past, but to dedicate ourselves with an earnest will and without fear to that work which our era demands of us, pursuing thus the path which the Church has followed for twenty centuries." As a historian he knew that the understanding of doctrine had always been developed through meeting the questions raised in each phase of human civilization, and that Councils have played a vital part in this process, especially during times of crisis. This Council was not called upon to repudiate what had been decided in past centuries, but it was expected to make "a step forward toward a doctrinal penetration and formation of consciences in faithful and perfect conformity to the authentic doctrine which, however, should be studied and expounded through the methods of research and the literary forms of modern thought. *The substance of the ancient doctrine of the Deposit of Faith is one thing, but the way in which it is presented is another."* And he added that this doctrinal renewal should have a pastoral orientation—it must be directed toward men as they actually are, living in the world today.

The sentence italicized above does not refer to new methods of teaching an agreed syllabus but, as the context reveals, to the historical and literary disciplines which have revolutionized the study of the Bible and are now being applied to dogmatic theology and the decrees of past Councils. Ancient formulations of Christian doctrine have to be evaluated in their full historical context and the substance separated from what belongs merely to the mental concepts of the period: primitive cosmology and anthropology, legendary history, the mythical expression of imaginative truth and the literary conventions of archaic tradition. Pius XII had already given cautious approval to these methods so far as the Bible was concerned in the encyclical *Divine Afflante Spiritu* in 1943, but in 1950, alarmed at some of the applications made, he put on the brake with *Humani Generis,* a directive which conservatives used to renew their attacks on the theologians and scholars committed to the new approach. During the '50s many of them were suspended from teaching by their superiors or moved to isolated posts. Apart from giving these harassed men new hope in his speech, John XXIII, who had experienced the situation in France as Nuncio, appointed many of them as *periti,* skilled theological consultants, to the Council, and they became moving spirits behind it. Pope Paul VI concelebrated Mass with some of them, in the last session.

It was no accident that the first theological crisis of the Council occurred on the introduction of the schema *De Fontibus Revelationis*—on the sources (plural) of Revelation. Drawn up in the terminology of post-Tridentine scholasticism it was attacked by bishops representing the Biblical and historical approach and a vote for its withdrawal and revision received a large majority, but not the two-thirds required by the rules of procedure. This was the only occasion when Pope John intervened—on the side of the majority. The schema was sent back to a new commission and later was passed under the title *De Divina Revelatione* (On Divine Revelation).

This was a victory for the bishops and theologians dissatisfied with the old formulations: God's revelation is in Jesus Christ, not a set of propositions, some deduced from Scripture and some from Tradition. There has to be a revaluation of the idea of Tradition in the light of the new understanding of history. The issues involved bear on the dialogue with Protestants and on the study of the Bible by Catholic scholars and theologians. It is interesting that it was the so-called progressives who forwarded the program which Pope John had broadly sketched for the Council; eventually they carried the rest of the Fathers with them, out of the enclosure of the European past and into the modern world. These men inherited many of the methods and insights of the scholars who had been suspected of Modernism. But if Modernism was a heresy, how is it that the heirs of the Modernists became the majority in the largest Council of Catholic bishops ever held? What *was* Modernism?

The decree *Lamentabili*, published by Pius X in July 1907, condemned, in the manner of the 1864 Syllabus of Errors, sixty-five erroneous propositions, mostly extracted from the writings of the Abbé Alfred Loisy, a famous French Biblical critic. Some are so awkwardly expressed as to suggest that the assessors of the Holy Office scarcely understood what they wished to condemn. Loisy pioneered the application of historical method to the interpretation of Scripture and much of his early work is now generally acceptable. But in controversy with the Protestant scholar Harnack, who separated historical Catholicism from the Christianity of the New Testament, Loisy was led to disconnect dogma altogether from historical fact, maintaining that the Catholic religion developed in response to the psychological needs of humanity. It was inevitable that the Church should repudiate such a dichotomy of fact and theory. After he was excommunicated Loisy said that he had only believed Catholic doctrine in this symbolic sense ever since 1895, though this statement may represent a later realization of what his early position implied. He gradually gave up all form of Christian belief and died unreconciled to the Church.

Loisy's limelit career into skepticism made things difficult for other scholars who used similar methods but remained faithful Catholics. To some people Loisy's apostasy justified condemnation of his methods of exegesis, just as the rumor (untrue) of Abbé Houtin's marriage was said to prove that Moses wrote the Pentateuch! The excitement in France was extraordinary; ferocious battles were waged in newspapers and pamphlets. The protagonists were usually anticlericals and anti-Modernists; the so-called Modernists spent more time anxiously writing to each other than to the papers.

Lamentabili was a trial to Biblical critics but did not much affect the philosophers, let alone Catholic writers. But on September 8, 1907, the Feast of the Blessed Virgin's Nativity, Pius X published his encyclical *Pascendi Gregis*, making it clear that the Modernists the Holy See wished to condemn were not a mere handful of Biblical scholars but many laymen "and even priests" who were trying to subvert the Church under the pretense of reform.

"The Modernist sustains and includes in himself a manifold personality," announced the encyclical; "he is a philosopher, a believer, a theologian, a historian, a critic, an apologist, a reformer." As nobody could be all these in one the condemnation effectively included almost anyone who advocated reform in the structure or doctrinal formulations of the Church. Priests were suspended from preaching or writing; laymen were in danger of having their books censured or put on the Index. Worst of all was the ubiquitous atmosphere of suspicion engendered and the heresy hunt among the intellectuals. For although few held the Modernist theories in the form in which they were anathematized—immanentism, subjectivism, psychologism—yet it was not hard to throw suspicion on works which used modern historical and philosophical methods in examining the problems raised by advances in human knowledge.

Pascendi provided a powerful weapon for the heresy hunters. Not only were its terms vehement even for a Vatican document (for the Curia uses the vocabulary of a bygone era), but it exhorted religious authorities to search out the hidden Modernists in seminaries and other institutions: instructions for an ecclesiastical purge which was carried out with enthusiasm, especially in France. Of course the extreme antagonism between Catholics and the anticlerical government gave added ferocity to the pursuit of supposed traitors within the ranks. An anti-Modernist oath was imposed on all Catholic bishops, teachers, and priests; it continued to be taken seriously at least until the Second Vatican Council. Modernism became a dirty word and people were afraid of any opinions which might be considered Modernist.

The language of *Pascendi* breathes fear, for it is fear which suspects conspiracies among opponents who have little in common but their opposition. The Modernists were referred to as a secret society of cunning agitators, only remaining in the Church in order to poison it from within, the agents of a heresy as insidious as an epidemic. The image of heresy as a disease is very ancient; it witnesses to the Church's consciousness of itself as an organic community. But treatment consisted in cutting out the diseased member and shunning contact for fear of contagion. Even diseases can be cured, or arrested, better if they are understood. Heresies are cured by truth, not by the persecution of heretics.

Nor is every new idea necessarily heretical; under the heading of Modernism much was included by Pius X and his advisers which merely seemed novel to them and when some opinions seemed to contradict each other the Pope sadly declared that this must be done deliberately to deceive. The Modernists were credited with a conscious plan to destroy Catholic doctrine. Even Loisy had originally wished only to defend it, yet sometimes one has the feeling that the Integrists projected their image of Loisy's subtle, ingenious, and secretive mind on to all others suspected of Modernism, most of whom were quite different, both from him and from each other. The Abbé Lucien Laberthonnière, for instance, who was forbidden to preach or publish, but remained faithful, used to make trouble for himself by his frank delight in shocking the brethren. He once remarked that Thomas Aquinas had done more harm to the Church than Martin Luther . . . and this was taken seriously.

But who were these Modernists, conspiring to subvert the Church? There was Loisy in France, George Tyrrell in England, and in Italy Ernesto Buonaiuti and the "social Modernist" Romolo Murri, who was reconciled to the Church before he died. None of these men founded a school, nor were they followed out of the Church by many friends or disciples. Most of the suspects lived and died as faithful Catholics. Such were the philosopher Maurice Blondel, the Abbé Laberthonnière, F. M. Lagrange O.P., the founder of the Biblical School at Jerusalem, the historian Monsignor Duchesne, Father Pierre Battifol, Baron von Hügel, the Abbé Brémond, and many others. As Blondel's recently published correspondence shows they were made anxious by the papal condemnations and harried by the heresy hunters, but they lost neither faith nor intellectual integrity. So far as they were allowed to work, they worked; out of their patient persistence they created anew the tradition which came into its own only in 1962, long after they were all dead, in the Council called by John XXIII.

There was no Modernist conspiracy, but there was an anti-Modernist conspiracy, a secret society whose inner ring within the Vatican was run by a certain Monsignor Umberto Benigni who worked in the Secretariat of State under Cardinal Merry del Val. The fantastic story of *La Sapinière* (*The Fir Plantation*), the nickname of the respectable *Sodalitium Pianum*, only came to light after the First World War because the Germans happened to discover a cache of papers in Belgium, at first thought to be the work of spies, as they were letters full of code names and phrases. They turned out to be Benigni's communications with some of his ecclesiastical spies. "Michael" was Pius X (sometimes Michelet or even Lady Micheline), Merry del Val was "George," bishops were aunts and priests were nephews. Benigni called himself Ars, Arles, Charles, Charlotte, and other names, including "Lady Friend of O."

The *Sodalitium Pianum* was a pious sodality named after St. Pius V, the rigorist ex-Inquisitor Pope who "deposed" Queen Elizabeth in 1570. Benigni had been professor of History and Diplomatic Style at the Accademia dei Nobili Ecclesiastici, and he had many contacts. Merry del Val gave him a place in the Secretariat in 1906. A year later he started a paper, at first known as *Corrispondenza Romana* and later as *La Correspondance de Rome*. Benigni kept in touch with several satellite papers in different countries and was able to run successful smear campaigns, with all these papers quoting each other. *La Correspondance* was known as Nellie in Benigni's code. Merry del Val was probably not aware of all Benigni's activities, though he knew about the paper and did not suppress it till 1913. In later years Merry del Val admitted to an English Oratorian that at the time they did not understand what they were dealing with; exactly the conclusion produced by reading the letters and official pronouncements of the period. Pius X received the members of the *Sodalitium Pianum* but he can hardly have known of the extensive campaign of insinuation and informing that was carried on from the Vatican itself. Nevertheless it was the papal encyclical which had first given encouragement to the heresy hunters and sincere though the Pope may have been in his conviction that a wicked conspiracy of Modernists existed, this did not justify the revival of the Inquisitorial spirit in the attempt to impose uniformity of opinion by force. Torture and death were no longer employed but intimidation and intrigue are not honorable substitutes.

Although it was Benedict XV's first act in 1914 to repudiate Integral Catholicism, in his encyclical *Ad Beatissimi*, and though he suppressed the *Sodalitium Pianum* in 1921, he could not remove all the anti-Modernists from high office. There they remained, exercising a more cautious but far-reaching influence and training suitable juniors to carry on the same inflexible system. "Modernism" remained a condemned heresy and "veterism (as Blondel called it) continued to be the criterion of orthodoxy. Those who did not conform were still liable to sudden transfers and interrupted careers. It was not till the Council began that the world became aware of these influential guardians of (non-historical) orthodoxy—and they discovered that they were a shrinking minority among the bishops of the world. But when the man who became Pope John was young, this tradition dominated the Vatican and the Catholic world and made things difficult for those who longed to modernize the Church.

Angelo Roncalli was not quite twenty-six when the encyclical *Pascendi* was published and had been a priest for only two years. Not a philosopher, nor attracted to theology as taught in the seminary, he was not directly affected by it. But no one could live through the years that followed and not be touched in some way by the ecclesiastical passions aroused.

After his ordination Roncalli's notes in his spiritual journal were confined to his yearly retreats and were no longer an outlet for religious emotion. They were short and practical. But in the autumn of 1910 the style suddenly reverted to a youthful outburst of feeling—and the subject was Modernism. Roncalli's reaction was conventional and naïve.

"Jesus has deigned to give me an even clearer understanding of the necessity of keeping whole and intact my 'sense of faith' and 'being of one mind with the Church,' for he has shown me in a dazzling light the wisdom, timeliness, and nobility of the measures taken by the Pope to safeguard the clergy in particular from the infection of modern errors, which in a crafty and tempting way are trying to undermine the foundations of Catholic doctrine." These papal measures were concerned with Roman and other Italian seminaries. "The painful experiences of this year, suffered here and there, the grave anxieties of the Holy Father and the pronouncements of the religious authorities have convinced me, without need of other proof, that this wind of modernism blows very strongly and more widely than seems at first sight, and that it may very likely strike and bewilder even those who were at first moved only by the desire to adapt the ancient truth of Christianity to modern needs. Many, some of them good men, have fallen into error, perhaps unconsciously; they have let themselves be swept into the field of error. The worst of it is that ideas lead very swiftly to a spirit of independence and private judgment about everything and everyone."

Roncalli reminded himself that "it is the Church which transforms and saves the peoples and the times, not the other way round." He determined to guard his faith, "the holy, pure, simple faith of my parents and the other good old folk of my family" and to take particular care in the seminary, where he was teaching history and apologetics, to show his loyalty to the Church and the Pope.

One of the painful events of the year to which he referred may have been the expulsion from the seminary staff of Don Giuseppe Moioli, who had followed Roncalli to the Roman Seminary and later specialized in Biblical studies. The published facts are not sufficient to reconstruct the episode with any clarity. The bishop was reluctant to take action but pressure was put on him and the newspapers entered the fray, with more passion than knowledge. Moioli was removed, and with him a friend who had defended him. Roncalli was upset by the whole episode but he defended the bishop in the diocesan magazine (anonymously) though in such guarded terms that only those familiar with the circumstances could interpret the references. It seems that Roncalli himself was suspected by some of holding Modernist opinions, but he retained the bishop's confidence and continued to teach in the seminary.

The spiritual journal can be misleading, since it does not contain the whole of Roncalli's mind. His devotional habits were always more conservative in form than his general opinions. In 1910 he could be convinced by a retreat preacher (Padre Moretto S.J.) that Modernism was an insidious disease, more widespread than he had supposed. But by the autumn of the next year, when he was nearly thirty, he had realized that the issues were not so simple and that the campaign against "modern errors" was being carried on in some questionable ways. The evidence for this development is contained in an article he wrote for *La Vita Diocesana* (*Diocesan Life*) which is reprinted as an appendix to the edition of his *Life of Radini-Tedeschi* passed by him for publication before he died in 1963. It was written at the request of his colleagues on the staff of the seminary, dated September 29, 1911 and signed with his name and status as Professor of Apologetics. The article dealt with a course of lectures given at the Bergamo summer school of social sciences by a priest designated simply as Padre M.

Padre M. had evidently come to Bergamo to denounce the errors of Modernism, whether or not this had any relevance to the subjects under study. Roncalli was careful to say he had not been present at every lecture; nevertheless he had attended seven or eight. He began by praising the culture of Padre M., who contributed to "the best periodicals," but confessed himself disappointed by his performance. He was at once surprised and disconcerted by the "impulsiveness and lively general tone, to call it nothing else" which the lecturer used, referring to specific persons and mixing up with valid observations "others which seemed to me exaggerated and not well attested." Roncalli said he could not reconcile these polemics with the quiet atmosphere of a summer school. "Certainly Padre M. rightly stated many hard and searing truths, especially against those who in a certain measure favour modernist ideas: but are there any of these in the Social School?" Surely, Roncalli surmised, he could not be directing his thunders against the seminarians present, brought up by himself and his colleagues on the pure milk of Roman doctrine? Moreover: "If the truth and the whole truth had to be told I do not see why it had to be accompanied by the thunders and lightnings of Sinai rather than by the calm and serenity of Jesus on the lake and on the mount."

Here he put his finger on the point which betrayed the motives of the anti-Modernists; they were attacking out of fear and it blinded them. He said he had tried to find good in the method but that it was too uncongenial to his own habit of mind. He even wondered if his discomfort might not be due to himself till he discovered that others felt the same.

Having thus politely criticized the manner rather than the matter of the distinguished lecturer, Roncalli proceeded, still courteously, to demolish the performance piece by piece. Padre M.'s "fire" not only led him to indulge in what seemed like personal innuendo (of course it could not be, he added) but played havoc with the order of the course, involving him in long digressions in pursuit of Modernists which had nothing much to do with the school of social studies. Roncalli slyly suggested that it looked as if Padre M. had not made enough preparation for the school, relying merely on his extensive general knowledge; what a contrast, he observed, to the careful attention given to its needs by the other visiting professors.

Worse still, in the "dizzy fever" of the lecturer's polemics, some of his judgments had been expressed in an absolute and one-sided way, unsuitable for the immature minds of young men who were unlikely to see how to reconcile his dogmatic principles with others equally true and Catholic. Roncalli picked two examples: Padre M.'s account of the value of internal and external proofs; and of the worth of human reason according to Kant and according to St. Thomas Aquinas. But, said Roncalli, wishing to be fair, it may have been the speaker's vehemence which left this impression of one-sided dogmatism.

However, in his next criticism he made no excuse for the Padre's intemperate language. The enthusiastic integrist had allowed himself to speak critically of the ninety-year-old Leo XIII's relations with youth and with Christian Democracy. Everyone went out shocked at such a judgment on a Pope—expressed in Bergamo too, "most Catholic of cities." From the safe distance of half a century we may be amused at this playing off of one supreme pontiff against another, Leo against Pius. But in that age of exaggerated deference to papal authority Leo's pronouncements were the only fortification behind which the Christian Democrats could safely entrench themselves. This was the year of the condemnation of *Le Sillon*.

Some further comments from this clarification, as Roncalli called it, reveal just how fantastic were the polemics of Padre M. The works of an eminent prelate were attacked for their "drop of Kantism" and soon afterward it appeared that this crypto-Modernist was none other than the great Désiré Cardinal Mercier of Belgium! Mercier was the hero of all those, like Bishop Radini-Tedeschi and his secretary, who wished to open a new approach to the modern world; in England he is chiefly remembered for his pioneer efforts toward Christian Unity. Again, Roncalli disliked the lecturer's attacks on Monsignor Duchesne, the Church historian, suspected of Modernism because he used modern methods of scholarship to explode old legends. Much might be said on this subject, Roncalli commented, but even so far as there might be some errors in some of Duchesne's works, at least the exposition could have been orderly and calm.

Finally, Padre M. had chosen his last talk to denounce *en*

bloc all the Catholic newspapers of Lombardy; these were not parochial newssheets but the major Italian dailies of the democratic tradition. Roncalli ended by expressing his sorrow that Padre M.'s undoubted gifts had not succeeded in serving altogether usefully either the cause of pure doctrine or "the harmony of the hearts of all Catholics in following with docility and love the directions of our Holy Father Pius X."

In his retreat notes of 1911, made only a few days after the article summarized above, Roncalli simply confirmed his last year's intention of guarding his "loyalty of heart and mind to the Church and to the Pope." He added only: "In days of uncertainty and sadness St. Alphonsus used to say: 'The Pope's will: God's will!' This shall be my motto and I will be true to it. O Lord, help me, for I desire you alone!" This brief entry contrasts with the emotional tone of the retreat made the year before. The significance of St. Alphonsus' exclamation, which Roncalli said was often on the lips of Bishop Radini-Tedeschi, is that it expressed the saint's anguish when the Pope of his day suppressed the Society of Jesus at the instance of the rulers of eighteenth-century nations still officially Catholic. The founder of the Redemptorists deplored the Pope's act and only accepted it under religious obedience. Radini-Tedeschi, and so to a certain extent his secretary, chose this way of expressing similar feelings when they could not believe the papal policy the best for the Church.

Reading only the two entries in the spiritual journal we might conclude that Angelo Roncalli simply rejected the Modernism of his youth without understanding the issues. The article of 1911, together with his speech at the Council, and other public comments, show that he was not so naïve. The philosophical theories, the denials of the historic facts of the Christian revelation, that were condemned in *Pascendi*, certainly had no appeal for him. On the other hand, even as a young man, he understood those who felt the need to open the Church to the modern world and he saw how dangerous the narrow rigidity of Integral Catholicism could be. Typically he was most distressed at the savagery displayed and at the dogmatic imbalance of the heresy hunters; here his study of history gave him an intellectual base for a fair appraisal. But he was not passionate in response to the passion of

militant conservatives. Much of their violence derived from
fear of the modern world, fear that its skepticism would destroy the faith of the Church. Roncalli was not afraid of the
modern world. Nor did he fear the prophets of doom in the
Vatican, trained by the anti-Modernists of his youth. He was
not afraid in 1911. He signed his criticism of the integrist
Padre who wrote in the best periodicals.

7   At Work in Bergamo: 1905–15

On the Feast of St. Francis de Sales, January 29, 1905, Angelo
Roncalli was present at the consecration of Monsignor
Radini-Tedeschi in the Sistine Chapel of the Vatican. It was
the first consecration performed by Pius X after his election
to the papacy. During the ceremony it was Roncalli's duty to
hold the book of the Gospels—"the yoke of Christ"—on
Radini's neck while the Pope stretched out his hands to confer
the gift of the Holy Spirit special to a bishop's function in the
Church. It came back to Roncalli's mind when he was praying beside the dying Bishop in August 1914 and Pius himself
was on his deathbed. The Pope had whispered to Radini-
Tedeschi that after his own death he would come back to fetch
him to paradise; the Bishop did in fact die two days after
the Pope. Their personal relationship was affectionate, in spite
of differences of outlook, and Pius always wrote to Radini in
his own hand. After the consecration the new bishop was
given many gifts and a banquet in the Borgia apartments.
In just this way his friend della Chiesa was to be honored—
and removed from the center of power.

Bishop and secretary entered Bergamo on April 9 and soon
afterward they went on pilgrimage to the shrine of St. Charles
Borromeo at Milan and then to France: to Lourdes, where in
1858 Bernadette Soubirous saw the Blessed Virgin in a cave
by the river; to Ars, home of the saintly Curé, Jean Vianney;
and to Paray-le-Monial where at the Visitation convent, in

the seventeenth century, Margaret Mary Alacoque had seen her vision of Christ's Sacred Heart. It was Roncalli's first visit to France, which he was later to know so well. Radini-Tedeschi did not give up his pilgrimages on becoming a bishop. In September 1906 he led one to the Holy Land, a great experience for Roncalli and the first time he went east.

On his return from France in 1905 the Bishop set to work in earnest. He opened a canonical visitation which was to include all the 352 parishes and churches of the diocese; it was triumphantly concluded at Pentecost 1909. It was his secretary who prepared the list of inquiries and the follow-up after the episcopal visits to make sure decisions were taking effect. Bergamo was a fairly exemplary diocese already, but Radini had high ideals. He wanted to revive the custom of holding diocesan synods, which had fallen into disuse since 1724. He succeeded in holding a synod from April 26–28, 1910; it was not so much a miniature council as an assembly of the clergy for mutual encouragement and the dissemination of episcopal ideals. Pope John's synod in Rome was to turn out rather similar. But even the revival of the *form* was something, and Radini-Tedeschi's visitation was certainly more than a formality.

Roncalli began his active priestly life in an atmosphere of reform and modernization. Bishop Guindani had already introduced a reorganization of studies at the seminary and Radini included further modern subjects in the curriculum. He also embarked on the modernization of the buildings, installing electricity, piped water, baths and showers and laboratories for physics and other natural sciences. Roncalli related with pride (in his life of the Bishop) that during the war, when the seminary was used as a hospital, an army general had said to him: "They say priests are retrograde and obscurantist, but here they are in the avant-garde of progress!"

Much admired, too, was the hall built by Radini-Tedeschi for special occasions and named after Pius X. The bishop was a builder in the renaissance tradition, though he preferred space and proportion to luxury. Finding the curial offices inconvenient, dark and damp, he immediately transferred them to the old Bishop's palace and built a new episcopal residence, into which he moved in November 1906. The cleaning and restoration of the cathedral was completed in 1908. If there was any defect, Roncalli shrewdly observed, it was in "too much"—there was perhaps too much decoration, too much light, too much brilliance. Roncalli, who had a Bergamasque appreciation of the arts, learned much from the Bishop's culture and taste. Radini had brought his piano-forte but he scarcely ever had time to play. As to painting he had that primness which in England we call Victorian; there was in the palace a picture of St. Sebastian which he thought somewhat improper and he had it removed as soon as he arrived.

Roncalli took a special interest in the renovation of the seminary, not only because he had so recently been a student, but because from October 1906, on his return from the Holy Land, he was teaching there. First he taught history to boys aged twelve to eighteen; later he was appointed professor of apologetics and patrology—the study of the early Fathers of the Church. Although it was only a diocesan seminary it had a good educational record which the Bishop was keen to extend. The new regulations, the modernized discipline and timetable were sufficiently admired to be adopted by the other Bishops of Lombardy, one of the best organized ecclesiastical districts of Italy. Radini arranged burses for young priests at Louvain, Jerusalem, and Rome, to do further studies, especially in history and archaeology, Holy Scripture, Canon Law, and of course in social sciences. Radini himself had been professor of Christian sociology in the new Pontifical Leonine College in Rome from 1902–4, a foundation which owed almost its existence to him.

Roncalli was a popular lecturer, kind to his pupils and communicating his own enthusiasms. His students remembered him hurrying in a little late from his other duties, out of breath from rushing up several flights of stairs. Leone Algisi, who was able to read some of his lecture notes, commented that he was familiar with the controversial questions of the day. "Sometimes he would not hesitate to give a searching account of problems, leaving the door open, wherever possible, to bolder solutions even where his sympathies lay nearer to a more definite orthodoxy." This is what one would suppose from his article on Padre M.'s shortcomings, quoted in

the preceding chapter. The history of the Church provided
Roncalli with a solid base from which to explore the controversies of his own time. It gave balance and depth to his
judgment.

The Bishop encouraged his secretary to continue his own
historical studies. In December 1907 he gave a lecture, afterward published as a monograph, in honor of Cardinal Baronius the Church historian, on the tercentenary of his death.
Caesar Baronius, one of the first disciples of St. Philip Neri
and earliest members of the Congregation of the Oratory, had
been a favorite of Roncalli's ever since his days at the Roman
Seminary. In the vacations he used to wander round Frascati
and imagine the learned Cardinal in his villa there. His
tribute was nothing extraordinary, but it was honestly written.
To set forth his hero's character he had to refer to the ecclesiastical scandals of the late sixteenth century. He introduced a few words of apology to his own contemporaries, so
prim in comparison with those of Baronius. "But history is
history," he added sturdily. It was better not to hide the
truth, however unpalatable. And Baronius' virtue, his recoil
from riches and power, shone more brightly in contrast with
the ambition and intrigue then rife in papal Rome.

In the next year, 1908, with encouragement from the formidable new Prefect of the Ambrosian Library in Milan,
Achille Ratti (later Pope Pius XI), Roncalli began working
on manuscripts he had discovered in the Library, the Acts of
the Apostolic Visitation conducted in Bergamo in 1575 by
St. Charles Borromeo, the contemporary of Baronius and
most famous of the reforming prelates of the Tridentine
Catholic reformation. Accompanying his Bishop, Roncalli had
already met Andrea Cardinal Ferrari, the successor of St.
Charles in the see of Milan, and a saintly man who took a
personal interest in this young priest, advising him at a critical
moment of his career. The links with Milan were always close.
Roncalli conceived an admiration for Achille Ratti and was
impressed by his efficiency. He had told the Prefect about the
Bergamese manuscripts; the next time he came Ratti had already been through them, had the relevant ones ready on his
desk for photographing and offered suggestions on the work
of editing them.

Roncalli embarked on what was to become a life's work, so much was he to be interrupted and taken away from it. The priest friend, Pietro Forno, who assisted him after he had left Bergamo, died in 1938, two years after the first volume appeared. The final volume (of five) was completed only in 1958, the year of Roncalli's election to the papacy and half a century after the work was begun. It was a labor of love, but an exacting one, for the *Atti* were edited with a full apparatus of notes which involved careful research. These records interested him because they revealed in detail the state of his home diocese as it emerged from the middle ages into the modern period, but the work was in no sense designed for popular appeal. Roncalli always modestly disclaimed the title of scholar, but had he remained all his life teaching in Bergamo seminary this is the sort of scholarly historical work he would have done, and earned for himself an honorable position in that useful but unspectacular field.

Writing to Don Giuseppe de Luca, the priest writer and publisher, who brought out new editions of his works when he became Pope, Roncalli gave his reason for undertaking this work; he thought "immense profit could be derived from the accurate publication of ancient documents to illustrate the most interesting periods for the spiritual life of which the Church is the perpetual animator." He hoped that many more would follow his example. This was obviously the inspiration behind another monograph which he published in 1912 on the *Misericordia Maggiore* of Bergamo and other benevolent institutions administered by the Congregation of Charity. This was printed in Bergamo by the San Alessandro press, and was a carefully researched account of the history of Bergamo's principal charitable foundations. It may not be inappropriate to observe that one of the best ways to moderate the fanaticism of the anti-reform integrists was to document the past history of the Church. Superficial theories as to what constituted unalterable tradition would not stand up indefinitely to the accumulation and organization of indisputable facts. "History is the teacher of life," Roncalli was to say when he opened the Council in 1962.

Meanwhile things continued to be difficult on the social and political front. Radini-Tedeschi, in his first pastoral,

showed himself faithful to the principles of the Christian
Democrats, though he was now compelled to reorganize the
local committees on the diocesan basis demanded by the
Holy See. He set about the reconstruction with great care, for
he wished the social action movement to retain as much freedom as possible. He worked in close collaboration with Professor Nicolo Rezzara, then about sixty and his senior in years,
who had given the best of his life to the *Opera dei Congressi*,
now disbanded. In June 1905 a papal encyclical, *Il Fermo
Proposito*, was issued, laying down the norms for Catholic
Action; in July the following year the Pope, in *Pieni l'animo*,
deplored the unrest, especially among young priests, which
had resulted from the first. The Pope's suggestion was that
bishops should be more careful in their selection of candidates for the priesthood, with emphasis laid on the duty of
submission to ecclesiastical authority. In *Pieni l'animo* much
was said of the dangers of a spirit which welcomed everything
new: new orientations, new enterprises, new ideas. It was an
anticipation of the thunders of *Lamentabili* and *Pascendi* in
the next year, 1907. Radini-Tedeschi congratulated himself
that *his* young priests were not rebellious. This was certainly
not due to any docility peculiar to Bergamo, that city of independent men. The reason why the young priests of Bergamo
did not rebel was that their Bishop involved them in social
action, practical and theoretical. It was a better way than
refusing young men with minds of their own.

The summer schools of social studies have already been
mentioned, in connection with Roncalli's article on the anti-
Modernist lecturer. The diocesan journal for which he wrote
it was founded in January 1909, with Dr. Guglielmo Carozzi
as managing director and Don Angelo Roncalli as editor.
Carozzi was Roncalli's contemporary, in the Roman as well
as in the Bergamo seminary, and was generally considered
the more brilliant of the two. The editor probably had the
more arduous task.

The Bishop continued to employ him in many different
capacities. In January 1910 a new Catholic Action committee
was formed, for Italian Catholic Women—the first women's
organization in Italy. Roncalli was appointed its ecclesiastical
adviser and when, in October, the new statutes of the dioce-

san Catholic Action were approved, he became president of
the fifth section, the women's action. As such, he sat on the
central co-ordinating committee. As he was only twenty-eight
when first given this responsibility, it shows the extent of the
Bishop's confidence in his sense and judgment. After the war
Roncalli continued to help the women to organize themselves,
and years later, as Pope, he told the Roman section of his
long association with their efforts and how he had been present at the opening of their office in Rome in 1922. He managed to combine the traditional Italian respect for mother-
hood with an understanding that women have other duties in
society; the rights of women as persons even get a mention in
his last great encyclical *Pacem in Terris* (1963).

In all the political issues with which Catholic Action was
concerned, Roncalli was in the thick of things. In the early
autumn of 1909 eight hundred workers at Ranica, just outside
the gates of Bergamo, went on strike for their right to organize
themselves into unions. They remained out for fifty days,
but none of the incidents predicted by pessimists occurred.
The Bishop had immediately given them his support and
headed the list of subscribers for the assistance of the strikers'
families. This action was criticized, but Radini was supported
by Cardinal Ferrari of Milan and by other northern prelates.
Professor Rezzara, of course, was also on the side of the
strikers.

Roncalli defended his bishop's action in *La Vita Diocesana*.
He said that a priest should be a master of truth, a minister
of peace and an apostle of love, but also and above all master,
minister, and apostle of justice—"because justice makes great
peoples and nations." He pointed out that the clergy could
not stand aside from these issues of social justice without
becoming strangers in their own house, unfamiliar with the
modern situation of their people, who were likely to be led
into socialism. (At that time socialism was not only anticlerical but anti-Christian.) Typical of the period was Roncalli's insistence that the Church opposed liberalism in economics just as strongly as it opposed liberalism in politics.
We have to remember not only the professed irreligion of
Continental liberalism but its capitalist laissez-faire econom-

ics. Christian trades unions were then the obvious answer both to the capitalists and the socialists.

In 1910 the liberal government forbade religious instruction in schools and Radini-Tedeschi took a leading part in the Catholic campaign against this measure. In a sense the Popes had brought these difficulties on Catholics by refusing to allow them to take part in the national elections, thereby ensuring a government which made no secret of its hostility to the Church. Indeed it was the schools issue and the fear of socialism which combined to persuade Pius X and his advisers to allow a partial lifting of the ban during the last years before the war. Radini did not criticize papal policy; indeed he had always boasted of being "intransigent" on the Roman Question. He became much involved with the schools question, wrote two books on the subject and spoke on it in the last year of his life, at the Social Week in Milan in 1913.

From April till October 1913 a prolonged crisis was going on in Bergamo over the national elections. These were the first in which Catholics participated after the law granting universal suffrage to men. In 1904 Bergamo had won the Pope's consent to their using the vote and had elected two Catholic candidates. But in the national elections of 1907 the Holy See had made it clear that it did not want Catholics elected, since the Roman Question remained unsettled and they could not be neutral upon it. Rather, the Vatican favored the support of moderate liberal candidates. Of course this directive went out in the name of the Pope; consequently Bergamo, *cattolicissima città*, obeyed. But by 1913 the electors were restive. Some of the liberals had gone back on their promises; worse, since 1907 some had made common cause with a group of conservatives. It was not to be expected that this would please the electors of Bergamo, with their well-known sympathy for the left wing of Christian democracy.

Electoral policy in the province was decided by the central commission of Catholic Action; Rezzara was president and Roncalli sat on it in his capacity as president of the fifth (Women's) division. He signed the statement of policy prepared for Rome in the spring; it was approved and all seemed in order. But during the summer there were dissensions about the candidates. Roncalli, unconvinced that there was any principle at stake, and embarrassed by his close relationship with the Bishop, obtained permission to abstain from signing further statements. At the elections there was a fiasco in one of the districts; the Catholics were divided and the recommended candidate failed to get in. Roncalli wrote for *La Vita Diocesana* a long and detailed report on the election and emphasized the importance of sticking to one policy, once it had been decided by the central committee. In other districts the recommended candidates got in. They were the moderate liberals supported by the Holy See, politically inclined toward conservatism—not a contradiction in Italy!

Connected with these elections there was an episode revealing Radini-Tedeschi's difficulties with the Holy See. Rome had asked Count Medolago-Albani for an independent report on electoral affairs in Bergamo. For some years the Count had been in disagreement with Professor Rezzara and time had increased his conservative sympathies. He made severe criticisms of the conduct of political affairs and accused the leaders in Bergamo of ambition, of creating divisions between Catholics and of embittering relations with the moderate liberals. Medolago-Albani was a personal friend of Pius X and his report would carry weight, especially against Rezzara, the Christian Democrat leader.

Until that moment Radini-Tedeschi had been trying to keep clear of political involvement; in past crises he had maintained silence on controversial issues. But now, realizing that Rezzara's reputation was in danger, and with him the whole effort of the diocese on the political front, he went straight to Rome and took up Rezzara's defense. It was not the first time he had done so; there were letters from earlier years in which he had praised Rezzara, to the Pope and the high curial officials, and emphasized his devoted and Christian life. Now he spoke out frankly and firmly. Apparently the immediate situation was clarified, for no action was taken by the Holy See.

But Radini's great grief in these later years, which he confided to his secretary, was that he felt he had lost the confidence of the Holy Father. His personal affection and veneration for Pius X made this hard to bear; he knew his own loyalty and how hard he had worked to inspire obedience in others, no easy task in the crises of this disturbed pontificate. He thought that there were those at Rome who were listened to more attentively than himself, and he was probably right. As one of the group who had worked so wholeheartedly under Leo XIII he could not but be suspect to the opposite party, in the ascendant under Merry del Val. In his biography of Radini-Tedeschi, written in the year after his death, Roncalli suggested that the bishop's fears may have been unjustified with regard to the Pope himself, who always wrote to him kindly, and in his own hand. But the secretary added that there were those who occupied "other cathedra" as it were and employed themselves in "hurling stones at the backs" of any they could implicate in "modernist errors." They succeeded in creating in the Bishop of Bergamo the sense that the Holy Father did not fully trust him, and this saddened his last years.

Radini-Tedeschi was not old, barely fifty-seven, but he was already mortally ill. He had begun to lose his health in 1910, but holidays seemed to restore him. On the orders of his doctor he visited monasteries every summer, for a rest, particularly Einsiedeln in Switzerland. His secretary went with him. Radini continued working as hard as ever, writing books, delivering speeches, conducting pilgrimages and attending to diocesan affairs. Mentally he was full of energy, but his attacks of pain became more and more frequent. When at last the surgeons made an exploratory operation a large malignant tumor was discovered. The cancer had already progressed too far for any possible cure and Radini lived only a few days afterward.

In the fashion of the day Roncalli wrote a long account of the Bishop's illness and death. It was August 1914; the European War had just broken out and the Pope was dying—of a broken heart, people said. "I do not bless war," he said to a militant Christian, "I bless peace." Pius X died on August 20; Radini-Tedeschi two days later. "The Holy Father is calling me, he's calling me," he murmured to his secretary. And he would say, "Poor Belgium, poor Cardinal Mercier!"

At the beginning of the last phase of his illness the knowledge that he was expected to die came as a shock to him and he broke down, feeling he could not face the judgment of

God. Roncalli tried to comfort him with the reminder of all
the good he had done. After this Radini composed his mind
and everyone was impressed with his calm in the face of
death. He insisted that everything must be done in accordance with the ceremonial of the Church, which lays down
certain regulations for a Bishop's deathbed. During his last
hour Radini's friend, an older priest who had been assisting
him, broke down and Roncalli was called to take over the last
prayers. *"Ecco qua, il mio uomo coraggioso e forte,"* whispered
the dying man. ("Here he is, my strong and courageous
man.")

So died Giacomo Radini-Tedeschi, at the beginning of that
terrible war which was to end an era in Europe, at the same
time as the Pope he had honored so much, but whose policy
had caused him so much trouble and pain. For Roncalli he
remained the ideal Bishop; he kept Radini's photograph in
his room for the rest of his life. "Was he perfect then?" he
asked in his biography and proceeded to draw his portrait,
affectionately pointing out that he had the defects of his good-
qualities. His powers of leadership, of inspiration and organization, of quick decision, meant that his manner was sometimes brusque, even authoritarian; he often cut short other
people's doubts and queries. His warmth of feeling made
him sometimes precipitate in action and as he thought that
changing his mind was a sign of weakness he could be obsti-
nate. His frankness and his outspoken comments, especially
on "the enemies of the Church," occasionally disconcerted
people more gentle than himself, observed his secretary—who
was probably one of them! ("The Church has no enemies,"
Roncalli was to say, as Pope.)

But the younger man admired Radini's continual efforts to
pull himself up, to correct his own faults and to teach himself
the patience which was by no means natural to him. He
recorded an interesting aphorism of Radini's: "There is a
prudence which is boldness and a wisdom which consists in
breaking through all the obstacles which impede a straight
road." As Pope John XXIII, Roncalli himself, so different in
temperament, was to exercise this bold and wise prudence,
quietly bulldozing his way through the obstacles to reform
the Church.

But now, at thirty-three, no one could have envisaged Angelo Roncalli's future. He was a strong stocky man with thick short dark hair. In the group photographs of this period his face is basically serious, even earnest, though breaking into cheerfulness with his wide smile. He was already beginning to put on weight, and this worried him because it impeded his activities. It was before the days when slimming and exercises became fashionable and as he decided in every retreat to cut down on food he must have found it difficult to do so. Each year, too, he reminded himself that he must get up at half-past five. A willing horse, he was heavily overburdened in these years. Besides his secretarial duties he had the responsibility of the women's Catholic Action and his teaching in the seminary, the editing of the diocesan review and all the innumerable tasks arising out of the Bishop's requirements.

No wonder then in 1912 he wrote in his spiritual *Journal:* "I must not try to follow or find new ways of doing good. I live under obedience and obedience has already overburdened me with so many occupations that my shoulders are sagging under the weight." The next year, 1913, he recorded: "I wanted to rid myself of some of the burden of my responsibilities and to indicate which of these I would prefer to retain. But I have decided not to do anything about it. My Superiors know everything and that is enough. As I have not been asked about this I will be careful not to show my preference for one kind of work rather than another. I must proceed, as my spiritual director tells me, with my head in the sack of divine Providence."

The new Bishop could have kept Roncalli on his staff but it was expected that he would follow a different line from Radini's and Roncalli moved out of the episcopal residence to leave the field free. He shared rooms with his contemporary Carozzi and continued to teach in the seminary. From the career point of view the death of Radini-Tedeschi was a blow to his prospects; he had already seen others "getting ahead" of him and had resigned himself to the fact. Now that he seemed no longer in the running for advancements he could concentrate more on his scholarly interests. But he was not left in the seminary for long. In May 1915 Italy entered the war on the side of the Allies and Angelo Roncalli was called up.

8 Soldiers and Students

Whether Italy should enter the European War was the subject of much debate within the country. In the preceding years agreements had been made with the Central Powers but Austria was the old enemy of the Risorgimento and the cause of the Allies was the more popular. Italy would have done better to remain neutral but the war party prevailed. It was perhaps more an assertion of nationhood on the part of the government than a matter of conviction for the people.

War was declared on Austria and Germany on May 23, 1915, and the next day the reserves were called up, among them Angelo Roncalli. It was Whitsun. He went to Milan and there an old pupil saw him, thought he looked embarrassed in his unaccustomed civilian clothes and helped him through the formalities. Roncalli gave his token day's pay to this ex-student to buy himself a drink. He was now a sergeant in the Medical Corps and was sent back to Bergamo to work in the hospitals there. The main fighting was in the north and Bergamo was near enough to the front to be a receiving center for the wounded, so that although he never saw any fighting Roncalli was in direct contact with the soldiers.

As a sergeant he grew a thick black mustache. Looking at a photograph in after days he is said to have remarked, "That mustache was a mistake!" But, like the unusual hats he wore as Pope, this mustache had its significance; it indicated that he liked to do as others did. According to present discipline priests are not allowed to grow mustaches but soldiers are. Not that Roncalli wanted to hide the fact that he was a priest; even as a mere medical orderly he exercised his ministry among the wounded and the hospital staff. In Bergamo he organized a special Mass for soldiers and co-ordinated religious assistance to troops in the district. In March 1916 the government overcame its anticlerical prejudices so far as to appoint chaplains to the forces; Roncalli then became chap-

lain to the Reserve Hospital (the New Shelter) in the lower
town and stayed there till the end of hostilities in 1918. In
March 1917 he opened a Soldiers' Home in Bergamo, and in
June 1918 started an association for the mothers and widows
of soldiers.

The northern battle was conducted on mountainous terrain
and in appalling weather conditions. After the disastrous defeat at Caporetto in 1917 the Italian Army succeeded in reforming and held the Austrians at bay for another year. This
engagement of a considerable enemy force was of great assistance in lowering the pressure on the front in France, but
to the ordinary Italian soldier it seemed a prolonged and
almost pointless agony.

Little evidence is available for this period of Roncalli's life,
so important for him. It was very different from his youthful
introduction to barracks life. He was now a mature man in his
thirties, acting rather than being acted upon. His brothers
were also called up and La Colombéra was left to the old and
the very young.

Roncalli's position in the hospital was not an easy one.
Many of the officers and doctors were anticlerical and prejudiced against him from the start just because he was a priest.
One lieutenant colonel was particularly sarcastic and let himself go so far that Sergeant Roncalli found it difficult to exercise any control over his subordinates, who took their cue from
the sneering officer. At last he was driven to protest, in a
written report. The colonel made a half-hearted apology, re-
marking that while he was unlikely to get further promotion
the chaplain would probably end up a cardinal. Remembered
as prophecy, this was more likely to have been a sneer.

As long as there were any students in the top classes at the
seminary, Roncalli continued to give lectures there in the
evenings. One of them, Simone Bottani, recalled later how
curious they had been to see this Professor of Apologetics
who was also a military chaplain—this curiosity reflects the
novelty of the situation at that time.

"When Lieutenant Chaplain Don Angelo Roncalli entered
the classroom he was dressed as any other priest, but on his
hat and the cuffs of his coat were two gold stripes. He put his
hat down and smiled at us, made the sign of the cross and

began with the quotation from St. Peter's epistle: (I Peter, 4:15) 'Let none of you suffer as a murderer, or a thief, or a slanderer, or as one coveting what belongs to others. But if he suffers as a Christian, let him not be ashamed; let him glorify God under this name.'

"The course that he gave us was reduced from two terms to one. At the end of that one term we all left, but that one term remains unforgettable because his apologetics was based on a sound knowledge of modern science. We knew that in order to give us this course he had to study night after night."

Many years later when he was Patriarch of Venice, Roncalli sent a letter to a congress of military chaplains in which he thanked God for giving him this experience. "How much I learned about the human heart during this time, how much experience I gained, how much grace I received to be able to dedicate myself to the performance of my duties as military chaplain." And he added, in the style typical of his old age: "The military chaplains who are now in service should not be afraid to come and see this old chaplain, not celebrated for arduous military action, but one who keeps happy memories of a spiritual work." At the end of the letter he warmly invited any of them to visit Venice and to let him know in advance, so that he could "prepare a feast" for them.

If there was ever any danger of Roncalli's becoming a professional ecclesiastic, cut off from ordinary life, his war experiences prevented its realization. Working with the wounded gave a new depth and confidence to his character which is shown by his activities at the end of the war. He was not yet officially demobilized when, in November 1918, he opened a hostel for students at Palazzo Marenzi in the Città Alta. These were not seminarians but lay students attending the university or other courses of higher education. As well as accommodating some of the young men the hostel, which had a big recreation room, served as a center for others. Roncalli ran the place himself; for the first year he was even responsible for the finances. Such a venture for a priest was something new; this hostel may even have been the first of its kind. The Bishop took an interest in the experiment and later set up a committee to enlarge the scope of the project, though when it came to planning further hostels in the lower town it was

Roncalli who found himself left with the actual work. In his view, this was what always happened on committees!

As far as the students were concerned Roncalli's hostel was a great success, but he had to endure a good deal of criticism from outside. There was too much turbulence, there were not enough pious exercises, the rules were too lax, the students did not have the discipline they would have had in an ordinary Christian family, Don Roncalli was naïve and consequently things went on which he knew nothing about . . . Don Roncalli was not as naïve as some people thought and in spite of criticism he did not alter his methods in the least. He did not want to introduce the seminary regime with its rigid discipline and compulsory spiritual routine. There was daily mass, with prayers and a short commentary on the Gospel. With the students he maintained a friendly personal relationship and he was determined that they should have as much freedom as possible. Since it was Roncalli who ran the place, it was unlikely that the students' natural interest in politics and social action would be suppressed.

After he left, not much over two years later, the hostel ran into trouble and the experiment was brought to an end. Roncalli was unhappy about it, but he could no longer take any action. But the idea caught on; other student hostels were opened elsewhere in Italy. The interest of Roncalli's is that it gives a glimpse of the sort of work that attracted him and which he might have developed further had he been a free agent. In 1919 Roncalli made a six-day retreat from April 28 till May 3 at the house of the Priests of the Sacred Heart, a diocesan association restored by Radini-Tedeschi, to which he belonged. His notes reveal the spirit in which he approached his postwar work in Bergamo.

"During these last years there have been days when I wondered what God would require of me after the war. Now there is no more cause for uncertainty, or for looking for something else; my main task is here, and here is my burden, the apostolate among students. When I reflect on the manner, the circumstances and the spontaneity with which this plan of God's Providence, through the medium of my Superiors, suddenly took shape and is now evolving, my heart is touched and I feel bound to confess that truly the Lord is here. So often, in the evening, when I turn over in my mind the events of the day spent in looking after my dear students, I feel in me something of the awe which fell upon those two disciples on the way to Emmaus, as if in contact with the divine."

As usual, he had accepted wholeheartedly what turned up, but on these days during the war when he wondered about the future, what was in his mind? In this retreat, made when he was thirty-seven, he wrote down some thoughts full of feeling on the subject of ecclesiastical careers. "I will never say or do anything, I will dismiss as a temptation any thought, which might in any way be directed to persuading my Superiors to give me positions or duties of greater distinction. Experience teaches us to beware of responsibilities. These are solemn enough in themselves if assumed under obedience, but terrifying for whoever has sought them for himself, pushing himself forward without being called upon. Honors and distinctions, even in the ecclesiastical world, are 'vanity of vanities' . . . Anyone who has lived in the midst of these stupidities, as I did in Rome, and in the first ten years of my priesthood, may well insist that they deserve no better name." This throws a retrospective light on the more mundane aspects of living at the center of the Bishop's Curia. Roncalli was a shrewd observer of his fellow men and also of himself, since he recognized the temptation to make his own way in the ecclesiastical world. He had the energy, convictions, and ability to carry him far, if he chose. But he would not choose, if it meant pushing himself forward.

In this connection it is noticeable that he was given no teaching post in the seminary at the end of the war. In December 1918 he was made spiritual director, and was able to help the demobilized clerical students to adjust to their training for the priesthood. It was certainly a responsible post; yet it made no use of his intellectual abilities and earlier teaching experience. This was the more surprising as in 1916 he had published his life of Radini-Tedeschi, written in his spare time at the hospital, and had been to Rome, on August 22, 1916, to present a copy to Pope Benedict XV. Roncalli made no complaint, but it is impossible not to feel that he had been passed over. He did not give up his historical and cultural interests; from July 1919 he became an active member of the Athenaeum of Sciences, Letters and Arts in Bergamo.

In reading the retreat notes of 1919 one receives the impression that Angelo Roncalli was the type to have founded some new religious society. "The work I have set my hand to is enormous; the corn is already golden in the fields, but alas! the reapers are few. I will try, with prayers to God and my own endeavors, to inspire in young clerics and priests a love and enthusiasm for this form of ministry which excels all others. I will try to make it attractive especially to those to whom nature and grace have granted a special aptitude for working with the young. Who knows but that the right word and still more a good example may succeed, and I may soon find myself surrounded with a fine circle of brothers, all eager for the apostolate among young people?"

It was not to be; yet it is easy to imagine Angelo Roncalli as the founder of a modern congregation devoted to the needs of young people. Monsignor Loris Capovilla has recorded a note made by Roncalli on June 19, 1919. "The Corpus Christi procession moved in beauty and majesty near the Students' House. I was there with my boys near the wall of the garden in the direction of Via Arena. I watched the banners. I saw one of them, white, beautiful, gay; but alas, not a soul followed it. It was the banner of the Catholic Youth. I hurried immediately to Santa Maria to ask Jesus, as he blessed me, to accept and make fruitful my promise to work with my whole being so that next year that banner would not be alone, but would be followed by a band of bold young men singing Hosanna to the triumph of Jesus."

He succeeded; the next year forty young men followed the banner. It was 1920, the year when the National Eucharistic Congress was held in Bergamo. Roncalli had planned this great occasion with Radini-Tedeschi before the war and he delivered the address on the theme originally chosen by his revered bishop: "The Eucharist and our Lady."

In September 1919 he had given a retreat to some young people at San Vittore in Bologna. He had devoted himself completely to this new work. He thought of it as "the formation of the new generation in his (Christ's) spirit." In the retreat notes of 1919 he added: "Nothing could be finer or more honorable for me than this, nothing more important, especially at this time, in the whole Church of God." He was sure that the future of the Church was with these young laymen. He wanted them to be "apostles of truth and goodness" in the disturbed times that followed the disasters of the war. He was sure that this could only be achieved by kindness and understanding. "I will recognize no other school than that of the Divine Heart of Jesus. 'Learn from me, for I am gentle and lowly in heart.' Experience has also confirmed the supreme wisdom of this method, which brings real success. I will love my young students as a mother her sons, but always in the Lord . . ."

Nevertheless the students did not monopolize his time and energy. He continued to be ecclesiastical adviser to the women's Catholic Action and after the war, when women were doing so many jobs they had not done before, he organized welfare and educational associations for saleswomen, nurses, refugees, tram conductresses, and telephonists. It is said that in the Città Alta gossips complained: "This good man Don Angelo wants to organize even the telephone girls! Couldn't he be satisfied with the sacristans?" But true to the principles of Christian Democracy, Don Angelo found the telephone girls just as important to the life of the Church as the sacristans. It is interesting that so much of his early work was in assisting women to organize themselves—an innovation in European society at that time.

There were women who needed a different kind of care. Monsignor Capovilla mentions one "poor girl, sick in body and spirit" to whom Roncalli ministered, and quotes the note he made on May 11, 1917: "I think with sadness of the many similar cases and of all the innumerable hidden miseries, and I ask myself if we priests—and with us, good laymen—are generous enough. If only at times we had more tact, more constancy, greater magnanimity, how many more victories (we would have) among so many! We do something, but we get tired of it quickly. We don't know how to understand, especially, or sympathize, or wait. And to remember that the first thing St. Paul says in praising charity is, 'Charity is patient, is kind.'" Patience and kindness were the secret of Angelo Roncalli's enduring success with people.

We shall never know if Roncalli might have become the founder of a society devoted to the needs of modern youth, for at the end of the year 1920 he was called from this promising field and his life thenceforward took a wholly different turn. The call came from Willem Cardinal van Rossum, the Prefect of the Congregation of *Propaganda Fide* (in charge of missions), known as the "Red Pope," who invited him to take up a directing post in connection with an organization named the Association for the Propagation of the Faith.

The title suggests a missionary body, but in fact it was a fund-collecting society started at Lyons in France in 1822 by Pauline Jaricot, whose brother was a missionary priest. In that mission-conscious age her penny-a-week fund spread rapidly and in 1843 a similar effort, the Society of the Holy Childhood, was started to collect the pennies and prayers of children for the children of the mission lands. Under Leo XIII a rather different venture was launched to raise money to train the natives of mission countries for the priesthood: the Society of St. Peter the Apostle for Native Clergy. Founded in Paris, its headquarters were removed to Fribourg in Switzerland in 1896, to escape the hostility of the anticlerical French government.

Propaganda had decided to amalgamate these three societies, of French origin but for long international in scope, and transfer their headquarters to Rome. To effect the plan someone with tact and organizing ability was needed. Looking over the list of suggested names Benedict XV noticed that of his old friend's secretary. "*Questo, questo*" ("This one"), he said at once, with characteristic quick decision. He had read Roncalli's book on Radini-Tedeschi and had probably been informed of his recent activities. For the job contemplated Roncalli was an excellent choice.

But apparently Roncalli himself was not sure whether he ought to accept. What about his work with the students, so important for the future? To go to Rome, to become a member of the staff of the Congregation of Propaganda, part of the central administration of the Church, was certainly a step forward in an ecclesiastical career, but was it right to leave the pastoral ministry to which he had devoted himself, in order to reorganize the machinery of the missionary fund-raising societies? Was it not abandoning a real and necessary work for an administrative career, with all the dangers of ambition which he was so anxious to avoid? In his perplexity Roncalli turned to the saintly Cardinal Ferrari, Archbishop of Milan, friend of Radini-Tedeschi and of Benedict XV. Ferrari, who was dying of cancer of the throat, wrote to him: "Dear Professor, you know how fond I am of you. The will of the red Pope is the will of the white Pope, and therefore the will of God. Drop everything and go; a great blessing will go with you."

Roncalli obeyed. He accepted the call as from God and gave up the work, so congenial, which he had launched in his home town, the position he had made for himself there and the house he had bought and furnished as a hostel. For it was his own and in the retreat notes of 1919 he had reminded himself to be ready to give it up at any moment—the only condition on which a Christian can hold the goods of this world. Now, so soon, the time had come.

He obeyed Ferrari's advice so promptly that when he arrived in Rome, on January 18, 1921, and walked into the College of Propaganda, then still in the Piazza di Spagna, he found that there was no office allotted to him. Monsignor Camillo Laurenti (afterward a Cardinal) welcomed him in a friendly way but evidently no one had expected him to turn up so soon. On the steps as he went out he met Monsignor Bugarini, the ex-Rector of the Roman Seminary, who offered him a room till he could find accommodation. Soon afterward it was to be Roncalli who took Bugarini into his house.

For the time being Roncalli returned to Bergamo to finish the academic year, but in the interval he came to Rome several times, in the attempt to get things moving. As usual, the decision being made, he threw himself wholeheartedly into his new work which, from the first, he regarded as part of the missionary effort of the Church. His official title was President for Italy of the Central Council of the Papal Missions—which sounded a great deal more important than in fact it was. But on May 7 he was made a papal prelate. When he went back to Sotto il Monte in the summer, wearing his monsignorial purple, several old women thought he had been made a bishop. The dangers of office and honor were already upon him!

Bergamo had made him an honorary canon of the cathedral on March 13. Before that, in February, he attended the funeral of Cardinal Ferrari, in whom he lost a kind adviser and patron. In April he began the first of many tours in Italy, and while working towards the reorganization of the APF, he always tried to stir up interest in the missions. In October 1921 he visited a Marian shrine in Sardinia, and several other towns there; in November he visited Rovigo and Genoa, and on December 5–7, Montecassino. The rest of December was spent traveling in France, Switzerland, Belgium, Holland, and Germany, meeting representatives of the APF. He stayed with the Redemptorist Fathers in Paris, Brussels, and at Witten in Holland, where he spent Christmas; he also said Mass in Aachen, Cologne, and Munich cathedrals. Radini's pilgrimages had started him traveling and he always preferred to go and see people rather than direct their affairs from a distant office.

He had barely returned to Rome when Benedict XV, who had been coughing painfully for weeks, developed bronchitis and became seriously ill. Curiously enough, this diminutive, slightly deformed man had rarely been ill. On this occasion it amused him to remark that in the whole of his life he had only spent two and a half lire on medical expenses. In fact, his days may have been shortened by his insistence on carrying on with his usual routine until the last possible moment. On January 12, 1922, he spoke on the missionary ideal to the students of Propaganda College, after saying Mass for them; his cough was excruciating and his hands very hot, as the students noticed when they kissed his ring. On January 17 he was still receiving important visitors, but the next day he was unable to rise from his bed. It was the first day of the octave of prayer for Christian unity, which he had done much to promote.

Benedict remained alert, dry, and humorous as usual until the last of the three more days that he lived. It was in a rare moment of lightheadedness that he tried to get out of bed to continue his work—"I must deal with those important letters." He died at six o'clock in the morning of January 22, 1922, astonishing those around him by his unexpectedly fervent response to a conventional request that he should bless the people. He used almost his last breath to pronounce aloud the great blessing of the Trinity.

So died this great little Pope who, in seven war-shadowed years, laid the foundation for much that was done by his successors. He was sixty-seven. To understand Roncalli's even shorter, and greater, pontificate, we have to remember that of Benedict XV, whom he loved and admired. Pope John XXIII took up many of the themes of Benedict's encyclicals, shared his enthusiasm for international peace, for unity among Christians, for Christian social democracy, for a new attitude to missionary endeavor and the modern world and against all narrowness of mind within the Church. John, like Benedict, looked at things from a historical angle and spoke with an evangelical emphasis. Even in small things he showed that he followed in the tradition of Benedict; early in his pontificate he appeared in the close-fitting renaissance cap which Benedict also wore and the wonderful stole with ships is also seen in the pictures of the earlier Pope. To wear a stole emphasized the priesthood of the Pope, and perhaps helped to restore the ministerial image, in community with all priests, and to get away from the idea of monarchy and the absolute power of the papal office.

So a new Pope had to be elected in February 1922, with Italy in a ferment of social unrest which many feared would lead to a revolution on the Russian pattern.

9   Pope and Duce

Conclaves for the election of a Pope are supposed to be secret, but secrets shared by so many men usually leak out sooner or later. It took fourteen ballots to elect a successor to Benedict XV. The two main parties, one led by Merry del Val and La Fontaine, Cardinal Patriarch of Venice, and the other by

Cardinals Maffi and Gasparri, Benedict's Secretary of State, were almost evenly matched; in the first ballot they scored twenty-three and twenty-four votes respectively, while Achille Ratti, Cardinal Archbishop of Milan, secured only six. It was to break the deadlock that Pietro Cardinal Maffi, the Archbishop of Pisa, recommended his supporters to vote for Ratti, who then commanded enough conservative votes to gain the necessary two-thirds majority. The fact that when he was elected he chose the name of Pius must have reassured the party headed by Merry del Val.

Considering the even balance between the two opposing factions, Achille Ratti was a good choice. He was progressive in that he had no fears of the modern world of science and technology and was to give scholars support and encouragement throughout his reign. He restored the Papal Academy of Sciences and summoned to it scholars of all faiths and no faith. Yet in other respects, theologically and politically, he was conservative. He believed in Pius X's form of Catholic Action, "above political parties" and run under diocesan supervision. He had little interest in Christian Democracy and no favor for the new *Partito Popolare* founded after the war by Don Sturzo, with the approval of Benedict XV. Pius XI was anxious to settle the Roman Question; his view was: "We are no longer living in 1870." He took as his papal motto *Pax Christi in regno Christi:* the peace of Christ in the kingdom (or reign) of Christ. In 1925 he instituted the Feast of Christ the King—Christ honored as the true Head of the human race, its leader and ruler.

Achille Ratti was sixty-four when he was elected Pope on February 6, 1922. He was born in 1857 at Desio, a small village near Milan, of a middle-class family engaged in industry. He was ordained in 1879 and after six years teaching in the Milan seminary became one of the college of Doctors of the Ambrosian Library and eventually its Prefect. He was an extremely efficient administrator; his scholarly interest was in local research—hence his encouragement of Don Angelo Roncalli's similar tastes. During his long period at Milan he acted as chaplain to the Cenacle nuns and took an active interest in their apostolate of retreat work for women and girls. His recreation was mountain-climbing and in his youth he made several notable ascents. He developed a somewhat formidable personality of the upright headmaster type, but his undoubted authoritarianism was tempered by a fine sense of justice, a dry wit, and remarkable courage. In 1910 he was summoned to the Vatican Library by Pius X and in 1914 became its Prefect. He was then fifty-seven and it must have seemed unlikely that he would ever leave this academic career.

Yet in 1918 Benedict XV chose him for a difficult mission to Poland. He went as Apostolic Visitor and was later made Nuncio. His common sense and cool head during the siege of Warsaw in 1920 won him respect, but it seems that his sudden recall was due to political misunderstandings or mismanagements in which the Polish hierarchy also played a part. However, Ratti was made Archbishop of Milan, in succession to Ferrari, and in June 1921 (no waiting!) Benedict made him a Cardinal. He was in fact the most junior of the Cardinals at the conclave which elected him Pope barely six months later. Thus he had rather a narrow experience of the world, though he spoke French and German (with a strong accent) and could read English. Italians were puzzled how to place him; he was not a diplomatic Pope like Leo XIII and Benedict XV, nor a pastoral Pope like Pius X. He himself was delighted to receive a letter from the head of a great American library expressing pleasure "that one of us has become Pope." Pius XI's outspoken manner alarmed the Curia, yet it was this frank integrity which won him respect even from enemies. Strange that this splendid Victorian headmaster was called to face some of the most powerful demagogues yet thrown up by the twentieth century!

As Pope, Pius XI's chief personal interest was in the missions. He began to accelerate the establishment of native hierarchies, consecrating the bishops himself in St. Peter's and encouraging the modernization of method and approach. It was not possible to rectify at once the effects of the original mistaken Europeanization and Latinization of the new Christians of Asia and Africa, but much was done to help the churches to become relatively self-governing. As soon as he became Pope, Pius told Cardinal van Rossum to conclude the business of transferring the headquarters of the Association for the Propagation of the Faith from France to Rome. It was effected by a *motu proprio* of March 3, 1922: *Romano-rum Pontificorum*. The organization was now to be known as the Pontifical Society for the Propagation of the Faith. The headquarters of the other two societies were transferred two or three years later and the amalgamation completed.

Angelo Roncalli had prepared the *motu proprio*; it was the result of his year of work since his appointment. The direction of the new body was tactfully left to the French, but he remained on the supreme council as president of the Italian national branch. In this capacity he started on his travels again, reorganizing local groups and beginning new ones. In March he was in Naples, in November in Calabria and the Campagna; in May 1923 he visited Sicily. In order to promote interest in the missions he started a magazine: *La Propagazione del Fede nel Mondo* (*The Propagation of the Faith in the World*). In a letter to a colleague in September 1922 he urged him to speak often about the association and to send in reports, adding a typical request for prayer "because the most important thing is: *adveniat regnum tuum; fiat voluntas tua* [Thy kingdom come; thy will be done]. This is the quintessence of everything."

When Roncalli was elected Pope the Pontifical Missionary Union of Priests issued a little book in which fifteen of his articles from this magazine were reprinted, together with the *motu proprio* and some addresses given in 1957–58 while he was Patriarch of Venice. Pope John XXIII wrote a little preface for the book, briefly telling his connection with the work; it was actually done before his election and is signed as a Cardinal. The articles from the early twenties are simple and short, telling the story of Pauline Jaricot, or of saints connected with Propaganda, and urging the importance of forming groups to support the missions. Roncalli certainly increased the revenue; it was 400,000 lire in 1920; in 1921 it went up to 700,000 and in 1922 reached 1,000,000.

What he said as Patriarch, in his seventies, is of greater interest, showing the development of his mind during the long intervening years. He spoke of baptism as initiating apostolate for all Christians, of lay missionaries; he laid emphasis on fraternal cooperation and said he spoke not as Patriarch but as a brother; he quoted the Fathers, Leo the Great,

St. Ambrose, St. John Chrysostom. Yet the same approach was already there in 1925, the Holy Year, missionary year, when he wrote of the new fraternity, of Christ our brother. Helping to organize the big missionary exhibition, the first of its kind in Rome, which Pius XI wanted for the Holy Year he decreed for 1925, was Roncalli's last task before his appointment to Bulgaria. The work for it was done in the autumn of 1924.

These years, during which Roncalli was based on Rome, were critical for Italy. In 1922 the country was in a state of unrest; there were paralyzing strikes in the north; young men roamed about in gangs, seeking and making trouble. The postwar liberal government was weak, but the *Partito Popolare* was rapidly expanding. In the first elections after its foundation it won one-fifth of the seats in the Chamber of Deputies; 1,200,000 votes were cast for it and 1,500,000 for the Socialists. In the 1921 elections the Popolari won seven more seats, while the Socialists declined. The *Partito Popolare* had been founded as "nonconfessional" so as to escape episcopal direction, and Benedict XV favored this autonomy. But the program included points of interest to Catholics and naturally it appealed to them more than the anticlerical and anti-Christian Socialists.

Into this situation erupted the *Fasci di combattimento*—the original Fascists who had been organized as a party by the ex-socialist Benito Mussolini, but who had few seats in Parliament. In Rome itself they were defeated in the municipal elections. They used violent methods and at first there was a considerable anticlerical element in their organized riots. In Mantua in March 1922 the bishop appealed to the central government because there had been so many Fascist attacks on priests. In Pisa the Corpus Christi procession was "forbidden" by the party chief and when it was held in spite of him, gangs were placed along the route to create disturbances. In Catania a procession was broken up by Fascisti with cries of "*Abasso il Papa!*" ("Down with the Pope!")

Nevertheless Mussolini himself, once he had switched from socialism to nationalism, realized the advantages of coming to terms with the Catholic Church. In 1921 he told his followers: "Catholicism can be used for national expansion."

This is the clue to his attitude to the Church throughout his ascendancy. He was not himself a believer, though his brother Arnaldo, editor of the party paper *Popolo d'Italia*, always remained (in his own opinion at least) a Catholic. In a less literary and historical way than Charles Maurras, but yet in a similar style to the *Action Française*, Mussolini recognized that Catholicism was part of the Italian nation and that it conferred on Rome an international importance greater even than the city commanded as the capital of the new Italian state. In spite of the anticlerical elements in his party and in his own past he therefore set out to conciliate the Church —or rather the Pope, since he saw the Church as a kind of religious nation ruled by the Pope. Unfortunately the authoritarian tradition of the papacy lent itself to this conception.

In October 1922 when the Fascist companies made their "March on Rome" Mussolini stayed in Milan till he was summoned to Rome by King Victor Emmanuel III and asked to form a government. He arrived, not in uniform but in the frock coat of the old-style politician. In his government he included members of various parties, among them several of the conservative wing of the *Partito Popolare*. Just before the famous March, a secret instruction from the papal Secretariat of State to the Italian bishops was leaked to the *Giornale d'Italia*; in directing the episcopate to keep Catholics outside party commitment, it was taken, not without reason, to indicate that the Popolari no longer enjoyed papal favor, as they had done under Benedict XV. When Mussolini immediately began to make polite gestures to the Pope and the Church, and to take over most of the religious program of the *Partito Popolare*, the support of the more conservative members began to waver. Mussolini played the Catholics off against each other, conciliating the rightist elements by adopting a policy which appeared favorable to the Church, and then accusing the Popolari of treachery to religion when they combined with the Socialists to defend Parliamentary liberty.

Pope, Curia, and conservative Catholics generally were induced by this behavior to believe that Fascism was less dangerous to Christianity than Socialism, and that liberal democracy was too feeble to stem the tide of revolutionary

Communism. For the Russian Revolution must never be forgotten: it was certainly not forgotten by Pius XI, who had seen it in action against Poland only two years earlier. Mussolini's later course and his alliance with Hitler's National Socialism makes it hard to understand the period when he was admired not only by patriotic Italians but even by Winston Churchill and other Englishmen who, when the final clash came, had no doubts which side they were on. Pius XI himself was to learn before he died the sort of power he had at first preferred to the Christian Democrats of the *Partito Popolare*.

The Popolari held a congress in April 1923 in Turin, where the internal strains were manifested in the open opposition between the right wing, pledged to the new government, and the left, absolutely hostile to it. Don Sturzo tried to unite them behind a program of collaboration on condition of independence: "One collaborates standing, not kneeling." Mussolini's answer was to sack from his government all who were members of the *Partito Popolare*. Next, a violent campaign against Don Sturzo was carried on in the press. Even the *Giornale d'Italia* joined in, accusing him of creating embarrassment for the ecclesiastical authorities. In June, he resigned from his post as General Secretary of the party. The next year, May 1924, he resigned altogether from the Directorate and finally left Italy. Vatican pressure on Don Sturzo has not been ruled out, though he himself would never say anything on the subject.

Don Sturzo's successor was Alcide de Gasperi, an Italian from the Trentino whose first political experience had been gained in the Austrian Parliament. Under De Gasperi the *Partito Popolare* made a last stand at the elections of 1924. By this time Mussolini had consolidated his position and was able to rig the elections; a campaign of intimidation was carried on. Even so the Popolari won forty seats. But they joined with the liberals in walking out of the Chamber in protest against Mussolini's illegal measures and in consequence of the notorious murder of Mateotti, who had openly attacked the new regime in the Chamber. Unfortunately this form of protest removed the opposition from the center of action. In this crisis the King refused to ask for

Mussolini's resignation, just as, in 1922, he had refused to proclaim martial law and defend Rome against the Fascists. Without these acts, negative as they were, Mussolini could hardly have established himself so easily.

The only result of this crisis was that Mussolini was granted "full powers" and from the beginning of 1925 he took a more definitely antidemocratic line. The freedom of the press was progressively reduced. Local elections were stopped and local officials were appointed by the government. In 1926 still wider powers were assumed by the dictator and he began to act by orders-in-council; Parliament had lost control. The opposition disintegrated, its leaders imprisoned or exiled. Alcide de Gasperi spent four years in detention. Yet Mussolini never altogether eliminated the Christian democratic tradition, as his frequent denunciations of "survivals of Popolarismo" showed. When his power collapsed in the Second World War, the party was quickly built up again, with De Gasperi, who had been sheltered in the Vatican as a cataloguer to the Library, during the worst period, once more in the lead.

Pius XI rendered a negative assistance to Mussolini by withdrawing support from the *Partito Popolare,* first in the affair of Don Sturzo and later by sending a circular to the bishops on the eve of the 1924 elections. This did not condemn the Popolari, but insisted that Catholics must not collaborate with Socialists. Attached to the circular was a copy of the Pope's speech to university students in which he had drawn a distinction between collaborating with Socialists already in power, which was allowable, and assisting them to power by collaboration, which was not. The danger of Socialism, with its openly atheistic creed, was much more evident to him than the danger of Fascism, which seemed a patriotic movement with violent elements which respectable conservatives hoped would be moderated by the responsibilities of power. Very much the same illusion assisted Hitler's rise to power, as the Catholic Franz von Papen's *Memoirs* so clearly show. By that time Pius XI had realized something of the danger of a regime which swept away Parliamentary safeguards, though he could still congratulate Von Papen on the new Chancellor's stand against Communism and

"Russian nihilism." It is impossible not to wonder what would have happened in Italy if Benedict XV had lived just a few more years. At any rate he would not have been so suspicious of the *Partito Popolare*, since he had encouraged its lay autonomy.

It is curious that it should have been Pius XI who in 1926 condemned the *Action Française* because its philosophy of life was incompatible with the Catholic Faith, while he seemed not to be aware of the similar faults in Fascism. It was not till the Fascists began to attack, sometimes violently, the Catholic Action groups, that Pius XI seems to have realized the un-Christian elements in the movement. His reason for withdrawing favor from the Popolari was that Catholics had their own "nonpolitical" form of social action. But once Mussolini had eliminated the Christian democratic party, he could not allow any local organizations but his own. Particularly bitter to the Pope was the loss of the Boy Scouts in favor of the militaristic Balilla. But by the time this became clear the Italian Church was tied to the Italian State by the Lateran Pacts of 1929, and the Pope himself had tied some of the knots.

The Lateran Treaty between the Vatican and the Italian government finally settled the Roman Question. The Pope renounced his rights over the former Papal States and the Italian government recognized the independence of the Vatican City state, with certain church buildings and property in Rome, and the summer villa at Castelgandolfo. Paul VI, at the United Nations Assembly in 1965, referred to his "minuscule" state; the bare necessity for maintaining his sovereign independence. In effect, the settlement recognized the existing situation and legalized it. The Holy See received large sums in recompense—Pius IX had refused similar indemnities under the Law of Guarantees because they were unilaterally decreed. A high proportion of the payment was in Italian State Stock. The negotiations for this settlement began officially in October 1926; there were many delays, but the pacts were signed on February 11, 1929, at the Lateran Palace, on the fourth anniversary of Pius XI's coronation, the Feast of our Lady of Lourdes.

The settlement of the Roman Question after nearly sixty years was greeted with rejoicing in Italy and satisfaction abroad. Though the Treaty was made with the Fascist government it was confirmed by the Republic after the war. But it was linked with a further pact, about which opinions were divided, and still are: a *concordat* on the position of the Catholic Church in the Italian State. Pius XI would not hear of one question being settled without the other; when it was concluded he felt that he had "given Italy back to God." Whether or not this was so, the Church in Italy became linked with the Fascist State in the minds of many. Its privileged position continues today, with the ambiguities attendant on all forms of ecclesiastical establishment.

Mussolini called Pius XI "a good Italian." While he kept up a wary sparring match with the dictator himself, the Pope did not curb the patriotic fervor of some Italian prelates and clerical journalists, who lavished praise on Mussolini and his regime. Much worse was clerical complicity in the oppression of the non-Italian and non-Catholic minorities in the territories perpetually quarreled over with Yugoslavia; there were attempts to Latinize the Slav Christians by force. There were also outbursts of clerical enthusiasm for the Abyssinian War. Where the Italian Church was thus compromised with Fascism the papacy could not fail to be suspected, especially as the Popes had for so long interfered with the politics of Italian Catholics. The whole situation is too complex for the kind of apologetics which stress only the Pope's caution in the international sphere. The Pope was primate of Italy as well as chief shepherd of the Church, and what he did in one field of action affected what was done in others.

Angelo Roncalli was in Rome during these crucial years, 1922 till 1924. He supported the *Partito Popolare* from its foundation. But since 1921 he was employed directly in the service of the Holy See and could take no open part in politics. He must have known what was happening; he must have had feelings and views on it all, but there is nothing yet in print from which a reliable estimate can be formed. There is even a gap in his spiritual journal—nothing between April 1919 and January 1924. On January 18, the third anniversary of his arrival in Rome, he wrote down some reflections while in retreat at the Villa Carpegna.

The first thing that came into his mind was this: "To my sorrow, I left behind in Bergamo what I loved so much: the seminary . . . and the students' hostel, the darling of my heart. I have thrown myself, heart and soul, into my new work. Here I must and will stay, without a thought, a glance or a desire for anything else, especially as the Lord gives me indescribable happiness here." The happiness the Lord gives is spiritual life and peace; it is not incompatible with other, less happy feelings. No one who is utterly content makes resolutions not to give a thought to anything else.

In the next paragraph he wrote: "Anyone who judges me from appearance takes me for a calm and steady worker. It is true that I work; but deep in my nature there is a tendency toward laziness and distraction," and he warned himself against procrastination. Later in these reflections he returned to this "sluggishness," again adding that others told him he was working too hard. Yet he knew that mere hurry and bustle accomplished nothing. "I will not worry if others are in a hurry. He who is always in a hurry, even in the business of the Church, never gets very far." Roncalli already practiced what he later brought to a fine art, the delegation of responsibility, "to make others work, and not keep everything, or almost everything, in my own hands." He quoted St. Gregory's Pastoralia and added, "Fortunately this does not go against the grain with me, and moreover the Lord has given me excellent collaborators."

It is clear that he was working not only hard but intelligently and cooperatively. In drawing up anew his daily timetable he only suggested to himself that after meals less time should be spent in talk. Yet obviously he felt the "sluggishness" as real. It may have been the kind of emotional reluctance we feel when we are not doing the work which is our own. Would not Roncalli have preferred to work with his students in Bergamo? He had to make himself accept the task laid on him in Rome. He told himself that everything must be subordinated to this mission; he must not accept other priestly work unless it could serve this first duty—"which is the only reason for my presence here in Rome." Yet how-

ever much he tried to make his job a missionary one, it was
essentially administrative.

Not long after this retreat Monsignor Vincenzo Bugarini,
the ex-Rector of the Roman Seminary, died in Roncalli's
house at Santa Maria in Via Lata, a street that turns off the
Corso. Pitocchi, his old spiritual father, had died in June
1922. The reminiscences he wrote then have a touch of nos-
talgia in them. He was in his early forties. In May and June
1924 Roncalli was off again, touring Piedmont and Tus-
cany; in July he went through Venetia, Umbria and the
Marches. What did he think about the state of Italy? About
the elections that September, the fate of Don Sturzo and of
the *Partito Popolare?*

Then he was appointed Professor of Patrology at the
Pontificio Ateneo Lateranense—now the Lateran university,
and began to lecture on the Fathers in November 1924. His
audience consisted of young clerics of university age and from
many nations. His lectures were popular and it is said they
were even applauded. Yet after only one term Roncalli was
relieved of this post and suddenly appointed Apostolic Visitor
to Bulgaria. As representative of the Pope he would be
consecrated bishop, and take the titular rank of an Archbishop. It was a promotion. Or was it?

One rainy spring day Roncalli stood on the doorstep of the
Greek College in the Via Babuino, when a thin leathery-
faced Benedictine monk joined him and shared the shelter
of his umbrella. Roncalli joked about the dilatoriness of
porters in religious houses and then said that he had come
to find out something about the Christian churches in the
Balkans, where he was shortly to be sent. The Belgian monk
said at once: "I've got the very man for you!" He was Dom
Lambert Beauduin, who told the story of this meeting to
Père Louis Bouyer, many years later. The monk he introduced to Roncalli actually accompanied him to Bulgaria a
few weeks later.

At the beginning of 1925 Angelo Roncalli was forty-three
and Octave Beauduin (Lambert in religion) fifty-one. Beauduin's father had been burgomaster of his town, Rosoux-les-
Waremme, in the Liège district of Belgium. One of a large
family, he went to the seminary at Liège and was ordained

in 1897. His earliest interests were in the industrial scene, guided by seniors keen on the principles of Leo XIII's social encyclical *Rerum Novarum,* but with the death of the bishop and the reversal of papal policy under Pius X there was a great reaction. In 1906 Beauduin entered the abbey of Mont-César as a postulant, at the age of thirty-three. Always considered something of an eccentric, his wartime experiences as a spy (the monastery was evacuated) did nothing to obliterate this reputation. His life was full of ups and downs.

Dom Lambert's three guiding loves were: the liturgy for the people; a return to true Benedictine simplicity; and the rediscovery of the tradition of the eastern churches. At the time when he met Angelo Roncalli he was about to launch an experimental monastic community at Amay (now at Chevetogne) where all these objectives were to be combined. He was a pioneer in all three fields and suffered the usual fate of the genuine pioneer, being misunderstood and harried by colleagues and superiors. At one time he was sent off for a long spell of isolation at the austere and remote monastery of En Calcat—and converted the monks there to many of his ideas. This dry, tough, dynamic little monk made a deep impression on Roncalli, who was later to say: "Dom Lambert's idea is the right one." He remained his friend for life. Dom Lambert Beauduin returned to his own community in 1951 and died there at the time of Roncalli's election as Pope.

It was providential that on the eve of his sojourn in the East, which was to last twenty years, Roncalli should meet one of the few western Catholics who was really open to the influence of the eastern churches and who was able to guide him toward a new approach to Christian unity.

Dom Lambert Beauduin used to say that Roncalli had been relieved of his teaching post at the Lateran on suspicion of Modernism. This could have been true; the Lateran has always been rigidly conservative and the ultra-orthodox were still inclined to label as Modernist any opinion which did not conform to their own. If Roncalli's students applauded his lectures, it suggests that they found his views of ancient history not irrelevant to the affairs of 1924. Certainly to appoint a professor and then remove him after scarcely more than a term was a curious proceeding.*

It was not as if Roncalli had particular qualifications for the mission to Bulgaria. He had proved himself a good organizer and an indefatigable traveler, but he had no experience of the special problems of eastern Europe. In those days Apostolic Visitor was a temporary appointment; a Visitor was not necessarily a member of the Vatican diplomatic service, either before or after his special mission. Roncalli's journal for several years to come contained restrained comments on the vague terms of his appointment and his difficulties in getting instructions from Rome. At this distance of time it looks very much as if someone was wanted to fill an obscure position which might or might not turn out to be useful, and Roncalli was picked for a variety of reasons, not all complimentary.

However that may be, he accepted his new task in the spirit of obedience and at once began to study the milieu in which he would be working. He did not have long. His appointment was made public on March 3, 1925 and he was to leave at the end of April. As later notes show, he did not expect to stay long in Bulgaria. He was sent to report on the situation and he imagined he would be back within a year. Whatever he thought about the nature and manner of his appointment, he took with deep seriousness his consecration to the office of a bishop in the Church. In his case it would confer only a titular rank and not, as in a diocese, the care of particular people. Yet to him it could never be other than a pastoral office.

He was to be consecrated on the Feast of St. Joseph, March 19, and made a brief retreat first, March 13–17, at the Villa Carpegna. "I have not sought or desired this new ministry," he began his notes: "the Lord has chosen me,

---

* Shortly after he became Pope in 1958, Roncalli visited a certain Congregation's offices and asked for his personal file. He said that he wanted to find out why a routine promotion had been so long delayed. Looking back to those early years he found against his name the damning words: "suspected of Modernism." Seizing a pen he wrote with a flourish: "I, John XXIII, pope, say that I was *never* a Modernist!" This story, related to me by one who was present, confirms the suggestion outlined above.

making it so clear that it is his will that it would be a great sin for me to refuse. So it will be for him to cover up my failings and supply my insufficiencies. This comforts me and gives me tranquillity and confidence."

For his meditations he used the *Pontificale*, the rite for the consecration of a bishop, and drew his resolutions from it. And he added what now seems not so much a resolution as a description of what he became, so faithfully did he carry out its spirit. "May my ministry be one of reconciliation 'in words and deeds,' and my preaching 'not in persuasive words of human wisdom but in the manifestation of the Spirit and power' and the authority conferred on me by the Church never used for my own glory—used not to break down but to build up."

It was now that he chose his episcopal motto: *Oboedientia et Pax*—the motto of Cardinal Baronius, disciple of St. Philip Neri. For the place of his consecration he chose San Carlo al Corso, the great Spanish Church where the heart of St. Charles Borromeo is venerated. It was quite near where he lived, in Santa Maria in Via Lata. He was consecrated by Giovanni Cardinal Tacci, Secretary of the Sacred Congregation for the Eastern Church. It was Benedict XV who had removed the care of Catholics in predominantly Orthodox countries from the charge of Propaganda (officially concerned with *missions*) and placed them under this Congregation, formed in 1917 especially to deal with churches of rites other than Latin, and with Catholics in the east. Catholics in Bulgaria came under this new Roman Office.

At the end of his retreat Roncalli had written: "The Church is making me a bishop in order to send me to Bulgaria, to fulfill there, as Apostolic Visitor, a mission of peace. Perhaps I shall find many difficulties awaiting me. With the Lord's help, I feel ready for everything. I do not seek, I do not desire the glory of this world; I look forward to greater glory in heaven."

Five years later, in 1930, he was to write: "The profound and lasting impression I received during the whole ceremony of my consecration as Bishop in Rome in San Carlo al Corso on March 19, 1925, and since then the difficulties and trials of my life in Bulgaria during these five years as Apostolic

Visitor, without any consolation save that of a good conscience, and the rather sombre prospect for the future, convince me that the Lord wants me all for himself along the
royal road of the Holy Cross and it is along this way and
none other that I wish to follow him."

In later years he said much of his love for the people of
Bulgaria, little or nothing of the profound personal trial endured during those ten critical years.

10   Beginnings in Bulgaria

After a holiday in Sotto il Monte, Angelo Roncalli left for
Milan on the Simplon-Orient Express and arrived in Sofia
on April 25, 1925. With him went Dom Constantine Bos-
schaerts, the Belgian Benedictine introduced to him by Dom
Lambert Beauduin. The house where the Apostolic Visitor
was to live was small but new—so new that it was unfinished
—and next door to the Catholic church of Sveta Bogoriditza:
the Holy Mother of God.

Nine days earlier, on April 16, a bomb had exploded in
the Orthodox cathedral, bringing down the cupola and killing
and injuring many of the people gathered there. King Boris
III escaped but his chief minister, General Kimon Gheorgiev,
was killed. This incident was all too typical of that period
of unrest and violence in the Balkans. One of the first things
Roncalli did was to visit the victims in hospitals—and one of
the principal hospitals in Sofia was run by Catholic nuns.

The Apostolic Visitor had been sent to report on the situation of the Catholics and on possibilities of union with the
Orthodox, some of whose leaders had made approaches to
recent private visitors from Rome, including Monsignor
Eugene Tisserant (later Cardinal), who had been there on
behalf of the Vatican Library. It is reckoned that 85 percent
of the people of Bulgaria at that time were Orthodox, 800,000
Moslems and only 50,000, or less than 1 percent Catholics.

Most of these were of the Latin rite, but there were about 5000 of the Byzantine rite, called by the Orthodox "Uniates" and generally despised as such. To understand why, in these circumstances, there could be any talk of union, we must briefly survey Bulgarian history, fascinating in itself and too little known in other parts of the world.

In ancient times the area, or part of it, was known as Thrace, the country north of Macedonia, with the Black Sea to the east. The Danube divides Bulgaria from Rumania to the north. Thrace was conquered first by Philip of Macedon and then by the Romans. The Emperor Constantine once thought of making Sardica (Sofia) his capital, but moved on to Byzantium. Thrace became part of the eastern Roman Empire, ruled from Constantinople. In the sixth and seventh centuries pagan Slavonic tribes invaded and settled there. In the last quarter of the seventh century a militant Turkic tribe, the proto-Bulgars, who came from Central Asia, erupted into the Slavic settlements and led the people in successful revolt against Byzantine rule. Although the Bulgars' language disappeared, they left their name to the Slav nation in which they were absorbed; by the ninth century it had become independent and powerful with Czars (Caesars) of its own. At this point the rulers decided to become Christian.

In the Balkans Christianity has always been associated with national politics. Long before the ninth century the Roman Empire, officially Christian since the fourth century, had fallen into two parts, and eastern and western tradition, both civil and ecclesiastical, began to develop differently. In the Church, while doctrine remained essentially the same, customs, liturgy, and discipline crystallized into two separate systems. In their missionary outlook, however, Old Rome and New Rome were all too similar: Rome Latinized its barbarians and Constantinople Hellenized them. To the Slavs, therefore, it was a matter of discovering whether Rome or Constantinople could offer the greater advantages.

The great apostles of the Slavs were Saints Cyril and Methodius, born in Salonika but of Slav origin. In their Greek monastery on Mount Olympus they began translating the liturgical books into Slavonic and used these vernacular versions when they were sent as missionaries to Moravia. It seems that it was not St. Cyril himself, but a later member of the mission, who invented the "Cyrillic" alphabet, adapting and adding to the Greek letters. There was much controversy about introducing the Slavonic languages into the liturgy. It upset one of those legendary theories which always seem to hypnotize Christians: that only Greek, Latin, and Hebrew, the three languages inscribed on the Cross, were fit for liturgical use. Saints Cyril and Methodius sturdily opposed this pious conservatism.

After the deaths of these enlightened missionaries the ruler of Moravia suddenly reverted to the German and Latin sphere of influence. The Slavonic clergy, rudely ejected, were welcomed by Czar Boris I of Bulgaria, who saw them as the perfect answer to the question of how to be Christian without being either Latin or Greek. The Greeks disapproved the whole proceeding and the ecclesiastical struggle for independence went along with political and ethnic opposition to Constantinople all through Bulgarian history. Bulgaria became the cradle of Slavonic Christian culture and it was from the Church there that Prince Vladimir of Kiev received Christianity in A.D. 988. Such was the beginning of Holy Russia.

In the century after its conversion the power of Bulgaria expanded till it included much of what is now Serbia, Albania, and southern Macedonia. The Czar Simeon even dreamed of ruling in Constantinople itself, but by the end of the tenth century Byzantium was again in the ascendant and in 1018 Bulgaria became a province of the empire. Its Church was forcibly Hellenized; the higher clergy were replaced by Greeks and the Greek language imposed on the liturgy and in the schools. This situation was never accepted by the Bulgarians and when they regained independence in 1185, the Archbishop of Turnovo was proclaimed Patriarch and Slavonic restored.

In medieval times Bulgarian culture flourished but the country became divided into factions, so that it fell the more easily to the Turks in the fourteenth century—for Bulgaria was under Turkish rule before Byzantium fell. The Turkish conquest reduced the Christian population to second class status, delaying the national development for centuries. Once more the Slavonic Church was subjected to the supervision of the Patriarch of Constantinople—simply to facilitate government for the Turks. In the Ottoman Empire the Greeks of the Phanar (the lighthouse district) in Constantinople became, even in their secondary status, extraordinarily rich and powerful. Balkan bishoprics became so many counters in the game of influence and Bulgars were often employed merely to collect the dues for the absentee hierarchy of their country.

Thus in the Balkans the Greeks became almost more hated than the Turks. In the nineteenth century, when the Bulgarians were trying to throw off the Ottoman yoke, there were occasions when flirtation with Rome could be politically advantageous. But by that time the gulf between eastern and western Christendom had become so wide that Bulgarian Orthodox, no less than Greeks, could find little in common with the Catholics of western Europe. Moreover Rome had become ever more imperial in outlook and Latinizing in practice. The Popes protected Catholics of Oriental rites on principle, but missionaries tended to westernize them, tidy up ancient customs and teach them alien habits of devotion. Consequently the Bulgarians turned to Russia, and it was with Russian aid that they at last won independence from the Turks, after the famous and terrible massacres provoked by their first revolts. Backed by the formidable Orthodoxy of Russia the Bulgarian Church once more threw off the rule of Constantinople and elected an independent Patriarch. There had been scenes in churches, when enthusiasts had shouted the Gospel in Slavonic, rebelling against the Greek liturgy. So nationalism and Slavonic Christianity were associated in Bulgarian history, much as nationalism was linked with Roman Catholicism in Poland and Ireland.

It is essential to realize the anti-Byzantine force in Bulgarian Orthodoxy if one is to understand the ambivalent attitude to Rome. There had always been minorities of Latin-rite Catholics in Bulgaria, often of German origin, and so there were always channels of approach. In the nineteenth century, when the western European powers used the Balkans as a political maneuvering ground, Catholic missionaries were often encouraged by their governments—and they were "missionaries" in the sense that they regarded the Orthodox, culturally depressed by centuries of Turkish rule, as fair game, much as Protestant missionaries regarded the superstitious peasantry of Catholic countries as ripe for conversion. Political influence helped to found the Catholic hospitals and schools in Bulgaria, run largely by foreign nuns and brothers; hence the ambivalent attitude to these institutions on the part of the local people. The services were needed and welcomed, but propaganda for Rome was suspected, not without reason. In Bulgaria it was doubly suspect. The Latin liturgy was expected of Latins (and even Old Slavonic was hardly vernacular) but the prayers of the people and the rosary were conducted in *French*. A Christian may well be tempted to despair of the divisive tendencies of human nature.

Roncalli did not despair. But he had to learn about unity the hard way. He took to the country at once and to the people, who reminded him of his own countrymen of Lombardy, a sturdy and independent peasantry. In the war Bulgaria had been allied with Germany and was involved in its defeat. The King, Ferdinand (German by birth), had abdicated in favor of his son Boris, and after a period of government by the radical agrarian party, with continual unrest and fears that Bolshevik Communism would spread from Russia, Boris had allowed General Gheorgiev to take over the government. It was this representative of a military regime who was blown up in Sofia's cathedral a week or so before Roncalli arrived. It was a mark of great respect for the Pope, therefore, that the King received his representative on April 30 and talked to him for three hours. Among other things, he told Roncalli he was glad the Pope had given him the title of Archbishop —it showed his sense of Bulgaria's importance. Such considerations explain the custom of the Vatican diplomatic service in raising all the representatives of the Pope to the rank of Archbishop. Whether ecclesiastical offices should ever have become titular honors is another question.

Not that Roncalli had the status of an official diplomat; as Apostolic Visitor he was merely a temporary personal representative of the Pope. But as the Pope had not been represented in Bulgaria since the thirteenth century, and since the King wished to maintain friendly relations with the Vatican, the Visitor was in fact treated more or less as a diplomat by the court. On the first Sunday, when he celebrated Mass in the Church of the Latins, many officials and reporters were present. He made his sermon a kind of declaration of policy, of friendliness to Bulgaria and of his mission to the Catholics, recently increased by the many refugees from Macedonia. He apologized for speaking in Italian and said he was going to start learning Bulgarian straight away. This delighted everybody, for Bulgarians are inured to the fact that few trouble to learn their language. Roncalli did learn it, but he had to rely a good deal on French. This was particularly trying to him as he wanted to get away from the idea that Catholics in Bulgaria were a kind of French colony; one of his first acts was to insist that the prayers of the people after Mass and at Benediction should be said in Bulgarian, and not in French.

Roncalli lost no time in using his favorite method of getting to know a situation—going to see the people. He started his first tour on May 19, less than a month after his arrival. He traveled by horse-drawn carriage over the dusty roads through the beautiful and well-tended countryside toward the Black Sea; his first visit was to Burgas, the second seaport in the kingdom. Then he went inland to Yambol, and to Stata Zagora, where the Resurrectionist Fathers were working. Another journey took him among the eastern-rite Catholics living in villages near the Turkish border, along the banks of the river Maritza. While he was there he went over the border to visit Adrianople, once part of Bulgaria and the scene of the Uniate movement of 1860.

For the eastern-rite Catholics of Bulgaria had come into being then as a result of another politico-religious crisis, when thousands, rebelling against the Phanar, had been received into communion with Rome. When the Russians interfered, carrying off Bishop Sikolski in a battleship, most, but not all, reverted to their old allegiance. These Slavonic Catholics were later increased by influxes of refugees, not always of the same nationality. They were very poor and relations with the Orthodox were antagonistic. In Adrianople, Roncalli sadly viewed the decaying and neglected churches; for the Christian population had largely emigrated after Turkey claimed the area.

Everywhere he went among these scattered groups of Catholics the people crowded to see the Pope's representative. He always went to the church, where he celebrated Mass, gave communion and confirmation and spoke to the people, by means of an interpreter, giving them simple words of encouragement. Often there was a group photograph taken, with everyone trying to cram into the historic picture. It was exhausting, but in this way Roncalli saw for himself how the people lived, the state of the communities and the churches, and he met all the priests, whether foreign missionaries or local men.

On one journey he took to a motorcar (then still rather a rare vehicle) but after thirty miles, driving into the mountainous country on the borders of Macedonia, he and his companion, Father Privat Belard, an Assumptionist, had to take to horses; the wooden saddles were covered with goatskin. In one village the presbytery was simply a small stone barn with unplastered walls; the two priests there insisted on giving up their beds and sleeping on the floor. The visitors were told terrible stories of the massacres of 1913 and alarming tales of brigands in the present. When they got back to the place where the car should have been waiting for them it was not there; the chauffeur had taken fright. They stayed at a frontier post and the soldiers telephoned for transport; two days later a cart drawn by oxen arrived to fetch them. The officer advised Roncalli to hide his pectoral cross and ring; brigands had attacked a mail coach the day before and left the driver injured in the road. However, Roncalli and Belard saw nobody but a long train of refugees. Most of this hazardous journey took place in torrential rain.

Scarcely less alarming was the visit to Malko Ternovo, a Catholic enclave near Burgas on the Black Sea. Roncalli was advised against going there, for Catholics and Orthodox had recently come to blows; in the past there had been fatal casualties. Determined to meet all the Catholics in Bulgaria, Roncalli ignored the warnings. During his sermon he felt he was being watched by hostile eyes, so he was careful to speak even more pacifically than usual. As a result, the vice-prefect of the town, who had wounded a Catholic in a fight the year before, came next day to pay his respects.

This visit took place in the middle of July; Roncalli traveled north after that and on July 27 he visited Bucharest, capital of Rumania, and stayed overnight. He made another tour at the beginning of August and then returned to Sofia. His adventurous travels had drawn attention to himself. An interview, published in *La Bulgaria*, describes how Roncalli rose from a desk covered with papers to greet his visitor, who noticed on his bookshelves the works of the Greek Fathers along with Dante, Petrarch, and the beloved Manzoni. "The monsignor is still quite young," the journalist reported; "there is in his face a striking energy, simplicity, and gentleness. His welcome was friendly and without fuss. He explained to us, with a vivacity common to his countrymen, the objects of his journey to Bulgaria and his first impressions of the country." He said he had come to transmit the Pope's blessing to "the noble Bulgarian people" and to organize the affairs of the Catholics. He praised the country and the people, their industry and hospitality. "The face of Monsignor Roncalli lights up with real joy when he is speaking of our country and its simple, gentle peasants." He was careful to mention the Turks "who also prostrate themselves before God" and the tolerance he had found in Bulgaria.

Roncalli had been able to give a large sum from the Pope to help with the problems of the refugees. In the Sobranie, the national assembly, a complimentary reference was made to the tact of the Apostolic Visitor. On August 26 Roncalli paid a courtesy visit to the Holy Synod and met the Metropolitan Stefan Gheorgiev. This was entirely his own idea. He soon realized that the Bulgarian Orthodox leaders had no real wish for union; they inherited all the ancient prejudices against the Latins. He was disappointed to find them ignorant of the mystical and devotional riches of the west; for though Dom Lambert Beauduin had opened his eyes to a similar ignorance in the west of the treasures of the east, he himself had always been familiar with the great Greek Fathers. But his sense of history helped him to understand the reasons for Orthodox intransigence and he persisted in all possible friendly contacts. Whenever he could, he attended the Slavonic liturgy.

The Metropolitan Stefan had sent a secretary to return the Apostolic Visitor's call on the Holy Synod. This was considered in Rome a loss of prestige and Roncalli, in some trepidation, was sent to see the Pope himself. "Was it not lowering the prestige of the Holy See, when they sent only a secretary to return your call?" Pius XI demanded sternly. "Oh no, Holy Father," replied Roncalli, "it was only because they were so busy." The Pope scrutinized him for a moment and then said enigmatically: "One sows and another reaps."

On this visit to Rome, in October 1925, Roncalli presented his report, the fruit of six months of hard work. Details are not available but in essentials his plan seems to have been directed at the *Bulgarization* of the Catholic Church in Bulgaria. Effective administration was divided between the three principal religious orders, Capuchins, Passionists, and Assumptionists. Hospitals and the girls' schools were run by various congregations of nuns. Consequently the scattered groups of Catholics appeared to the bulk of Bulgarians as missions run from western Europe, not only Latinized but Frenchified. Roncalli's ideas were practical. He wanted a central seminary in Sofia where clergy of both rites could be trained together in their own country, with a proper appreciation of eastern and Slavonic tradition. He thought this seminary should be run not by the existing orders but by "new men"—probably he was thinking of Dom Lambert Beauduin's monastic venture. He recommended that the eastern-rite Catholics should no longer be ruled by an Apostolic Administrator sent from Rome but by a bishop chosen from among themselves.

In this last aim he succeeded; Stefan Kurteff, the man he recommended, was appointed in 1926 Exarch Apostolic of the Bulgarian Catholics of the Byzantine Rite. Kurteff, a Bulgarian priest of about thirty-five, was living in Roncalli's house in Sofia when he arrived and had accompanied him to Malko Ternovo. Born of Orthodox parents, it was only after he had lost them that Kurteff received his training through the Assumptionist order. Roncalli took him to Italy and in November 1926 they made a retreat together in the monastery of St. Paul in Rome, under the direction of the Abbot, Dom Ildefonso Schuster, afterward Archbishop of Milan. A few days later, December 5, Stefan Kurteff was consecrated bishop in the ancient church of San Clemente, built over the house of the early Pope Clement. St. Cyril is buried there.

They returned to Bulgaria via Istanbul, where Roncalli was later to spend so many years. On January 28, 1927, Kurteff was feted at his old seminary at Kadikog, the ancient Chalcedon, seat of the famous Council when several national churches had gone into schism, resenting the imperial claims of Constantinople as much as they opposed the new definitions of doctrine. A few days later the new Exarch was enthroned in Sofia and the Apostolic Visitor expressed satisfaction at the accomplishment of the first task set him by the Holy Father. Kurteff went off to visit his parishes and Roncalli wrote in his praise to Father Saturnin Aube, provincial of the Assumptionists in Constantinople, a letter full of quotations from Scripture.

La Croix, the Assumptionist paper, once accused Roncalli of prejudice against the order, but he had chosen a pupil of theirs for a responsible position and used their houses in Plovdiv and Yambol for retreats and congresses of the eastern rite priests. He was on good terms with the Brothers of the Christian Schools in Sofia, and celebrated their founder's day with them in May 1927. Although he was anxious to build up the indigenous elements of the Church in Bulgaria, he always respected the hard self-sacrificing work of the priests and nuns from the west. Nevertheless the fact that he wanted "new men" to run his proposed central seminary is not without significance.

He never got them. He never got the seminary either, though in 1929 he actually negotiated for a site in Sofia. It was not the Bulgarians who put difficulties in the way. At the retreat before Kurteff's consecration he wrote in his journal: "I have been a bishop for twenty months. As I clearly foresaw, my ministry has brought me many trials. But, and this is strange, these are not caused by the Bulgarians for whom I work but by the central organization of ecclesiastical administration. This is a form of mortification and humiliation that I did not expect and which hurts me deeply. 'Lord, you know all.' I must, I will accustom myself to bearing this cross with more patience, calm and inner peace than I have so far shown. I shall be particularly careful in what I say to anyone about this. Every time I speak my mind about it I take away from the merit of my patience. 'Set a guard over my mouth, O Lord.' "

Because it was not necessary for the purpose of examining his conscience Roncalli did not specify his difficulties in his spiritual journal, but it is not hard to guess some of them. He had been sent to report on a situation but his recommendations were not followed. Possibly they were thought too novel; there were also excuses about finding money. More trying still, he was not sent further instructions. He failed to get answers to his questions. He still had no diplomatic standing, and after Kurteff's appointment he had practically no pastoral duties. In this anomalous situation he was left to get on as best he could, year after year. He was useful enough not to be recalled but not important enough for his position to be clarified or his advice implemented. For an active man in the prime of life this uncertainty and frustration were exceedingly hard to bear.

At one point Roncalli wrote to a curial friend about his difficulties and the friend, not with the greatest tact, showed his letter to the officials of the Eastern Congregation under whose jurisdiction he came. Some people were very annoyed indeed. When Roncalli heard of this he wrote a twenty-page letter on the subject; he spent two pages apologizing for hurting anyone's feelings and the other eighteen in showing he had grounds for his complaints. This letter eventually reached the Pope himself. Pius XI read it through and remarked, "*Ecce ira Agni!*" ("Behold the wrath of the Lamb!")

It was all too easy for the officials in Rome to ignore this Lamb-like wrath. Roncalli's frustration continued. In November 1926 he had written: "I must take great care to show charity in my conversation. Even with trustworthy and venerable people I must be very chary of mentioning things which refer to the most delicate part of my ministry and concern the good name of others, especially if these are invested with authority and dignity. Even when I feel the need to confide in someone, in hours of solitude and loneliness, silence and

meekness will make suffering for the love of God more pro-
ductive of good . . . I must think of myself as the man
bearing the cross [Simon of Cyrene] and love the cross that
God sends me without thinking of any other."

The next year, November 1927, he made his retreat in a
Jesuit house in Ljubliana (Slovenia) where he wrote: "If I
cannot do all the good I think is necessary for the benefit of
souls in the mission entrusted to me, I must not let myself be
in the least worried or anxious about this. To do my duty in
accordance with the promptings of charity, that is enough.
The Lord knows how to use everything for the triumph of
his kingdom, even my not being able to do more, even the
effort it costs me to remain comparatively inactive."

He repeated his admonitions to himself not to talk too
freely, even in his own household. It was exactly the situation
where gossip and small jealousies easily become rife. "It is
my nature to talk too much. A ready tongue is one of God's
good gifts, but it must be handled with care and respect,
that is, with moderation, so that I may be welcome and
not found a bore."

Again he decided to study Bulgarian and French more carefully. He noted that he was growing old. He was then within
a few days of his forty-sixth birthday. He had recently been
ill, but men of forty-six do not usually consider themselves
old. Roncalli increased heavily in size during these years and
it may be worth noting that many people put on weight
when they are frustrated or unhappy. In the group photographs
he is always smiling, but the formal episcopal portraits of
these years reveal a look of withdrawal and disappointment,
even sadness in his eyes. By the end of his time in Bulgaria
this had changed to a look of cheerful resignation, even of
shrewd amusement, but the transformation was not easily
achieved. Not to be able to do for God work seen to be
necessary is a rare trial for a Christian; only a person of great
apostolic energy is capable of feeling this hidden suffering.
It was this frustration which he struggled with during his
first five years in Bulgaria. And because he was there under
obedience he would not allow himself to ask for a change.

In retreat during December 1928, at the villa of the
Lazarist Fathers at Babek on the Bosporus, he wrote: "I will

never take any step, direct or indirect, to bring about any change or alteration in my situation, but I will in all things and at all times live from day to day, letting others say and do, and suffering whoever so desires to pass ahead of me, without preoccupying myself about my future . . . May the Lord help me in this matter never to succumb to the fascination of any ecclesiastical circles in which love of this world may sometimes play a part."

This sort of self-sacrifice is quite invisible to other people. Probably nobody thought twice about leaving the uncomplaining Roncalli in his obscure post. A Bergamasque peasant had no reason to complain, in any case, of such a respectable position. Not many people want to do more work than they are given.

Although these years seemed inactive to Roncalli because there was so much he could have done, had it been allowed, he did not sit back and do nothing. In April 1928 there was a very bad earthquake in Bulgaria. Roncalli went at once to visit the stricken areas in Cirpan and Baltzagi. He secured a gift from the papal funds and in May set up relief soup kitchens in Papazlji. About this time he wrote to Don Giovanni Birolini, parish priest of Sotto il Monte, telling him to take no notice of rumors that he might be transferred; there was more need than ever for a representative of the Pope and "as Scipio was called Africanus [the African], so I'm ready to become *il bulgaro* [the Bulgarian]," he added. On June 24 that year, writing to the Rector of the college at Celana, he asked him to pray for *il fratello lontano* (the brother far away), who in his humble way had taken up the ministry of St. John the Baptist, filling up the valleys *et facere aspera in vias planas* (making the rough ways smooth). Perhaps he was again thinking of this mission of the Baptist, thirty years later, when as Pope he chose the name of John.

The first Bulgarian convention of Catholic Action was held under his auspices at Plovdiv on March 3, 1929. On his holiday the year before he had attended the 15th Social Week held in Milan and took part in a discussion on *Mortalium Animos*, Pius XI's conservative encyclical on Christian Unity. The Vatican still looked at the Christian world with the eyes of the sixteenth century, seeing the descendants of the Reformers simply as men cut off from the one true Church and misled by false ideas. While Roncalli shared the Pope's belief that the Catholic Church maintained the true faith and that its unity was the gift and work of the Spirit, he had begun to discover how Christians of the East, separated from Rome, regarded these questions. He realized the long legacy of hate left by the Crusaders who had sacked the Greek cities, the difficulties of western theological development for eastern minds. Yet in spite of this he had met men whom he knew to be brothers. One was the Armenian primate in Bulgaria, Stepanosse Hovagnimian, Archbishop of Nicomedia, whom he met in August 1927 and who said to him with tears in his eyes that perhaps the division of the Church was the "unforgiveable sin" of the Gospel.

When he spoke to the non-Catholic observers at the Council on October 13, 1962, Pope John referred to this "venerable old prelate" to whom he had given, as an act of courtesy, a medal of Pius XI's pontificate. "A short time afterward when he was dying he asked that after his death the medal should be placed on his heart. I saw it there myself," said Pope John, "and the memory still moves me."

But as well as his sympathy with separated brothers Roncalli had the gift of drawing together his own colleagues, united in faith but, as Catholics know too well, by no means always united in charity. St. Joseph's Day in March 1927, the anniversary of his episcopal consecration, was celebrated with a dinner in the Capuchins' refectory at which both the Catholic bishops of Sofia, Monsignor Peeff and Monsignor Kurteff were present, with secular and regular priests to the number of thirty. It was a great success. Roncalli wrote to the Provost of San Gregorio in Bergamo: "Everybody was happy: 'Monsignor Roncalli is the salvation of Bulgaria: a true Angel (Angelo) of the Lord, sent here . . . etc etc etc.' Joking apart, the feast of St. Joseph has turned out an affirmation of that spirit of charity and brotherhood which is too rare merchandise in the Balkans and which I should like to leave as the most precious and dear memory and teaching of my poor work in Bulgaria."

Roncalli traveled about a good deal, not only in Bulgaria. He visited Istanbul twice in 1927, once with Kurteff and again at the end of March when he consecrated Monsignor Giovanni Battista Filipucci, Latin Archbishop of Athens. From December 18, 1928, till February 1, 1929, he was in Turkey, making an Apostolic visitation of the Georgian Catholics; and he was to make further visits to Istanbul before his appointment there. On one of these, in 1930, he visited the ruins of Troy. Meanwhile in the spring of 1929 Dom Lambert Beauduin stayed in Sofia on his great tour through the eastern Christian countries. In August of that year Roncalli went off via Prague for Poland, where he visited the shrine of Our Lady of Czestochowa, Warsaw and the Redemptorist Fathers in Poznan. On his way back he stayed two days in Berlin where Eugenio Pacelli, the future Pope Pius XII, was then Nuncio. In December 1929 Pacelli was made a Cardinal and when Gasparri retired in 1930 he was made Secretary of State. In September 1929 Roncalli led the first Bulgarian Catholic pilgrimage to Rome where Pius XI was holding another Holy Year, to celebrate his own jubilee as a priest. While he was in Italy Archbishop Roncalli consecrated the new parish church at Sotto il Monte, on September 21, 1929.

At the beginning of 1930 it was confidently rumored that Monsignor Roncalli would be sent as Apostolic Delegate to Istanbul, a post for which he was now well-qualified, and which would be a promotion from his still temporary rank as Apostolic Visitor. But it was Monsignor Carlo Margotti who was appointed, a northern Italian whose energy and zeal seem not to have been matched with equal tact; five years later Roncalli was to be plunged into the cross-currents he had started among the Catholics in Istanbul. So in 1930 Roncalli was rather obviously passed over for promotion. At the same time he had to admit defeat in his plans for a central joint seminary in Sofia, even though he had purchased a site for it.

It was not surprising then that in April 1930, when he went to retreat in the house of the Passionist Fathers at Rustchuk, Angelo Roncalli had to meet an inner crisis of the spirit. He was forty-eight. The way he endured and overcame this trial was crucial in his development as a person.

Toward the end of his retreat at Rustchuk, Roncalli gave a description of the scene, a rare event in his spiritual journal. "All around me in this great house is solitude, absolute and magnificent solitude, amid the profusion of nature in flower; before my eyes the Danube; beyond the great river the rich Rumanian plain, which sometimes at night glows red with burning waste gas. The whole day long the silence is unbroken. In the evening the good Passionist bishop, Monsignor Theelen, comes to keep me company for supper. My soul is absorbed all day in prayer and reflection . . . O Jesus, I thank you for this solitude, which is giving me a real rest and great peace in my soul."

But the peace was not easily won. This is what he wrote of his personal situation: "The trials, with which in recent months the Lord has tested my patience, have been many: anxieties concerning the arrangements for founding a Bulgarian seminary; the uncertainty, which has now lasted for more than five years about the exact scope of my mission in this country; my frustrations and disappointments at not being able to do more, and my enforced restriction to my life as a complete hermit, in opposition to my longing for work directly ministering to souls: my interior discontent with what is left of my natural human inclinations, even if until now I have succeeded in holding this under control: all this"—(what? torments me, he might have said, but no)—"all this makes it easier for me to enjoy this sense of trust and abandonment, which contains also the longing for a more perfect imitation of my divine Model."

But though the basic resignation of the will was there, he still had to come to terms with the thoughts and emotions his situation continued to arouse. What he said about his natural inclinations is interesting; it is plain that his life in Sofia was lonely. Till then he had no companions who could be friends. Living in his house was a certain Father Methodius Ustichkoff, who had translated the *Imitation of Christ* into Bulgarian. Algisi's description of him (which must have come from John XXIII) is charitably phrased but does not quite disguise the fact that he must have been a trying person to share a house with. He was "volatile," always surrounded by people "who took advantage of his kindness," a great cigar smoker, emotional (bursting into tears easily), and he enjoyed poor health. No wonder Roncalli had to watch his conversation. Father Ustichkoff eventually went to end his days in the Assumptionist house at Lyons and when Roncalli was Nuncio in France he visited his grave there.

He repeated his intention to take no notice of "worldly gossip" about his affairs and added: "I am willing to live like this even if the present state of things were to remain unchanged for years and years. I will never even express the desire or the slightest inclination to change, however much this may cost me in my heart." He reminded himself of his episcopal motto of *Oboedientia et Pax* and of St. Ignatius' prayer of oblation, of willing indifference to all things for God's sake, which he said every day after Mass. "To tell the truth, I find it rather hard to say this prayer." This admission shows that it was a prayer which he tried to live. Later, he wrote to a friend who was also experiencing frustration, to encourage him to persevere in patience and he mentioned this prayer. "Well, one morning when I was suffering more than usual, I became aware that my state indicated precisely that my prayer had been granted." A few lines above, in the same letter, he had said: "It is not that the reasons for my troubled mind last year has ceased to exist; no, they are all still there, almost as powerful as before. But I found a reason for life and a reason for suffering; and so I live and suffer willingly."

He realized that just because he was unwillingly subject to frustration he was in the state of voluntary indifference to what happened to him. Although this may sound simple, it is in fact difficult to realize. It was necessary at the same time to stand by and watch a situation deteriorate which he knew he could remedy, given the means, and yet not either waste energy fretting at inactivity, nor sink into personal lethargy, seeking satisfaction in private life. How easy it would have been to become the comfortable easygoing prelate that to the unobservant he may have already appeared! It is often what people do *not* do, in such crises, that illuminates the meaning of the outcome. A spiritual victory is not at once observable, even to the one who has made it.

It was on this occasion that Roncalli recalled his consecration five years earlier and the profound impression he then received that he was being called to the way of the Cross. Ten years later, when he was in Turkey and meditating on the verses of the Psalm *Miserere*, at the beginning of the war, he recollected both this retreat at Rustchuk and the ceremony of consecration and added to his earlier memories. After his prostration before the altar, he said, "I arose bearing with me a clear impression of resemblance, at least in my soul, with Christ crucified." Yet again in 1950, in retreat at Oran (Algeria) during his time as Nuncio in France, he once more reminded himself of this lasting sense that in his episcopal consecration he had been sealed to the carrying of the cross. If he felt it first in St. Carlo al Corso, it was in Bulgaria that he came to know the weight of it, invisible though it might be to others. At Oran he wrote: "In Bulgaria, the difficulties of my circumstances, even more than the difficulties caused by men, and the monotony of that life which was one long sequence of daily pricks and scratches, cost me much in mortification and silence. But your grace"—he was addressing the Lord—"preserved my inner joy, which helped me to hide my difficulties and distress."

It was at Rustchuk that he deliberately met the full impact of this distress and came through to a new kind of confidence, a new maturity, which was only to deepen as he grew older. The retreat in the great spring solitude by the Danube brought him a deep peace, of which he was conscious at once; he resolved to try to preserve this cheerfulness, inwardly and outwardly. "One must learn to bear suffering, without letting anyone even know it is there." In this he surely succeeded. "I am like a bird singing in a thicket of thorns," he quoted from St. Francis de Sales. "So, I must say very little to anyone about the things which hurt me. Great discretion and forbearance in my judgments of men and situations: willingness to pray particularly for those who cause me suffering, and in everything great kindliness and endless patience . . . I will be patient and good to an heroic degree, even if I am to be crushed."

For all he knew then, his life would continue indefinitely in this lonely frustration. Some may think his resolve to do nothing to change a position in which his powers were wasting unused, an unnecessary submission, encouraging his superiors to leave things as they were. His self-imposed silence suggests that his constant watch against ambition was not undertaken without reason. Even though it was not promotion, but a field of action for others, which he desired, he evidently distrusted his own latent energy of will. It was morally safest simply to accept the tasks given him, when they were given; under the rule of obedience they could then be taken as God's will, not his own. The fact that he found this passivity hard reveals the active force of his character.

In the autumn of 1930 Roncalli suddenly but uncomfortably emerged from his obscurity as a victim of the religious cold war between Catholic and Orthodox. King Boris, whose mother was a Bourbon Parma, was to marry Princess Giovanna, daughter of the King of Italy, and he promised to marry her in a Catholic Church and to bring up his children as Catholics. The marriage duly took place at Assisi on October 25, but as soon as Boris brought his bride home to Sofia it was celebrated again according to the Orthodox rite in the cathedral of Alexander Nevsky.

Pius XI was exceedingly annoyed. When he published his encyclical *Casti Connubii*, on Christian marriage, in the consistory at Christmas he addressed some pointed remarks to the Cardinals about people who did not honor their promises. Naturally this was not well received in Sofia.

Monsignor Roncalli had to protest to the King on behalf of the Pope. It was expected that he would be asked to leave Bulgaria; a member of the diplomatic corps even told him that his expulsion would probably take place the day after Christmas. But after all, nothing happened, probably because the King liked Roncalli. He stayed on.

He took it all remarkably calmly. In his retreat notes for June 1931 he wrote that the "profound meditation" at Rustchuk the year before "had not been without its fruit. Since then I have felt and still feel more composed and ready for whatever the future may bring, willing to accept the most diverse things, successes or defeats, with equal calm, considering it a great triumph for me simply to be doing my duty in the service of the Holy See." He determined once more, but in slightly different terms, "lovingly to accept my present inactivity without being impatient to do more, and to love this semiobscurity in which the Lord keeps me, prevented as I am by circumstances from doing anything else, although this would be my inclination and my desire."

Roncalli went to Istanbul twice in 1931, once in June for the sixteenth centenary of the Council of Ephesus and once in August for the consecration of a bishop. In September 1931 his position in Bulgaria was at last clarified, when he was made Apostolic Delegate. This, though not on a par with a Nunciature, is a more permanent form of papal representation than that of Apostolic Visitor. In February 1932, on the tenth anniversary of the coronation of Pius XI, he received the diplomats and ministers in Sofia, reading his speech in Bulgarian as well as in French. This reception was held in the new and larger residence acquired to suit the recognized status of a Delegation. The gloomy entrance was transformed by the skill of Luigi, known as Roncalli's factotum, who exercised his Bergamasque craftsmanship not only in Sofia, but later in Istanbul and in Paris. Italian friends helped Roncalli with the cost of decorating the chapel. He secured for it a copy of one of the three tapestries of the Trinity which used to be hung above the altar of the Sistine Chapel in the Vatican. In this choice he showed his understanding of Orthodox piety and iconography.

He was now sent a secretary, Giacomo Testa, a young priest starting on his diplomatic career. Like all Roncalli's secretaries of every nationality he became a devoted friend and a disciple of his methods—the friendly approach to everyone, no matter how diverse their beliefs, seeking always what was held in common as the basis for further unity. *Monsignore Vogliamoci bene*, Roncalli was nicknamed in the east, because he said it so often: "Let's wish each other well"—a real goodwill, not more good manners.

On January 13, 1933, Queen Giovanna gave birth to a

daughter and the baby was almost immediately baptized with Orthodox rites by the Metropolitan Stefan Gheorgiev. Understandable as this was, it contravened Boris's solemn promise and the Apostolic Delegate had to inform the Pope and once more make a formal protest at the Palace—where he was not received. As the Queen had nothing to do with the affair Roncalli advised her to come to Mass in the chapel of the Delegation, instead of in the Catholic Church as she usually did, in order to avoid possible insults from loyal Catholics who might think she had deliberately disobeyed the Pope. Feelings ran high. Roncalli said ruefully of the King: "He deceived me!" But he found excuses for Boris's behavior in the pressure put on him by patriotic Orthodox prelates and in what he called "the original mistake"—King Ferdinand's consent to his son's being brought up as an Orthodox. Ferdinand himself, as well as his wife, and Boris's sisters, were Catholic; it was less a religious than a political question. That did not make things any easier for the Pope's representative.

Pius XI was again deeply offended and said so, as was his wont, in no uncertain terms, at a consistory in March 1933. St. Joseph's Day that month was the anniversary of Roncalli's episcopal consecration and Queen Giovanna insisted on attending Mass in the church on that day. So, to show that the Pope's displeasure did not include her, the Delegate presented her there with a beautiful missal; a typically thoughtful gesture. All the same he was not received at court for a year. He gave communion to the Queen publicly in the church at Christmas, at the end of a course of sermons he had been giving to commemorate the closing of the Holy Year of 1933, held in honor of the traditional date of the death and resurrection of Christ.

At the height of the baptism row the *Popolo d'Italia* announced that Roncalli would be sent as Nuncio to Bucharest in place of Monsignor Angelo Dolci, who was being made a Cardinal and returning to work in Curia in Rome. Even in Bucharest this news was accepted as true. Such a transfer to Rumania would be not only a promotion but a gesture of the Pope's confidence. But as before, in the case of Constantinople, the gesture was not made. The appointment went to

He followed the Ignatean method

Monsignor Valerio Valeri, Roncalli's contemporary at the Roman Seminary and one who was strangely destined to "pass ahead" of him in the diplomatic career, until the last surprising event. To have this promotion so publicly proclaimed and then not to receive it, was something of a humiliation, if not a disgrace. Once more, Roncalli was left where he was.

In June that year he went to Istanbul to deputize for Monsignor Carlo Margotti at Pentecost and Corpus Christi; on July 30 he had the pleasure of meeting some Bergamasque workers at Kniagevo in Bulgaria. Writing to Don Carlo Marinelli on May 18 he had apologized for delay in answering his letter, adding in excuse: "Notwithstanding appearances to the contrary I am like a beast of burden always harnessed to his cart. I don't carry much weight, but I'm always at work." The diminutives (*somarello, carrettino*) suggest a smile at his own insignificance.

It was in Sofia that year that he made his retreat in September, with the Capuchin Fathers. "Great calm and peace," his notes begin, but continue: "I have to do everything myself because the good preacher Samuele had prepared some fine discourses for his colleagues but without any knowledge of the Ignatian method." He remained always faithful to the pattern of the Jesuit spiritual exercises in which he had been trained. "My prolonged mission as papal representative in this country often causes me acute and intimate suffering," he admitted, "but I try not to show this. I bear and will bear everything willingly, even joyfully, for the love of Jesus . . ."

In August 1934, once more at Rustchuk, he found again that the preacher knew little of the Ignatian method. But he could write: "My soul is tranquil. This year was remarkably calm." Not knowing that it was his last year in Bulgaria he told himself: "Do not be concerned about your future but think that perhaps you are drawing near to the gateway of eternal life. At the same time be ever more content to live like this, hidden from the world, perhaps forgotten by your Superiors, and do not grieve at being little appreciated but try to find an even greater joy in 'being esteemed of little worth.'" The quotation is from the *Imitation of Christ*.

"What has Monsignor Roncalli been doing during these monotonous years at the Apostolic Delegation? Trying to make himself holy and with simplicity, kindness, and joy opening a source of blessings and graces for all in Bulgaria, whether he lives to see it or not.

"This is what ought to be. But these are grand words and still grander things. O my Jesus, it shames me to think of them; I blush to speak of them. But give me the grace, the power and the glory of making them come true. The rest does not matter. All the rest is vanity, worthlessness, and affliction of soul."

At this point, when he had reached a serene resignation to his enforced inactivity, he was summoned to a life of ever-increasing action. Because he had done nothing to change his circumstances himself, he knew he could take the summons as coming from God. In November 1934 he received notice of his appointment as Apostolic Delegate in Istanbul. It was not promotion such as would have been the Nunciature in Bucharest; in fact, as he realized, it was a post even more beset with difficulties than his position in Sofia. Turkey was now a secular Republic under the dictator Mustafa Kemal and the Delegate also had the responsibility for the Catholics in Greece; in neither country were they any more numerous than in Bulgaria and there were even more complex divisions among them. As well as problems inherent in the situation there were those created by the overhasty zeal of Monsignor Margotti, whose reorganizations had upset the local Catholics. It was probably Roncalli's reputation for tactful good humor which landed him with this difficult assignment.

Now that the time had come to leave Bulgaria he was sad to say goodbye to all the friends he had made there. His farewell speech to the Bulgarians has often been quoted—the Irish story of the Christmas candle in the window to show Mary and Joseph that a family was waiting to receive them, and the application: "Wherever I may be, even though it be at the ends of the earth, if a Bulgarian away from his country comes past my house, he will find in my window the lighted candle. He has only to knock on my door; it will be opened to him whether he be Catholic or Orthodox: friend of Bulgaria, that title will be enough. He can come in and I will extend to him a very warm welcome." Less often noted is the fact that he also told the Bulgarians he was full of friendly feelings toward the Greeks and the Turks too—their hereditary enemies! Peace to all.

As a gesture of affection to Bulgaria he got the title of his bishopric changed from Areopolis to Mesembria—one of the ancient cities of the country, which he had visited in 1926 when he was trying to assist the refugees from Macedonia. Apart from farewell ceremonies Roncalli's last public occasion in Bulgaria had been in September, before his nomination to Istanbul, when he had presided over an international congress of Byzantine studies in Sofia. In moving to Constantinople he was moving towards the ancient center of the eastern Church, still, after the rest of the Orthodox had long been liberated from it, under the rule of the Turks. "You will not mistake me for Constantine," he remarked, with his usual humor, observing that he was following in the steps of that Emperor who had wished to make his capital in Sardica (Sofia) but had moved on to Byzantium.

So, with the goodwill of the people, Angelo Roncalli left Bulgaria, where he had faced and overcome the deepest psychological crisis of his life. He left on January 4, 1935. He was fifty-three.

12   Istanbul and Athens

Although he had been given an official send-off from Sofia, with representatives of the King and the Patriarch at the station, Roncalli arrived at Istanbul as a private visitor and was met only by the secretary from the Delegation. Scrupulous in obeying the law, he registered with the police the very day he arrived. He was not accredited to the government and so there was no question of official diplomatic contacts; even privately his approaches would have to be cautious and tactful.

"As it is pouring with rain in that country, I shall have to keep to the walls and get along as best I can," he had written on December 20, 1934 to Monsignor Adriano Bernareggi, the Bishop of Bergamo, who had sent good wishes. Bernareggi, incidentally, was an outstanding man, devoted to social action. There was a real friendship between him and Angelo Roncalli. "Each of us has his own cross to bear and each cross takes its own particular form," Roncalli wrote in this letter. "Mine is fashioned entirely in the style of this century." Circumstances had led him to live in that modern world, repudiated by so many of his senior Roman colleagues, where Catholics were considered a peculiar and tiresome minority group. This was particularly true in Turkey, which Mustafa Kemal was turning into a westernized modern state where not even Islam was to retain special privileges. In this year the president decreed that every Turk must adopt a surname and set an example by becoming Kemal Atatürk—Father Turk.

The creation of the national state of Turkey out of the ruins of the Ottoman Empire is an extraordinary story. Mustafa Kemal, the only undefeated Turkish general at the end of the First World War, was its architect and inspiring genius. He belonged to the military élite of the last era of the Ottomans and his chief supporters were drawn from the ranks of the Young Turks, the westernizing liberal party. The Turks entered the war as the allies of Germany and were involved in its defeat, with almost the total loss of the remnants of their European Empire.

Encouraged by the apparent demoralization of their hereditary enemies the Greeks in 1920 launched an attack on Asia Minor, coming within miles of Ankara, the new capital, before Mustafa Kemal began to drive them back. The invasion ended in 1922 with the complete repulse of the Greek army and the Turks were able to modify the harsh terms of the Treaty of Sèvres (never put into force) for those of the Treaty of Lausanne, which left them with the mainland, their home country since the defeat of Byzantium. Kemal became the first president of Turkey, the Sultan fled to Malta and that was the end of the Ottoman Empire.

Religiously, it was ended with the exile of the Caliph. Kemal had first separated the Caliphate from the Sultanate, giving it to another member of the Osman family, but he soon realized that the function of Caliph, as traditional leader of the Muslim faithful all over the world, was incompatible with the modern national state he wanted to build. The Caliph went, and with him the old order of Islam, where sacred and secular were inextricably one. Islam was officially "disestablished" in 1928. The roman alphabet was adopted and this certainly simplified the task of educating a largely illiterate population, since the Arabic script had always been unsuited to the Turkish language. But as the Koran was written in Arabic the script, even apart from the language, had hallowed associations and the change was unpopular with religious people. The main opposition to Atatürk's program came from orthodox Muslims, but after a rebellion by the Kurds had been severely put down in 1925 there was no open revolt. Kemal himself was immensely popular and could always appeal to the patriotism even of the orthodox. His right-hand man, Ismet Inönü (who took his surname from a victory against the Greeks) remained always faithful to Islam and when he succeeded Atatürk many Muslim customs came back into favor.

There was an amusing side to Atatürk's program of westernization. In spite of his own military prowess he gave up wearing uniform and appeared in a morning suit and top hat, which he regarded as the correct civilized dress. He was determined that the hat should replace the fez, a relatively recent Turkish adaptation of the turban, which has always had a strong religious symbolism for Islam. "Gentlemen," he said in October 1927, about two years after this reform had been introduced, "it was necessary to abolish the fez, which sat on the heads of our nation as an emblem of ignorance, negligence, fanaticism, and hatred of progress and civilization, to accept in its place the hat, the headgear used by the whole civilized world, and in this way to demonstrate that the Turkish nation, in its mentality as in other respects, in no way diverges from civilized social life."

After the Greco-Turkish war it was decided to exchange minority populations. Between 1923 and 1930 about two million of Greek descent were sent to Greece and a rather smaller number of Turks repatriated from territory now under Greek control. (Kemal himself had been born in Salonika.) This tremendous upheaval was over by the time Roncalli arrived to take up his post in Istanbul, but its effects were not. The most noticeable was the enormous reduction in the Greek population and the consequent isolation of the Orthodox Ecumenical Patriarch, who from time immemorial had exercised some kind of ecclesiastical control over all the main groups of Orthodox in the Balkans. We have seen how this was resented in Bulgaria (as in other Balkan countries) and how the nations, on becoming independent, invariably nationalized their churches, making them autocephalous (self-governing) though still maintaining communion with the Ecumenical Patriarch. Often it was a long time before the Patriarch officially recognized these unilateral declarations of independence.

With the Greek nation, however, the situation was different. The Greeks on the mainland of Europe as well as those in Turkey regarded themselves as the heirs of the Byzantine Empire and the Turks as interlopers. The Patriarch of Constantinople had always been the head of the Greek Church and under the Ottoman Empire he had been the head of their nation too. Inevitably the Turks regarded him as a center of disaffection. At the negotiations of Lausanne in 1922 they wanted to remove the Patriarchate from Istanbul, but the Greeks would not endure such a break with tradition. A compromise was reached; the Patriarch was to concern himself solely with religious affairs and not with politics. But so many things, marriage suits, disputed inheritances and so on, came into both spheres of influence. In the years after the war there were expulsions and flights from the Phanar, and the continual threat of violence. After all, under Ottoman rule a Patriarch had been hanged in reprisal for a Greek rising. But Atatürk wanted peace with Greece and by 1930 the position had been stabilized. The Greek Prime Minister, Venizelos, visited Ankara and Kemal went to Athens. But the Patriarchate was shorn of almost all its old power and influence.

In 1940 the total population of Turkey was reckoned at 17,900,000. After the exchanges there were left about 180,000 Greeks, 80,000 Armenians, 70,000 Jews and perhaps 20,000 Catholics of all rites, about 10,000 of which lived in

Istanbul itself. Those of the Latin rite in Istanbul were organized in a Vicariate Apostolic and ruled direct from Rome; the Delegate, as Apostolic Administrator, was in fact their bishop, with full pastoral responsibilities. For the Latin rite Catholics in the south there was an Archbishop of Smyrna. There was also a Mission "Sui Juris" of Samsun on the Black Sea, ruled by an Italian Capuchin who had all the powers and jurisdiction of a Bishop except that of conferring orders. For these two territories the Apostolic Delegate was the representative of the Pope and the normal channel through which they carried on their business with the Holy See. He fulfilled the same functions toward the Catholics of Oriental rites: an Armenian Exarchate comprising about 7500 Armenian Catholics in Turkey, with their own Archbishop resident in Istanbul; and a Greek Catholic Exarchate of about 1000, also with a Bishop resident in Istanbul. There were also a few scattered priests and faithful of the Chaldean Rite living close to the frontiers of Iraq; they were subject to the Chaldean Patriarch in Baghdad but Monsignor Roncalli was their Apostolic Delegate.

This complex human mosaic was the work of a long history; ancient schisms had divided the Armenians and Chaldeans from the Byzantine Orthodox long before the great schism between Greeks and Latins. Then in the centuries after Trent missionaries in communion with Rome had won back various groups to the papal allegiance. Sometimes these reunions were influenced by politics, but often the people became genuinely convinced of the duty to be in communion with the successor of St. Peter and remained faithful under conditions of the greatest difficulty and danger. They were called "Uniates" and despised by the Orthodox, who regarded them as especially instituted to undermine their own church, because they kept their ancient liturgy and customs. As in the Balkans, there had been a certain amount of westernization—easy to understand when we think of Kemal Atatürk's identification of civilization with western Europe.

Although the breakdown of the Ottoman Empire and the subsequent events had borne most hardly on the Greek community in Turkey, the miscellaneous Catholic groups were also affected, chiefly because Kemal Atatürk was determined to be free of the influence of the great European powers which had for so long interfered in Turkish affairs. The Latin rite Catholics had relied greatly on the protection of France and Italy. Religious orders, staffed mostly by French and Italian missionaries, ran the parishes and schools. In Istanbul itself the Vicariate was divided into seven parishes and all but one—the Cathedral of the Holy Ghost itself—were entrusted to the orders. Two were run by Dominicans; one by Friars Minor (Brown Franciscans); one by Capuchins; and two by Friars Minor Conventuals (Black Franciscans). Most of the priests in charge in these parishes were Italian, but there were always some French members of the orders to deal with French-speaking Catholics. The Jesuits had a retreat house and they were nearly all French. The several schools, primary and secondary, were run by De La Salle Brothers, mostly French, and Vincentians, also French, with one Austrian community. The Minor seminary was run by French Capuchin Fathers.

Apart from the Italian Sisters of Ivrea who ran the Italian hospital, most of the nuns in Istanbul were French: the Sisters of Notre Dame de Sion, the Sisters of Charity of St. Vincent de Paul (with one Austrian community and several French ones, each with a school), and the Little Sisters of the Poor. Of course many of the Latin rite Catholics were French or Italian, living in Istanbul for business reasons. There were also a fairly large number of diplomatic families, of all nationalities. In 1924 the government had threatened to close all the schools but Monsignor Dolci, who had been Delegate from 1914 till 1922, came back and successfully negotiated a settlement. The schools were to remain an anxiety, all the same, for various reasons.

Roncalli came into this complex situation well knowing its difficulties but determined to live in friendship with all its diverse human elements, including the Turks. The day after his arrival was January 6, the Feast of the Epiphany, commemorating the manifestation of Christ to all the nations. It is a more ancient feast than Christmas, and is more celebrated in the East. It was the best of times for Roncalli to inaugurate his new ministry. "If the sun did not shine," wrote the cathedral archivist in French, "it was largely compensated for by

the face of the hero of this family feast day which was radiant
with kindness." Everyone was impressed by the Archbishop's
reverence when he kissed the crucifix held out to him by the
Archdeacon of the Cathedral of the Holy Spirit, Monsignor
Collaro. The papal bulls were read and when the clergy came
to kiss his ring in token of obedience: "in his paternal way
he gave them a kiss of peace accompanied by an appropriate
word or two which no one will ever forget." In 1958 the world
saw him do the same thing with the Cardinals at his coronation. It was Pope John's style, already his own in 1935.

In his address Roncalli emphasized that his functions were
purely religious: "I have not been sent here to deal in politics
or to look after material interests." He knew that within the
Catholic community a good deal of friction had been caused
by the overhasty reforms imposed by his predecessor. So he
was careful to praise all his predecessors, especially Dolci, but
he added: "Each had the spirit proper to himself, but every
spirit praises the Lord." Even though he went on to say that
he felt small beside them he had thus tactfully indicated that
he too would follow his own spirit. Again this was to have an
echo in his pontificate.

Roncalli's way was always to take people as they were and
to expect the best of them; he did not criticize except in dire
necessity. Already in February 1935 he wrote in a letter: "I
find myself surrounded here by people of the highest quality,
all of them anxious to help me in any way they can, even to
the point of being willing to swallow the pills ordered by
Monsignor Margotti to make them better and which in his
time they could not take without making faces. What more
could a man ask?"

In July the secretary of the Delegation, Angelo Dell'Acqua,
was recalled to Rome. Although Roncalli appreciated his personal qualities (he was to be one of the circle who worked
closely with him as Pope) his departure made it possible to
rectify one of those situations which had upset the local
clergy. For Margotti had made the young secretary his vicar-
general, taking the office away from Father Collaro, the archdeacon who had offered the Delegate the cross to kiss on his
arrival. The description of Collaro in Algisi's book (author-
ized by Pope John) stresses his holiness but suggests that the

long hours he spent in the confessional prevented him from
being a really efficient vicar-general. Roncalli respected his
goodness and long experience of local conditions more than
he deplored his lack of administrative ability. He gave the
post back to him. The official nomination from Rome did not
come through for two years! The delay may have been due
not to mere dilatoriness but to suspicions as to Collaro's
suitability. But in Roncalli's eyes it was wrong to pass over a
local man; inefficiency was not immoral. If the appointment
meant more work for himself, that did not deter him.

In the summer of 1935 the Turkish government brought
in a decree forbidding the wearing of any form of religious
habit; an edict which was to apply to Muslims as well as
Christians. The Catholic religious orders were so indignant
that they asked the French ambassador to lodge a protest.
When he did, he received the proud reply from the Turkish
government: "We are now the masters of Turkey." Let France
send a fleet if she wished; its reception would be very different from what it had been in 1914. The days of foreign intervention were past. In reaction, some of the religious decided
to leave Turkey rather than give up the habit.

Roncalli did not approve this attitude. He thought too
much was being made out of things of secondary importance.
Heads of religious communities were allowed to apply for
exemption and he joined the petition to express solidarity
with others but decided that if permission were granted he
would not make use of it. In this respect he seems to have
been unique. The Patriarch was said to have decided to stay
in the Phanar for the rest of his life rather than give up his
religious dress. In the event the only exemptions allowed were
for the heads of Turkish communities.

The decree came into force on June 15 and Roncalli decided to make its observance among Catholics a community
gesture. All the clergy assembled on that day in the church
of St. Anthony, in the center of the city, and came out in
procession, in ordinary dress. Roncalli had left everyone to
make his own choice, so long as his clothing was suitably dark,
so it was an odd collection that emerged from the church.
Smiling as usual, the Archbishop brought up the rear, in a
costume that made him look rather like a broad church Eng-

lish vicar. Except in his own house and in church he wore lay clothes for the whole of the time he was in Turkey. He believed in accommodating himself to the country in which he was living, in everything that was not a matter of principle.

It was in this spirit that he began to introduce the Turkish language into Christian devotions. On June 9 he had given his first sermon in Turkish, as well as in French. On January 12, 1936, introducing catechism instruction into the cathedral, he ordered the Divine Praises, the vernacular prayers at Benediction, to be said in Turkish. He also saw that official documents were written in Turkish. Such measures were not popular with the Christians, who regarded the Turks as religious enemies and the new government as atheist. But to Roncalli it seemed the Catholic thing to do, to say public prayers in the language of the country. On May 6, 1936, he noted in a diary: "When the *Tanre Mubarek olsun* (Blessed be God) was recited, many people left the church displeased . . . (But) I am happy. On Sunday the Gospel in Turkish in front of the French ambassador; today the litany in Turkish in front of the Italian ambassador . . . the Catholic Church respects everyone . . . The Apostolic Vicar is a bishop for everyone and intends honoring the Gospel, which does not admit national monopolies, does not become a fossil . . . looks to the future."*

Whatever the Christians thought, his attitude made a great impression on the Turks. It was recalled in their newspapers in 1958 when he was elected Pope. Roncalli persevered in learning Turkish, no easy task for a man in his fifties. He never became fluent, but had to rely a good deal on French. But his liking for the Turks was genuine; he mentioned it several times in his private retreat notes.

During his first year in Turkey Roncalli was struggling with the problem of the schools. Pius XI was particularly anxious that they should be kept open but the working of the state system, the continued emigration of Catholics and the tensions between the secular government and the foreign religious orders made it impossible to maintain them all. The Christian Brothers gave up four out of eight boys' schools

---

* The quotation, with the omissions, is as recorded by Monsignor Loris Capovilla in *The Heart and Mind of John XXIII*.

and two out of three girls' schools were closed by the Sisters of Our Lady of Sion, though the remaining one, near the cathedral, was expanded. Roncalli succeeded in persuading some of the other orders concerned in education to stay on, but it was a situation which did not seem likely to improve.

At the end of his first year in Turkey, in December 1935, Angelo Roncalli made a retreat in the Delegation, with the priests of his cathedral. The Superior of the Jesuits, Father Paolo Spigre, took it; Roncalli, in his brief notes praised him, but commented that there were too many distractions for him when he attempted to make the exercises at home. The journal, however, breathes the happiness he was finding in his new mission, with its pastoral duties. "There is so much work waiting for me here! I bless God, who fills me with the joys of his sacred ministry. I am determined, however, to order all my affairs with greater precision and calm."

He included a footnote on those long years in Bulgaria: "By sending me here the Holy Father has wished to point out to Cardinal Sincero the impression made on him by my silence, maintained for ten years, about being kept in Bulgaria, without ever complaining or expressing the wish to be moved elsewhere. This was in order to honor a resolution I had made, and I am very glad I was always faithful to it."

He was soon to discover that his difficulties with the central administration were by no means over when he left Bulgaria, but in this year he did not get back to Italy. This was in itself a personal sacrifice, for his father died on July 28, 1935. He thought of flying home for the funeral, but decided that there were too many reasons against it. Giovanni Battista Roncalli was eighty-one, and his son comforted himself with the hope of a meeting in heaven, as he told Davide Cugini, the lawyer who had been at the college at Celana when Roncalli was secretary to the Bishop, and who visited him in Istanbul early in August. After his father's death, his mother joined his two sisters at Camaitino.

Curious as it may seem, in view of the hostility between the two nations, the Delegate in Turkey was also responsible for the affairs of the Catholics in Greece, not pastorally, but in relation to the Holy See. Until 1932 the Bishop of Syra, an island in the Aegean with a largely Catholic (Latin rite) population, had acted as papal delegate; at that date Monsignor Margotti was appointed. The Greek government mistook this for a diplomatic appointment, made by the Pope without previous consultation. Monsignor Margotti was refused a visa.

When Roncalli asked for a visa he simply stated that the religious affairs of Catholics in Greece needed attention. He was given a permit for eight days only, provided that he traveled as a private person. Accepting the condition, he went to Athens on May 3, 1935, and returned on May 12. The whole time he was in Athens he was aware that he was watched and followed. He behaved with the utmost circumspection, avoiding any contact with the diplomatic corps and, as far as possible, any special reception from the Catholics. He met as many of the bishops as had been able to come to Athens, heard their difficulties, and discreetly retired. In consequence of this cautious approach he was allowed to return to Greece on August 30 and stay a few days, and then again from November 4 till 18, when he visited the islands, Syra, Santorin, Naxos, and also Piraeus, the port of Athens.

The situation of Catholics in Greece was exceedingly difficult. When Greece gained independence, in the war finally concluded by the Treaty of London in 1832, it was with the help of Great Britain, Russia, and France. The Greeks, who had throughout the war been much divided among themselves, accepted Otto of Bavaria as their first king. After the prolonged Ottoman rule the country was much in need of assistance and Catholic religious orders were allowed to found schools and hospitals, at first staffed chiefly by French fathers and nuns. There had been groups of Latin rite Catholics in Greece ever since the Crusades, especially in the ports and the islands, but the Greeks had never forgotten the misdeeds of the Crusaders and retained a strong hostility toward Rome. Foreigners were called Franks, and as such were suspect.

The tension between Greeks and Latins was increased during the two decades after the First World War by Mussolini's aggressive Mediterranean policy, which made Italians more unpopular than ever in Greece; and by an unexpected result of the exchange of populations with Turkey after the Treaty of Lausanne in 1922, when some two thousand Greek

Catholics of the Byzantine rite arrived from Asia Minor. These Uniates, as the Orthodox called them, were unacceptable because they kept the Greek liturgy and customs while acknowledging the primacy of the Pope. Roncalli, of course, had met this difficulty in Bulgaria, and understood the situation with greater sympathy than most of his Italian contemporaries, outside the ranks of scholars, would have done. He was anxious not to antagonize the Orthodox still further. He felt his way, slowly and cautiously.

Just after he left Greece in November 1935 King George II of the Hellenes was recalled from London, where he had been living in exile, by a plebiscite, which was afterward said to have been managed by the army. In April the next year General Joannes Metaxas became Prime Minister and shortly afterward assumed the powers of a dictator, a position he held till his death early in 1941. His type of dictatorship was perhaps more like that of Franco in Spain than Mussolini's in Italy, military rather than demagogic. It was accepted by the King as the only efficient means of uniting a politically divided nation—the changes of government had become chaotically frequent—in the face of what was believed to be a real threat of revolutionary Communism. King George, member of a cosmopolitan royal family, received the Apostolic Delegate on May 25, 1936, and was not unfriendly; this meeting helped to facilitate Roncalli's work in Greece.

It took place at the end of a tour, beginning on April 18 and ending May 29, when Roncalli visited Corinth, Nauplia, Mycenae, Epidaurus, Delphi, Boeotian Thebes, and Mount Athos. Of course there were no Catholics on the famous monastic mountain; his visit was made privately, because of his intense interest in the life and prayer of the Orthodox. The monks were surprised to meet a representative of the Pope, but since he came only in a private capacity, they welcomed him as they would any other visitor.

He made two more visits to Greece in 1936, once in September, when he met General Metaxas, and once in December. In 1937 he was there several times and in August traveled to the islands of Tenos, Delos, Syra, and Corfu. Off Patras, on board the *Kephallinia*, he succeeded in meeting the Orthodox Archbishop, John Chrysostom Papadopoulos. He was always eager to make personal contact where he could. He continued the tour on the mainland, visiting Patras, Aghis Laura, Olympia, Sparta, Messene and Tripolis. On July 25 he had consecrated an Assumptionist, Monsignor Antonio Gregorio Vuccino, as Bishop of Syra.

During these years things became even more difficult for the Catholics in Greece. Measures were passed by the government making all but Orthodox marriages illegal and putting restrictions on other activities of Catholics. The Uniates were refused permission to build themselves a church. The regulations on mixed marriages told heavily against Catholics, a fact that may provoke wry smiles from Protestants. Added to these problems there were troubles among the Catholics, whose diverse elements did not always pull together. In all these delicate situations Roncalli moved with exceeding caution and he did much to prevent unwise Catholic reaction to government measures. Even on the marriage bill he counseled restraint. He negotiated endlessly about the site for the Uniates' church, trying to find a solution acceptable to the Orthodox hierarchy.

"In Athens we don't ride in a carriage!" he said to Davide Cugini. "The bombardment of Corfu is still sounding in Greek ears. My illustrious predecessor was certainly very acute, but perhaps just a little optimistic. Certainly the encounter with the reality of things is sometimes . . . another thing." The lightly punning style did not conceal the shrewdness of his appraisal.

It was in 1937 that for the first time Roncalli succeeded in meeting a member of the Turkish government, M. Menemencogliu. It was the first of several conversations, on neutral subjects. But after that the Delegate spent a few days in Ankara every year and left cards on suitable people. Yet he never attempted to procure any sort of official recognition.

It was not a spectacular method. It was obscure, quiet, slow work. Roncalli called it "ant's work, bee's work"—the perfect description and typical of the countryman he was.

He made his retreat in 1936 during his holiday in Italy, in the villa of the Daughters of the Sacred Heart at Ranica, just outside Bergamo, the place of the famous strike in 1909. It was "full of peace and silence," he recorded in the journal.

"I am pleased with my new ministry in Turkey, in spite of many difficulties." Nevertheless he reverted to the subject of his relations with the central administration in Rome, which he had now visited for the first time since taking up his new appointment. "I feel quite detached from everything, from all thought of advancement or anything else," he wrote. "I know I deserve nothing and I do not feel any impatience. It is true, however, that the difference between my way of seeing situations on the spot and certain ways of judging the same things in Rome hurts me considerably: it is my only real cross. I want to bear it humbly, with great willingness to please my principal Superiors, because this and nothing else is what I desire. I shall always speak the truth, but with mildness, keeping silence about what might seem a wrong or an injury done to myself, ready to sacrifice myself or be sacrificed. The Lord sees everything and will deal justly with me. Above all, I wish to continue always to render good for evil, and in all things to endeavor to prefer the Gospel truth to the wiles of human politics."

Taking into consideration the resolution of obedience and the calm tone, these are strong words. He was writing, not about some clash of temperament, but about differences with curial officials on method and policy. They did not understand his ant's work, carrying away tiny pieces of the barriers between men, his bee's work, filling the cells of mankind with small doses of honey. Because he did nothing spectacular, they may have thought he was not doing anything significant. The comparison between human politics and Gospel truth is one which Roncalli was to use again in this connection and he referred to the curial politicians as "the other school." He had no use for political planning in the affairs of the Church and he stuck to his principles till the end. From this point his spiritual journal records a new anxiety: whether he was doing as much as he ought. But he never had any doubts on his method. In a world where Catholics were a minority with a history of religious imperialism to live down, the way of the Gospel was the only way to lay foundations for future peace and unity.

"I want to study Turkish with more care and perseverance," he went on. "I am fond of the Turks, to whom the Lord has

The Ant and the Bee

sent me: it is my duty to do what I can for them. I know that my way of dealing with them is right; above all it is Catholic and apostolic. I must continue in this with faith, prudence, and sincere zeal, at the cost of any sacrifice."

The men in Rome may have had other ideas on how to deal with the Turks—and the Greeks. It is interesting to see how Roncalli's motto of obedience, which he adhered to so faithfully, did not prevent him from persisting in his own approach when he considered it right and appropriate to the Gospel. He did what he was told, but he had his own way of doing it.

At Sotto il Monte, that year, he saw his mother settled into his house at Camaitino, with Ancilla and Maria. The house is neither large nor small, a simple comfortable place with a tiny chapel where Roncalli said Mass when he was at home. In the middle of the ceiling is painted the small dove of the Holy Ghost descending, seen from below, with feet neatly tucked up. Roncalli's bedroom is small, holding not much more than his solid wooden bed; the window looks straight up the steep green hill to the tower of San Giovanni. Here, from his far-flung travels, Angelo came back to his family who worked on as they had always done, brothers and sisters and children all together. Away in Sofia or Istanbul he was always thinking of Sotto il Monte, corresponding with the parish priest, making suggestions about the road to the cemetery, remembering the old sacristan when he died, reminded by the Feast of St. John the Baptist in June of this green hillside, "blessed with the scent of spring in flower and rich with the gifts of summer," as he wrote in 1937 to Don Carlo Marinelli.

In that year of 1937, as well as his tours in Greece, he visited in May some monasteries of Asia Minor, at Yalova, Gemlik, and Bursa. He also went to Mudanya and Nicea, where the first great Council of the Church was held, called by the newly converted Emperor Constantine and attended by many bishops who bore in their bodies the scars of recent persecutions. Few Popes can have visited the sites of so many Councils as Pope John.

In September 1937 he was in Bergamo for a regional Eucharistic congress and gave four talks for the eighth centenary of beautiful Santa Maria Maggiore there. In November he had an audience of Pius XI, then, in his old age, battling against the menace of Nazism. Already in 1936 he had denounced "neo-paganism" along with "atheistic Communism." He deplored Mussolini's increasing commitment to the idea of an "Axis" with Hitler. When Hitler visited Rome, Pius XI pointedly left for Castelgandolfo. Roncalli, who understood Achille Ratti's northern Italian patriotism and, from his involvement with Christian Democracy, was less deceived by Fascism, must have sympathized with his efforts to halt the rush to the abyss. He always had a great admiration for Pius XI, whose best qualities came out more strongly in old age.

Although he was only in his fifties Roncalli himself began to feel the approach of age. In 1938 he would be fifty-seven, the age at which the revered Bishop Radini-Tedeschi had died, whose years he hardly felt it proper to outlive. In December 1936 he had been suddenly taken ill. He had already written in his journal that year: "For my health's sake I must stick to a diet as regards food. I eat little in the evenings already but now I must eat less at midday too. It will do me good to go out for a walk every day. O Lord, I find this hard and it seems such a waste of time, but still it is necessary and everybody insists that I should do so. So I shall do it, offering the Lord the effort it costs me." In fact, he scarcely ever walked without an object in view, even if it was only to visit bookstalls. As to his size, it never diminished; it was probably too late for that. But it never seemed to stop him getting about the world as actively as any thin person.

Although there were some difficulties in his position, it was not frustrating, as it had been in Bulgaria. He had the pastoral work he wanted and life in Istanbul was fascinating to anyone with an interest in past history and present people. One of the first people to call on him was the Reverend Austin Oakley, the chaplain to the British Embassy and the Archbishop of Canterbury's personal representative to the Patriarch of Constantinople. Roncalli soon returned his visit and they became friends. Austin Oakley was the first Anglican Roncalli came to know well. He was on very good terms with the Phanar. He had traveled even further afield than

Roncalli, for he had been director of a mission school in Basutoland, South Africa, and an Archdeacon in Central America. Father Oakley arranged a meeting between his own Bishop, Harold Buxton of Gibraltar, and the Apostolic Delegate at the house of a mutual friend on Prinkipo, one of the Propontic islands. It was a great success; Catholic and Anglican bishops embraced and talked happily together.

Roncalli used to visit Oakley's chapel and prayed with him, showing that he was no stickler for niceties of ecclesiastical procedure. At that time such an unconstrained friendship between a papal delegate and an Anglican priest was unusual; they met often during the nine years they were in Istanbul together and did not quite lose touch afterward. In 1961 Father Oakley visited Pope John, who received him in private audience with a warm embrace. Minor officials at the Vatican were puzzled and one asked Father Oakley: "You're not an Archbishop, are you?" Pope John knew what he was doing when he called the Council with reunion as its ultimate aim and when he set up the Secretariat for Promoting Christian Unity. He never expected sudden reunion of long-separated communities, but his principle was always to emphasize what unites rather than what divides. He was fond of the aphorism: *gutta cavat lapidem* (the drop of water hollows the stone). Thinking of the centuries-long barriers between Christians, he said to Oakley: "I try to pull out a brick here and there." It was his ant's work again, his bee's work.

In January 1938 there were celebrations for the fifteenth centenary of the tanslation of the relics of St. John Chrysostom from Cappadocia to Constantinople. Because his letters have been preserved, St. John's human qualities make him one of the most accessible of the early Fathers. He was ever a favorite with Roncalli, who frequently quoted him. In Febraury the Delegate consecrated Giuseppe Descuffi, an Italian Vincentian, as Archbishop of Izmir (Smyrna); Monsignor Descuffi was to speak on several occasions during the Council. In March Roncalli was making pastoral visits to the scattered groups of Catholics in Turkey, sometimes only a few hundreds of people. He stayed in Smyrna and took the opportunity of visiting the ancient ruins of Pergamum. At the beginning of May he attended a meeting of the Greek

Episcopate at the monastery of the Pammacaristos and spent about a week in Crete. Later in May he made a pastoral visit to Ankara, where the Catholics were mostly those attached to embassies. In June he was at Adrianopoli; in November he was in Greece once more, visiting Volos, Phthiotic Thebes, and Chalcis. As a private visitor he went to see the famous monasteries of the Meteora, perched on their inaccessible rock fastnesses.

On the day he returned to Istanbul Kemal Atatürk died: November 10, 1938. Roncalli saw to it that Catholics joined in the national mourning. The Turks did not forget the admiration he expressed for their great leader; it was recalled twenty years later when he was elected Pope. Whatever his faults Atatürk had made a new nation of the Turks out of the ruins of the Ottoman Empire. The new president, Ismet İnönü, continued his work and showed more favor to Islam, the religion of the majority of Turks.

Roncalli saw Pius XI for the last time in September 1938; he was eighty-one, the same age that John XXIII was to reach. Pius XI died in February 1939 and, after one of the shortest conclaves recorded, his Secretary of State, Eugenio Pacelli, was elected and took the name of Pius XII. Roncalli arranged a Requiem for the dead Pope in Istanbul for February 19, 1939. It was a measure of the success of his unobtrusive methods that there were present at it members of the diplomatic corps, civic officials, a representative of the Patriarch, two bishops representing the Armenian Patriarch of Kum Kapu and the Great Rabbi. Roncalli arranged the ceremonies to emphasize the variety of traditions within the Church; the absolutions at the catafalque were delivered by the Melkite Patriarchal Vicar, Greek and Armenian bishops, and a Bulgarian priest (Slavonic), the Delegate himself giving the last in Latin. He also delivered the panegyric on the dead Pope, which he kept simple and straightforward. He recalled the faith and courage of Pius XI and his desire for the peace and unity of mankind. The last time he had seen him the Pope had said: "I have no fears for the future of the Church, I have no fears. God keeps his promises." The faith of Pius XI, said Roncalli, was "a reflexion of the assurance of the divine promises." The Pope's fears were only for the nations, under the threat of imminent war.

There were accounts of the ceremony and of the Delegate's speech in the Istanbul papers the next day. In his circular to the faithful, announcing the election of Pius XII, Roncalli emphasized the nonpolitical function of the Pope in the world. "His ministry is one of reconciliation and peace." He added: "And even beyond the Christian flock which is his more especial care, he sees only the children of God, worthy of respect, understanding, and love."

After these public occasions Roncalli made his first official visit to the Phanar, to thank the Patriarch Benjamin I for his courtesy in sending a representative to the Requiem. This meeting had been prepared for by others between the Delegate and the Grand Vicar. An unprecedented event, it took place on May 27, 1939, the first sign of a crack in the wall of prejudice that had lasted even longer than the nine-century schism. Undoubtedly Roncalli's links with the Phanar played their part in later efforts to draw Orthodox and Catholics closer together. It is known that Pope John had wished to meet Patriarch Athenagoras, who later met Pope Paul VI in Jerusalem and by a symbolic embrace began a new era. At the end of the second Vatican Council the mutual anathemas between Constantinople and Rome were repealed simultaneously in both cities, leaving the way open for closer relations. On this occasion the Patriarch's representative at the Roman ceremony, Archbishop Meliton, left nine white roses, one for each century of the schism, on the tomb of Pope John.

The day after the Requiem for Pope Pius XI Angelo Roncalli's mother died in Sotto il Monte, at the age of eighty-five, and was carried to burial from La Colombéra, the *casa paterna*. His old school friend of Celana, Pietro Donizetti, now a professor, wrote to tell him how everyone in the village seemed to be at Marianna Roncalli's funeral, so greatly was she respected. Roncalli replied that he was much moved by Donizetti's account and by that wish of hers to be carried to burial from the house where her husband had died and "where for so many years she had lived for and loved her family. *Basta questo gesto a rivelare le altezze e le finezze di un'anima cristiana*—(that gesture is enough to reveal the heights and the refinements of a Christian soul)."

He wrote this little verse about his mother.

> *La sua umile vita*
> *Pura come ruscello di fonte montana*
> *Corse tranquilla per vie piane e consuete.*
> *Semplicità e bontà*
> *Fra consolazioni e tristezze*
> *Della lunga fatica materna*
> *La resero a tutti cara e veneranda*
> *Più cara a suoi figlioli*
> *Che crebbe numerosi e robusti*
> *Al timore di Dio ed all'amore degli uomini*
> *Ed ai figli dei figli*
> *Che vide in gaudio moltiplicati*
> *Nella sua casa*
> *Fino alla terza ed alla quarta generazione*
> *Benedicenti alla sua memoria.*

> Her humble life
> Pure as a stream from a mountain spring
> Ran quietly by level and habitual ways.
> Simplicity and goodness
> Through the joys and sorrows
> Of a mother's long toiling
> Made her dear and respected by all,
> Dearer to her children
> Who grew up numerous and strong
> In the fear of God and the love of men
> And to the sons of her sons
> Whom she saw multiplied in joy
> In her home
> Even to the third and fourth generation
> Blessing her memory.

A few days after his visit to the Patriarch, at the beginning of June 1939, the Delegate traveled to Beirut for the Eucharistic Congress presided over by Eugene Cardinal Tisserant. He returned through Palestine and Syria, visiting Jerusalem, Jaffa, Palmyra, Homs, and Aleppo, but rapidly, for he was back in Istanbul by June 10. In October there were other tours, to Adana, Alexandretta, Antioch, Aleppo, Mersina, Tarsus, Konia, and Smyrna again. As Pope he referred to his visit to Tarsus, St. Paul's home town, and the little Catholic chapel in that ruined place.

Meanwhile, the Second World War had started in northern Europe, in September 1939. Roncalli was in Italy at the time. He had his first audience with the new Pope, Eugenio Pacelli, who, since 1930 had been one of his principal superiors as head of the Secretariat of State.

In November that year Roncalli succeeded in making a retreat away from his home, at the Jesuit residence Ayas of Pasa; his priests were with him, but there was more chance of detachment from immediate affairs. When meditating over his own position he noted in the journal that his holiday in Italy had been all too brief and "spoiled by the need to return soon." But, he reflected, "in compensation I received an extremely benevolent and encouraging welcome in Rome from the Holy Father, the office of the Secretary of State and the Congregation of the Eastern Church. I thank the Lord. This is more than I deserve. But I do not work for men's praises."

This warm welcome in Rome may have given rise to rumors of promotion which had come to his ears. "There is no lack of rumor around me, murmurs that 'greater things are in store,'" he had written earlier in these notes. "I am not so foolish as to listen to this flattery, which is, yet, I admit it, for me too a temptation. I try very hard to ignore these rumors, which speak of deceit and spite. I treat them as a joke: I smile and pass on. For the little or nothing that I am worth to Holy Church, I have already my purple mantle, my blushes of shame at finding myself in this position of honor and responsibility when I know I am worth so little. Oh what a comfort it is to me to feel free from these longings for changes and promotions! I consider this freedom a great gift from God. May the Lord preserve me always in this state of mind."

These rumors did not come to anything. The accelerating tempo of the war and its rapid spread over the world meant that Roncalli's position in neutral Istanbul became more important than in peacetime. It was not the moment to move someone as tactful as he had proved himself to be.

13   War in the Eastern Mediterranean

Though the war which began in northern Europe in September 1939 did not immediately affect the eastern Mediterranean, the nations were maneuvering for position there. Before Hitler initiated the *blitzkrieg* Mussolini had carried out one of his own. On Good Friday, April 7, 1939, he launched an attack on Albania and almost at once succeeded in annexing it. The Greek government mobilized the army, expecting invasion over the border at any moment, but Mussolini made no further move, nor did he join Hitler's war till the fall of France in June 1940. Even then he did not attack Greece until the end of October.

In spite of the superior numbers and armament of the Italians, the Greeks not only forced them back over the frontier but by the next spring had occupied almost a third of Albania. But in March 1941 Bulgaria joined the Axis and Hitler invaded Yugoslavia and Greece. The German army reached Athens in April 1941. General Metaxas had died in the January of that year. The Greek government fled to start a resistance center outside the country and a puppet administration was set up in the capital. To the Greeks the most bitter result of the disaster was the occupation of their country by the Italian army they had defeated.

Turkey, meanwhile, was determined to remain neutral. The German attack on Russia, the Turks' hereditary enemy, inclined the nation's sympathies toward the Axis; on the other hand, there were trade links with Britain and Atatürk is said to have advised, from his deathbed, that in the event of war Turkey should not place herself in opposition to Britain. Both sides tried to influence the issue, but Turkey succeeded in maintaining a precarious neutrality until February

1945 when, since it was clear that Nazi Germany was on the verge of defeat, the Turkish government declared war on Hitler so as to join the United Nations as one of the victors.

Turkey's neutrality meant that Istanbul became a great center of intrigue and espionage, as well as a clearing house for communications between belligerents on prisoners of war, refugees, and other questions. As representative of the Pope, even though not diplomatically recognized, Roncalli found himself in a position of more importance than hitherto and of even greater delicacy. The Pope, of course, remained neutral and his representatives also, whatever their own nationality. A central information bureau was set up in the Vatican, headed by Bishop Evreimoff, a Byzantine rite Catholic of Russian origin. For this office Roncalli transmitted much information; couriers of the Holy See passed through Istanbul en route for many countries. The Chief Rabbi of Jerusalem sent requests concerned with the fate of European Jews through the Palestine Agency in Istanbul for the Delegate to forward to the Pope or to the Nuncio in Budapest. Although he was anxious to help, the political situation became so complex that he was later warned against too much involvement, in particular with the German ambassador to Turkey, Franz von Papen.

Von Papen was a devout Catholic who had made the fatal mistake of backing Hitler's Chancellorship under the impression that Nazism was a patriotic movement strong enough to ward off the threat of revolutionary Communism, which could yet be guided by conservatives to drop its violent elements. Von Papen was the German equivalent of the Catholic collaborators with Fascism in Italy. None of them realized in time that the appeal to violence and hatred was just what gave these movements their popular power; on the psychological level they shared much with the destructive element in Communism, while the Communist *ideal* remained superior to the narrow cult of nationalism.

Von Papen wrote in his *Memoirs* (published in London in 1952 when Roncalli was still Nuncio in Paris): "The Papal Delegate, Monsignor Roncalli, who had arrived in Istanbul for a confirmation service, tried to assuage our fears. He could see no alternative to a German defeat, but he had confidence in the judgment of the Western Allied statesmen and their intention of taking all the measures necessary for European security. At my request he forwarded to the Vatican my pleas that the Allies should recognize the difference between the Hitler regime and the German people." This was a legitimate request, but when "Operation Cicero" is recalled, the most complex spy game of the war, in which von Papen was closely involved, it is understandable that Roncalli was warned about his relations with the German Ambassador. After the war von Papen asked Roncalli to testify for him at the Nuremberg trials.

Many of the Catholics under the Delegate's care were members of the diplomatic corps or belonged to nations at war with each other; he had to maintain peace as best he could. After the fall of France the large French colony was indignant with Italy for joining Germany at that critical moment; a few months later it was the Greeks who had cause to hate the Italians. Mussolini had made his country-men unpopular everywhere and had renewed the age-old antagonisms of the eastern Mediterranean. In an Easter address of 1941 Roncalli reminded his mixed flock that every-one tended to judge events from the standpoint of his own nation, but that they must try not to dispute about the blame. No one will ever admit he is wrong "but actually every one of us is at fault; there comes a time when every individual is involved in what happens to all the rest."

After 1940 even the French in Istanbul were divided against each other; some supported the government Marshal Henri Pétain set up at Vichy and others backed General Charles de Gaulle and the resistance movement. The conflict spread even within the religious orders. A Lazarist went off to Cairo to contact the Free French; a Carmelite organized a liberation group; some Assumptionists who had fled from Plovdiv when the German army entered Bulgaria were anxious to do the same. Each side wanted the Delegate to declare in its favor. A French priest who had preached the Lenten ser-mons in the cathedral went after Easter to join the Gaullists in Beirut; returning later, he wanted the Delegate to speak to the French colony in favor of de Gaulle. Roncalli let him talk but he used Scripture to show the necessary base for his neutrality. "I read in the Bible that the patriarch Jacob also had sons who disagreed among themselves. But he, the father, *rem tacitus considerabat*—considered the matter in silence." And silent he remained on the political issues.

But he could always see the humorous side of any situation. He was constantly watched and followed by spies of all the nations. "I never knew whether they were spying on me or each other," he used to say.

That he remained on friendly terms with so many people at enmity with each other was a measure of the success of his efforts to work for the alleviation of suffering during the war. During the Greek famine he appealed to everyone for the starving children of Greece. "Who's that fellow in a dark suit and string tie?" asked somebody at the British Embassy and was surprised to hear from a high official that he was the papal Delegate and one of the few who was "really doing something."

Roncalli arranged to begin his sixtieth year in retreat. He could not go to the Jesuits again because of the war situation, so he went to the villa of the nuns of Our Lady of Sion at Terapia on the Bosporus, where, as he put it in his *Journal*, he had "come to act as chaplain to the good sisters, old and in retirement, who have fled here for shelter from their houses at Jassy and Galatz in Rumania." His priests from the cathedral were to follow him one by one, going into retreat separately. This left him more freedom.

He began his retreat on his fifty-ninth birthday, November 25, 1940, on purpose to dedicate to God "that period when a man begins to be old, and admits it." Pope Pius XII had asked all Catholics to join him in the Litany of the Saints and in reciting the penitential psalm *Miserere*, so Roncalli decided to write down some meditations on each verse of the psalm, beginning with the mourning of the nations. Some people thought one nation or another would be preserved "because of the righteous people who live there or because of the good they do." But he knew it was otherwise. God made the nations, but he left the constitutions of states to the free decisions of men, hence their actions brought the natural consequences upon them. God did not arbitrarily intervene. "And even his assistance to his Church, although it preserves her from final defeat, does not guarantee her immunity from trials and persecutions." War was the fault of man. He went on to meditate on the state of war within all souls, including his own, and to pray that the mercy of God would transform the evil situation for good. There are twenty long meditations altogether.

Preceding them in the *Journal* are some comments Roncalli made on himself. "Even without exaggerating the importance of entering upon this last, possibly rapid and brief, period of my life, I feel something more mature and authoritative within me in relation to all that interests and surrounds me. I think I notice greater detachment from all that concerns my own future, a more marked indifference 'to all created things,' a slow and slight blurring of the outlines of things, persons, places and undertakings to which I was formerly more strongly attached, a more evident inclination to understand and sympathize and a greater tranquillity and clarity in impressions and judgments."

In the next paragraph he wrote: "Every now and then a thorn pricks me, sometimes very sharply. I ought, strictly speaking, to make stern decisions. By doing so I should pull out the thorn. Would I then not deserve others, and sharper ones? And then, what about truth, charity, and mercy? And the spirit of Christ in dealing with the souls of men? In dealing with my own soul?" He left the questions unanswered in writing but answered them in practice. He never could bring himself to make stern decisions on those under his authority. He knew that this was sometimes regarded as weakness, not charity. Nevertheless he would try every method to appeal to the conscience of the one causing trouble, except the stern decision. In Venice, years later, he was urged to proceed against a priest. He said, "If you drop a glass, it's smashed. You can't put it together again." Colleagues thought him weak, in this case. Yet the priest afterward returned to the line of duty.

Roncalli noted that in 1940 he had received a considerable sum of money for his personal use. Instead of investing it he gave it all away: "some to the poor, some for my own needs, and the needs of members of my family, and the rest, the main part, for the restoration of the Apostolic Delegation and some of my priests' rooms at the Holy Spirit"—the cathedral church. The residence of the Delegation was a gloomy house "with an unprepossessing entrance," as Austin Oakley remembered it. Under Luigi's artistic skill it was greatly improved and the hall became "a pillared atrium." The chapel also was enriched with Byzantine icons and decoration.

This transformation Roncalli intended as a gift to the Holy See and he was quite hurt when he was told to send in the bill. So when the refund came he decided to spend it on a gift for the new library being built for his beloved seminary in Bergamo. So he bought from an Armenian convent, with assistance from another Bergamasque, Monsignor Gustavo Testa, the Delegate in Cairo, and not to be confused with Giacomo Testa, a set of the 350 volumes of Migne's edition of the Greek and Latin Fathers. It was a typical as well as a generous gift.

As to the original sum, which could have been invested for the future, he wrote, during this retreat: "According to the world's judgment, which can penetrate even the sacred inner recesses of clerical life, and according to the criteria of human prudence, I have been a fool. In fact, now I am poor again. Blessed be the Lord. I think that, by his grace, I did the right thing. Again I trust in his generosity for the future. 'Give, and it shall be given unto you.' "

Earlier in 1940, before the invasion of Greece, Roncalli had been there twice. In January he visited Salonika and Alexandropolis, and during a tour of about three weeks in April and May he was in the islands of Naxos, Syra, and Rhodes. After the fall of Athens in 1941 the Greek population was in danger of starvation. Crops had not been sown and the Allies were maintaining a blockade against the German and Italian armies of occupation. When he was in Ankara Roncalli approached the German and Italian ambassadors to find out if their governments would cooperate if a way could be found to bring food to Greece. They assured him of their assistance and he set out in June on his mission of mercy, driving to Sofia by car.

There he met again King Boris and Queen Giovanna, and the Orthodox Metropolitan Stefan Gheorgiev. They offered all the help they could. On July 8 he flew to Athens. Here his earlier caution and friendliness stood him in good stead; in spite of being an Italian he was able to act. He at once set up a bureau co-ordinated with that in the Vatican for the exchange of information about prisoners, and began to dispense funds in collaboration with the mayor of Athens. He visited English and Greek prisoners of war in hospital, and also the Italian wounded. Among these he found a Bergamasque contingent and his own nephew, Assunta's son, who had been wounded on February 5. With Father Richard Liebl, the head of the Capuchins in Athens, he started a clinic at the Delegation. It was known as the Good Samaritan and continued in existence for four years after the war.

But Roncalli was anxious to do something more effective about the famine and managed to get in touch with Archbishop Damaskinos, head of the autocephalous Greek Orthodox Church, who was acting as Regent for the absent King, now with the Allies. Roncalli's intermediary and assistant was Monsignor Calavassy, Exarch of the Byzantine rite Catholics. In spite of his invidious position as head of the Uniates, Monsignor Calavassy had won the respect of the Greeks, and a decoration from George II, for his work among the refugees from Thrace. In his message to Archbishop Damaskinos, Roncalli asked him to designate the place of meeting, partly out of courtesy and partly to protect the Regent from possible charges of treason for dealing with an Italian.

The first formal meeting between the head of the Greek Church and nation, and the Pope's representative took place in the Paleophaleron Palace, in the apartment of Clement Maneas, president of the Greek chamber of commerce. The second meeting was held in the same palace but in the apartment of a friend and legal adviser of the Archbishop's. Damaskinos had already approached the German general who had agreed in principle to contact being made with the Allies about the blockade, but insisted that he must know who was going to be in touch with the enemy. The Archbishop told him he was going to work through a Christian Church which had once been in communion with the Orthodox. The German leaders understood that the Holy See was to be the intermediary, and accepted.

At the final meeting Damaskinos handed to Roncalli a

letter for the Pope, signed by the highest lay leaders in Greece. The Delegate offered to take a letter for the exiled Greek government in London; this letter contained the details of the appalling state of the Greek population as a result of the blockade. Roncalli's first meeting with the Archbishop had been on September 10, 1941. After the last, when the two principals parted with the kiss of peace, Roncalli flew to Rome and had an audience of the Pope on October 10. Pius XII was keeping up the tradition established by Benedict XV of doing his utmost to moderate the rigors of war and encourage moves toward peace, and the Holy See was able to contact London via Lisbon. The Greeks had capital reserves in Turkey, America, and Australia, and could pay for the necessary shiploads of grain; what was needed was safe-conduct through the blockade. The plan was put into action, the ships passed through, and the Greeks were saved from the worst effects of the famine. And at the end of the war, at the victory celebrations, the Catholic Exarch and Latin Archbishop stood with the Orthodox Church leaders.

This intervention was the most important service Roncalli succeeded in doing during the war but he was engaged on many lesser activities. For instance, he administered confirmation to Italian soldiers, relieving Greek Catholic bishops who would have been suspected of treason in undertaking religious duties with the enemy. On one occasion he visited the Italian 64th Infantry, stationed at Kalamata on the Greco-Albanian border. The troops, who were paraded to receive a bishop with the honors of a lieutenant general division commander, expected a grand arrival with an entourage. But Roncalli arrived in an inconspicuous black car and talked to them in a friendly and natural way, with no eloquence on military glory. He remembered his own service in the army! When it was time for him to go a soldier shyly advanced; he had been deputed to embrace the Archbishop "from all of us"—a typically Italian gesture which must have warmed his heart.

In 1942, at the end of October, he again had to make his retreat in his own house in Istanbul; for security reasons it was inadvisable to go to the Jesuit residence. He invited the

Testa

Archbishops of the Armenian and of the Byzantine rite Catholics, who each brought three priests. Melkites, Syrians, and Bulgarians were also invited. Father Folet, a French Jesuit, preached.

In his notes Roncalli accused himself of "the same old problem" of being too slow, of not getting so much done as he wanted to, although he admitted that possibly he now had more work than he could manage, especially in the delicate situation in which he was placed. There were so many people to offend if he acted hastily.

"My ministry in Greece is the one more beset with difficulties," he wrote. "For this reason I must love it more. Moreover in recent months it has given me the greatest consolation. When I am here, in Istanbul, I never wish to leave for that country which today has become 'a place of torments,' but once I get there I am like a fish in water."

During that year he had been in Greece twice already, from March 10 till 27, and then from May 30 till July 31, when he visited Kolokastron, Tripolis, Kalamata, Nauplia, and Argos. After this October retreat he went there again, from November 14 till December 21. The military situation prevented further visits. The Greeks, with Allied help, turned against the occupying armies. Monsignor Giacomo Testa, once Roncalli's secretary, who had spent two years in the Vatican Secretariat of State after his recall from Istanbul, was stationed in Athens, though Roncalli was still, as Delegate, officially responsible. Testa was still in Athens when the British army was there in 1944–45; later he was to follow in Roncalli's footsteps as Delegate in Istanbul, always faithful to the methods he had learned from the man to whom he remained devoted. But he died before Pope John, in 1962.

In 1943 Mussolini's government collapsed and under new leadership Italy was accepted by the Allies as a co-belligerent. In their own country the Italian partisans took an active part in expelling the German army, not least Roncalli's fellow countrymen in Bergamo. But it was too late to improve Greek-Italian relations. Before the war in Greece a Catholic priest was usually referred to as *gallikos papas* (Frankish, or French father); but in 1945 an English Catholic army chaplain heard himself called *italikos papas* (Italian father). Mussolini's nationalism had transferred to his people all the generalized suspicion of the Franks which had existed in Greece since the Crusades.

In his retreat in October 1942 Roncalli reminded himself of the evils of nationalism. He thought Italian priests less corrupted by nationalism than others; an opinion which all might not share. But he warned himself to be watchful. "It is one thing to love Italy, as I most fervently do, and quite another to display this affection in public. The holy Church, which I represent, is the mother of nations, all nations. Everyone with whom I come into contact must admire in the Pope's representative that respect for the nationality of others, expressed with graciousness and mild judgments, which inspires universal trust." This was good training for the papacy.

"We are living through great events," he wrote, "and chaos lies ahead. This makes it all the more necessary to return to those principles which are the foundation of the Christian social order, and to judge what is happening today in the light of what the Gospel teaches us . . ." He felt that it was particularly the duty of a bishop to meditate on the events of the day in the light of the Gospel and of history, if he were to exercise his proper function among the faithful. It may sound simple, but it is not often carried out. It is a temptation for bishops, as for other rulers and administrators, to act according to political and ecclesiastical habit. Meditation on the Gospel and history in the Council produced a reorientation that surprised many of the bishops themselves. Roncalli ended this retreat, typically, by copying out the views of St. Isidore of Seville (d. A.D. 636) on the perfect bishop.

The capitulation of Italy came in September 1943. In the following year the Allies invaded German-occupied France and by August 1944 Paris was liberated. Armistice was made with Bulgaria and Rumania in September; in October the British army landed in Greece. Suddenly the tide had turned; Hitler was losing, the end of the war was in sight.

On December 6, 1944, a coded telegram from the Vatican arrived at the Delegation in Istanbul. The person who usually decoded the messages was not there, so Roncalli laboriously worked it out for himself. To his astonishment it was an official notification that he had been appointed Nuncio in Paris.

Nuncio to France! This was one of the highest posts for a Vatican diplomat and here was Roncalli, who had never been even an Internuncio, never been more than Delegate in countries which did not extend official diplomatic status to a papal representative, nations where Catholics were unimportant minorities, here was Roncalli, who was now sixty-three and had given up expecting further promotion, to be sent to France, "the eldest daughter of the Church." No wonder he was surprised, and unable to believe it fully until the confirmatory letter arrived on December 22, even though he had to make preparations to leave before that happened. The letter was signed by Giovanni Battista Montini, now Pope Paul VI, but then one of Pius XII's two *sostituti* (substitutes for the Secretary of State). After the death of Luigi Cardinal Maglione in August 1944 the Pope had not appointed another to the office, resuming the reins he had held so long before and keeping them till his death. The senior *sostituto* was Monsignor Domenico Tardini, who had long been one of Roncalli's superiors in the Secretariat of State.

It was Tardini whom Roncalli met when he arrived in Rome on December 28. He began, hesitantly, to thank him for the unexpected promotion—such a surprise to him. "It was a surprise to us too," said Tardini drily. The appointment had been the personal decision of Pius XII.

Since Angelo Roncalli eventually became Pope himself there has been a tendency to overlook the extraordinary nature of his assignment to France. It is taken for granted that it was merely modesty which made him express surprise; that he was really an obvious choice. Tardini's attitude should indicate otherwise.

What made Pius XII decide to send Angelo Roncalli to Paris in 1944? When the capital was liberated France was psychologically divided between those who had accepted the government set up by Marshal Pétain at Vichy and those who had fought by underground methods in the Resistance, in support of the Allies and the Free French under General de Gaulle. Since the fall of France in 1940 the representative of the Holy See had resided at Vichy. He was none other than Monsignor Valerio Valeri, Roncalli's old colleague who had so often "passed ahead" of him, moving steadily up the diplomatic scale, Nuncio to Rumania, Nuncio to France, while Roncalli for so many years had remained an obscure Delegate in the East. Now, however, Valeri's connection with Vichy made him *persona non grata* to de Gaulle, who asked that he should be recalled to Rome. But the Nuncio was by tradition the doyen of the diplomatic corps in Paris and as such would deliver their good wishes to the general, as head of the provisional government, on New Year's Day 1945. The next senior member of the corps was the Russian Ambassador, and General de Gaulle, a good Catholic, preferred to receive the message from a representative of the Holy See. There must be a replacement for Valeri at once.

The Pope had to find someone to throw into this awkward situation, someone who knew French well, who could be tactful and who had no connection with any authoritarian regime, for Pétain's paternalist discipline had been all too well received by some of the French higher clergy. In wartime Istanbul Roncalli had proved his ability to keep clear of embittered factions; in his youth he had had connections with Christian Democracy, now suddenly reviving in France as in Italy. Roncalli also had a negative qualification not so often mentioned: he was sixty-three and not at all well known. How easy, if anything went wrong, simply to retire him to some harmless post in the Curia! Cynics would say that Roncalli was expendable.

He had to go at once. On December 23, the day after the confirmatory letter arrived, the bishops of the various rites gave a farewell dinner for him, but he had to leave directly afterward to catch the train to Ankara. At the station members of the diplomatic corps came to see him off—as in Bulgaria he had arrived unheralded but left with public expressions of goodwill. He traveled overnight to Ankara, to find that M. Menemencogliu had just left, appointed Turkish Ambassador to—Paris!

Roncalli said his Christmas Masses in the French Embassy chapel and in St. Paul's Church. On December 27 he left in a plane put at his disposal by the French government and disembarked at Cairo. From Cairo he went, on December

28, via Bengasi, Cyrenaica, and Naples to Rome where, the next day, he had an audience with Pius XII. The next day he left the Rome-Ciampino airport at ten in the morning and arrived at two in the afternoon at Paris-Orly. Nobody had been able to come to meet him. He went straight to the Nunciature at 10 Avenue President Wilson and the same day he visited the Quai d'Orsay. On the last day of 1944 he met Emmanuel Cardinal Suhard and on the first day of 1945 he presented his credentials at the Elysée and, in the name of the diplomatic corps, offered good wishes to General de Gaulle as President of Free France.

Sofia, Istanbul, Greece, the east—suddenly it was all past, that long twenty years, and here he was in the middle of the troubles of northern Europe.

14   *First Steps in Liberated France*

"To feel myself seized without any warning like Habakkuk and suddenly transported from Istanbul to Paris seemed to me, too, to be almost an act of magic," Roncalli wrote to his friend Bernareggi, Bishop of Bergamo, on March 23, 1945. "It was the last thing I expected or wanted." And he added that his amazement had only been increased when he learned that it was the Pope himself who had chosen him. The suddenness of his translation is mentioned in several letters written at this time. He told Don Fortunato Benzoni, chaplain of the mission to the Italians in France and a Bergamasque, that he understood his feelings at having to leave Paris for Annecy, since he himself had suffered at having to leave Constantinople. But he quoted his own motto *Oboedientia et Pax* and observed that the great thing was to know how to give up one's own wishes and tastes to serve the will of God. When he had first heard of his appointment he had been quite overcome—"*rubuit vultus meus*" (my face was red). But he had left Turkey with great calm and confidence. "*Caro don Benzoni, corraggio.*"

To others he joked about it. "I flew here on the quiet, just like a little bird," he told one visitor, according to Louis Chaigne. To someone else he quoted: "*Ubi deficiunt equi trottant aselli*" ("When there are no horses the donkeys trot out"). He was aware of the importance of his new post and knew that his career so far had hardly marked him out for such prominence. On February 20 he told Giovanni Birolini, parish priest of Sotto il Monte, that when he met clergy and lay leaders in France memories of Radini-Tedeschi were revived and Bergamo was called "the most fervent diocese in Italy." When he had been to Notre Dame for the first of the Lenten sermons, the Jesuit preacher, Father Paul Panici, had addressed him by name and by his ecclesiastical titles in front of "that august assembly, full of men of the highest rank." "*Oh! povero me!*" ("Poor me!") he exclaimed to Don Birolini. "I thought of La Colombéra and Sotto il Monte." He ended this letter by offering help for any urgent necessity in the parish "notwithstanding the fact that at Paris my means will be much diminished from what they could be, and sometimes have been, in Istanbul."

This mixture of genuine surprise at his appointment, suppressed regret for Istanbul, with its pastoral work and network of friendships, determination to accept the Pope's choice as the will of God and his half-humorous, half-fascinated awareness that he, Angelo Roncalli of Sotto il Monte, was now moving among the great ones of the earth, is a revelation of the nature of the man, naïve and yet shrewd, directly involved and yet inwardly detached. This detachment was something he had to fight for all his life; in a brief retreat during Holy Week 1945 at the famous Abbey of Solesmes he began his notes: "The events of my life during the last three months are a constant source of amazement and confusion to me. I have had to renew very frequently my resolution not to preoccupy myself with my future or to try to obtain anything for myself!" It was strange that just when he had thought the battle won, and was resigned to spend the rest of his life in obscurity, he should have been put in a position where detachment would be particularly hard of attainment. For the

Pope's Nuncio in France was almost inevitably involved in politics, civil and ecclesiastical. From the start Roncalli was determined to keep clear of any kind of intrigue, to be friendly to everyone, to suppress his own opinions as far as possible, to observe all but to refrain from interference.

At the beginning of 1945 the war was still in progress. Indeed, General Karl von Rundstedt's offensive in the Ardennes in December 1944 proved a setback to the Allies even though it was not possible at that point to do more than delay the final victory. Although Italy was no longer a belligerent with Germany, the French did not forget the way Mussolini had taken advantage of the collapse in 1940. On March 18, 1945, Roncalli wrote an interesting letter to Monsignor Francesco Borgongini Duca, the first Nuncio to the Italian government after the Lateran Pacts of 1929. He apologized because his passage through Rome had been too rapid to admit of a visit, and wrote at length, joking that Monsignor Gustavo Testa, their mutual friend, "will begin to say I am always preaching and don't correct myself." People in France were saying to him: "Poor Italy! Poor Italy!" All the nations, France included, seemed at present "poor" but Roncalli felt that this poverty was the beginning of a resurrection in which the servants of the Holy See were particularly called to collaborate. The end of the war would mean the beginning of the reconstruction of Europe.

Roncalli added that he was rereading the *Mémoires* of Domenico Cardinal Ferrata, Leo XIII's Nuncio to Paris from 1891 to 1896, and finding that the book took on a new dimension when read on the spot. His choice of Ferrata is significant of his own preference for the policy of collaboration with the Republic, rather than the intransigent attitude which had by no means died with *Action Française* and had even enjoyed a kind of resuscitation under Marshal Pétain. The marshal's government had given state grants to Catholic schools, a concession that was to be strongly contested in the postwar years. The hierarchy had for the most part supported Pétain, though that did not of itself make them collaborators with the Nazis. But this was the accusation made by the victorious Resistance, politically left in sympathy.

Many Catholics had shared the vicissitudes and triumph

of the Resistance and of the Free French, and at the liberation a new party was formed, the *Mouvement Republicain
Populaire* (MRP), which represented a resurgence of the
Catholic left similar to that which was forming in Italy under
Alcide de Gasperi, and was shortly to appear in Germany
under Konrad Adenauer. Half a century after Leo XIII's policy
of *ralliement* had failed, Catholics in France suddenly did
rally to the Republic. Many of the leaders, including Georges
Bidault, the new foreign minister, had started their political
career in the *Sillon* movement, under the leadership of Marc
Sangnier. The old man was still alive; when he died in 1950
Roncalli wrote to his widow a tribute to his memory and all
he had tried to do for Christian Democracy.

Roncalli had no difficulty in sympathizing with the Catholics of the left, but when considerable pressure was put on
to force the resignation of no less than thirty bishops on the
charge of collaboration, he thought the demand unjustifiable.
He did not protest; he merely asked to be shown the evidence
against the bishops. On examining the dossier he mildly observed: "But these are only newspaper cuttings." By courteous
delaying tactics he managed to prolong the affair till feelings
had died down. In the end, instead of thirty bishops, only
three were forced to resign. "I got the nought knocked off,"
said Roncalli, with sly modesty.

One of the suspected was no less than Cardinal Suhard,
Archbishop of Paris, who had taken up his office in 1940 at
the very time of the debacle. When Paris was liberated General de Gaulle attended a Te Deum in Notre Dame, but
Suhard was not allowed in his own cathedral; he was ordered
to remain in his residence. The new Nuncio succeeded in
getting the Cardinal Archbishop extricated from the proscrip-
tion, but only at the cost of his auxiliary, Monsignor Beaussart. To ease the blow for Beaussart and to show his own
confidence in him, Roncalli asked him to be his confessor.

Some of the bishops had spoken out against the Nazi domination, in particular Jules Saliège, Archbishop of Toulouse.
During the occupation Saliège, although paralyzed, had himself carried into his cathedral in order to protest against the
application of the Nazi racialist policy in France. The new
French government let it be known to the Nuncio that they

would appreciate recognition for Saliège from the Holy See. The intermediary was Giuseppe Saragat, the new Italian Ambassador in Paris, a Social (not a Christian) Democrat. He has since become President of the Italian Republic. The Nuncio therefore strongly recommended Saliège for a Cardinalate. It was granted in the first consistory held by Pius XII on February 18, 1946. Incidentally the Pope was determined to internationalize the College of Cardinals. When he was congratulated on his courage in naming three from Germany he is said to have replied: "It is nothing to the courage I needed to create only four Italian Cardinals!"

Jacques Dumaine, appointed chief of protocol at the Quai d'Orsay in 1945, told this story in his journal, published in 1955, after his death and before Pope John's election. A man of the world, he liked the new Nuncio, but did not penetrate beneath the surface. Roncalli joked to him about the difficulties in the way of the three new French Cardinals: " 'Monsignor Saliège has been paralyzed for six years and can't utter a word, while Monsignor Petit de Julleville, Archbishop of Rouen, suffers from agoraphobia and must always have someone with him. Only Monsignor Roquer is active and able to speak, so things are not very promising, are they? Your Ministers tell me that a priest should be judged by his intelligence, his priestly virtues and his courage. I tell them that his physical presence is also important, even within the precincts of the Church—and especially at his consistory . . .' and so on with his amusing chatter," recorded Dumaine.

Nevertheless Roncalli had a genuine admiration for Saliège, to whom he himself brought the red biretta from Rome at the beginning of March 1946. As Pope, he once read out the words of Saliège on Christian unity, spoken in 1943: "Union will be achieved. It is the design of God. It is what all fervent Christians pray for. It will not happen tomorrow. But there is a general presentiment that Christian Unity will be achieved."

Of course Roncalli himself had shared these feelings ever since he had met Dom Lambert Beauduin in 1925. Almost the first thing he did in Paris was to attend the January Unity Octave at the church of St. Joseph des Carmes—the church of the *Institut Catholique* and of the *seminaire universitaire*.

Here he presided at pontifical vespers and gave his first public address in French.

"I am happy that the first words I speak before an altar in Paris should be the continuation of those I spoke for the last time in Constantinople (today Istanbul): an invitation to unity, desire for peace. Between these two luminous points which mark two worlds and two forms of civilization, Constantinople and Paris, rises a bright rainbow in which shine the last words of Jesus at the moment when he was leaving his friends and comforting them: *Ut unum sint* (that they may be one)."

The new Nuncio drew attention to Pius XII's encyclical *Orientalis Ecclesiae decus*, written in 1944 for the fifteenth centenary of the death of St. Cyril of Alexandria, which encouraged prayer for unity of the type then acceptable to Catholic authority, unity envisaged as a simple return to the existent Roman Church. It was not till he himself was Pope that Roncalli suggested that the Church itself must "return" —renew itself at the sources, so as to become so clearly the Father's house that all Christians would find their home in it. In 1945 he merely emphasized that unity could not be forced, but must be made in "liberty, love and trust" and in a spiritual obedience which brought peace. This reminded him of his episcopal motto, *Oboedientia et Pax*, and its originator, Cardinal Baronius, the Oratorian Father of Church history—not forgetting to work in a graceful reference to Père Louis Bouyer of the French Oratory, who had preached the sermon.

Bouyer, a convert from Protestantism, was a friend and admirer of Dom Lambert Beauduin and in his book on the founder of Chevetogne he tells how Beauduin called on the Nuncio, not sure what his reception would be, since Roncalli had graduated to a position of importance while Beauduin, who was only allowed to return to his community in 1951, was still not considered quite a safe person. But he had hardly opened the door when he heard the joyful welcome: "*Lamberto! Venga, venga!*" ("Come!") And he was enfolded in the well-known warm embrace.

In his short Holy Week retreat at Solesmes Abbey in 1945, when he had recorded his amazement at his translation, Roncalli continued: "Here I am now, transported from Istanbul to Paris, with the initial difficulties of introduction overcome, I hope successfully. Once again my motto *Oboedientia et Pax* has brought a blessing . . . The first cardinal virtue is prudence. This is what Popes, Bishops, Kings, and commanders have found difficult, and it is in this that they frequently fail. It is the characteristic quality of a diplomat, so I must cultivate it with particular care. Every evening I must examine myself strictly on this point. My ready tongue often betrays me into saying far too much. Beware, beware! Know how to preserve silence, how to speak with moderation, how to refrain from judging people and their attitudes except when this is an obligation imposed by Superiors, or for grave reasons. On every occasion say less rather than more and always be afraid of saying too much, remembering St. Isidore of Seville's praise of St. Fulgentius. And be particularly careful to preserve charity. This is my Rule."

It was a Rule he kept in a way all his own. No one could maintain that he managed to say less rather than more, but he certainly succeeded in preserving charity and moderation, perhaps just because of the genial flow of his conversation. If he made any gaffes he was able to cover them up and he often covered other people's gaffes in the same way. Though he did not exactly keep silence, he kept a certain reserve, not only on ecclesiastical and political affairs, but on his private thoughts and feelings. It is this that makes his time in France the most difficult period for a biographer. Great controversies were fought out in those years, while all that is available of Roncalli's own mind is contained in a few retreat notes and a great many occasional speeches which naturally steer clear of current problems. He talked happily to everyone—but gave little away.

It was this reserve, which went unrecognized in a talkative man, that made his radical pontificate such a surprise to people in France, who had put him down as a conservative. This is a well-known fact, attested by all French writers on Pope John. Reading his addresses it is easy to see why. He continued to express his religious feelings in the style of his youth and he liked to refer to the past history of the places, persons, or events he was commemorating. Yet French people who visited him in Venice were struck with his retrospective enthusiasm for pastoral initiative in France and how he spoke of it to his Venetian clergy.

Canon Berrar of St. Germain-des-Prés, who remarked on this in a letter to the author, also recalled a conversation on the way to Chartres, where there was to be a concelebration of Mass, when Roncalli defended private Masses and maintained that he had always derived spiritual comfort from the daily recitation of the last gospel (first chapter of St. John) at the end of Mass. On the other hand, in Venice he immediately took steps to involve the people more actively in the liturgy, according to the norms then acceptable and Monsignor Capovilla, his secretary in Venice as well as in the Vatican, says that he was always open to the idea of liturgical reform, especially of simplification. Probably the truth is that he was content with the forms he had known all his life, but pastoral considerations gradually convinced him of the necessity for reform in this, as in other fields. He was always more radical in action than in idea; he was a practical man and, in a good sense, an opportunist.

In June 1945 the Nuncio went to Lyons for the seventh centenary of the Council held there in the middle ages. The war in Europe was just ending; it was a moment full of hope. Pierre Cardinal Gerlier and fifteen Bishops were gathered in the basilica of St. John the Baptist and the Nuncio gave the address. It was a subject which interested him and, as he wrote to Don Fortunato Benzoni, the chaplain of the Italian mission at Annecy, he had been reading it up in Mansi's *Conciliorum amplissima collectio*. He noticed that in 1260 the Bishop of Valence ordered his priests and friars to teach the people the *Pater Noster* and *Credo*, "as it seems that in those days few knew them from memory." "*Caro don Fortunato,*" Roncalli continued, "we live in times and in circumstances where it seems even priests and friars, if they know how to say them, don't understand the *Pater Noster* and *Credo* and don't know the spirit of them. Let us remain faithful to these two résumés and symbols of the thought and life and apostolate of the Catholic Church." Benzoni was celebrating the silver jubilee of his ordination and his friend concluded: "And then let us go on, I in front and you behind, with the staff of old age, imminent for you, already begun for me, and with great faith in the Lord and in his blessed Mother and ours. I write to you on the night of the Sacred Heart . . ."

In his address in the cathedral Roncalli also linked the occasion to himself with a personal touch, recalling his two earlier visits to Lyons, first with Radini-Tedeschi in 1905, when they heard a Te Deum sung for St. Joan of Arc, just declared "Venerable"; and again in 1921 when he had come to the center where the Association for the Propagation of the Faith had been started. Indeed, the day before, he had visited the local headquarters once more. "*Et me voici revenu parmi vous,*" he said in the basilica, "*cette fois avec les marques du declin sur une tête qui blanchit, mais le coeur demeurant vif et jeune.*" ("Here I am among you again, this time with the signs of decay on my whitening head, but with a heart still lively and young.")

Then he meditated on what had happened at Lyons seven centuries ago, on the liberty of the Church and on Pius XI's last words to him in 1938. The old Pope had said that he was not afraid for the Church, because in all tribulations there was Christ's promise that he would sustain it, but that he was afraid for the nations, powerful and menacing as they then were, because there was no promise to them; states would only survive to the extent that their governments reflected the ideals of the Gospel. This was a favorite theme with Roncalli; it had occupied him in Istanbul at the beginning of the war.

The Nuncio recalled Matthew Paris's description of the end of the Council of Lyons, when Pope Innocent IV declared the Emperor Frederick deposed and threw down on the paving the taper he held, smoking, in his hand, symbolically quenching its light. We have been through days of wrath, said Roncalli, but now we must pick up the blessed candles which the hurricane has put out. "Let us light a new flame." And because it was the church and the feast dedicated to St. John the Baptist, he recalled the words of the hymn of Zacchary, praising God for deliverance from enemies and asking him to guide our feet into the way of peace.

Perhaps this occasion may stand for the many he attended

eight years in France!

during his eight years in France. It would be tedious to rehearse them all. The addresses were always adapted to the occasion, with a historical basis, a personal reminiscence and a cogent reference to the Gospel. The style does not translate well into English. Oratory in English tends to sound pompous, where in Italian or French it is the exercise of an art and has a musical propriety of its own. Roncalli's addresses are not sentimental or inflated, indeed they are simple and straightforward, but they are best read in the language in which he wrote them.

The Mayor of Lyons in 1945 was Edouard Herriot, a politician in the old anticlerical tradition. Roncalli met him first in his capacity as Mayor on June 25; in Paris later they became increasingly friendly, to most people's surprise. There is a letter of November 9, 1948 from the Nuncio to Herriot when he was President of the Chamber of Deputies, thanking him for the gift of the first volume of his reminiscences, *Jadis*, which he had sent with "such simple and touching" expression of friendship. "I thank you with all my heart," wrote Roncalli warmly. He told Herriot he was following him with lively interest, often with a smile and often edified (he gave references for the occasions of edification); "and so I have accompanied you as far as the great door of the *mairie* at Lyons." He was sure that when he got to the end he would be waiting eagerly for the second volume.

Roncalli became even more friendly with Vincent Auriol, who was made President of France in January 1947 and so remained for the rest of the Nuncio's stay. Auriol was professedly a nonbeliever. Reading through the messages which it was the Nuncio's duty to address to the President every new year in the name of the diplomatic corps, one senses the growing friendship between them. Auriol was to present the red biretta to Roncalli before he left France, and to be much moved by the occasion. When he afterward visited him in Venice, bystanders were surprised at the warmth of the embrace with which the Patriarch greeted this distinguished unbeliever. Roncalli's ability to make friends with men who repudiated Christianity is one of the characteristics that most clearly demonstrates the depth and quality of his personal faith.

Best known of these unexpected friendships was that with M. Bogomoloff, the Russian Ambassador. As the Nuncio was doyen of the diplomatic corps and the Russian Ambassador next in seniority, they were often placed side by side on public occasions and were seen in animated conversation. Once, attending a review at the Arc de Triomphe, it began to rain heavily. Roncalli had no umbrella, but he was soon seen sheltering thankfully under the large umbrella wielded by M. Bogomoloff. This was at the period when relations between the Soviet government and the Vatican were at their worst. The Nuncio invited the Russian Ambassador to lunch and the invitation was accepted, but at the last moment a polite excuse was made and he did not come. But their personal relations continued friendly.

Back in Paris in the summer of 1945, with the war just over, Roncalli wrote on July 9 to a colleague, Monsignor Cesare Orsenigo, Nuncio in Germany, whom he had just discovered, contrary to rumor, to be alive. "We live in times when the devil takes all sorts of shapes," he said, "but he's always the devil: *princeps huius mundi* (prince of this world), who has just had five years of triumph." It is an interesting letter, full of contrasts. Of his new position he wrote that he had been a bit stunned at first, but that at present he felt only the pricks of straws in his nest, not of thorns. He told of a predecessor as Nuncio, Monsignor Antonio Garibaldi (1797–1853) who had died in Paris; the Austrian Ambassador had said in his memoirs that he was such an amiable character he had only inconvenienced his friends once—at his funeral. "In fact, he was very fat, and when they arrived at Notre Dame it was only after much time and labor that his coffin was extracted from the hearse . . . As you see," Roncalli added gaily, "I am looking back to find my models."

Immediately afterward in the same letter he noted the contrast between an official dinner for thirty given in his honor at the Quai d'Orsay and the scene a little earlier when he had assisted at an open-air Mass for prisoners returning from Germany and their relatives; many women in mourning and holy communion distributed by a hundred priests still in prisoners' uniforms. "So we live among tragic visions of grief and death and the contrast of life reborn." He ended by hoping he would meet Monsignor Orsenigo soon "by the friendly banks of the Adda." He too had not been home for nearly five years.

Some six months later, January 15, 1946, he was writing to Monsignor Giuseppe Descuffi, Archbishop of Smyrna, whom he had consecrated in 1938, and he said: "If I can judge by the affection shown me by these French people, Bishops, priests, and laymen, and also by the good terms I am on with state authority, I have reason to take courage. Here, consolations are not missing, but the road is difficult and every step has to be watched. It is necessary to be ready for anything."

Shortly after this, on February 4, 1946, Jacques Dumaine, the head of protocol at the Quai d'Orsay, visited the Nuncio and recorded in his journal: "Monsignor Roncalli took off his skull cap and purred: 'My role in France is that of St. Joseph, because I discreetly watch over and protect the interests of our Lord. I show myself as rarely as possible to your government, only meeting them when they ask to see me; but M. Bidault has reproached me for making myself so scarce, so now we have agreed to meet every fortnight. When Cardinal Ferrata was Nuncio at the beginning of the century' [actually, at the end of the last] 'he used to meet the Quai d'Orsay every week.' Monsignor Roncalli murmured on, 'But in those days your ministers were usually anticlerical and the Nuncio had to remind them of his existence. I am more fortunate because I find myself among friends whom I have no desire to embarrass.'" He then joked about the new cardinals, as referred to above.

On November 20, 1946, Dumaine recorded: "I paid a call on the Nuncio, who always amuses me. Although Monsignor Roncalli is more artful than subtle, he has had much experience and radiates a lively bonhomie. He is at great pains not to become involved in internal politics nor to exceed his functions as diplomatic representative of the Sovereign Pontiff. Indeed, he is well aware of the reproach habitually cast at the Nuncio in France, which is that of interfering with the domestic affairs of the French clergy and of meddling with the bishops' prerogatives. I am not convinced that his apparent discretion really succeeds in ensuring his detachment, because one of our worst faults is that of inveigling foreigners to take part in our domestic problems. Our Communists do not realize how traditional their behavior can be."

At the end of that year Dumaine was extremely amused because the Nuncio, having lost his voice with laryngitis, mimed his speech to M. Léon Blum, the then President, while the words were read by a member of his staff. In a different context, it was Dumaine who recorded, May 18, 1949, a story now famous: "A sly remark of the Nuncio's: 'In the course of the official dinners I attend, I have often observed that when a lady appears wearing a daringly low-cut dress, people are more apt to look at the Nuncio than to gaze admiringly at the lady.'"

Superficial though these comments may be, they indicate something of Angelo Roncalli's diplomatic style; an extremely personal style, yet quite as shrewd as it was light in touch. He had a double problem: relations with the French government and with the French hierarchy. Both relationships had a troubled past, though the violent storms of the decade before the First World War had subsided into occasional outbursts on the schools question. But religion could still complicate and embitter the political situation. In March 1947 there was a public outcry over an alleged clerical conspiracy to hide wartime collaborators in religious houses. The police published their investigations, religious bodies defended the right of asylum and Père Riquet pointed out that members of the Resistance had also found shelter in churches and monasteries. Roncalli took care to keep out of this dispute, but the excitement engendered showed that tensions still existed between the Church and the Republic, and within the Church itself.

Dumaine, as a trained diplomat, knew the delicacy of the Nuncio's position in France when he speculated on whether he would succeed in maintaining the detachment he professed. Some of his duties inevitably entailed involvement in ecclesiastical affairs. For instance, he had to advise the Pope on the nominations of new Bishops and discover if the government had any objections to candidates. During his first three years in France he was instrumental in the appointment of twenty-seven Bishops and of Cardinal Suhard's successor as Archbishop of Paris, Monsignor Maurice Feltin. In view

his tact

of the important role played by the French hierarchy in the Council, it is interesting that Roncalli had a hand in their selection. Of course, as Pope, he made further appointments himself.

His attitude is expressed in his retreat notes of December 1947. He wrote in his spiritual journal: "The longer I stay in France the more I admire this great country and the more sincerely fond I grow of 'this most noble Gallic people.' I am, however, aware of a contrast, which sometimes gives me a twinge of conscience. I am delighted to praise these dear brave Catholics of France, but I feel it is my duty, one inherent in my mission, not to conceal through a desire to be complimentary and not to give displeasure, a certain amount of disquiet concerning the real state of this 'elder daughter of the Church' and certain obvious failings of hers. I am concerned about the practice of religion, the unsolved question of the schools, the insufficient numbers of the clergy and the spread of secularism and Communism. My plain duty in this matter may be reduced to a question of form and measure. But the Nuncio is unworthy to be considered the ear and eye of Holy Church if he simply praises and extols all he sees, including even what is painful and wrong. This means a continual watch over what I say. A gentle silence, without severity, kind words full of mercy and forbearance, will do more than statements, even if made in confidence and for a good purpose. For the rest, 'there is one who discerns and judges.' "

Something over four years later, in April 1952, he wrote on the same subject when in retreat at Montmartre during Holy Week. "I must have a great understanding and respect for the French people. My prolonged stay with them enables me to appreciate the very noble spiritual qualities of this people and the fervor of Catholics of every school of thought. At the same time however it has enabled me to see their failings and excesses also. This means I have to be very careful in what I say. I am free to form my own judgment, but I must beware of any criticism, however slight and friendly, that might wound their susceptibilities. Oh, this never doing or saying to others what we would not wish to have done or said to us! We are all rather remiss about this. Great care then to avoid the slightest expression that might lessen the effectiveness or dignity of our conduct. I say this for myself, but I must be a guide and example of those around me, my colleagues. In every case, a caress is always better than a scratch."

The bonhomie that amused Dumaine and made Roncalli so popular in Parisian society was not as simple as it looked. Much care, restraint, delicacy of feeling, sensitivity to atmosphere, went into it, even though he certainly did enjoy the company of other people. As to the problems of the day, he watched, he went everywhere, but he bent as much energy to the task of nonintervention as some of his predecessors had given to intrigue, political and ecclesiastical. Undoubtedly it was his ability to get on with all sorts of people which made him increasingly popular in France. His calendar of engagements became more and more crowded as the years went on; it is amazing that a man of his age could stand the pace, but he thrived on it. Of the eighty-seven dioceses of France he visited all but two; to some he went several times. Towns large or small, shrines, monasteries, convents, schools, seminaries—there he was, smiling and talking to everyone from Bishops to children, eager to see everything there was to be seen. In 1950 he even made a tour in Algeria, then a scene of war and dissension. Again he kept clear of politics, but he did not travel with his eyes shut.

It is from his engagements that something of Roncalli's activities and interests can be gained; they were by no means narrowly ecclesiastical. He was at the reopening of the Louvre in July 1945; at the Institut Catholique on November 17 the same year for the centenary commemoration of Cardinal Newman's reception into the Catholic Church; in March 1947 he was at the première of *Monsieur Vincent,* the film on St. Vincent de Paul, the seventeenth century founder of the Sisters of Charity; at the Academie Française on March 3, 1947 for the reception of the poet and playwright Paul Claudel and again on May 29 for that of the Catholic philosopher Etienne Gilson; in August that year he went to the Scouts' Jamboree; in March 1948 he attended the gala of Paul Claudel's play *L'Annonce fait à Marie;* at Notre Dame in October he was present at a performance of Berlioz's *L'Enfance du Christ;* on February 24, 1949, he was at the Sorbonne for the solemn UN proclamation of the Rights of Man; at the end of March 1949 he went up the Eiffel Tower; in May he attended a recital of poetry at Latin America House; he went to public lectures, for instance one on Gandhi on January 13, 1950; to military reviews; in August 1950 he found time for the exhibition of treasures from Italian Libraries; in October he went to hear Verdi's Requiem in the Champs Elysées Theatre. He met Winston Churchill (May 11, 1947); Pandit Nehru (January 19, 1951); Alcide de Gasperi (July 25, 1952) and other famous statesmen. In June 1951 he went to the Music Festival and to the Goya exhibition; in 1952 he was appointed permanent observer for the Holy See at UNESCO, whose sessions he had already attended.

This is a mere selection of his ordinary engagements; religious occasions far outnumber them. Running like a thread through them all was his attendance every March at the dinner given for old men by the Little Sisters of the Poor. This was his way of celebrating St. Joseph's Day, the anniversary of his episcopal consecration. Another permanent engagement was the annual *Semaine Sociale*, the summer school of Catholic Social Action; he never failed to be there. Again, he was always present at the opening of the academic year at the Institut Catholique in Paris. He went regularly to the charity sale held by Catholic authors. He always attended the course of Lenten sermons at Notre Dame, usually given by Père Riquet S.J.   *Read these*

There is a mass of other engagements, far too many to list here. Some show only his readiness to oblige, others reflect his personal interests. He was always saying Masses for cultural or academic groups on special occasions. Any event connected with Catholic social movements, including women's organizations, could claim his presence. Eastern rite Catholics in Paris soon discovered his interest in them; Armenians, Ruthenians, Rumanians, and other groups invited him ever more frequently as time went on. The Italian colony, of course, claimed him often; he loved to be given the pastoral task of confirmation and of giving the children their first holy communion.

Unobtrusively Roncalli continued the "ant's work, bee's

Ange Joseph

work" he had done in Istanbul. In September 1945 he visited the German prisoners of war in France and assisted the Abbé Franz Stock to carry out a scheme whereby the seminarists among them could continue their studies for the priesthood behind barbed wire. Later, he was able to use his influence to get the Germans repatriated, for the French delayed for too long the release of their former enemies. Yet while he was in France he signed himself "Ange Joseph" instead of Angelo Giuseppe. And when, after Cardinal Suhard's death in 1949, he ordained forty-nine priests on June 29 in Notre Dame, during the vacancy of the see, he wore the late Cardinal Archbishop's stole. Such gestures may seem small, but they are significant of his deep consciousness of the implications of Christian brotherhood.

All through the summers he traveled about France, on visits and on pilgrimage; to Lourdes, of course, but also to lesser known centers, such as the mountainous La Louvesc, where a holy Jesuit missioner, St. John Francis Regis, lies buried, and where, in the nineteenth century, the Cenacle order of nuns was founded. Wherever he went Roncalli visited any historic buildings or ruins in the vicinity, and prayed at the tombs of the dead, whether saints of old or of men he had honored in his youth. On his way to Belgium and the Netherlands in 1950 he stopped to pray at the tomb of Monsignor Tiberghien, a friend of Bishop Radini-Tedeschi and a great man in the pre-1914 Catholic social movement. Perhaps this selection from a mass of factual detail may convey something of Roncalli's wide-ranging interests and his loving attention to individual persons and human occasions.

His colleagues remember some of the incidents of his travels with keen enjoyment. For instance, when he went to the Camargue for the gipsies' festival he was invited to a bull-fight and accepted because he did not want to offend his hosts. In the French bullfights the bull is not killed, but even so Roncalli found it hard to sit through. He took the side of the bull in every encounter and grumbled to himself all the time. "Poor beast! Look at those darts—no wonder he's angry! Poor creature!"

Another time, going to a fishermen's festival in La Vendée, the boot of the car was left open and the parcel containing the *cappa magna*, a cloak of watered silk with a long train, had fallen out. It was an expensive item, but when someone commented on the servant's carelessness, Roncalli said, "Be quiet! I've already 'made my detachment.'" However, as they passed the spot on the way home he said pensively, "But what could anyone who found it *do* with it?" "They could make curtains of it," suggested his secretary, "or a ball dress!" "Quiet, quiet!" said Roncalli hastily, between anguish and amusement.

This secretary accompanied him once to Venice in 1950. They stopped at a restaurant overlooking the sea on a terrace and Roncalli ordered a good meal, *antipasto*, pasta, with meat to follow. The driver, who was at the table, wondered why everyone was staring at them. A Capuchin Father, of the party, said, "It's Friday, and here are we priests all eating meat." Roncalli looked up. "Nonsense!" he said firmly. "It's obvious that we're traveling." (This excuses from the rule of abstinence.) He looked at his Swiss secretary who was wearing a clerical suit, not a cassock. "It's your suit they're staring at, of course!" And he set to, with a good appetite.

Incidentally, Roncalli once discussed his size with his secretary. "I'm too fat," he said, sighing. "Too much here, and here." He patted his stomach and cheek sadly. "What can I do?" Monsignor Bruno Heim began to explain about calories. "Why, in every cup of coffee you take six lumps of sugar," he said, "and each one represents a thousand calories." Roncalli looked worried. Then his face cleared. "I'll tell you what I'll do," he said. "I'll take only *five* lumps of sugar in my coffee!"

Pius XII came to disapprove of all this traveling, and in particular of the Nuncio's habit of walking informally about Paris, poking into bookstalls. Pius did not think this correct behavior for a papal representative. When he had been Nuncio in Berlin he had confined his outdoor exercise to riding on Saturdays. Pope Pius's intervention on this point reveals his personal style: he liked to keep his eye on everyone and his hand firmly on the wheel. He *ruled* the Church; there was no mistake about that. Some people liked it and some did not. *Oboedientia et Pax*, said Roncalli. But when he became Pope himself he walked, or drove, about Rome as much as he liked.

Roncalli still had his troubles with the Roman Curia. He

knew quite well that he was called, dismissively, *il buon Roncalli* (our good Roncalli) by those who thought him insufficiently versed in the ways of diplomacy. He called these men "the other school," indicating not merely disagreement but the fact that he thought of himself as representing a different tradition. He too acted on principle. *Veritatem facientes in caritate* (doing the Truth in charity) was a favorite text of his, expressing what seemed to him the only diplomacy worthy of the Gospel of Christ and suitable for a priest. He could be reserved, but not devious. There must be no ulterior motives behind his goodwill to all; it was worth nothing if it was not genuine. He knew that "the other school" believed in making use of the ways of the world, the usual channels, and criticized him for not being more secretive, for not being busy with plans, protests, meetings behind the scenes, diplomatic notes and so on. Yet an ecclesiastical diplomat of this kind would scarcely have lasted long in the explosive situation of postwar France. Roncalli lasted just because people liked and trusted him, even if perhaps some underestimated him. Nor was he intimidated, as some might have been, by the knowledge that influential men in the Roman Curia did not understand or appreciate what he was doing. It could hurt him, but did not alter his convictions. With the least possible fuss, he went his own way.

15 *Upheaval and Revival*

On the big questions of the day which concerned the Church in France, Roncalli's attitude was quite extraordinarily reticent. Indeed, his public silence on the dangers of Communism at the time of the Cold War, his refusal to comment on the much publicized experiment of the worker priests or on other burning issues is in itself evidence of an attitude different from what was expected of a representative of Pius XII. Because he talked much and was friendly to everybody, this reticence went unnoticed. It was not his habit to put forward views of his own; he knew how to let others talk and act, he knew how to wait and let time resolve tensions. Had he not become Pope and pursued a policy of "openings to the left" which many found surprisingly radical, what he said, or did not say, in France, would by now be forgotten. Yet in spite of his silences, it is plain that Roncalli did a lot of thinking in France in those eight years between the end of the war and the death of Stalin; it was there he met once more the problems of the modern world which had pressed on him as a young priest, so many years ago.

The worker priests were only one expression of a new wave of vitality in the French Church, but the movement serves to focus the confused situation of Catholics in France as they became aware of their changed relationship to the modern world. The crisis of the Modernist period, with its aftermath of the condemnation of *Action Française* in 1926, had never been properly resolved. Relations between Church and State had improved so much after the First World War that a great many Catholics seem to have settled into a position of non-established establishment, a self-contained religious world functioning alongside, rather than within, secular society. But within this body the two divergent attitudes noted by Blondel at the turn of the century continued to exist, one turning toward and one away from the modern situation, as it presented itself both in idea and action. It was during the thirties that a new generation grew up who were to influence the way things developed at the Second Vatican Council, taking up the problems of the Modernists with a greater understanding of history and society.

In estimating the growth of movements it has to be remembered that in any organized community, and especially in the Church, the leaders are usually old. In any period the men in authority are those who were trained from thirty to fifty years earlier. Between the two wars not only the French politicians but the French Cardinals, Bishops, rectors of seminaries, and eminent laymen were all trained before 1914 and most preserved the outlook of the nineteenth century. When Pius XI condemned *Action Française* in 1926, he threw French Catholics into confusion, because so many of them supported its right wing politics either actively or passively. The hierarchy conformed (though Ludovic Cardinal Billot had to resign his post in the Roman Curia) but many remained in sympathy with the "good Catholics" who lived without the sacraments rather than desert the standard of Maurras. There were scandals about the deathbeds of these disobedient but virtuous reactionaries. Italian clerics were surprised at the severity with which the condemnation was applied in France; in Italy verbal warfare was expected on political differences, but in practice an arrangement could always be made. When Eugenio Pacelli became Pope in 1939 the excommunications were withdrawn.

In spite of the action taken by Pius XI against the political right, the *intellectual* right continued to dominate the ecclesiastical scene, partly because the neo-scholastic revival had attracted genuine scholars and thinkers, so that there was a real opening up of the theology of St. Thomas and not simply the perpetuation of a system derived only remotely from his work. Nevertheless the dominance of Thomism still made it difficult for those who were trying to work in philosophical traditions which had developed since the break-up of medieval Europe. Outside the circle of genuine Thomist scholars there was also a tendency to accept not only the theological system but a whole view of the world, only superficially modernized, which had been conceived (even if by a genius) in the thirteenth century. Hence some of the strange attitudes to the theory of evolution expressed by Catholic authorities up to the middle of the twentieth century, sometimes almost schizophrenic in dissociating body and soul. Fear of Modernism encouraged this hiding behind the name of St. Thomas, and lurked in the disproportionate suspicion of Biblical studies and perhaps in the rebarbative official attitude to Christians of the Reformation traditions. If the outline of Catholicism were not kept hard and clear, would it not open the way to the horrors described by Pius X, the crumbling of the Church from within?

But the danger of trying to preserve intact the organization and theology of the medieval Church was that men were all the time becoming more and more different from the men of the middle ages. In France the violent split in the nation caused by the Revolution has never entirely healed, but for a long time the line between believers and non-believers was clear and there were parts of the country where people went on living in the religious pattern of their ancestors undisturbed by challenges which they did not really understand. It was only after the First World War that even in these areas things began to change, and only with the Second that Catholics became fully aware of the change. The realization was crystallized by the report of two young Abbés, Godin and Daniel, which was published in 1943 under the title: *France—pays de mission?* Cardinal Suhard read the book and it kept him awake all night. It was partly out of the shock of this report that the worker-priest movement sprang, but it was only one of many efforts on several fronts directed toward a renewal of Christian life which, pioneered between the wars, became active and publicized after the second.

The discovery of the "dechristianization" of France was made by means of an historical and sociological survey. The contact of the people with the Church in different areas was noted, there were statistics of priestly vocations which showed a constant decline in relation to the population, there were attempts to map the degrees of conformity with Catholic norms in morals and practice. The survey disclosed that in many regions, especially in the big towns (and Paris in particular) most of the working class had no religious affiliation whatever. Church attendance, such as it was, had become a bourgeois affair except in a few country places. In some cases the attitude to Christianity was hostile, in others indifferent. The Church had somehow become irrelevant to the life of the people.

Of course this situation is not confined to France. Indeed it happened sooner, or was noticed sooner, in England. Recently (1966) a French Catholic journalist reported to *Informations Catholiques* that dechristianization in France was nothing to what it was in England. It used to be common for Anglicans to compare their situation with that of the Catholics in France—both had a long tradition of establishment behind them, of patriotism, aristocratic patronage and national culture; in both countries the clergy had come to live lives somewhat remote from those of the working class. Sim-

ilarly both groups began to find their beliefs not only actively
questioned by the few but passively ignored by the many.
Population increased, effective and committed Christians de-
creased. Sacraments survived only as social occasions. Politics
aroused passion and interest but religion was a hobby or a
bore, snobbery or nonsense, according to taste. But in France
the Church attracted more political attention and overt hostility than the Church of England. The contrast also appears
in secular politics. A Communist party as large and efficient
as that in France has never shown any signs of coming into
existence in England. The conflict of left and right exists, but
muted; nor does Christian allegiance affect political affiliation. There are Anglican Bishops who support either party
and the number of Catholic candidates for each side in the
last election was equal.

The priest-worker movement in France reveals to the English all the differences, religious and political, between their
situation and that across the Channel. The British working
classes may have become indifferent to religion but they have
never taken up the ideology of Communism, which was the
creed, fanatically held, of thousands of French workers at
the end of the war. The class war was a reality to them and
the Church appeared to be on the side of the bosses. Social
alienation coincided with religious alienation. The expression
monde ouvrière (workers' world) so often used reveals the
extent to which this class had become divided from the rest
of the French nation. Yet for all the internationalism of the
Communist creed the workers remained very French, as
Jacques Dumaine noticed. Now, with the progress of the common market and the increased prosperity of France much of
the old Communist solidarity has broken down. But in those
postwar years the workers did indeed inhabit a world of their
own, feared by the other classes and by the rulers, whose eyes
were fixed on the Stalinist imperialism of Russia and on the
satellite countries of eastern Europe.

It was this world the priest workers entered, to bring Christ
to men who knew almost nothing of him. Many found this
vocation when, like Henri Perrin, they volunteered to go as
workers with the young men conscripted for German factories,
because priests were not allowed to go with them as chaplains.

The working priests found out two things: what factory life was really like and that most of their comrades had no interest in Christianity. Demobilized and repatriated, they could not forget their new insights, and they found in Cardinal Suhard a leader ready to authorize an experiment to recover, or to discover, the masses. Some worked in groups, especially the Jesuits and Dominicans, others as single secular priests. Although they were scattered over France it was the *Mission de Paris* which attracted most attention.

They led hard lives. It was difficult to fit the reading of the long Latin office into the working day; Mass had to be said in the evening, in their lodgings, though this was a moving experience for the participants. But it was more difficult to manage the difference of social background. A workman's life was totally unknown to most of these idealistic young priests, who usually came from bourgeois homes. At that time workers in Paris were very badly housed and there was little social security. The contrast with English Catholics is evident here. Many workers in the northern industrial towns are Catholics, who vote Labour and till recently have accepted their religious parish life quite naturally; priests, coming from the same background, have fitted in well—often better than the Anglican clergy, for instance. Problems exist, but they are different. But in Paris the priest workers had to overcome the double barrier of class and faith. That they did so is a tribute to their dedication and persistence, but to achieve identification with the workers' life in that time and place meant a virtual identification with Communist politics, and this led to trouble.

Appalled by local conditions the priests became involved in strikes, in anti-American demonstrations and political meetings. Because the Communist-controlled CGT was the largest and most effective union they joined it, to the chagrin of laymen who belonged to the Catholic unions. This division of unions along religious lines, inconceivable in England, was dictated by the militant anti-Christianity of Socialism and Communism on the continent—itself in reaction to the old alliance of "Throne and Altar." In this way worker priests became isolated from lay workers of the Catholic Action movements, though in some cases there was more communication than in others.

Even more complete was their isolation from the existing parishes, with their pious associations of elderly people and children, the scales of fees for funerals (recently abolished) and Sunday attendance at incomprehensible Masses in Latin. If the worker could be interested in Christ, it was virtually impossible to make him see the relevance of parish life. Yet Christianity is essentially social and must be lived in community. The renewal of parish life, of social and liturgical participation, had already begun then, but it was still a matter of a church here and there, run by a few avant-garde priests or religious. Later it became less difficult to integrate parish and community life, but in the 1940s the gap was in most places unbridgeable.

The idea of priests working in factories and living in slums appealed to journalists and an ever increasing stream of reports, articles, and even novels appeared in print. As usual, the celibacy or otherwise of the priests distracted attention from the aims of their mission. Conservatives accused the priests of betraying the faith: instead of converting the workers to Christ they themselves were being converted to Marx. Yet Cardinal Suhard and other Bishops continued to sanction the mission, trying to ease the difficulties and to pacify the suspicion aroused in Rome.

It was certainly part of the Nuncio's task to keep Rome informed on this experiment; it is equally certain that Monsignor Roncalli's reports are not yet available for study. However, it seems clear that so far as he was in a position to advise, Roncalli advised delay. Wait and see, give them time: this seems to have been his own attitude. At the same time he appears to have been doubtful of the ultimate value of this type of approach. He knew the very different Italian industrial situation, where there was not such a gap between priest and worker and much had been achieved with industrial chaplaincies and well-organized Catholic unions and Catholic Action groups. Though the Italian Communist party was (and still is) vast in numbers, many of its members were less committed to its atheist ideology than was the case in France. Roncalli was working class himself, and proud of it, but he had grown up in a tradition where priesthood was regarded as a full-time working profession with its own regulations. His was not the temperament to rebel against the current priestly discipline. But in spite of his doubts as to the effective worth of this new apostolate, he was not the man to advise suppression, especially when the mission had the backing of the French hierarchy.

It has been several times pointed out by experts that the condemnation from Rome came only after Monsignor Roncalli had been translated to Venice and some have even suggested that he was promoted to make way for the introduction of sterner measures. At any rate the first task of the new Nuncio, Monsignor Paolo Marella (now a Cardinal) was to prepare the way for a Roman intervention which more or less forced the French hierarchy to suspend the experiment by imposing conditions impossible of fulfillment, such as that no priest should do more than three hours manual work a day. The first moves were in the summer of 1953 and the religious orders had withdrawn their priests from the mission before the end of that year; the final blow came at the beginning of 1954.

The majority of worker priests submitted to the Bishops, but a large minority did not. The French hierarchy prolonged the time for submission and did their utmost to ease the way back for those who later changed their minds. Of those who did not obey, many got married and left the factories. The marriages were noticed more than the abandonment of the workbench. In spite of all the public outcry the French Bishops continued to believe in the necessity for a special mission to the workers and when Roncalli became Pope the question was reopened. It is said that Pius XII had a great respect for Cardinal Suhard, who had been at the Gregorian university with him; Suhard insisted on seeing the Pope himself and so, until his death in 1949, the curial opposition was kept in check. But after Pius' serious illness in 1954 the curial congregations became more powerful. When Cardinal Feltin arrived at the Vatican in June 1959, he found the question already settled, in the negative. John XXIII had not been able to manage the Curia for him, as Pius had managed it for Suhard. Now, at the end of the Council (1965) the French

Bishops hold authority from Xst
not the Pope
216   POPE JOHN

Bishops have announced the resumption of the mission in a modified form. It took a Council to break the power of the Curia.

For one of the most important aspects of the whole affair is the relationship between local hierarchy, Papacy and Curia. It was clear in 1953 that of their own accord the French Bishops would not have stopped the experiment. They were forced to do so and the orders came through the papal Nuncio. The sequence of events right up to the decision of 1959 illustrates the dominance of the Roman Curia and confirms the suspicion that the Nuncio was often the instrument through which Pope and Curia ruled the Bishops. The decrees of the Council have recalled the Church to a more serious contemplation of the rights of Bishops who hold their authority direct from Christ and not through the Pope, although he is the center of communion and the chief shepherd of the flock on earth. This reaffirmation is now being used to reorganize the structure of government in the Church. It remains to be seen how successful the reform will be; it needs to be co-ordinated with reform of the priest-bishop and laity-clergy relationships. But the Roman intervention in France of 1953–54 could not have taken the same form ten years later.

There are other aspects of the "dechristianization" of Europe besides that of an alienated urban proletariat. The necessity for a new intellectual approach to the doctrine and application of Christianity in the modern world became more urgent in the changed world situation after the war. Encouraged by Pius XII's encyclical *Divine Afflante Spiritu* (1943) Catholic scholars and exegetes plunged boldly into the newest currents of the Biblical movement. At the same time theologians were making new historical and philosophical approaches to dogmatics, while moralists and educationalists made extensive use of psychological and sociological techniques. These movements still encountered a stiff opposition, even within the Jesuit and Dominican orders, which were the most directly concerned. Again we must remember that the men in positions of authority had been trained during the anti-Modernist reaction.

In the Holy Year of 1950, when Rome was once more surging with pilgrims, Pius XII issued the encyclical *Humani*

Generis, which was intended to put a brake on these new developments. Pius was seventy-four in 1950, but extremely active, physically and mentally. In some ways it was his year of triumph, crowned on the first of November (All Saints) by the proclamation of the doctrine that the Blessed Virgin Mary is body and soul with her divine Son in heaven. The dogma of the Assumption finds its true place in relation to the community history of the Church and the ultimate destiny of human persons, but to those not familiar with Catholic theology it often appears as an incongruous pagan myth and explanations are listened to with suspicion, especially by those familiar with superstitious aberrations of Marian devotion. Pius XII's interest in Mariology, his turn toward theological conservatism in *Humani Generis* and his extreme commitment against atheistic Communism all militated against those who were attempting a new approach to modern problems. At that time the Church in eastern European countries under Russian domination was suffering extreme persecutions: Cardinals were tried, priests and editors imprisoned, professors arrested, convents, monasteries, seminaries closed, orders disbanded. Faced with this external pressure the Pope evidently feared that too much latitude within the Church might produce a dangerous disunity.

The tone of *Humani Generis* was nothing like that of Pius X some thirty years earlier, but the encyclical was used by conservatives to discipline progressives. The Holy Office intervened frequently. In France men as famous as Yves Congar O.P. and Henri de Lubac S.J. were removed to the provinces and forbidden to publish. There and in other countries men lived under suspicion who, scarcely a decade later, were to become *periti* at the Council and exercise a considerable influence on the shape and content of the decrees. The man ultimately responsible for this unexpected development was Angelo Roncalli, since the creation of the Secretariat for Christian Unity was entirely his own idea, and it was largely through this extra-curial organization that he brought the progressive theologians of many countries into the Council preparations.

Yet, in France as Nuncio, Roncalli was put down as conservative, even as anti-intellectual. It is true that he was not

Italy is Peter, France is Paul

himself a theologian, but the appearance of conservatism was
more likely due to his caution, as representative of Pius XII,
not to interfere, unless he was ordered to do so, with French
affairs. Canon Berrar recalls this diplomatic reticence when
he visited the Nuncio in connection with the *Semaines des
Intellectuals catholiques*, held annually from 1946 onward.
Yet even in the difficult atmosphere engendered by *Humani
Generis* he never discouraged the meetings of those who were
considered avant-garde. He only insisted that they should keep
the authorities in Rome informed of the intellectual controversies in France and he gave his personal assistance to
their efforts in this direction. He showed his usual common
sense here, for the chief trial of French progressives was to
be denounced behind their backs by conservative fellow countrymen in Rome. It was the old Modernist-integrist situation, played out with less ferocity, if with equal duplicity.

As a footnote to his recollection of Roncalli's attitude
Canon Berrar told of the visit of Romano Guardini, the German priest writer who, in his generation was most sensitive to
the ordinary man's difficulties of faith in the modern era. He
called on the Nuncio in 1950 and stayed talking nearly three
hours. He came away deeply impressed and told Canon Berrar that he had found a man who, under a show of bonhomie,
hid a mind cultured to the point of scholarship, but above
all, a person of exceptional goodness. "And," added Guardini,
"a goodness and human warmth of such a quality are rare
enough in our world."

"Italy is St. Peter, France is St. Paul." Roncalli liked to
quote this aphorism of Louis Cardinal Pie, a French ultramontane at the First Vatican Council. He thought France's
mission in the Church akin to that of the most intellectual
of the Apostles. He used to say: "In France ideas are born
with wings"—a perceptive comment. But he could not resist
making mild jokes about the French passion to get into
print. Here, he said, no priest is happy till he has got the
presses groaning to bring forth a book, whereas in Italy
priests tend to shun the publicity of print.

There was a great deal of talk in Paris about the Jesuit
Pierre Teilhard de Chardin, who was forbidden to publish his
works. Private copies were in circulation among his friends.

Roncalli, who could make little of these ideas, nevertheless got one of his juniors to find out about them. The fact that Cardinal Saliège gave support to Teilhard was enough for Roncalli. It is true that it was during his pontificate that the Holy Office issued a Monitum on the subject of Teilhard's books, which were published after his death, from 1955 onward and aroused some remarkably fierce controversy. But the Monitum of 1960, which was not signed by Pope John, was couched in mild and general terms. Although he himself was content with a comparatively old-fashioned theology, Roncalli's historical sense made him always aware that there must be development of doctrine and that it could not take place without controversy. "Without a touch of holy madness the Church cannot grow," he used to say. He knew that the mind of the Church was bigger than his own; and this is remarkable enough in a high prelate.

It seems certain that Roncalli did a good deal of thinking in France, even though he did not express his thoughts. But he was the Pope's Nuncio; he had to carry out the policy of Pius, even though it was transposed into the key of Roncalli. Meanwhile he watched and listened; he read a great deal and he went on with his own labor of love, the edition of the *Atti* of St. Charles Borromeo's visitation of Bergamo in 1575, when he began to put into effect the decrees of the epoch-making Council of Trent. "I work at it in the hours of night," he wrote on July 5, 1951, to Père Baudouin de Gaiffier of the famous Société des Bollandistes in Brussels. He was modestly pleased at the interest shown by these scholars in his work, while still insisting he was really no scholar himself.

The retreat notes of this period, though not very detailed, yet give some indication of his thoughts and feelings. By now his first preoccupation was preparation for death. He revised his will. For spiritual reading he was content with the Missal, Breviary, *The Imitation of Christ* and Bossuet's Meditations on the Gospel. "So I am simplifying everything more and more," he wrote in the Jesuits' house at Clamart between December 8 to 13, 1947, "and find it is better so."

There is an interesting paragraph in which he wondered if his general reading was not taking up too much of his time. "What is the use of all this anxiety to read and to know, if it is detrimental to my immediate responsibilities as Apostolic Nuncio?" Yet it is a sign of his immense vitality that he was still, at sixty-six, eager to learn. Undoubtedly this continued expansion of the mind was to assist him in his pontificate.

Evidently Roncalli had some difficulties during his first years in France with the members of his household. He again quoted to himself St. Isidore's praise of St. Fulgentius as the perfect Bishop, never alienating his subordinates but never allowing unsuitable behavior. Roncalli wrote: "I must keep a careful watch on conversation, which must be free from all rash judgments, and show no disrespect to anyone's episcopal dignity, or to our ecclesiastical superiors, of high or low degree, on whom the Nunciature depends. Even if this costs me inner mortification and personal humiliation I am determined to succeed in this. My colleagues will understand and this will be a source of satisfaction."

However, this situation was not so easily settled. The next year, in retreat at the Benedictine monastery of En Calcat (where Dom Lambert Beauduin was exiled) in the days of November when his birthday fell, Roncalli wrote in his *Journal*: "My own temperament inclines me towards compliance and a readiness to appreciate the good side of people and things, rather than to criticize and pronounce harsh judgments. This and the considerable difference in age, mine being more full of experience and profound understanding of the human heart, often makes me feel painfully out of sympathy with my entourage. Any kind of distrust or discourtesy shown to anyone, especially to the humble, poor or socially inferior, every destructive and thoughtless criticism, makes me writhe with pain. I say nothing, but my heart bleeds. These colleagues of mine are good ecclesiastics: I appreciate their excellent qualities, I am very fond of them and they deserve all my affection. And yet they cause me a lot of suffering. On certain days and in certain circumstances I am tempted to react violently. But I prefer to keep silence, trusting that this will be a more eloquent and effective lesson. Could this be weakness on my part? I must, I will continue to bear this light cross serenely, together with the mortifying sense of my own worthlessness, and I will leave everything else to God, who sees into all hearts and shows them the refinements of love."

Renewing his intention to keep a watch on the conversation, he broke out with retrospective admiration for Radini-Tedeschi's household, forty years before. "Never was there a single reference to a Vatican official, from the Holy Father downward, that was lacking in reverence, affection or respect. As for women, and everything to do with them, never a word, never; it was as if there were no women in the world. This absolute silence, even between close friends, about everything to do with women was one of the most profound and lasting lessons of my early years in the priesthood; and I am most grateful to the kind and illustrious man who taught me this discipline."

In this context he referred to women in their sexual role and his tone is that of someone brought up at the end of the nineteenth century. It is possible that he misjudged younger generations, accustomed to more frankness of speech on the subject, though it is unfortunately true that what starts as honesty may end as license. But in his boyhood at the seminary he had learned to equate the sexual instinct with "evil impulses." In Turkey in 1940, entering his sixtieth year, he had written in his *Journal* of "the internal impulses of carnal desire, the result of our 'natural infirmity,' of the tainted blood which mankind has inherited from its first source in fallen Eve. Advancing years, when one is in the sixties like me, wither the evil impulses to some extent, and it is a real pleasure to observe the silence and tranquillity of the flesh, which has now become old and irresponsive to the temptations which disturbed it in the years of my youth and vigorous maturity." Chastity was not the hardest of virtues to Roncalli; at eighty he could write of sins against chastity: "nothing serious, *ever*." But it is clear from his own notes that he had his difficulties in this connection, as every human being must.

It is doubtful whether Radini-Tedeschi's Victorian silence would be possible or effective in the changed world of today; in this respect Roncalli belonged to a pre-Freudian era. As far as his colleagues were concerned, the problem of free speech about sex was probably less pressing than free criticism of superiors. Roncalli had been trained to regard such criti-

to be simple with prudence

cism as shocking, even sinful. It is interesting to have from one of his junior colleagues an example of what happened when the criticism was directed against himself. One day he was late for lunch and his subordinates were criticizing him for his mildness. "He is too good—he can't say no—sometimes it's weakness." Suddenly the Nuncio came in and the conversation stopped dead. "How silent you are! I suppose you were criticizing me," he remarked shrewdly. Seeing he had guessed right he went on: "Well, priests have to give up so much—marriage, family, theatres—so many pleasures forbidden. They must be allowed the greatest clerical sport—criticism of superiors!"

Yet he did allow himself one form of criticism—of bringing into the Church the ways and wisdom of the world. In this 1948 retreat at En Calcat he wrote of the simplicity of the Gospel and commented: "All the wiseacres of this world, and all the cunning minds, including those in Vatican diplomacy, cut such a poor figure in the light of the simplicity and grace shed by this great and fundamental doctrine of Jesus and his saints! This is the surest wisdom, that confounds the learning of this world and, with true courtesy and true nobility, is consistent, equally well or even better, with the loftiest achievements in the sphere of science, even of secular and social science, in accordance with the requirements of time, place and circumstance. 'This is the height of philosophy, to be simple with prudence,' as was said by St. John Chrysostom, my great patron saint of the East."

In applying this to himself he had written in the preceding paragraph: "The more mature I grow in years and experience, the more I recognize that the surest way to make myself holy and to succeed in the service of the Holy See lies in the constant effort to reduce everything, principles, aims, position, business, to the utmost simplicity and tranquillity; I must always take care to strip my vines of all useless foliage and spreading tendrils, and concentrate on what is truth, justice and charity, above all charity. Any other way of behaving is nothing but affectation and self-assertion; it soon shows itself in its true colors and becomes a hindrance and a mockery." The image of pruning the vines is apt; he knew what he was talking about.

This year, 1948, marks the point in his journal where the question of his colleagues, senior and junior, pressed most strongly. Whether or not it did in the next year, there are no notes to show; by 1950 his tone on the subject was not only resigned but cheerful. In 1950 he was in Algeria and made a brief retreat in Holy Week at Oran. He recorded: "Some people feel admiration and affection for my humble person; but thanks be to God I still blush for myself, my insufficiencies and my unworthiness in this important position where the Holy Father has placed me, and still keeps me, out of the kindness of his heart. For some time past I have cultivated simplicity, which comes very easily to me, cheerfully defying all those clever people who, looking for the qualities required in a diplomat of the Holy See, prefer the outer covering to the sound ripe fruit beneath. And I keep true to my principle which seems to me to have a place of honor in the Sermon on the Mount: blessed are the poor, the meek, the peacemakers, the merciful, those who hunger and thirst for righteousness, the pure in heart, the suffering and persecuted."

"I end these notes," he wrote, "to the sound of the Easter bells ringing from the cathedral of the Sacred Heart nearby, and I remember with joy my last Easter homily in Istanbul, when I preached on the words of St. Gregory Nazianzen, 'the will of God is our peace.'"

Although he was happy in France, Roncalli was aware that he was still something of an anomaly in the Vatican diplomatic service. He used to say to his secretary: "I am the oldest Nuncio who has ever been in France. At my age they have usually been Cardinals or dead and buried." Then he would add cheerfully: "Well, nowadays we 'arrive' later, but we live longer!"

Roncalli's last retreat in France was made at Montmartre, with the Carmelite nuns, on the sacred three days of Holy Week, April 1952. It was rather an active retreat, for on Holy Thursday the nuns of the Nunciature came to the Mass and in the afternoon the Nuncio went on foot to four churches: Saint-Pierre, Saint-Jean, Notre Dame de Clignancourt, and the Martyrium. On Good Friday afternoon he went to preside at the liturgy in the Byzantine rite at Saint-Julien-le-Pauvre. On Easter Eve he took part in the restored Vigil.

These notes simply recapitulate all his recurrent themes: simplicity, charity to all, greater concentration on essentials. And he set down the hope to "gather speed as I near the end."

But the end was not yet. Monsignor Carlo Agostini, Patriarch of Venice, was seriously ill. On November 10, 1952, Pope Pius XII asked Roncalli to accept that see when it fell vacant. On November 29 it was announced that his name was among those of the new Cardinals. On December 29, Monsignor Agostini died and on January 15, 1953, the day Angelo Roncalli received the red biretta from Vincent Auriol, President of the French Republic, the Pope announced his appointment to the Patriarchate of Venice.

These events followed very quickly one after the other. Monsignor Valerio Valeri, Roncalli's predecessor in Paris, was made a Cardinal at the same consistory. On December 22, 1952, Roncalli wrote to Valeri, assuring him that his elevation was as much appreciated in France as his own. On Sunday, December 7, the head of the government himself, M. Pinay, came alone and on foot to the Nunciature to congratulate Roncalli, who told him what Georges Bidault had said in 1945, that the French government had nothing against Valeri personally, and Pinay agreed. Then Roncalli described to Valeri how he sat next to Monsignor Feltin, also to be made a Cardinal, in Notre Dame: *"ambiente assiderata: ma folla immensa"* ("atmosphere glacial: but the crowd immense"). The preacher made a poetic tribute to "the four Cardinals of France" and at the name of Valeri, said his kind successor, there was a *frisson*, felt rather than seen, of affection and universal rejoicing.

Whatever the French people felt about Valeri, they were certainly delighted to honor Roncalli. Auriol recorded later what a moving experience he found it to place the red biretta on the new Cardinal's head, for Roncalli knelt humbly before him on the carpet, accepting the non-Catholic head of the Republic as the representative of the Pope. His simplicity and the friendship between them made this curious ceremony, a relic of the bygone age when the monarch of France was called "the Most Christian King," the sign of a new relationship between sacred and secular.

There were many farewells to make, many letters to write.

But all the time, as Roncalli put it in letters to personal friends, there was a thorn in his heart. Almost at the very time he had heard of his promotion he also heard from Sotto il Monte that his sister Ancilla was gravely ill and expected to die. In fact she lived another year, dying on November 11, 1953. But her brother knew her illness was incurable: it was cancer. Ancilla was perhaps the closest to him of his sisters, who lived in his house at Camaitino.

So, after eight years in France, Roncalli at last returned to Italy. He was seventy-one when he became Cardinal and Patriarch of Venice.

16 Venetian Patriarch

On the Cardinalate Roncalli wrote: "It is neither a sacrament nor a sacramental, and yet it is a kind of sign that providence has responsibilities in store for me which will require me to give a serious account of myself." The Patriarchate was a different question. He was old to undertake a pastoral office but he was still active and in good health. He had no desire at all to be a Cardinal in Curia, whereas he had always been happiest in a pastoral ministry. "I came in the end to the conclusion that it is also a grace for which I should bless the Lord and which will earn me some other grace." Typically, he recalled another Bergamasque who had been made Patriarch of Venice just a hundred years before, in 1852: Aurelio Mutti di Borgo di Terzo. On April 10, 1958, he celebrated the centenary of the death of this predecessor, on the island of San Giorgio.

Roncalli left France on February 23, 1953, noting in his diary: "A separation stamped with sadness, but sweet in its union with God, in the serene consciousness of having made goodness loved. 6 o'clock: Holy Mass. 7:30 silent and moving farewell, some tears . . . I bless the Lord and thank him *pro universis beneficiis suis* (for all his kindness)."

He spent the first few days of March in Rome, then returned to Bergamo. From March 11–14 he was in retreat at Padua, and on March 15, after celebrating Mass at the altar of Blessed Gregory Barbarigo, his favorite local saint, he went on to make his official entry into Venice in the afternoon. The speech he made introducing himself has often been quoted. He wrote down the notes for it on three pieces of paper. It is characteristic; in it Roncalli speaks of himself almost as if he were another person. He headed his notes: *Ecce homo, ecce sacerdos, ecco pastor* (here is the man, the priest, the shepherd).

"I want to talk to you with the greatest frankness. You have waited for me impatiently. Things have been said and written about me that greatly exaggerate my merits. I humbly introduce myself.

"As does any other man on earth, I come from a family and from a particular place. I have been blessed with good physical health, with sufficient good sense to see into things quickly and clearly and with an inclination to love men, which keeps me faithful to the law of the Gospel and respectful of my own rights and those of others; it prevents me from doing evil to anybody; it encourages me to do good to all.

"I come from a modest family and was brought up in a happy and blessed poverty which has few demands, a poverty which fosters the truest and highest virtues and prepares one for the great adventure of life.

"Providence took me away from my native village and led me along the roads of the East and the West; it permitted me to approach people of different religions and ideologies, to observe grave and menacing social problems. Yet Providence allowed me to maintain a calm and balanced judgment. I have always been more concerned with what unites than with what separates and causes differences, keeping firm my belief in the principles of the Catholic Credo and of moral law.

"Here I am, at the end of much experience, turning again toward Venice, the land and the sea familiar to my ancestors for a good four centuries, and familiar to me through my studies and personal sympathies. I do not dare to apply to myself what Petrarch, another lover of Venice, used to say of himself; nor have I the tales to tell you that Marco Polo told returning among his own. But strong bonds tie me to Venice. I come from Bergamo, land of St. Mark, land where Bartolommeo Colleoni was born. Behind the hills of my youth lies Somasca and the cave of St. Jerome Emilian.

"You see what a simple man I am!

"No doubt the great position entrusted to me in Venice exceeds all my capacities. But above all I commend to your benevolence the man who wants simply to be your brother, amiable, approachable, and understanding. I have made a firm resolution to remain faithful to what has always been the source of my self respect. This characteristic was probably responsible for my appointment to Venice among people noble and generous of expression and especially sensitive to sincerity, to simple manners, words and deeds, to those qualities that mark a man of integrity . . .

"Such is the man, such is the new citizen whom Venice has been good enough to welcome today with such festive demonstrations."

As Patriarch of Venice Angelo Roncalli became Metropolitan of nine dioceses and on April 8, 1953, he held his first meeting with the bishops. In May he spent six days in retreat with them at Fietta, the villa of the Venetian seminary below the mountains. Here he wrote in his *Journal*: "In April last year I sought shelter under the roof of the Sacred Heart at Montmartre in Paris, and May this year finds me here at the foot of the Grappa, Cardinal, and Patriarch of Venice. What a transformation in all that surrounds me! I hardly know what to dwell on more: on how 'I rejoiced when they said unto me . . .' with all that follows, or on the sense of insufficiency which inspires feelings of humility and trust in the Lord. It is he who has really done all, and done it without my help, for I could never have imagined or desired such greatness."

This was Angelino of Sotto il Monte speaking, unable to believe he could really have become Cardinal Patriarch of Venice, at the top of the ecclesiastical tree in the province where he was born. It was indeed a surprising journey, with none of the steps chosen by himself, except the very first: to be a priest. As he wrote at the end of these notes: "The arc of my humble life, honored far beyond my deserts by the Holy See, rose in my native village and now curves over the

domes and pinnacles of St. Mark's." As to honors: sees are
honored (or not) by their holders, not *vice versa*. Roncalli
knew this well enough in the case of others; he lovingly celebrated his saintly predecessors, especially St. Laurence Justinian and St. Pius X.

"I am beginning my direct ministry at an age—seventy-two
years—when others end theirs," Roncalli wrote in his *Journal*.
"So, I find myself on the threshold of eternity. O Jesus, chief
Shepherd and Bishop of our souls, the mystery of my life and
death is in your hands, close to your heart . . . In the few
years I have still to live, *I want to be a holy pastor*." It was
he who underlined these words. He had fulfilled pastoral
duties before, especially in Istanbul; but in Venice this was
his whole work and he came into his own.

Venice seemed the ideal setting for Angelo Roncalli's last
years. That strange city, floating between water and sky, red
and golden in the flood of Adriatic light, with its green sea
roads opening away to the East, was the perfect place for this
wise, smiling old Patriarch, so ready to recall his farming
forebears and yet himself so inveterate a traveler. So many
ancient churches, so many relics reminded him of eastern
countries; even St. Mark's was built on the plan of the church
of the Holy Apostles in old Constantinople. For an Italian of
the north, a historian by predilection, a lover of the Orient,
what more suitable resting place could be found? And almost
as soon as he got to Venice Angelo Roncalli decided to be
buried there, under St. Mark's. He at once put in hand the
restoration of the crypt and the tombs of the Patriarchs, making sure that there would be a place for his own body when
the time came. But God willed otherwise.

No one could be more fascinated by the past than Roncalli,
but he lived in the present. His ancient diocese was beset with
modern problems. In 1915, when Cardinal La Fontaine became Patriarch, it contained under two hundred thousand
people. Forty years later the population had almost doubled.
Yet in Venice itself numbers were constantly declining, as
the younger generation went to the mainland in search of
jobs. Marghera and Mestre had become large industrial towns.
Venice, in spite of the naval arsenal, was almost too much of
a tourists' paradise, a lure for parasitic moneymakers.

he loved music and art & opened the way for priests to know them

Roncalli's immediate predecessor, Carlo Agostini, had been younger than himself, only sixty-five when he died after four years of intensive activity, initiating the building of many churches in the new mainland districts. It appears that he was brusque and hasty in manner and Roncalli was regarded as the complete contrast—never in a hurry and always in a good humor. When he said he wanted to be a brother to the Venetians, he meant it. He was approachable in his residence, next to St. Mark's, but he was not always in it. He walked about the city and hired motorboats without fuss. A journalist who called watched members of his entourage coming in and out freely, though they kissed his ring as they did so. But when the journalist was leaving and began to do the same, Roncalli would not let him, but rose and shook hands, seeing him to the door himself. A quarter of a century earlier journalists in Sofia had been impressed with just the same friendly courtesy and informality.

Roncalli started a special Mass for journalists, held annually in St. Mark's on January 29, Feast of St. Francis de Sales, patron of Catholic writers and long a favorite with him. He read several newspapers daily, a habit from his days as a diplomat. He was not uncritical, though his expression of opinion was mild. "You put a little too much salt in it," he told the editor of a Catholic weekly.

More unusual for a cleric in Italy was Roncalli's attitude to art. The famous Biennale, the exhibition of modern art held in Venice every two years, had been denounced as indecent by the ecclesiastical authorities ever since the days of Giuseppe Cardinal Sarto (St. Pius X), who had forbidden priests to visit it. Roncalli held a reception for the distinguished visitors in the hall of the Patriarchal palace and lifted the ban on the exhibition for his clergy. He had a genuine interest in painting and a wide knowledge of pictures—something that, owing to his habit of disclaiming expertise, was only known to personal friends. He enjoyed the musical festivals too. It was he who arranged for the first performance of Igor Stravinsky's oratorio: *Canticum Sacrum in honorem Sancti Marci Evangelistae*, to be held in St. Mark's itself and he was present for the occasion, in September 1956. Two years later Stravinsky came back to Venice to conduct his *Lamentationes*

Jeremiae Prophetae and Cardinal Roncalli was seen at a rehearsal, talking animatedly with the composer.

He had his own difficulties with artistic authorities, however, on the subject of the screen at St. Mark's, which interfered with communal participation in the liturgy. He wanted the panels removed so that the people could see the altar. The controversy outlasted his sojourn in Venice and it was only after he had left that the problem was solved by making the panels movable. Characteristically Roncalli would not exercise his authority to overrule the experts. "If I were told that to succeed I had only to kill a single ant, I would not kill it," he said.

Pastoral considerations alone could have moved him to alter anything in the historic building. Pastoral care again caused him to oppose the city authorities when it was suggested that the casino should be moved from the Lido to the center of Venice; in April 1957 it was proposed to move it to the Justinian palace. After Roncalli had gone the casino was brought into the town, but sited near the railway station. As Bishop of Venice Roncalli was also concerned with the habits of tourists who often treat Venice as if it were a holiday beach and walk about in unsuitable clothes, which they would not dream of wearing in Paris or London, New York or Berlin. Roncalli's rebukes were made in his own style. "We do not live in the tropics or in the arctic, so it is quite easy for women to decide what to wear." The visitor who is banned from St. Mark's merely for wearing a short-sleeved jumper and then has to queue in lavatories with men may sometimes wonder at the peculiarities of Italian modesty.

Davide Cugini records several recollections of Pope John in his Venetian days. A few days after his arrival he went to the Loggetta del Sansovino, to see the fifteen illustrated volumes on St. Mark's recently produced by the publishing firm of Ongania. He happened to meet there Giuseppe Cherubini, as well known for his long beard as for his pictures. Cherubini attempted to kiss the Cardinal's ring, but Roncalli shook him by the hand, saying, "We are two Patriarchs, you for your magnificent beard and I because I am so—*ad literam!*" (literally.) Signora Ongania was presented to the Cardinal, and a few days later, visiting the Patriarchal residence, she said,

"You may not remember me." To which the Patriarch replied gallantly: "*E come no!* (How could I not?) You were the first vision I saw on my visit to the Loggetta del Sansovino. Sit down here now in this armchair, and let's talk about ourselves." And he patted the cushions invitingly. No wonder the Signora remembered him as "*affabile, buono ed anche un po' lepido* (friendly and kind and just a bit facetious)."

Signor Cugini asked the Patriarch to sign some postcards for him; he looked at the addresses and then turned them over to examine the pictures. One, of a shapely lady, caused him to hesitate for a moment. "It's a work of art," murmured Cugini. "Oh, I can see it's the Santa Barbara of Palma il Vecchio," he replied serenely, signing it with added blessings.

Looking at the address on another card he remarked: "I don't know who this Signora Teresina Piccinini may be," and looked expectantly at Cugini, who replied that it was his wife. "*Ah! Allora, va benissimo!* (That's fine.)" And his blessings overflowed into the space reserved for the address.

Although he found time in Venice for friends, for painters, composers, and film-makers—he had a special Mass for the film-makers, reminding them of their responsibilities—Roncalli's principal work was to carry out ordinary episcopal duties. In February 1954 he picked up the pastoral visitation of the diocese where his predecessor had left it and completed it by December 1957. In that year, on November 24, he opened the thirty-first diocesan synod. Although the synod came near the end of his time in Venice his opening address on episcopal authority summarizes his aims and ideals, which he was to carry with him to the bishopric of Rome.

He began by saying that in the liturgy the bishop is called Father and Shepherd; he has to care for the spiritual welfare of his children and protect them from the dangers that might threaten their faith, and teach them how to play their part in a Christian society. This is in the traditional paternalist tone, but then he went on to say that the Bishop must avoid authoritarian arrogance and a patronizing manner. Authoritarian arrogance stifles truth and reduces everything to a desolate formalism dependent on external discipline. It curbs all wholesome initiative, makes one incapable of listening to anyone else, and confuses inward resolution with harshness, dignity with stubbornness. As for a patronizing manner, it is a caricature of true fatherliness. It often goes with an unjustifiable proprietary attitude to one's victim and a habit of intruding, together with a lack of proper respect for the rights of subordinates. It speaks with condescension and is an obstacle to any real cooperation. Here we have the considered conviction which underlay Roncalli's friendly manner, proof against even the highest human office and its inevitable protocol.

As Patriarch, Roncalli tried to fulfill his duties according to his own ideal. In spite of his years he was an active Bishop. In Lent 1955 a mission was held at which he himself spoke so often that his magnificent voice failed and he was left quite hoarse at the end of it. His list of engagements is full of visits to the new parishes among the workers on the mainland; his very first visit outside Venice was to the AGIP works. He went round the towns and villages of Venetia. He made a point of attending the Social Week at Trent, and the special occasions of the Catholic trades unions and Social Action. In his first year as Patriarch, August 1953, he went to pray at the tomb of Professor Toniolo, one of the original founders of the Christian Democratic movement in Italy.

Here we reach a complex problem: Roncalli's attitude in Italian politics. As Pope, he began an unprecedented "opening to the left," yet his public pronouncements in Venice followed the line of Pius XII, rigidly committed against both Communism and Socialism. This is the more puzzling when we read what he said soon after his arrival, visiting the Mayor and Council, many of whose members were Socialists or Communists. He stressed his good wishes to all.

"I find myself in the house that belongs to the population as a whole and I am glad to be here, for the place is in good order. I am happy to be among busy people, for only the man who works to good purpose is a true Christian. Indeed, the only way to be a Christian is by doing good. That is why I am happy to be in this house, even though there may be some here who do not call themselves Christians, but who can be acknowledged as such on account of their good deeds. To all I give my paternal blessing—to all without distinction."

This is unlike what he had to say in August 1956, when,

Alcide de Gasperi   great C D leader

like Montini at Milan and other members of the Italian hierarchy, he came out against any coalition between the Christian Democrats and the Socialists. The truth of the matter is
that it was Pius XII's directives that they were following. As
Pope, he had to maintain neutrality on political questions,
but he was also Primate of Italy, and when the Bishops came
away from their visits to the Vatican they had their instructions. Until the Second Vatican Council the Italian episcopate had never met as a whole, though there had been incomplete conferences; Roncalli attended one at the beginning
of 1955, held, improbable as it may seem, at Pompeii.

In the first years after the war the Christian Democrats
enjoyed an over-all majority, and in face of the enormous
Communist party it was natural that Catholics should give
them wholehearted support. But as time went on and the
first fervor of reconstruction faded, divisions appeared and in
order to retain power the Christian Democrats had to form
coalitions with other parties. The conservative wing became
stronger and favored combinations with the right. Professor
Gedda, the president of Catholic Action, who was much favored by Pius XII, was not only opposed to any cooperation
with the Socialists but in 1952 organized Catholic Action
committees in a powerful political campaign, known as Operation Sturzo, because Gedda tried to use the aged Don
Sturzo as a figurehead. At the last moment Don Sturzo realized what was happening, and withdrew his support.

The Christian Democrat leader, Alcide de Gasperi, was in
a difficult position. He did not enjoy papal favor to the same
degree as Gedda; for instance, Pius XII would not receive him
on the occasion of his wedding anniversary. (Roncalli sent
him a warm congratulatory letter.) De Gasperi, an Italian of
the Trentino who had gained his first political experience in
the Austrian Parliament, was fully aware of the dangers of
clerical intervention on behalf of his party. He disapproved
the use of Catholic Action as a political instrument, but did
not like to split the Catholic ranks by attacking Gedda. This
great and disinterested statesman, to whom Italy owes so
much, died in 1954. His monument, a fine modern relief
sculpture, is in the porch of the basilica of San Lorenzo.

De Gasperi died in 1954 and the same year Pius XII, who

was seventy-eight, was stricken with a severe illness. Against all expectation he recovered, but he was never the same man afterward. A bad illness at such an age cannot but have deleterious effects. These did not appear to the general public, but within the Vatican they were increasingly felt. Pius XII's authoritarian methods of government meant that as his powers began to fail and the single control weakened, the central curial group quietly built up their position. As far as Italian politics were concerned this curial party was even more to the right than the Pope, for whom, to the end, atheistic Communism was the enemy and Socialism merely its pawn. Although the world situation began to change after the death of Stalin, it must not be forgotten that the ruthless crushing of the Hungarian uprising by the Russians came in 1956. The Cold War atmosphere continued up to the time of Pope John's election and in Italy his attempt to allow elections to proceed without clerical direction aroused bitter indignation in conservative Catholic circles.

All this has to be borne in mind when considering Roncalli's public speeches in Venice, especially in 1956. In 1949, at the height of the Stalinist persecution of the Church in Eastern Europe, the Holy Office had issued an "Instruction" to the effect that joining the Communist party or voting for it automatically incurred excommunication. It was even reiterated in 1959, by the same authority, ultimately that of Alfredo Cardinal Ottaviani. It is interesting that now (1966) Cardinal Ottaviani has pronounced that only adoption of the specifically atheist Marxist ideology incurs excommunication; other forms of support are left vague. This change comes as a direct result of Pope John's personal policy, outlined in his two major encyclicals, *Mater et Magistra* (1961) and *Pacem in Terris* (1963) and his attitude to the Italian Socialist parties.

As Patriarch of Venice Roncalli's own views were indicated in February 1957, when a Socialist congress was to be held in Venice. The Patriarch had posters of welcome put up all over the city and went out of his way to be polite to the visitors. So marked was this attention that conservative Catholics were shocked. A Catholic editor, anxious to excuse his Bishop's lapse, put it down to a wish to win the socialists for

Christ. In the course of a statement he made to quiet the fuss Roncalli said: "Alongside purity of doctrine there open up fields for the exercise of charity . . . which begins with respect and courtesy." The newspaper controversy raised in Venice was nothing to the silent disapproval in the Vatican—silent as far as the public was concerned. Even as a Patriarch in his seventies Roncalli still had difficulties with "the other school." When he became Pope he was to authorize the use, in his encyclicals, of the word "socialization" in relation to the Church. He could not do so in Venice without disloyalty to Pius XII.

In view of his pontificate one of the most interesting ways in which he exercised charity toward those in disagreement with the Church was his continued effort in the cause of Christian unity, especially between Catholics and Orthodox. In January 1954, the first time he was in Venice for the octave of prayer for unity, he himself gave a series of lectures at San Basso, on the eastern Churches. "The road to unity between the different Christian creeds," he said then, "is love, so little practised on either side." He emphasized the need to study Christian doctrine together and spoke of how Joseph forgave the brothers who had ill-treated him, coming down from his throne to say: "I am Joseph, your brother." This Biblical story is a key image for the mind of Pope John. As Pope, he was to use it again, several times. Indeed, his whole papal apostolate consisted in coming down from the throne to say to everyone: "I am your brother."

In May 1956 Roncalli went back to Paris for the centenary of *L'Oeuvre de l'Orient* and in September 1957 he traveled to Palermo in Sicily to give the inaugural address at the seventh annual week of prayer and study run by the Association for the Christian East. On this occasion, speaking of the eastern schism, he pointedly asked, "Does the whole responsibility really lie with our separated brethren?" It was not mere warm feeling but a deep concern for the best way to approach Christians separated from each other for centuries which was the foundation for Roncalli's new ventures as Pope.

Although he was so busy in Venice and so happy there, Roncalli went abroad almost every year, often in answer to requests from the countries where he had been stationed, to

He goes to Fatima

speak on oriental or historical subjects. In June 1954 he conducted the pilgrimage of the three Venetian provinces to Lourdes and afterward made quite an extensive private tour in Spain. In October the same year he was sent as Papal Legate to the Lebanon for the closing ceremonies of a Marian congress. Pius XII had declared 1954 a Marian year, to honor the centenary of the dogmatic definition on the Immaculate Conception of the Blessed Virgin Mary. In 1958 he held another centenary year, in honor of her apparition at Lourdes. It was to be the year in which he died. In March 1958 Roncalli was chosen as the Pope's Legate to consecrate the great new underground basilica at Lourdes, dedicated to St. Pius X —canonized in Rome in 1954, at a ceremony at which his successor as Patriarch of Venice was of course present. In May 1956 Roncalli went on pilgrimage to Fatima in Portugal, where in 1917 three peasant children had visions of our Lady, who told them to pray and make sacrifices for peace. On one of these occasions the sun appeared to whirl round and fall from the sky; this curious phenomenon was well-attested, though a few who were present saw nothing. Pius XII is said to have seen a similar vision in the Vatican gardens; he was extremely interested in the Fatima apparitions, and intensely devoted to the Mother of the Lord.

Roncalli made many shorter journeys. He several times visited Assisi. On his way back from the episcopal conference at Pompeii he went to Montecassino, the great Benedictine monastery destroyed by Allied bombs in the war and entirely rebuilt after it with the assistance of pilgrims from all over the world. Then the Patriarch's visits to Rome were not all to see the Pope. In November 1957 he gave the introductory address at the first international conference of ecclesiastical archivists, a subject near to his heart since his student days.

There was time in Venice for Roncalli to pick up his historical studies. His one personal wish, to complete his edition of the *Atti*, the records of St. Charles Borromeo's visitation of Bergamo in 1575, was fulfilled: the fifth and last volume was in the press when he was elected Pope. He had to find the money himself, as he told Davide Cugini; he hoped to raise some in Bergamo "because I'm not a capitalist," he said. He called this lifelong work "a little sign of my affection for the land of Bergamo." His interest in his native city and province remained brisk; he liked to show visitors the shelves in his library loaded with Bergamasque books. He told Cugini he would like to leave them to the Vatican Library and exhort other Bishops to do the same. His face lit up as he said, "If they listen to me in Rome, the Holy See will have to build a new wing for the Library!"

There was a lively controversy in progress about the tomb of Colleoni in Bergamo; Cugini relates that the Patriarch would have liked to join in, but his other activities prevented him. "What a pity," he remarked, "perhaps I might have contributed . . . the tombstone."

Although Venice was a quiet city, without traffic, he moved his study to a position next to his bedroom, overlooking the courtyard. Here he could work undisturbed; sometimes when he woke in the night, he went there at two in the morning. He told Cugini he liked working at night, when there was no noise. As Pope he remarked, "I work in the night so as to be left in peace."

As a general rule, however, as he told Don Andrea Castelli of Bergamo in a letter of March 1957, he went to bed early, at ten, and rose at four. This gave him time to pray in peace and go to work with a quiet mind. "In my humble life I've never been a race horse," he said. "In these last years Providence has willed that I should be a modest pilot, encouraging and guiding younger men in the race: and that's enough for my littleness."

Younger men of all ages were much attracted to him. One with whom he began to correspond at this time was the priest writer and publisher, Don Giuseppe de Luca. Don Giuseppe met Roncalli when he went to lecture in Venice in 1955. By letter they discussed such subjects as the panels of the screen in St. Mark's, the Patriarch still quoting his favorite tag: *Gutta cavat lapidem* (the drop of water wears away the stone). Roncalli wanted an edition of St. Laurence Justinian's works published for the fifth centenary of his death.

Later, when Don Giuseppe was in difficulties with his publishing business, Pope John suggested that he bring out new editions of the early works of—Angelo Roncalli; they would have been forgotten, he observed, had he not been elected

Pope, but now they might save the fortunes of *Edizioni di Storia e Letteratura*. In his enthusiasm and admiration Don Giuseppe de Luca went too far for his modest patron. A long introduction to a new edition of the first volume of the *Atti* received a mild but firm criticism from Papa Roncalli. He did not think that anyone interested in the visitation of 1575 would want to be delayed by notes on the *curriculum vitae* of Angelo Roncalli, or by disquisitions on Federigo Cardinal Borromeo, Roberto Cardinal Bellarmine and "other vague digressions." With a kind wish that Don Giuseppe would understand the spirit of this criticism, the note was signed briefly: "Jo. XXIII." Don Giuseppe de Luca died in 1962. The correspondence was published by Monsignor Capovilla after the death of Pope John, but with his permission.

Roncalli wrote at length to Don Giuseppe about the centenary celebrations for St. Laurence Justinian. On Holy Innocents' day 1955 St. Mark's was full of wailing infants, when gifts were presented to the poor; in the afternoon there was a meeting of Sisters and at both Giacomo Cardinal Lercaro "who knows how to create at once an atmosphere of happiness" gave addresses. Then, round about Epiphany, they held a solemn Triduo at which all the Archbishops and Bishops of the three Venetian provinces were present in the sanctuary of St. Mark's though still, the Patriarch lamented, invisible to the people, because of the solidity of the screen . . . More was to come, in the way of lectures and functions. This letter was typewritten and so full that Roncalli had to finish it by hand on the back, with an apology for continuing "*All' antica*" (in the antique style).

The year after he came to Venice Angelo Roncalli kept a private anniversary, the fiftieth of his ordination, in August 1954. He spent it quietly at Sotto il Monte. "A wonderfully bright sky after beneficial night showers," he wrote in a private note. "The sound of the Angelus from S. Giovanni roused me at once with a '*Laus tibi Domini*' (Praise to thee, Lord). There followed an hour of prayer in the chapel, with the Breviary lessons about St. Laurence (the martyr deacon) in my hand, on my lips, in my heart: pages that are a poem. What is my poor life of fifty years of priesthood? A faint reflection of this poem: 'My merit, God's mercy.' "

His sister Ancilla had died in November 1953; Teresa, the married sister, in 1954, and Maria, who had kept his house at Camaitino with Ancilla, in 1955. In his retreat in May 1955 he wrote: "Losing them has been a great blow to me: it is my heart, not my reasoning mind that has grieved. Although I never cease praying for them, I love to think of them in heaven praying for me, even more delighted than of old to help and await me there. O Ancilla, O Maria, now reunited in the joyous radiance of eternity with the other two, Teresa and Enrica, so good and God-fearing all of you, I remember you always, I mourn for you and at the same time I bless you."

He felt that this separation would help him to devote himself all the more completely to the Venetians, and noted that it was better that he should live apart from his family "as an example to these good Venetian clergy who, for various reasons, some of them valid, have with them too many members of their families, who are a considerable encumbrance to their pastoral ministry in life, in death, and after death." Whether priests are married or unmarried, they still have families. Roncalli's wills, preoccupied with the determination that his family should not benefit from his ecclesiastical offices, while wishing to show his love and solicitude for them, witness to the difficulties of this situation in a traditionally Catholic country. It was a question of striking a balance between an inhuman isolation and an all too human involvement.

The two brothers nearest Angelo in age, Zaverio, who had married in 1907, and Alfredo, who had never married, survived him. Giovanni, ten years his junior, died in 1956. He liked his brothers to come up to Camaitino and sit and talk. He had never lost touch: he had even invited them to Paris and joked about acting as wife to them, tying their ties for them. In his letters there are many references to the younger generation, a nephew who became a priest, nieces who became nuns, the numerous children at La Colombéra.

The retreat in May 1955 was made in Padua, a special occasion when the preacher, the Jesuit Father Riccardo Lombardi, was appointed by the Pope. His campaign "For a Better World" was much favored by Pius XII. Roncalli had some reservations and was not quite at ease with Father Lombardi's aims and methods. Some of his notes on the subject are discreetly omitted from the *Journal*. He comforted himself with the knowledge that the Pope approved the movement. But he added: "Here also it is well to 'test everything: hold fast what is good.'"

"Of my pastoral life, my only life now, what can I say?" he wrote. "I am content, because it really gives me great joy. I do not need to use harsh methods to keep good order. Watchful kindness, patience and forbearance get one along much further and more quickly than severity and the rod. I have no illusions or doubts about this." Nevertheless he continued to be a little anxious lest he was too much inclined "to prefer a quiet life rather than making precarious moves" and perhaps "to fear that the reaction may cause an increase rather than a reform of the evils that are to be corrected." Yet he became more and more sure of his conclusion. "But the shepherd must above all be good, very good. On the other hand, though he does not, like the hireling, leave his flock to the wolf, he runs the risk of becoming useless and ineffective if he nods over his task. O Jesus, good shepherd, pour your own spirit into me, that these last years of my life may be a sacrifice and burnt offering for the souls of my beloved Venetians."

He recurred to the same problem the next year, June 1956. His words reveal a consciousness of the psychological difficulties of cultivating true simplicity—people are apt to equate simplicity with stupidity and ignorance, or at best, with a naïve bonhomie. But Roncalli was determined to pursue "the perfection of mildness, patience, and charity . . . and this at all costs, even at the risk of seeming to be, and being considered a person of little worth, with little to give." Even as Pope he was to feel, sometimes, this sense of being undervalued. In spite of the love he aroused in so many, there were some colleagues to whom he was always just *"il buon Roncalli."*

A small incident, related to the author by one who was present, illustrates his recurring trials with the top-ranking Vatican officials, even when he became a Cardinal. A predecessor in Venice had been extremely unpopular—even stoned on one occasion by his angry flock. When he died, Roncalli asked to celebrate his requiem. Usually the Cardinals were merely present at the requiem of a colleague, but Roncalli wanted to honor him just because he had been difficult. Roncalli's friends always said that the sure passport to favors from him, when he was Pope, was to have treated him badly in the past. At this requiem Roncalli forgot to change his silk skull-cap for a woollen one, which ecclesiastical etiquette demanded for the occasion. Afterward, in the Sacristy (a huge place full of people) a certain high curial prelate said loudly and publicly: "What sort of a Cardinal is this, who doesn't even know what he should wear for a requiem!" And this prelate often snubbed him on other occasions.

But he thought his sense of his own insufficiency a gift from the Lord. "It keeps me simple and saves me from making a fool of myself. I would not mind being thought a fool if this could help people to understand what I firmly believe and shall assert as long as I live, that the Gospel teaching is unalterable, and that in the Gospel Jesus teaches us to be *gentle and humble*: naturally this is not the same thing as being weak and easygoing. Everything that smacks of pretentiousness and self-assertion is only selfishness and comes to nought."

He scarcely felt this retreat in 1956 to be a real one, because he had to join his priests at the seminary at Santa Maria della Salute and of course all of them wanted to come and consult him. He had missed the Bishops' retreat, when he had been on pilgrimage to Fatima—the shrine of prayer for peace. But: "the memory of Fatima and of the joy I felt there makes me feel an even greater veneration for the Lord's command 'to preach the good news to the poor and to comfort the broken-hearted.'"

In 1957 he managed to retreat again with the Bishops, in June. He began by quoting the Nones hymn for the Sunday office: "'Give me more light as evening falls.' O Lord, we are now in the evening of our life . . . Three quarters of my contemporaries have passed over to the further shore. So I too must always be ready for the great moment." He thought of his beloved brother Giovanni, who had died recently. "Ah, what a good life and what a fine death!"

He thought again and always of the Lord, "to whom I am now turned as a child turns toward his father's open arms. My poor life, now such a long one, has unwound itself as easily as a ball of string, under the sign of simplicity and purity . . . The Lord caused me to be born of poor folk and he has seen to all my needs. As a young priest I was struck by the motto *Oboedientia et Pax* of Cesare Baronius, who used to say it as he bowed his head to kiss the foot of St. Peter's statue—and I have left everything to God and have allowed myself to be led in perfect obedience to the plans of Providence. Truly, 'the will of God is my peace.' And my hope is all in the mercy of God, who wanted me to be his priest and minister."

Curiously enough he added: "I think the Lord Jesus has in store for me before I die, for my complete mortification and purification and in order to admit me to his everlasting joy, some great suffering and affliction of body and spirit. Well, I accept everything and with all my heart, if it is for his glory and the good of my soul and for the souls of my dear spiritual children. I fear my weakness in bearing pain; I implore him to help me, for I have little faith in myself, but complete faith in the Lord Jesus."

At this time, of course, he thought this final suffering would come in Venice.

In September 1958 he again found his retreat beset with the human problems of his pastoral office; he had to give addresses to his priests. At the end of his brief notes he wrote: "My advanced age means that I must now be much more chary of accepting engagements to preach outside my own diocese. I have to write everything down first and this is a great effort, besides the humiliation of feeling my own insufficiency. May the Lord help and forgive me."

He was within two months of his seventy-seventh birthday. Before it arrived he had been elected Pope, the chief shepherd of the flock of Christ.

Eugenio Pacelli, Pope Pius XII, died on October 9, 1958, at the age of eighty-two. A few days later Angelo Roncalli, Cardinal Patriarch of Venice and only five years younger than the man he had served so long, set out for Rome, the funeral obsequies and the conclave. When he packed for the journey he left all his personal documents and even his Bible behind, expecting soon to return. But he took a last-minute look round St. Mark's. Off he went down the Grand Canal and there were crowds at the station to wave farewell. Inevitably people remembered how Giuseppe Sarto had taken a return ticket in 1903, but had stayed in Rome as Pope Pius X. When the same thing had happened to Roncalli, parallels were drawn—misleadingly, for they were only alike in their peasant origin and deep personal faith.

Roncalli was moved by the funeral of Pius XII, who for nearly nineteen years had guided the destinies of the Church on earth. To the rector of the Venetian seminary he wrote: "What impressed me most during my first days in Rome was the wax-like countenance of the Holy Father, laid out in state on his bier in St. Peter's, before the white silk veil hid it forever from the gaze of mortal men. What does life mean to a man to whom only the exterior has meaning? If then there is no consolation for our eyes, for our soul there is indeed consolation, gazing after that great and glowing spirit gone on into the land of eternal peace." He went on to say: "We must pray that his successor, whoever he may be, will not represent the end of the hierarchy but will progress in the spirit of the Church's eternal youth . . . The material world is indeed progressing, by dint of all those inventions and discoveries which make our lives so much more comfortable. But progress has no value in itself, it is but so much straw that a small spark can kindle and turn to useless ash."

From the Domus Mariae, where he was staying in Rome,

Roncalli also wrote to the Bishop of Bergamo—no longer Bernareggi, whose funeral he had attended in June 1953. "It matters little whether the new Pope be Bergamasque or not. Combined prayers should ensure that he be a wise and gentle man, and that he be a holy man and one who spreads holiness." After the event, those who thought this an excellent description of John XXIII, wondered whether he had expected his election. This seems unlikely, in view of his behavior during the conclave. He was an old man, not well-known in ruling circles; his name was not high on the list of *papabili* drawn up by the gambling Romans for the *Totopapa*.

Conclaves are supposed to be secret and measures taken by modern Popes have certainly made them more secret than they used to be, even in Rome, that city of inspired rumor. But in view of the extraordinary nature of John's pontificate it is necessary to appreciate the situation in which he was elected. It was the first conclave of the century when there were no external pressures of any kind. In 1903 the Austrian Emperor could still veto the choice of Mariano Cardinal Rampolla and the political situation in France was critical. In 1914 the First World War had just begun. In 1922 Italy was in the throes of a revolutionary crisis. In 1939 the Second World War was imminent. But in 1958 even the Cold War was not so intimidating as it had been, though the repercussions of the Soviet crushing of the Hungarian rising two years earlier had not died away in Europe. But as far as the world was concerned, the conclave was free.

Within the Church, however, the situation was not simple. There was a hidden groundswell of discontent of which the Cardinals from northern Europe were well aware. There was a complex of problems concerning the central administration. It was not just perennial irritation with curial bureaucracy. Pius XII, an efficient, methodical man with a long tenure of power in the Vatican even before his pontificate, tried to dispense with some of the human machinery of curial institutions. It was typical of him that when Maglione died he should have resumed control of the Secretariat of State himself, and told his two *sostituti* that he required executors, not collaborators. Under Pius XI he had increased the power of the Secretariat in relation to other departments, arranging the numerous concordats of that period. The heads of the curial congregations were accustomed to regular audiences with the Pope, but if Pius XII had nothing he himself wished to raise, he canceled their routine visits and referred queries to the Secretariat. In consequence it became difficult to approach the Pope through the usual channels and human nature being what it is, this opened the way to unofficial approaches through members of the Pope's private entourage. Meanwhile, since it was impossible for one man to control the whole administration, on matters in which the Pope had no direct interest the curial offices produced their answers in the time-honored way—which was increasingly out of touch with the realities of modern life.

After the Pope's severe illness in 1954 the situation worsened rapidly. During his last years Pius acted positively in the Church as a whole, easing the Eucharistic fast, introducing evening Masses and some reform in the liturgy, but he became isolated from the normal procedure of the Vatican. Toward the end it was said that no one could see him unless Sister Pasqualina, the nun in charge of his domestic arrangements, allowed it.

Pius XII held only two consistories for the creation of Cardinals; one in 1946 and the other in 1953. His laudable intention of making the Cardinalate more international meant that the Curia had a smaller proportion of members of the Sacred College than ever before. In October 1958 the College numbered only fifty-two, of which fifteen were Cardinals in Curia; only sixteen were Italian. It will be seen that in this conclave, even if the curial members acted as a body, they amounted to less than one third.

An additional complication was the fact that Giovanni Battista Montini, long regarded as the probable successor of Pius XII, was not a Cardinal. At the consistory of 1946 Pius had stated that he wished to make his two *sostituti* (Tardini and Montini) Cardinals, but that they had begged to remain working under him in the Secretariat of State. However, in 1953 Montini was suddenly sent to Milan as Archbishop; yet he was not made a Cardinal. Since Milan is a cardinalitial see and as Pius XII was said to be grooming Montini to succeed him, this was unusual. Some people said it was not unconnected with the unfortunate "Operation Sturzo." Montini has always defended the actions of Pius XII, but it is thought possible that he was not altogether at one with the Pontiff on this issue. In Milan he threw himself wholeheartedly into his work as Archbishop of Italy's most industrialized modern city and, like Roncalli in Venice, in public affairs he took his cue from Pius XII. As his rapid election in 1963 proved, the leaders of the Church considered Montini eminently qualified for the post of chief shepherd; but in 1958 he was not a member of the Sacred College. Technically speaking, any Catholic can be elected Pope but in practice he is generally a Cardinal. Efforts in past conclaves to break an impasse by importing some holy monk have hitherto been notable failures and in fact this expedient has not been adopted for centuries.

Montini, then, the obvious candidate, was not available in 1958. Someone was wanted who would restore the working machinery of the Vatican after the unhappy experiences of the last years of Pius XII, someone who would not be too managerial and would not, to put it bluntly, last too long and so queer the pitch for the probable succession of Montini. Hence the talk, when Roncalli was elected, of a caretaker Pope, a transitional Pope, a *papa di passaggio*. From Pope John's own words it is clear that he realized the reasons behind his election. He turned it into a joke and indeed it was to become more of a joke than his electors expected.

Of course Roncalli had positive virtues which explain why he and not some other old Cardinal was chosen to stop the gap. The French Cardinals are said to have supported him, knowing his gifts as a discreet and charming Nuncio. He was widely traveled, had long diplomatic experience. His goodness and kindness were apparent. But one cannot help feeling that few of the Cardinals can have realized just what they were doing. To the world at large Roncalli was virtually unknown and he always expressed himself in such traditional terms that nobody remembered much of what he had said. After all, everyone expects a bishop to talk about charity; what they do not expect is for him to practice it in a radical and realistic way.

The conclave was not concluded very quickly, but neither was it exceptionally long drawn out. In the very last notes

Pope John made in his *Journal*, just before the opening of the Council in 1962, he wrote: "Summary of great graces bestowed on a man who thinks poorly of himself." This was the first grace: "To have accepted with simplicity the honor and burden of the pontificate, with the joy of being able to say that I did nothing to obtain it, absolutely nothing; indeed I was most careful and conscientious to avoid anything that might direct attention to myself. As the voting in the Conclave wavered to and fro, I rejoiced when I saw the chances of my being elected diminishing and the likelihood of others, in my opinion truly most worthy and venerable persons, being chosen."

From this it is clear that the decision was not a simple one. After every voting session the Cardinals came out of the Sistine Chapel and Roncalli always stopped to chat and laugh with the group of secretaries and other officials, until the evening of October 27 when he hurried out in silence, making straight for his room. He had realized then that he might become Pope. Yet the thing was not settled in the morning. The election was made on the afternoon of the third day, October 28, the Feast of St. Simon and St. Jude. (St. Jude is known as the patron of lost causes.)

An elected Pope is formally asked if he accepts the decision; from the moment when he does he becomes Pope, with full powers. His answer is recorded and has come to constitute a little manifesto; it is a considered statement.

Eugene Cardinal Tisserant, Dean of the Sacred College, put the question to Angelo Giuseppe Roncalli, Cardinal Patriarch of Venice.

He said: "Listening to your voice 'I tremble and fear seizes me' and what I know of my poorness and insufficiency is enough to cover me with confusion. But seeing in the votes of my brother cardinals of our Holy Roman Church the sign of God's will, I accept the choice they have made. I bow my head and my shoulders to the chalice of bitterness and the yoke of the cross. On the solemnity of Christ the King we have all sung: 'The Lord is our judge, the Lord is our lawmaker; the Lord is our king: He will save us.'"

Then Cardinal Tisserant asked him: "By what name do you desire to be called?"

He answered: "*Vocabor Johannes.*" ("I will be called John.")

This was the first surprise. If the new Pope was hardly expected to choose the much favored name of Pius, because of the late Pope's formidable reputation, he might have looked back to Benedict, whom he admired, or to Leo, the great Pope of his youth. Not only had John XXII been an unattractive medieval Pope, but there had even been a possible John XXIII already, one of the rival Popes at the time of the Council of Constance, a crucial period which the modern Popes had preferred to leave shrouded in oblivion. The status of that earlier John XXIII was uncertain; in fact, Roncalli helped to settle it by fixing the number on himself.

John XXIII read from the notes he had written: "The name John is dear to me because it is the name of my father. It is dear because it is the title of the humble parish church where we received baptism. It is the solemn name of innumerable cathedrals throughout the world, and first of all the blessed and holy Lateran basilica, our cathedral. It is the name which, in the long series of Roman pontiffs, has been most used. Indeed there have been twenty-two unquestionably legitimate supreme pontiffs named John. Nearly all had a brief pontificate."

This was the nearest he could come to a joke on such a solemn occasion. He went on to give a little sermon, so typical that it must be quoted in full. It contains the essence of John XXIII.

"We have preferred to shield the smallness of our own name behind this magnificent succession of Roman pontiffs. And was not St. Mark the Evangelist, the glory and protector of our dearest Venice, he whom St. Peter, Prince of the Apostles and first Bishop of the Roman Church, loved as his own son, also called John? But we love the name of John, so dear to us and to all the Church, particularly because it was borne by two men who were closest to Christ the Lord, the divine Redeemer of all the world and Founder of the Church: John the Baptist, precursor of our Lord. He was not indeed the Light, but the witness to the Light. And he was truly the unconquered witness of truth, of justice and of liberty in his preaching, in the baptism of repentance, in the blood he shed. And the other John, the disciple and Evangelist, preferred by Christ and his most holy Mother, who, as he ate the Last Supper, leaned on the breast of our Lord, and thereby obtained the charitable love which burned in him with a lively and apostolic flame until great old age.

"May God dispose that both these Johns shall plead in all the Church for our most humble pastoral ministry which follows the one so well conducted to its end by our lamented predecessor of venerable memory, Pius XII, and those of his predecessors, so glorious in the Church. May they proclaim to the clergy and to all the people our work by which we desire to 'prepare for the Lord a perfect people, to cut straight the windings of every street and make rough paths into smooth roads, so that all mankind shall see the saving power of God.' (Luke 3, 4–6.) And may John the Evangelist who, as he himself attests, took with him Mary the Mother of Christ and our Mother, sustain together with her this same exhortation which concerns the life and joy of the Catholic Church and also the peace and prosperity of all peoples.

"My children, love one another. Love one another, because this is the greatest commandment of the Lord. Venerable brethren, may God in his mercy grant that, bearing the name of the first of this series of supreme pontiffs, we can, with the help of divine grace, have his sanctity of life and his strength of soul, unto the shedding of our blood, if God so wills."

This speech comes out of the deepest and most ancient tradition of the Church, the heart of the Gospel. Because Pope John's mind was like this the most diverse people instantly recognized in him the true spirit of Christ. It is not too much to say this; indeed, it has to be said if his pontificate is to be understood. Otherwise fruitless arguments arise about conservatism and innovation. The Gospel is always the same and always new. Christ said that he came not to destroy but to fulfill; yet he shocked the rulers of his people. Fulfilment is not always what it is expected to be. The Johannine impact was of a person, not a program. The only mystery about it is the mystery of the Holy Spirit, working in and through a human being.

From the moment when Roncalli surprised everyone by

taking the name of John everything became just that little
bit different. He immediately asked the Cardinals to remain
in conclave till the next day, so that he could consult with
them in private. This was so unprecedented a step that Monsignor Tardini and others who burst upon the scene were
astonished to be ordered off by Cardinal Tisserant and told
they had incurred excommunication by breaking into the
conclave. It was not exactly a solemn excommunication and
Pope John lifted it the next morning; but it was quite an
event.

Domenico Tardini was to be one of the first Cardinals
John XXIII made and he raised him to the full rank of
Secretary of State. He is said to have remarked, on visiting
the offices of the Secretariat, "Too many people have been
sostituti here for too long." The very first Cardinal, however,
was Monsignor Alberto di Jorio, the secretary of the conclave.
Pope John revived an old custom when he placed his discarded
red skullcap on di Jorio's head. Many of his first gestures
indicated his liking for old customs connected with the papacy, but they were such as emphasized the share that others
had in the government of the Church. He refused to play
another game with skullcaps, to which Pius XII had conformed—the custom that if anyone gave the Pope a white
cap he should receive the one worn at the time. Pope John
did not like this form of "personality cult."

From the start Pope John behaved in the natural and
simple manner which made him so popular. After his election he had to go out on the balcony to give his first papal
blessing *Urbi et Orbi* (to the city and the world). For this,
he had to be dressed in full pontifical vestments. For a start,
the Vatican tailors had not envisaged a Pope of Roncalli's
girth. Even the biggest of the three white cassocks prepared
would not meet down the front. Luckily the gap could be concealed by the surplice. Pope John murmured about "the
chains of office." In all this antique paraphernalia he at length
emerged from the Sistine Chapel with numerous officials
fussing round him. Suddenly his great voice boomed out:
"If you *want* me to trip over, this is the way to go about it!
Now, don't fuss me." Everyone scattered in surprise, and he
went out to give his blessing to the people.

It was soon apparent to those nearest him that he was not going to be an inactive Pope. Going over the speech for his coronation with Monsignor Igino Cardinale, his chief of protocol, Pope John saw him wincing at occasional modernisms of speech. He had been trained under Pius XII, a purist in language. John looked at him over his spectacles. "Well? What's the matter?" Hesitantly Monsignor Cardinale ventured that such phrases did not appear in Palazzi's dictionary. Pope John looked at him for a moment and then said: "Well, if necessary we shall reform *even* Palazzi!"

The coronation took place a week after his election, on November 4, 1958, the Feast of St. Charles Borromeo. The ceremonies, which are medieval with some relics of antiquity and some baroque additions, were unchanged: a curious mixture of the sacred and the secular, the pomp of the days of temporal sovereignty. Pope John, whose fame was to rest on his "coming down from the throne," was crowned with the heavy papal tiara used since the early nineteenth century. Of course, the triple-crowned mitre had been in use for centuries, though it would have surprised the early Popes. The three crowns now seem only a barrier to popular understanding of the function of the papacy—the Pope too easily appears merely the last of the absolute monarchs. Pope Paul VI, who was given a modern tiara by the Archdiocese of Milan, later sent it to be sold for charity. But he has not yet been able to dispense with all the Vatican regalia.

It is customary for the new Pope to suggest the aims of his pontificate in his coronation speech. Praising the achievements of his polymath predecessor, John XXIII said that he wished to be known simply as a pastor. This was not an unusual wish for a Pope, since it is the essence of his office. What was to be unusual in John XXIII was the way in which he carried out this pastorate. Although he was so unlike St. Charles Borromeo in temperament and training, Pope John's reference to him showed his lifelong admiration for this reforming Archbishop, who first made the decrees of Trent a reality.

Later that day, in the Hall of Benedictions, Pope John spoke to a gathering of people from Venice and Bergamo. He was carried in on the *sedia gestatoria*, borne by uniformed men, a form of locomotion he very much disliked. But in his speech he made the best of it. "Here we are again on a new journey. Here we are, carried high by our children. Seventy years have passed since the day our father bore us on his shoulders during the celebrations of Catholic Action at Ponte San Pietro. But it can be said that with divine help these were seventy years of generosity, of grace, of service to God, of the life of a good man. The secret of all this is to let oneself be carried by the Lord, and to carry Him." This simplicity in putting himself entirely into God's hands was the human occasion of everything that was to follow.

In the evening of his coronation day, as on that of his election, Pope John was talking in a homely way to his secretary, Monsignor Loris Capovilla, who had come with him from Venice. He told him that when he was first carried in this chair it made him think of his father and mother, his humble home in Sotto il Monte. Curious indeed how the child of that little country hamlet had been brought, without any planning of his own and by such roundabout ways, to the highest position in the Church. He would not have been human if it had meant nothing to him and yet he was able to accept it so simply as the gift of God and the choice of his brother Cardinals that he seemed to have no anxieties.

"He seems to have been Pope all his life," someone in the Vatican observed, right at the beginning.

This was not quite true. Most people have heard the story, first broadcast on Radio Television Française, of how, in the early days of his pontificate, Pope John was kept awake by some anxiety. "I will speak to the Pope about it," he said to himself. And then he remembered: "But *I* am the Pope!" His characteristic solution was: "Well—I will speak to God about it!"

In another story of the night watches he said to himself: "Don't take yourself so seriously, Angelo!" He certainly took his own advice on this point.

In one impromptu speech he remarked that he was going through his papal novitiate. Later, he said about the Council: "We are all novices." The last Council had been held in 1870, over ten years before he was born.

These stories indicate what enabled him to launch out on

his brief but epoch-making papal career: it was his lifelong habit of leaving to God the beginning and end of all he did. He tried, in speeches, and in his *Journal*, various ways to express this trust in God and attentiveness to the inspirations of the Spirit. In words, it is apt to sound either platitudinous or smug. His own personality, his presence brought out the meaning more clearly than words. There was no impression of a man straining to fulfill some superhuman ideal, but of someone doing the work given him by the Church, and so by God. It is the difference of approach that is crucial. By making the most of his ordinariness he showed that the Pope really was the servant of the servants of God.

In these first days, walking with his secretary in the Vatican gardens at sunset, Pope John was struck by the beauty of Michelangelo's great cupola, seen through a gap in the trees. The sun's red blaze, reflected from a window, made the great basilica look as if it were on fire. Fascinated, the Pope returned to the spot on the two following evenings. On the third he took up again the reading of a document soon to be published, and remembered a passage from St. John Chrysostom.

"Christ has left us on earth to become beacons that give light, teachers who give knowledge; so that we may discharge our duty like angels, like heralds among men; so that we might be grown men among the young, men of the spirit among men of the flesh, and win them over; so that we might be seed and bring forth many fruits. It would scarcely be necessary to expound doctrine if our life were radiant enough; it would not be necessary to use words if our acts were witness enough. If we behaved like true Christians, there would be no pagans."

After a moment's silence, Pope John said that if anyone wanted to know the nature of the new pontificate, he could be answered in those words, or with others like them. This was his idea of true Christian ministry and he began to put it into action in the way most natural to himself, but so unusual in Rome that it soon gained world-wide publicity. He went out of the Vatican, not just for special occasions, but again and again, visiting churches, visiting colleges, visiting people. He got out of his car and walked about on foot. (No wonder he spurned the white satin slippers the Popes had used for so long! He wore strong black or red leather buckled shoes.) His smiling interest in everyone, his good-humored straight-forward talk did the rest. First Rome and then the world was fascinated. Pope John stories multiplied so rapidly that it is now almost impossible to sort the true from the apocryphal. But the type and number of the *bon mots* attributed to Pope John show how completely his natural manner and shrewd but kindly humor had won people's attention and affection. Why was it all such a surprise? Why did John XXIII capture the hearts of thousands who had never felt any reverence for, or interest in the papacy?

Before the beginning of the quarrel between the Holy See and the government of united Italy, Popes naturally went about Rome, and not only on sacred occasions. Yet it was as sovereigns that they made these public appearances, surrounded, like secular rulers, with the signs of power and with ceremony. After the concordat of 1929 the presence of the Duce was not conducive to the Pope's leaving the precincts of the Vatican. If Pius XI had been feted by the Fascists, or if he had been cold-shouldered by them, the situation would have been equally difficult. Then came the war. When bombs dropped on the outskirts of Rome, Pius XII immediately drove to the scene of destruction, very much distressed by the suffering he witnessed. But he did not go much into Rome in the years after the war. Perhaps he was anxious not to cause political reactions, perhaps he considered it a waste of time. People—endless crowds and organizations of people— visited him; he did not go out to them.

Then suddenly Pope John was there, standing up in the back of his car, or walking about without fuss, talking to everybody. It was impossible to think of him as a sovereign, a rival statesman to the rulers of Italy. Nor was there any sacred mystique about this shortish, stout, smiling old man in his big hat and sturdy shoes, so obviously happy and enjoying the opportunity to bless and encourage the people he met.

Two of the earliest and most famous of these visits took place at Christmas 1958. On Christmas Day, after offering the eleven o'clock Mass in St. Peter's, the Pope went to the Santo Spirito and Gesù Bambino Hospitals to visit the sick children. In a very short time the children were all excitedly calling: *"Papa! Papa! Vieni qui!* (Come over here!)." It is a pity that the ugly English word "pope" disguises its origin in the homely word for "father." To the children, this Papa really was a papa. "Quiet, now! I'm coming, I'm coming," he said to them. He asked one little boy his name and received the reply: "Angelo!" Pope John was delighted. "That's my name—that used to be my name, but now I'm called John."

He certainly had a way with the children. They used to write to him. One said he had not made up his mind whether to be a pope when he grew up, or a policeman. "It would be safer to train for the police," Pope John replied. "Anyone can be Pope, as you can see since I have become one." A little girl suffering from leukemia was brought a long way to see the Pope. There is a photograph of them sitting and talking, serious and absorbed. At that time, Pope John was already ill himself.

On December 26, 1958 the Pope went to the Regina Coeli prison. "You can't come to me, so I have come to you," he told the prisoners, who clapped at his entrance and knelt down for his blessing. A man who had committed a murder said, "Can there be forgiveness for me too?" Pope John opened his arms to embrace him. Talking informally to the prisoners he remarked that he had early realized what a serious thing it was to be sent to prison, since one of his cousins had been sent to jail for poaching (hunting without a license). The Vatican newspaper, the *Osservatore Romano*, shocked at a Pope's admitting to a poaching relative, discreetly omitted this observation in its report. Editing Pope John's impromptu asides must soon have become a fulltime job with the official scribes of the Holy See.

This newspaper was accustomed to writing of the Pope with the pompous elegance of a bygone age and a solemnity now more likely to amuse than to impress. At his first interview with the editor, Count della Torre, Pope John requested him to abolish this turgid style. "Just say: 'The Pope said this, did that.'" But it would take more than a Pope to change the terminology of the Vatican.

Apparently the reporter from the *Osservatore* had been in the habit of taking dictation from the Pope on his knees. When Pope John told him to get up, he was quite taken aback, and assured him he was used to the posture. But the independent Bergamasque Pope could not stand it. He threatened to leave the room if the reporter did not rise to his feet.

It was the custom for everyone in the Vatican, even those who worked all day in close contact with the Pope, to genuflect three times whenever they entered his room. John XXIII soon stopped this. "Have you got St. Vitus's dance?" he teased one of them. "Once is enough! Don't you think I believe you the first time?"

It is interesting that his predecessor, a Roman born and used to Vatican customs from his youth, apparently never thought of altering this antique code of manners, modern though he was in certain things—witness his keep-fit exercises, experiments with hormone injections, his electric razor (white) and his fondness for speeding on the road to Castelgandolfo, when he used to time the performance of car and chauffeur with a stopwatch. It is said that the kneeling routine was so ingrained at the Vatican that officials even fell on their knees when Pope Pius rang them up on the internal telephone system.

To Monsignor Heim, who had been his secretary in France, Pope John said, "It makes me nervous to see people kneeling!" he made him get up and insisted on giving him *"un' bacetto"* (a little kiss) and then he was to sit down and talk naturally. Monsignor Heim, a Swiss, and an expert in heraldry, had drawn a coat of arms for the new Pope. But he had depicted the Lion of St. Mark rampant, with claws extended. "Don't you think he is too fierce?" Pope John said. "A little Germanic? He would have done for Gregory VII! Can't you make him more *human?*" The final result was that homely Venetian lion which, as Pope John said at an audience in April 1963, "wouldn't frighten anyone."

Another custom John XXIII altered was that which decreed that the Pope should eat alone. Originally this had been a reform, introduced to do away with the often unseemly banquets in the Vatican. But the high moral character of modern Popes it had become instead one more way of isolating them from normal human intercourse and emphasizing the unique solemnity of their office. Pope John said he found nothing in the Bible which forbade Popes to eat with other people, and soon had his secretary and others round his table.

It was not easy to change even trivial customs, far less the pomp and ceremony of official occasions. Pastor Roger Schutz of the Protestant monastic community in Taizé, France, once asked why the baroque splendors of Vatican ceremonial could not give way to Gospel simplicity. "Patience, patience!" said Pope John. "I can't do everything at once." Incidentally, these brothers of Taizé appeared in white habits, but explained that they did not wear them for work, but only in choir. "Oh," said Pope John, in his white cassock, his eyes twinkling, "I'm not jealous, you know!"

John XXIII combined a real determination to reform the Vatican with an easygoing lightness of touch which prevented him being solemn about it. He loved beautiful things, including, for instance, the papal rings, the pictures and other ornaments. But when he saw the room in which all the treasures given to Pius XII were kept he said, "We must get rid of some of this." He gave presents to all those who had been close to Pope Pius. Sometimes this caused an awkward situation, as when a member of a Roman association recognized a picture on the desk of a Vatican official. "It looks just like the one we gave Pius XII," was the suspicious comment.

Pope John himself was an adept at coping tactfully with such tricky situations. When, as Cardinal, he was sent as Papal Legate to consecrate the underground basilica of St. Pius X at Lourdes, he took with him as the Pope's gift a relic of the saint which had been put into a fine reliquary case from the Vatican's treasures. Among those who saw it at Lourdes was a prominent member of the Society of St. Vincent de Paul, which is the most famous of Catholic charitable associations. "But that is the reliquary we gave to Pope Pius XII!" he exclaimed. Without hesitation Cardinal Roncalli said, "Yes: and now he has sent it back to you with a relic of his holy predecessor."

Pope John said, "We must blow off the dust from the

throne of Constantine, which has been lying too long on the Chair of Peter." He meant it. But it was more important to blow that dust from the minds where it still lodged than to sweep away external splendors. When someone asked him what he expected a Council to do, he flung open a window to let in the fresh air. This was how he worked, opening up ways for the Spirit to enter. He did not try to impose a program. The Spirit must work through the men who were there.

We know from Pope John's own *Journal* that he had endured much from the officialdom of the Vatican ever since his first post in Bulgaria. Yet this did not lead him to continue the somewhat autocratic rule of his predecessor. On December 15, 1958, only some six weeks after his coronation, he created twenty-three new Cardinals, passing the limit of seventy set by Sixtus V in the late sixteenth century. Of these, eleven (nearly half) were from the Roman Curia. The next year, of eight new Cardinals, seven were curialists. John XXIII continued to create Cardinals frequently; in just over four years he made fifty-four and at one time the Sacred College numbered eighty-five. He followed the two Popes Pius in extending its international composition; he created the first Indian Cardinal, Valerian Gracias, and the first African, Laurian Rugambwa of Tanganyika, in March 1960. But about half of all his creations were from the Curia, though some were very old men, receiving the red hat as a final accolade.

But though Pope John wanted to restore the curial machinery and revive the idea of the Cardinalate as an advisory body, he did not want to perpetuate the system-within-a-system which operated as an oligarchic instrument of power, with a few men holding key posts in each Congregation. Addressing his first new Cardinals he said tactfully that he hoped these creations would help to make the burdens lighter and nearly a year later, in October 1959, he pointed out that by this he had meant not merely for individuals but for a more equal distribution of duties which would facilitate the dispatch of affairs in the Roman Curia, with advantage to the whole Church. At that point (1959), when he found no one had taken the hint, he was forced to ask those high curial officials who held several top posts to resign from some of them. Needless to say, there were heart-burnings over this reshuffle. Pope John's letters of thanks to Cardinals Eugene Tisserant and Giuseppe Pizzardo were printed in the *Acta*. Not printed there was the fact that certain others refused to relinquish their pluralities of office. Pope John, who had lived by his motto of *Oboedientia et Pax*, could hardly believe it. "They have refused the Pope," he was heard to say. "They have refused the Pope!"

The situation was a curious one. John was Pope, but for most of his life these men had been his superiors. They were "The other school" who had called him *"il buon Roncalli,"* who thought him not much of a diplomat but a useful man to smooth down angry foreigners, who had been surprised by his ever being made a Nuncio. They must have expected him to make a kindly but unexacting Pope, behind whose capacious back the bureaucratic machinery would run excellently according to plan. It did not turn out like that.

Yet it was not Roncalli's way to reach his goal by removing men from office or by imposing a new order from above. He worked toward it by widening the distribution of power at the top and by a personal and visible renunciation of autocratic methods and privileges. That he had to pay for this is clear from the notes in his *Journal*, restrained though they are. But even before the Council's discussions on the principle of collegiality John's historical mind was already imbued with it; he knew himself to be a bishop among bishops, even if he held the primacy, the eldest brother in a family; and he knew that the episcopate, essential to the maintenance of the sacramental Christian community, must think and act together for the good of the whole. To believe this was to deny himself the exercise of autocratic authority, even over the Curia.

In smaller things too Pope John discovered his powerlessness. When he first went out into the Vatican gardens the gardeners all scuttled away. Pius XII had used his walks for meditation and did not like to be disturbed. John XXIII was different. He liked talking to gardeners and to anyone else who worked for him. As soon as they discovered how approachable he was, the gardeners began to tell him their grievances. There was one, who had worked there a long time, but had never been taken on to the permanent staff. Pope John said he would fix that. But when he met the man again some weeks later he found that his recommendation on the subject had not been followed. He was hurt by this discovery, hurt that the man's hopes should have been raised for nothing. Afterward, he was wary of promising things. "You must go to Archbishop Principi," he would say, naming the prelate in charge of the domestic affairs of the Vatican. "He's much more powerful than I am!"

Nevertheless he did succeed in getting the wage scale for Vatican employees raised. From being lower than the average in Rome it became higher, and jobs in Vatican City were sought after. The Bergamasque Pope was faithful to the principles of Catholic Social Action.

His going out into the gardens whenever he felt like it, instead of at a set time, upset the officials in charge of the cupola of St. Peter's. In Pius XII's time it was always shut during the time of his walk in the garden. The officials complained to Pope John of his irregular sorties and when he asked why it had to be shut they replied that otherwise the tourists would see him.

"Why shouldn't they?" he said, amused. "I'm not doing anything disedifying!"

This common sense, this refusal to become an object of cult or a figure of mystery, was the base on which Pope John built a new image of the papacy which instantly appealed to men of goodwill in the modern world. The Pope was suddenly seen to be human. "I am Joseph, your brother."

Incalculable revolution, effected by one person! For while it is true that the great changes now coming to birth in the Church have been put into effect through the Council, it must not be forgotten that the first breakthrough to the *world* was made by John himself.

18 *Papal Apostolate*

On the eve of the opening of the Council, Pope John, in retreat in the renovated Torre San Giovanni in the Vatican, wrote in his *Journal:* "A summary of great graces bestowed on a man who has a low esteem of himself but receives good inspirations and humbly and trustfully proceeds to put them into practice." The first grace, concerning his election, has already been mentioned; the second refers to the Council. "To have been able to accept as simple and capable of being immediately put into effect certain ideas which were not in the least complex in themselves, indeed perfectly simple, but far-reaching in their effects and full of responsibilities for the future. I was immediately successful in this, which goes to show that one must accept the good inspirations that come from the Lord, simply and confidently.

"Without any forethought I put forward in one of my first talks with my Secretary of State, on January 20, 1959, the idea of an Eoumenical Council, a Diocesan Synod and the revision of the Code of Canon Law, all this being quite contrary to any previous supposition or idea of my own on this subject. I was the first to be surprised at my proposal, which was entirely my own idea." In a note written in 1959 and quoted in the *Journal* he recorded: "This is the mystery of my life. Do not look for other explanations. I have always repeated St. Gregory Nazianzen's words: 'The will of God is our peace.'"

Pope John often insisted that the idea of the Council came to him as a sudden inspiration. The Secretary of State was Domenico Tardini, once Pius XII's right-hand assistant and Roncalli's superior. It was John XXIII who had made him a Cardinal at his first consistory. According to Pope John he replied enthusiastically, "*Si, si, un concilio.*" But it may be doubted if he took the idea seriously, for he did not lead a chorus of approval when the Pope announced it to some eighteen Cardinals assembled for St. Paul's day, January 25, at the end of the Unity Octave held in the basilica of St. Paul's-outside-the-Walls. It was typical of Pope John to launch his great venture in such a place—at the tomb of the Apostle of the Nations—and on such an occasion, the week of prayer for Christian Unity. It was typical, too, that he should ask the Cardinals for their advice.

No one had a word to say.

"Humanly, we could have expected that the Cardinals, after hearing our allocution, might have crowded round to express approval and good wishes." But there was dead silence. In recording this disappointing reaction Pope John was careful to put the best construction on it. "Instead there was a devout and impressive silence. Explanations came on the following days."

The silence was probably one of simple shock. Now that the Council has met, deliberated in a blaze of publicity and come to far-reaching decisions, it is strange to remember that in 1959 nothing was further from the minds of Catholics. Councils were associated with the settlement of debated points of doctrine and nothing seemed to require dogmatic definition. Moreover, since the definition of papal infallibility in 1870 it had been tacitly assumed that Councils were thereby rendered unnecessary. Any problems which came up could be settled by the Pope. Catholics said to each other: "A Council? What will it be about?" Skepticism as to its usefulness continued in some quarters right up to the opening session. No wonder the curial Cardinals in St. Paul's that January day were made speechless by the new Pope's extraordinary and (as it seemed to them) unnecessary inspiration.

One of the greatest things accomplished by Pope John was to have broken up this image of a Church which, because its chief pastor had been given special divine assistance in exercising his function as final arbiter, did not need the collective wisdom of occasional extraordinary assemblies, such as had been held ever since the Emperor Constantine had granted freedom of worship to Christians. Precisely because of the centralizing effects of Vatican I, the implications of Vatican II are far-reaching indeed. Pius XI examined the possibilities of calling a Council but political difficulties forced him to give up the idea. Pius XII took it up but did not pursue it. A Roman born, who had spent a lifetime in the Vatican service, he foresaw the repercussions a Council might cause within the Church and feared for unity. In spite of his interest in modern technology his mind had been formed in the nineteenth-century Curia; he was thirty-eight when the First World War began. Toward theology and Biblical studies he followed a stop-go policy which reflected both his open-mindedness to scientific progress and his anxiety about theories and activities which broke out of the Roman mold. Yet John XXIII, who belonged to the same generation, called the Council with unity specifically in mind; nor was he ignorant of the kind of upheavals Councils usually cause.

In his first radio message at Christmas 1958 Pope John summed up his predecessor's chief concerns as Unity and Peace, and adopted them as his own. Yet he used different methods in pursuing both aims. The difference lies in the way each thought of unity, and of peace. It is not immediately obvious from John XXIII's speeches, especially at the beginning of his reign, when he often began with a quotation from Pius XII. He is said to have remarked that, faced with some public occasion, all he had to do was to look up the subject in his predecessor's voluminous output. Yet as the months went by and he discovered, to his surprise, his own immense popularity, the references to Pius became less frequent and his own simple, Gospel style more confident. The great turning point was the reception of *Mater et Magistra*, the encyclical of social problems sponsored by Pope John, which appeared in May 1961 on the seventieth anniversary of Leo XIII's *Rerum Novarum*. Reassured by the acclaim his social teaching received Pope John went ahead in his own way, gathering momentum till the very last weeks of his life. Thus began the great two years in which, as Mr. Edward Hales has demonstrated in *Pope John and His Revolution*, the whole papal policy entered a new dimension.

The simplicity of Pope John's speech has sometimes disguised its depth. In August 1961, knowing the success of *Mater et Magistra*, he made a retreat at Castelgandolfo in preparation for his eightieth birthday; the notes in his *Journal* are the longest made during his pontificate and essential for an understanding of it. In the course of them, writing on "Ideas for a good apostolate" he returned to a favorite theme —the tiresomeness of clever, self-sufficient men who think it possible to pursue the ends of the Church by the means of the World. He called them *saccenti*, know-alls, wiseacres. "Wiseacres may show disrespect, if not scorn for the simple man. But those wiseacres are of no account; even if their opinion and conduct inflict some humiliations, no notice should be taken of them at all: in the end everything ends in their defeat and confusion. The 'simple upright God-fearing man' is always the worthiest and strongest. Naturally he must always be sustained by a wise and gracious prudence. He is a simple man who is not ashamed to profess the Gospel, even in the face of men who consider it to be nothing but weakness and childish nonsense, and to profess it entirely, on all occasions and in the presence of all; he does not let himself be deceived and prejudiced by his fellows, nor does he lose his peace of mind, however they may treat him." He knew well enough that for some people, even in the Church, simplicity is equated with lack of practical ability in human affairs. And some of those *saccenti* were inside the Vatican.

He went on to distinguish from these worldly wise men the character of the man prudent in the Gospel sense, concluding with "the man who, having chosen a good, or even a great and noble objective, never loses sight of it, but manages to overcome all obstacles and see it through to the end. Such a man in every question distinguishes the substance from the accidentals; he does not allow himself to be hampered by the latter, but concentrates and directs all his energies to a successful conclusion; he looks to God alone, in whom he trusts, and this trust is the foundation of all he does."

He ended this section with some general observations. "Simplicity is love: prudence is thought. Love prays: the intelligence keeps watch. 'Watch and pray': a perfect harmony. Love is like the cooing dove; the active intelligence is like the snake which never falls to the ground, because before it glides along it first probes with its head to test the unevenness of the ground." This perceptive elaboration of the Gospel image reflects once more his countryman's wisdom.

Pope John was not original in thinking these thoughts; his originality was in living them. The prudent snake was always there with the cooing dove. As ever, his acts reveal more than his words, though he used all public occasions to forward the project of the Council. He never lost sight of his great aim, in spite of the inauspicious reception of its announcement by those without whose aid it could not be carried out; and in spite of the increasing pressure of his own public engagements.

Heads of state and important visitors came ever more frequently, drawn by the lure of his personality. More came to the Vatican in John's four short years than in all the twenty of his predecessor. The first, in December 1958, was the Shah of Persia. Pope John genially recalled the visit of an earlier Shah at the beginning of the century when, as a seminarian, he had heard the Roman crowd shouting: "Long live the Shah! Down with the Pope!" Now, he remarked, times had changed and people were ready to include the Pope with the Shah in their goodwill. Pope John maintained the same natural, cheerful manner with all his grand visitors.

To be ready to meet everyone in this friendly way was part of his personal apostolate, but the Council was the great event toward which his efforts were directed. The first definite step was the setting up of an Ante-Preparatory Commission on June 18, 1959. Pope John chose Pentecost for the chief steps toward the Council because that feast commemorates the descent of the Holy Spirit on the disciples gathered together in prayer after the risen Christ had returned to the Father: the formation of the Church and the beginning of its mission to the world. He liked to call the Council "a new Pentecost" and to pray for a great outpouring of the Spirit in the hearts of men.

Cardinal Tardini appointed Monsignor Pericle Felice as Secretary General of the Council, a post which he held to the end. This first commission organized the circulation of preliminary literature to all the 2500 Bishops, prelates, and heads of men's religious orders and to the thirty-seven Catholic universities of the world, requesting suggestions for the agenda. The answers filled two thousand files. On the reports made from these documents the real preparatory commissions, created by Pope John at Pentecost (June 5) 1960, set to work. There were ten commissions, each headed by Cardinals from the corresponding curial congregations, a fact that filled progressive Bishops and theologians outside Rome with gloom.

No doubt aware of this, Pope John in his inaugural speech, made a distinction between the work of the Curia and that of the Council. "The Ecumenical Council has its own structure and organization which cannot be confused with the ordinary functions of the various departments that constitute the Roman Curia . . . The preparation for the Council will not be the task of the Roman Curia but, together with the illustrious prelates and consultors of the Roman Curia, Bishops and scholars from all over the world will offer their contribution."

Nevertheless it was inevitable that the men familiar with the everyday government of the Church from its Roman center were in the position to influence the way things developed. We can judge this from the fate of most of the original schemata presented to the Council, which were the work of the Curia-dominated commissions. They were criticized as too juridical, too rigidly formulated according to the theology systematized after the Council of Trent, which made few concessions to historical and scientific developments and was couched in the defensive-offensive language of apologetics. When some of the Council Fathers began to attack the schemata, the curial opposition was forced into the open. This was one of the most beneficial results of the first session of the Council, since it opened the eyes of ordinary Catholics to the mechanics of power within the Church. The fact that they learned what was happening was largely due to the journalists exasperated by the attempt to preserve absolute secrecy over conciliar proceedings. From what happened in the Council, it is possible to deduce what went on before it. Evidently the curial oligarchy intended the Council simply to endorse prepared positions and tighten discipline. *Aggiornamento*—the word Pope John used for modernizing the Church—meant to them a mere streamlining of old methods and statements of doctrine.

When the preparatory commissions were set up at Pentecost 1960, Pope John also announced the formation of a Secretariat for Promoting Christian Unity. This was entirely his own idea. The new organization was neither a curial department nor a conciliar commission (although it was later given the status of the latter) but a separate body. Its independence of existing ecclesiastical government allowed it to become the most flexible and influential instrument of the new papal policy, initiating approaches to Christian churches and communities not in communion with the Holy See. Augustin Cardinal Bea was appointed as its head. Bea was a German Jesuit, a Biblical scholar who had been Pius XII's confessor, and he was about the same age as Pope John. He immediately proved himself an able and active leader in promoting "dialogue" between Catholics and other Christians. The other members of the Secretariat, picked from different nations, were carefully chosen for their ecumenical experience.

Pope John's personality had drawn the attention of other Christians, who until then had tended to see the papacy as the antithesis of the Gospel—expressing formality, domination and rigidity. When they saw a Pope so evidently full of goodwill and good-humor, loving and lovable, stepping right outside the cultic image of sovereignty and mystery, the atmosphere at once changed. The members of the Secretariat were able to follow up with new contacts. When Dr. Geoffrey Fisher, then Archbishop of Canterbury, decided in November 1960 to visit the Pope in Rome, the meeting was arranged through the new Secretariat. Through it too the observers from other Christian communions were invited to the Council and its members looked after these important guests during the sessions. The idea of inviting the observers was Pope John's own, and it was he who insisted that they should be given the best places. Although the principal objective of the Council was renewal within the Church, Pope John wanted it always remembered that everything must be done with a view to ultimate unity.

Unhampered by age-old Roman customs the Secretariat adapted to the increasing pace of reform and soon became useful not only in approaching the "separated brethren" but also in introducing new ideas and a wider outlook to the conciliar commissions. Consequently it became a major preoccupation of the curialists to keep them out.

Some of the intrigues behind the scenes have been told by

"Xavier Rynne," the pseudonymous American author(s) of the first reports on the Council, later published as *Letters from Vatican City*. The brilliant introductory chapters make enlightening reading. Typical are the maneuvers of the curial conservatives against what they regarded as Biblical Modernism—echoes of the great campaigns under Pius X and Merry del Val! It is related here because it links with the debates in the Council, especially those on the Source(s) of Revelation, and illustrates the effect of the Roman *saccenti* and prophets of doom on the life of the Church.

According to Rynne there was a plan afoot to amalgamate the various institutes of higher education for the clergy in Rome under the Lateran academy, a conservative stronghold which was to be raised to the rank of a university. The chief object was to gain control of the Biblical Institute, run by the Jesuits, of which Cardinal Bea had been Rector. The Lateran was successfully upgraded and the attack on the Biblical Institute was launched in the Lateran journal *Divinitas*, December 1960, in an article by Monsignor Antonino Romeo, secretary to Cardinal Pizzardo, head of the Congregation for Seminaries and Universities. A free copy of this article was sent to all the bishops of Italy. A reply from the Rector of the Biblical Institute was not printed.

At this point an Italian bishop, making a routine visit to the Pope, innocently commiserated with him on the shocking state of Biblical studies in Rome. This was the first Pope John had heard of what was afoot. He at once sent for the Rector of the Biblical Institute and assured him of his confidence. Then Cardinal Pizzardo was asked to write to Cardinal Bea, disclaiming knowledge of the article by his secretary, Monsignor Romeo. Yet the affair did not stop there. At the beginning of the scholastic year in 1961 the Holy Office required the Rector to remove two of his professors, Lyonnet and Zerwick, on suspicion of unorthodoxy. When the Jesuit Father General intervened, the Holy Office dropped the case. But at the end of the year the Secretary of State was persuaded to suspend the two professors. Ramifications of this intrigue persisted right on through the Council, when Ernesto Cardinal Ruffini of Palermo revealed himself as one of the principals in the campaign against the Biblicists.

Ruffini was himself a Biblical scholar, but of an outlook almost fundamentalist. Xavier Rynne quotes Ruffini's front page article in the *Osservatore Romano* in June 1961, where the Cardinal indignantly rejected the idea that the modern studies in literary *genres* could make any significant contribution to the interpretation of the Bible. "How can one suppose that the Church has during nineteen centuries presented the Divine Book to her children without knowing the literary genre in which it was composed, if this is the key to exact interpretation?" To describe these shocking views, which he castigated so severely, the Cardinal used the very terms adopted by Pius XII, in the encyclical *Divine Afflante Spiritu* of 1943, to promote such modern studies! Such a direct contradiction of a pontifical document, if it had been made by anyone on the other side of the controversy, would have got him into serious trouble. It was typical of this conservative clique that they thought themselves so infallibly right that they could afford to ignore even the Pope. People who imagine that the *Osservatore Romano* is always directly inspired by the Pope, should take warning by this episode.

Of course these men of "the other school" were sincere. They believed that Pope John's way of doing things was leading to a dangerous weakening of the unity and discipline of the Church, in face of what they regarded as the implacable enmity of Communist nations and parties. There are some today who think they were right. It was only the Council which revealed that they were a very small minority; even so, they remained powerful out of proportion to their numbers because of their position in control of the central administration. Hence the sometimes fierce tone of the calls for curial reform, during the sessions. Before the Council it must sometimes have seemed to Pope John, who lived in the middle of them, as if the prophets of doom were in the majority. No wonder he told himself that the simple man trusts in God alone.

In Advent 1959 Pope John made a brief retreat in the Vatican and wrote in his *Journal*: "The experience of this first year gives me light and strength in my efforts to straighten, to reform, and tactfully and patiently to make improvements in everything." I do not think he ever elsewhere put on record so plainly his intention to attempt reform in the Church. It is unequivocal.

He went on to express gratitude to God for giving him a temperament which preserved him from anxiety and he showed an honest delight in the fact that his trust in Providence enabled him to act with evangelical simplicity. He knew what people felt about him; he read it in the newspapers as well as in their faces and in their cheers and applause. "The welcome immediately accorded to my unworthy person and the affection still shown by all who approach me are always a source of surprise to me. The maxim 'Know thyself' suffices for my spiritual serenity and keeps me on the alert . . . Above all, one must always be ready for the Lord's surprise moves, for although he always treats his loved ones well, he generally likes to test them with all sorts of trials such as bodily infirmities, bitterness of soul and sometimes opposition so powerful as to transform and wear out the life of the servant of God, the life of the servant of the servants of God, making it a real martyrdom."

This reminded him of Pius IX, whose "sufferings" from the Italian nationalists had been almost an article of faith in the world of his childhood. He said he would "like to be worthy to celebrate his canonization." Some may feel less devotion to the cause of Pius IX than to that of John XXIII; they may also suspect that he had his share of opposition, even if it was a hidden opposition.

Two years later, in the retreat of August 1961 (already mentioned) on the fifty-seventh anniversary of his ordination, Pope John wrote some words in his *Journal* which have often been quoted. "When on October 28, 1958, the Cardinals of the Holy Roman Church chose me to accept the supreme responsibility of ruling the universal flock of Jesus Christ, at seventy-seven years of age, everyone was convinced that I would be a provisional and transitional pope. Yet here I am, already on the eve of the fourth year of my pontificate, with an immense program of work in front of me to be carried out before the eyes of the whole world, which is watching and waiting."

When he wrote this he was determined that the Council, the preparations for which threatened to extend indefinitely into the future, should open as soon as possible. Delay has always been one of the methods by which the Roman Curia has remained in command of the internal apparatus of power. Pope John was encouraged by the fact that the Synod of Rome was held only one year after he had announced it. It is said that the idea of holding a Synod was suggested by Archbishop dell' Acqua, once secretary at the Delegation in Istanbul and now a prominent member of the Secretariat of State. But ever since the days of Radini-Tedeschi, Roncalli had been anxious to revive local Synods; he had held one in Venice in 1957. There had been no Synod in Rome since 1725, and even that had been a provincial, not a diocesan, Synod.

Pope John's Synod, which he opened in his cathedral church, the Lateran basilica, on January 24, 1960, was a disappointment to many. The contributions of the clergy were processed in the central offices and there was little visible *aggiornamento* in the resulting decrees. But at each session—others were held in the Vatican and at the Gesù—the Pope addressed his clergy as their bishop. He felt satisfied that a beginning had been made to deal with the pastoral problems raised by the sudden expansion of postwar Rome, with its large new suburbs.

In fact, John XXIII probably did more toward this in other ways. Even when the Popes were sovereigns of Rome they had rarely taken part in Corpus Christi processions in the city. In 1959 and 1960 Pope John did so, waiting for the Blessed Sacrament by the Colosseum, scene of the early Christian martyrdoms. There were his many visits to parishes, especially the new ones. Even by Easter 1959 he had been outside the Vatican more often than Pius XII in the whole of his reign. In September 1960 John went from Castelgandolfo to Roccantica to visit the summer villa of the Roman Seminary, where he had gone after his ordination in August 1904. Typically he went to pray at the tomb of a colleague of those days, now nearly sixty years away. No Popes had been to Roccantica, once a papal stronghold, for nine hundred years. His visits to the various colleges and institutions of Rome were too numerous to mention. Sometimes even his private calls on sick or dying colleagues got into the press.

On Ascension Day, May 26, 1960, Pope John went to the Lateran basilica to canonize his beloved local saint, Gregory Barbarigo, defying the eighteenth-century canonist Pope, Benedict XIV, who had decreed that all canonizations must take place in St. Peter's. John wanted Barbarigo to be patron saint for pastoral Bishops as well as for Bergamo, and so it seemed suitable to canonize him in his own cathedral of the Lateran. John liked to recall the witness at the Process for Barbarigo's beatification, two hundred years earlier, who had said: "If Cardinal Barbarigo had not died untimely, the Greek and Latin Churches with the Lord's help, would have been felicitously reunited." Whether this optimism was justified or not, the cause was dear to the heart of Pope John.

In 1961 Pope John wrote in his *Journal:* "The various initiatives of a pastoral character which mark this first stage of my papal apostolate have all come to me as pure, tranquil, loving, I might even say silent, inspirations from the Lord, speaking to the heart of his poor servant, who, through no merit of his own save that very simple merit of mere acquiescence and obedience, without discussion, has been able to contribute to the honor of Jesus and the edification of souls.

"My first contacts with high and low; the charitable visits here and there; the meekness and humility shown in the approaches made to clarify ideas and give warm-hearted encouragement; my Lenten visits to the new parishes; the unexpectedly successful outcome of the diocesan Synod, the closer links between the papacy and the whole Christian world, achieved by the repeated creation of new Cardinals and Bishops from every nation and of every race and color, and now this vast activity, of unforeseen and most imposing magnitude, for the General Council—all this confirms the wisdom of the principle of waiting on God and expressing with faith, modesty and confident enthusiasm the good inspirations of the grace of Jesus, who rules the world and guides it according to the supreme purposes of the creation, redemption and final and eternal glorification of souls and peoples."

Since meekness and humility are reckoned as virtues by Christians, and it is not considered humble to think yourself humble, some may be surprised at Pope John's way of referring to himself. But he was thinking of humility as a method of approach, not as something praiseworthy he had acquired for himself. For centuries the Pope has been called the servant of the servants of God, but the aspect of service was not readily visible while he was surrounded by the pomp and circumstance of earthly monarchy. The loss of temporal power in 1870 was offset by the increased emphasis on spiritual power and the intensive centralization made possible by modern communications. It was the mystique, not the doctrine, of infallibility which isolated the Pope in the popular mind and gave his every utterance the prestige of an apostolic command.

From the start John's approach to his office was different. He called it his papal ministry, his apostolate, his service; again and again in his speeches he used these chosen terms. Some people thought he was just a kind man who found it easy to smile. He knew they did. He did not try to impress them. His deepest thoughts on the Pope's function can be found in his retreat notes for August 1961, in meditation on the passage in St. John's Gospel where the risen Christ gives the command to Peter: "Feed my sheep."

"There is great authority in these words: the investiture of the Pope with his task as universal shepherd, in answer to his thrice-repeated assurance of love, an assurance he gives to Jesus, who has deigned to ask for it with gentle insistence. It is love, then, that matters: Jesus asks Peter for it, and Peter assures him of it.

"Peter's successor knows that in his person and in all that he does there is the grace and the law of love, which sustains, inspires and adorns everything; and in the eyes of the whole world it is this mutual love between Jesus and himself, Simon or Peter, the son of John, that is the foundation of Holy Church, a foundation which is at the same time visible and invisible, Jesus being invisible to the eyes of our flesh, and the Pope, the Vicar of Christ, being visible to the whole world."

In the days of Pius IX and Pius X this idea of the Pope as a sort of visible Christ had too often taken on overtones of submission of a kind that can only be given to the Lord himself. Here, Pope John makes the mutual *love* of Jesus and Peter the foundation which should be visible. "*It is love, then,*

that matters . . . this mutual love . . . is the foundation of
Holy Church." Too often the Pope has been seen as the Vicar
of Christ's power; John thought of him as the Vicar of
Christ's love.

By this orientation toward love and fraternal service Pope
John contributed toward a restoration of balance in the
Church's structures, strengthening the bonds of sacramental
communion and slackening those of the juridical institution.
Both are necessary to the Church, but organizational relationships had set in a rigid ruler-subject pattern and the
papacy was its supreme expression; hence the Protestant de-
testation of it as an institution. When John XXIII simply
stepped out of this power structure and showed himself the
successor of the real Peter of Galilee, in a ministry of love,
he was making an incalculable contribution to the renewal of
the Church and to the understanding between Christians.

There was nothing soft about this ministry of love; Pope
John's humor and shrewd good sense gave his words and actions a flavor of salt that delighted all kinds of people. "His
eyes would gently scrutinize but never intimidate," his secretary Loris Capovilla has written in his book *The Heart and
Mind of John XXIII*. "Whatever one said never seemed to
upset him. To someone in difficulty he would say, 'I shall
remember you in my rosary tonight and tomorrow when I
raise the chalice . . .' If he ever heard a bitter word, a look
of bewilderment came over his face, like a child when he first
hears a strange sound. Pope John would answer patiently
then, trying not to shame but to mitigate the impulsive anger
he had been witness to."

But his simplicity was not naïve; Monsignor Capovilla noticed that he did not like to be called a "country priest" because to him this implied a certain narrowness or parochial
outlook. After all, he had never been a parish priest, in the
country or anywhere else. As a young priest his ministry had
been to groups—Catholic Action, the women, the soldiers, the
students. This was not without its relevance to his understanding of the needs of the modern world. His subsequent
long service in the East and then in France had only widened
and deepened a pastoral spirit which was always more missionary than parochial.

Still considering Pope John's manner Monsignor Capovilla wrote: "He would always rise when a visitor came to see him; he tried to overcome the rigidity of protocol with the warmth of his gestures. Before he began a solemn act, there would always be a brief friendly word and look, as if to increase the 'circulation' of understanding among his listeners."

This constant awareness of others, of their need for affection and encouragement, the fruit of his long experience in Christian living, became an important part of his papal ministry because it helped to humanize the office. "We must come down from our throne," he said. So effectively did he come down that it seems unlikely that any future Pope will have to climb up again into that splendid isolation.

Small acts illustrate John's spirit of human understanding. On his first Good Friday as Pope he went to the stational church of the Holy Cross in Jerusalem (Santa Croce) to celebrate the liturgy and expunged from the prayer for the conversion of the Jews the adjective *perfidis* (faithless). Six months later he had a new text published to replace Leo XIII's act of consecration of the human race to the Sacred Heart of Jesus, because the references to Jews and Moslems had given offense.

Even the official speeches to important visitors show these personal touches, less noticeable in cold print than in his living presence. When the King and Queen of the Hellenes visited him, after making references (in French) to Plato and Aristotle, the early martyr-popes who were Greeks and his own sojourn in Greece, he spoke a few sentences in Greek. Similarly when the President of Turkey called, he congratulated him on the progress effected in his country and remembered a Turkish greeting: "May God guard you and roses bloom along your way." He repeated the first two of the Divine Praises which he had caused to be translated when he was in Istanbul: "Blessed be God: blessed be his holy name."

There were personal reunions too. Speaking to the veterans of two world wars he said how delighted he was to see among them a face he knew well—that of M. Vincent Auriol, who was honorary president of the group. In 1961 the Reverend Austin Oakley, friend of his years in Istanbul, was received privately with such warmth as to surprise the Vatican officials.

"You're not an Archbishop, are you?" one asked suspiciously. It was early days still for ecumenical encounters, though the famous visit of Dr. Fisher, Archbishop of Canterbury, had taken place. To two Anglican clergymen who visited him at different times, Pope John gave the volume of his breviary in current use, with cards still in marking the places. Besides Anglicans, ministers of the Free Churches visited him from England and America.

Pope John was always ready to enjoy personal reminiscences in his audiences. To French groups he spoke of his days in France; Italian journalists were given as model his favorite novelist "the great layman" Manzoni; to chaplains he was the ex-chaplain of the First World War; women of Italian Catholic Action were reminded how he had worked with them from the beginning and had been present at the opening of their new headquarters in Rome in 1922. When he was speaking to women's groups Pope John was fond of stressing their natural interest in peace and unity, the work of love; but he did not forget that the family is not the whole of a woman's life and spoke of their work and contribution to society too. Women's rights gained a special mention in his encyclical *Pacem in Terris.*

With his pastoral interests Pope John was often at his best in speaking to priests and students for the priesthood. One of his first encyclicals, *Sacerdotii nostri primordia* was addressed to them. To the Lenten preachers in Rome for 1959 (his first year as Pope) he gave three points: God has called us to illuminate consciences, not to confound or force them; God has called us to speak with the simplicity of the Apostles' Creed, not to complicate things or to flatter the audience; God has called us to heal the brethren, not to terrorize them. John XXIII used the first person plural here to include himself among his brother priests. Simplicity, wisdom and love for the brethren were always his themes in addressing priests.

But he understood the difficulties of priests in the modern world. He even referred, in an address to the Synod in January 1960, to the discipline of celibacy. What most afflicted his heart, he said, was *"il gemito, vicino e lontano . . . il gemito di anime sacredotale"*—the groaning, the lament from far and near of priestly souls, for the burden they had to carry, of prejudice, loneliness and of this law of celibacy. John had accepted this renunciation of family life and had never fallen from his ideal, but he had understanding and sympathy for those who broke down under the strain. In America there is a new order dedicated to helping priests who have failed to keep their vows. Pope John wrote to them: "These men are our brothers, pilgrims in life. In the dedication of their young lives they did not count the cost. If now they have been wounded in the fray, it is our duty to help them, for they are our brothers, our sick brothers. If the Good Shepherd will go after the sheep that is lost, how much more will he seek out the shepherd himself, should he stray in the mountain mists? Did he not do so for his first shepherd, Peter?"

In Rome itself John XXIII tried to ease things for priests who had left their duties simply because of the burden of celibacy, by allowing marriages to be regularized, so that they could, though not exercising their sacerdotal function, at least live as Catholics and receive the sacraments. This whole question of the celibacy of secular priests (monasticism is a different vocation) has been raised again by the changes in western society. It was shelved at the Council when Pope Paul VI decided it was not a suitable theme for discussion there. It will certainly come up again, since it is a matter of discipline, shaped by historical circumstances, and not of doctrine.

In November 1960 John XXIII celebrated the anniversary of his coronation with a Byzantine-Slav liturgy and in his address recalled "the dear peoples of Bulgaria, Constantinople, and Greece" and spoke of the "sweet prayer, slow, melodious, and penetrating of *Gospodi pomilui* and *Kyrie eleison* (Lord have mercy)." He spoke too of the coming Council and of the unity of the Church being always a unity in multiplicity: the varieties of nations, languages, liturgies, and activities enriched the catholicity of the Church. In the following April he himself consecrated Monsignor Coussa bishop in the Oriental rite and again used the occasion to point the same moral. A few days later he told the story of an old wandering monk he had met in Bulgaria, to the seminarians of the Oriental rites in Rome. The old monk had kissed Roncalli's hand and whispered: "O representative of the Pope:

the sweetness of David and the wisdom of Solomon!" Pope John asked them to pray that the successors of Peter should always show these patriarchal qualities. "On your lips, in your heart, in your lives, may these holy and blessed words resound!"

Shortly after this, on May 15, 1961, his encyclical *Mater et Magistra* appeared. Pope John had not written it himself, but sponsored it wholeheartedly and quoted from it for months afterward. In this document the principles of social policy first enunciated by Leo XIII, and elaborated in 1931 by Pius XI in *Quadrigesimo Anno*, were carried further and the "socialization" of human society approved, provided it was developed in accord with justice and freedom.

In the same summer of 1961 Cardinal Tardini died. He had tried to retire the year before, but had been persuaded to remain. As Secretary of State Pope John chose Amleto Cardinal Cicognani, who had been for some twenty years a popular Apostolic Delegate in America.

Of course there were special celebrations in November 1961 for the anniversary of Pope John's coronation and for his eightieth birthday. Cardinal Montini (now Pope Paul VI) celebrated Mass in the Ambrosian rite of Milan. Pope John spoke warmly and informally, quoting St. Charles Borromeo and remembering his own work on the *Atti*, encouraged by Pius XI when he was Librarian at Milan; quoting too his favorite early Pope, St. Leo.

"What happened on the evening of October 18, 1958, is a mystery of the goodness and mercy of the Lord," he said, "and everything since then has unrolled itself day by day accompanied by such consolations as have truly alleviated the suffering which consecrates the ministry and service of the Pope . . . *Sia lodato Iddio:* may God be praised. *E siate ringraziati anche voi, fratelli e figli, vicini e lontani, di ogni lingua, stirpe e nazione.*" ("And I thank you too, brothers and children, near and far, of every tongue and race and nation.") He repeated the text with which he had begun his reign: "The Lord is our lawgiver: he will carry us and save us."

A month or so later, on Christmas Day 1961, Pope John issued an Apostolic Constitution announcing that the Council would take place the next year. It was signed, according to custom: *"Ego, Joannes Catholicae Ecclesiae Episcopus."* ("I, John, Bishop of the Catholic Church.") But in face of the many delays and the rumors that the Council would be postponed for years, this act of faith was indeed his own.

19 A New Pentecost

Pope John liked to refer to the coming Council as "a new Pentecost." This idea evoked some skepticism among Catholics, popular though the Pope himself had become. Journalists were asking people what they expected from the Council. The story went in England that if the answer was "Nothing" the speaker was a Catholic. This cynical attitude, compounded of indifference and self-satisfaction, depressed those who shared the hopes of John XXIII. In these circumstances, when rumors went round that the Pope was ill, hearts sank still further.

In November 1961 John wrote in his *Journal:* "I notice in my body the beginning of some trouble that must be natural for an old man. I bear it with resignation, even if it is sometimes rather tiresome and also makes me afraid it may get worse. It is not pleasant to think too much about this; but once more, I feel prepared for anything."

This was written just after his eightieth birthday and may refer to the prostate trouble which was the least serious of the afflictions of his last year, but "tiresome" indeed to someone committed to such a heavy public program as the Pope. But it was during the summer of 1962 that he began to feel the effects of the disease which was to carry him off. He made several references to the possible shortness of the time left to him; in the most famous he observed that "any day was a good day to die on."

Yet the pace did not slacken. The whole year was crammed with activity, from the announcement at Christmas 1961 that the Council would be held the next year, with the addition of the opening date, October 11, 1962, given on February 2, Feast of the Purification, to the great day itself. Pope John lost no opportunity to appeal for prayers for the Council, and for sacrifice and mortification from the faithful. But he also appealed for peace in Algeria, received the increasingly frequent visits of statesmen and church leaders, and continued to go out into Rome. In Lent 1962 he visited twenty-four churches, almost all parochial.

It was in April 1962 that he achieved a further reorganization in the Sacred College. Seven "suburbicarian" sees were given to Bishops, so that direct pastoral care could be exercised in the rapidly growing suburbs of Rome; the Cardinals were left with the titles only. At the same time Pope John decreed that all the Cardinals should be Bishops and he himself consecrated the Cardinal-Deacons on Holy Thursday at the Lateran basilica. These actions demonstrate John XXIII's deep convictions on the nature of the episcopal office, apostolic in origin and only to be entered by sacramental consecration, and therefore essential to the Church in a way the Cardinalate is not. By giving the suburbicarian sees their own Bishops he emphasized the importance of pastoral care; by making all Cardinals Bishops he intended to underline the truth that the government of the Church should be a sacramental service. It put an end to the situation where Bishops all over the world virtually came under the authority of curial non-Bishops in Rome.

Of course it needed more than this to effect a real change in the balance of power between the Bishops and the Roman Curia. The excitement aroused by the debates on collegiality and the attacks on the Holy Office in the course of the Council reflect the vital importance of the issues involved. It remains to be seen what difference will be made by the Synod of Bishops, to be elected by the national hierarchies, which was announced by Pope Paul VI in September 1965. In the limited area in which he could act before the Council, Pope John did what he could.

A curious episode of the immediate pre-conciliar period was the issue of the Apostolic Constitution *Veterum Sapientia* on February 22, 1962, which not only proclaimed the pre-eminence of Latin but insisted that all lectures in seminaries should be given in that language. Outside Rome this caused consternation. In at least one college in England the decree was put into effect, with confusing results for the students. The framers, being Italian, probably did not expect such prompt and literal obedience. The Roman and the Anglo-Saxon attitude to law is notoriously different. There is an Italian proverb: "The law is for your enemies, the exceptions are for your friends." Italians announce principles but compromise in practice; the English mind likes to get its compromises legalized. This is a constant source of misunderstanding, and each side thinks the other is being dishonest. In England *Veterum Sapientia* was even hailed as putting a stop to experiments with the vernacular in the liturgy, even though it was not designed to cover liturgical matters which were to be discussed in the first session of the Council.

Pope John sent back the first version of *Veterum Sapientia* for revision, indicating that it was too severe, but he signed it and spoke on it when it was issued. All languages have right of citizenship in the Church, he said, before defending Latin as a useful medium of communication between diverse nations and "the august center of Christianity." With his experience of the East, John certainly had no wish to impose Latin on nations with a long tradition of Greek or Slavonic languages. On one of his visits to parishes he expressed the opinion that vernacular should be used more freely in the Mass; this was omitted in the *Osservatore Romano*. *Veterum Sapientia* was certainly out of line with the policy of *aggiornamento* and the Council soon made it a dead letter, as perhaps the Pope expected.

On July 1, 1962, the Feast of the Precious Blood (a devotion that attracted Pope John in old age: it symbolizes Christ's outpouring of his life for men), he issued an encyclical *Poenitentiam agere*, asking all Catholics to pray and make sacrifices for the coming Council. It was just about this time that he felt the onset of the disease that was to kill him, though he did not at first know what it was. The doctors were anxious but he was impatient of lengthy examination. When they spoke of "a gastropathic condition" he laughed and said, "Oh, they only say that because I'm a Pope! They can't call it stomach ache." However, he was persuaded to be X-rayed because it was suggested that it would give other people in the Vatican confidence if he was the first to use the new apparatus installed. The diagnosis of cancer was not in fact confirmed till the end of October, and then the doctors disagreed as to the advisability of an operation. They decided against it. They did not speak to him of cancer, but of ulcers.

Pope John's confessor and his secretary did not hide from him the gravity of his situation and before the Council opened he knew he might not live to see its end. He never would pray that he "might begin and end it." It became a favorite thing to quote St. Martin: "I neither fear to die nor refuse to live." Nevertheless he remained optimistic, even about this. He put all the energy he had into preparing the way for the Council.

On September 11, a month before the opening date, he delivered a radio message. He summed up his message as: *Lumen Christi: lumen ecclesiae: lumen gentium.* (The light of Christ is the light of the Church and the Church is the light of the nations.) "The world has need of Christ and the Church ought to bring Christ to the World." He said that the world in anguish seeks the solution to its own problems, war, hunger, injustice, poverty. The Church should be the Church of all, especially of the poor. Like all mothers and fathers the Church hates war. It must seek "an earthly existence more noble, just and worthy for all." Co-existence on the international scene is not enough; we must work toward *convivenza*—life together—a real coordination and integration, a fraternity of love. Pope John often used this word *convivenza*, the key to his concept of the way in which Christians could work with all other men.

The Pope broadcast this message from the retreat he was making in the Torre San Giovanni in the Vatican gardens. Earlier in his reign he had expressed a liking for this old tower and had agreed to the suggestion that it should be renovated for his personal use. He was somewhat taken aback by the extent of the work done on it, which included the installation of a lift. But there he was able to retire for a few days, seeing only his secretary and Padre Chiappi, with whom he practiced his Latin in readiness for the Council. Here he wrote the last notes in his *Journal,* recalling the two great graces given him:

the acceptance of his election and the inspiration to call a Council. "After three years of preparation, certainly laborious but also joyful and serene, we are now on the slopes of the sacred mountain. May the Lord give us strength to bring everything to a successful conclusion!"

The next surprise to the world was the news that the Pope was going on a pilgrimage to Assisi, to pray at the tomb of the great Italian apostle of love and poverty, St. Francis. Later, he decided to include Loreto, the shrine of our Lady which shelters the tiny house supposed, in the middle ages, to have been transported from Nazareth by angels. However unlikely the angelic flight the house symbolizes the humble and hidden life of Mary and Jesus, the mystery of the Incarnation.

Pope John set off on October 4 (St. Francis' feast day) in the papal train from the Vatican station, built by Pius IX but never used. His secretary has told us that he was in discomfort and some pain for the whole journey, which was one of fatigue and strain for an old man of eighty, already seriously ill. He did not show it. All along the line people turned out to see him, to cheer and wave. He stood at the window, smiling and blessing them. It was the same at Assisi and Loreto. After Pope Paul's journeys to Jerusalem, to India and to the United Nations at New York, Pope John's expedition may seem unimportant, but it was the first a reigning Pope had made outside Rome for a very long time. The little journey symbolized Pope John's concern that the Church should be true to the Gospel of the poor, to love, simplicity, labor, humility, and prayer. It expressed what he had said in his radio message but in even simpler terms.

Rome was already full of Bishops and prelates, journalists and theologians; in St. Peter's the tiers of seats were ready, the voting machines, the squads of seminarians who were to assist with the clerical work. There had been a scare—a homemade bomb found under the seats. Television crews were getting ready; for the first time people all over the world were to see the opening of a Council of the Church. All this extraordinary and multifarious activity had come into being at the inspiration of one old man.

On October 11 the great day dawned to which the whole of his pontificate had been directed. Ill as he already was, though the fact was not known, Pope John insisted on walking with the Bishops of the universal Church for a large part of the inaugural procession, including the descent of the Scala Regia's long flight of marble steps. It was another symbolic action, to emphasize that the Pope also was a Bishop, one among brothers, even if the first. His age and his natural manner helped him to manifest this fraternal aspect of his office with great conviction; no one who saw, on the screen, the slow, awkward, determined but almost painful descent of the stairs but will always remember this simple expression of brotherly love and true papal ministry.

He had to submit to being carried into St. Peter's on the *sedia gestatoria*; indeed, the crowds could not see the Pope unless he was carried shoulder high. But once inside he again walked up the nave. Then came the solemn Mass that opened the Council; in the old baroque tradition of pomp and ceremony, to the disappointment of some of those present. It suggested that the Council would be merely an occasion for pageantry and reaffirmation of principle. But then the Pope made his speech. In spite of discomfort and fatigue his voice was as strong and resonant as ever and he read in his usual businesslike way, flicking over the pages as he went.

This speech was of course delivered in Latin but Pope John had taken steps to see that his first, Italian, version was published as well. He wanted it to be read and understood by everybody, not merely by the Council Fathers. He wanted to inspire the gathering to real work and to ensure that there would be an audience outside watching for signs of action. For months beforehand he had been discussing the issues with Cardinal Bea, Cardinal Suenens, and others. Unexpected in its frankness and personal quality, Pope John's address instantly raised the spirits of everyone who sympathized with his ideal of *aggiornamento*. His comment on "the prophets of doom" whom he heard so often but would not listen to, caught the ear of the world outside the Vatican.

Some of what he said on the reformulation of doctrine has been quoted in the chapter on Modernism; but he also spoke on the subject of unity: "The unity of Catholics among themselves, which must always be kept exemplary and most firm; the unity of prayers and ardent desires with which those

Christians separated from this Apostolic See aspire to be united with us; and the unity in esteem and respect for the Catholic Church which animates those who follow non-Christian religion." While unity is here regarded from the point of view of Rome, Pope John, after quoting St. Cyprian, the great African Bishop martyred at Carthage in A.D. 258, went on to suggest that the Council's task was to prepare "the path toward that unity of mankind which is required as a necessary foundation in order that the earthly city may be brought to the resemblance of that heavenly city 'where truth reigns, charity is the law, and whose extent is eternity'"—a quotation from St. Augustine. Pope John's idea was that the Catholic Church should reform itself in every sphere, so as to become ever more truly catholic and evangelical; he trusted that other Christians would find their true home in this renewed Church of the future.

He ended with a prayer to God. "In Thee we place all our confidence, not trusting in our own strength. Look down benignly upon these pastors of Thy Church. May the light of Thy supernal grace aid us in taking decisions and in making laws. Graciously hear the prayers which we pour forth to Thee in unanimity of faith, of voice and of mind." And after an appeal to Mary, Help of Christians, to St. Joseph, the Apostles Peter and Paul, and to his own patrons the two saints John, he concluded: "To Jesus Christ, our most lovable Redeemer, immortal King of peoples and of times, be love, power and glory for ever and ever, Amen."

The Council had begun.

Pope John did not attend the daily congregations, but he had a closed television circuit on which he could observe what was happening in the *aula*. He continued with his own papal duties. On October 12 he received, in the Sistine Chapel, the extraordinary diplomatic missions to the Council. The next morning it was the turn of the journalists, who were warned of the temptation to sensationalism, though the Pope hastily added an aside to assure them he did not believe it was one they would succumb to. The journalists might well have replied that it was Vatican secrecy and inadequate information which led to sensationalism—which in the context of the Council meant reporting the clashes of opinions between the Fathers. Thanks to the journalists, the later sessions were held more openly, with consequent lowering of temperature and increase of understanding.

In the afternoon of October 13 the Pope received the non-Catholic observers and the guests of the Unity Secretariat, in the Consistorial Hall. The chairs were arranged in a square and the Pope left his throne unoccupied and sat on a chair with the others. He tried to get round Vatican protocol and present himself as a fellow Christian, not as a Sovereign. *Fratres sumus!* (We are brothers) he said it often. More than his words, his personal friendliness won the hearts of the observers. The importance of their presence at the Council has often been emphasized. It was Pope John who had insisted that they should be given the best seats, and remain present at the closed sessions of the congregations, supplied with schemata, translations, and the assistance of Catholic theologians. They soon became an integral part of the Council, taking part in many private discussions, in the coffee bars in St. Peter's and elsewhere in Rome.

This is not the place for an account of the first session of the Council except in so far as Pope John affected it. At the very beginning, through the initiative of Achille Cardinal Liénart of Lille, the Bishops refused to elect the prepared list of candidates for the ten conciliar commissions and the first working session ended unexpectedly in less than half an hour. It was time well wasted. With newly prepared lists the Bishops returned, confident that they were an independent assembly and not a mere organ of collective assent to the Roman Curia. Pope John added men to the commissions, including curial officials, but otherwise did not interfere with procedural changes.

Discussion began on the Constitution of the Liturgy, the only schema prepared on relatively progressive lines. The system was such that the speeches were unrelated to each other, each Bishop spoke only for himself, and subjects came up haphazard. Improvements were made in each subsequent session. But, as Pope John himself observed in his speech at the end of the first session, the Council had to find itself, the Bishops had to get to know one another.

This was the first and in some ways the most important

result of the Council. Before they ever debated the *idea* of collegiality the Bishops began to discover its reality. Until then they had dealt with the Pope and the Curia, but much less with each other. In some countries conferences of the national hierarchy were well-established; others only met for the first time during the Council. Outside these national groups Catholic Bishops had had little contact with one another. Now many international groups were formed, theologians from various schools were asked to give addresses, lively encounters took place everywhere. East met West, rich met poor, missioner met establishment-bishop. The Council became a reality.

This great activity had hardly got under way when the Cuba crisis threatened to plunge the whole world in war. On October 24 Norman Cousins, the editor of the *Saturday Review*, telephoned the Vatican and suggested that the Pope should make an appeal for peace. Pope John, although he had received good wishes from Khrushchev through the Russian ambassador in Rome earlier that year, was afraid that what he said might offend the Soviet government, but Cousins assured him that the terms could be checked by each side before publication. So Pope John stayed up till midnight, preparing a radio message which he delivered next day, October 25, 1962. It was given in French.

"Lord, hear the supplication of your servant, the supplications of your servants, who fear your name," he began, quoting Nehemiah 1:11. "This ancient Biblical prayer rises to our trembling lips today from a moved and afflicted heart." Repeating that the Church had nothing more at heart than peace and brotherhood among men, he appealed to the conscience of those who held power: "May they hear the anguished cry which rises to heaven from every corner of the earth, from innocent children to old men, from persons and communities: peace! peace!" He begged the rulers to try every method to save the peace, appealing to their conscience before history and he called to prayer all baptized Christians and all united by faith in God. To all who worked for peace he gave the great blessing "with love in the name of him who wished to be called the Prince of Peace."

Khrushchev afterward told Norman Cousins he was

moved by this appeal, because the Pope had no temporal ambition behind it. It contributed to the easing of tension, which became apparent the next day, October 26.

Two days later, on the anniversary of Pope John's election, the doctors confirmed the diagnosis of cancer.

On November 4, his coronation day, Pope John visited the church of San Carlo al Corso, where, thirty-seven years earlier, he had been consecrated Bishop, and received so strong an impression that inwardly he was called to the way of the cross.

He went on with his usual routine, receiving Bishops, giving general audiences, visiting colleges and going out into Rome to see sick friends and colleagues.

The first big crisis of the Council came in November, with the introduction of the scheme De Fontibus Revelationis (On the Sources of Revelation). This scheme had been drafted in the old style by a Theological Commission whose guiding members were accustomed to think on the anti-Modernist lines in favor under Pius X. It was severely attacked by Cardinals and Bishops from the northern European nations and by Bishops from the East. It was defended equally warmly by curial Cardinals and conservatives. Practically all the grievances of both sides came out in this debate, including the disclosure that members of the Unity Secretariat had been kept off the commission. One of the chief complaints of the attackers was that the scheme was couched in scholastic terminology unfamiliar to other Christians.

The curial defenders insisted that as the schemata were formally sponsored by the Pope they could not be rejected outright. An application to the rules disclosed that, on the contrary, rejection was allowed. According to those who best knew his mind, Pope John's pastoral concerns would be better served by an entirely new schema. On November 20 a vote was taken on whether the schema should be discussed or referred to a mixed commission for redrafting. A large majority voted for the latter course, but fell short of the required two-thirds by a hundred and five votes.

At this point Pope John made his decisive intervention. By his order, it was announced next morning, November 21, the will of the majority was to take effect and the schema was to be referred to a mixed commission on which Cardinal Bea, head of the Unity Secretariat, and Cardinal Ottaviani, head of the Holy Office, would sit as joint presidents. The spirits of the reformers rose and a joke went round Rome, where the posters of British European Airways (BEA) were familiar, that a notice had been hung outside the Holy Office: "*Travel with BEA.*"

On November 25, the Holy Father's eighty-first birthday, the Council sent him a message of good wishes, to which he replied with gratitude. On that day he celebrated Mass at the College of Propaganda, where there were students for the priesthood from all races and nations. On Monday, November 26, the schema on Ecumenism, entitled *Ut Unum sint* (That they may be one) was introduced in the Council. In the night that followed Pope John had a sudden and unexpected hemorrhage. Nothing was said about this, but rumors went about that he was ill. On Thursday, November 29, an announcement was made in the *Osservatore Romano* that all audiences had been canceled since Tuesday on account of the Holy Father's health; it was said that he was suffering from severe anemia. Much anxiety was felt and rumors gathered weight.

But on Sunday, December 2, Pope John appeared at his window as usual, to recite the Angelus at noon with the crowd in St. Peter's Square. Pale but cheerful he said: "Good health, which threatened for a moment to absent itself, is now returning, has already returned." He did in fact get over the hemorrhage wonderfully and it did not recur till the onset of the end, the next May. He found treatment tiresome and called it "complicated" but submitted to it as a duty. The word cancer had not been used by his doctors and he was to read it for the first time in the newspapers. But he knew his condition was grave and probably guessed the nature of his disease; after all, his sister Ancilla had died of it, ten years earlier.

On Wednesday, instead of the general audience in St. Peter's, it was announced that the Holy Father would give his blessing from his window. The Council Fathers came hurrying out of St. Peter's to mix with the huge crowd. When the Pope finished the Angelus there was a roar of cheering, bells ringing and horns tooting. Pope John said: "My children, Divine Providence is with us. As you see, from one day to the next there is progress, not going down but in coming up slowly—*piano, piano*." He was touched by their solicitude. Then he looked round and said, "What a spectacle we see before us today—the Church grouped together here in full representation: *ecco*, its Bishops; *ecco*, its priests; *ecco*, its Christian people! A whole family here present, the family of Christ!"

The Council was now discussing the original schema *De Ecclesia* (On the Church). On December 6 the Secretary General announced that by the wish of the Pope *all* the schemata were to be redrafted by mixed commissions and sent out to the Bishops for emendation and suggestion before the second session opened—the date was set for September 8, 1963, our Lady's birthday. A new co-ordinating committee was set up under Cardinal Cicognani. The last general congregation was held on December 7, a Friday. At 11:15 A.M. Pope John walked into St. Peter's by a side door, recited the Angelus with the Fathers, thanked them and blessed them, and then descended from the platform unassisted. Delighted applause demonstrated the feelings of the assembly.

The next day, the Feast of the Immaculate Conception, the first session of the Council was solemnly closed. Again Pope John arrived on foot. He was pale but vigorous, got out his glasses and began to read his closing address in his usual businesslike way. As he went on, he became more and more his old self, emphasizing his points with quick gestures and peering over his spectacles, delighting his audience.

Pope John said he felt a good beginning had been made. "The first session was like a slow and solemn introduction to the great work of the Council—a generous willingness to enter into the heart and substance of our Lord's plan. It was necessary for brothers, gathered together from afar around a common hearth to make each other's closer acquaintance; it was necessary for them to look at each other squarely in order to understand each other's hearts . . . In such a vast gathering, it is understandable that a few days were needed to arrive at agreement on a matter on which, in all charity, there existed with good reason sharply divergent views. But even this has a providential place in the triumph of the truth, for it has shown to all the world the holy liberty that the sons of God enjoy in the Church.

"It was not by chance that the first schema to be considered was on the sacred liturgy, which defines the relationship between man and God . . . And then five more schemata were presented, a fact which alone makes one realize the extent of the work thus far completed. Indeed, it is right to conclude that a good beginning has been made.

"It will then be a question of extending to all departments of the life of the Church, social questions included, whatever the Conciliar Assembly may decide . . ." Everyone must collaborate "in order that the acts of the Fathers be seconded by a joyous and faithful response."

The conflicts in St. Peter's had not shaken Pope John's great optimism. "It will be a new Pentecost indeed, which will cause the Church to renew her interior riches and to extend her maternal care in every sphere of human activity. It will be a new advance of the Kingdom of Christ in the world, an elevated and persuasive reaffirmation of the good news of redemption, a clarion call of God's kingship, of the brotherhood of men in charity, of the peace promised on earth to men of goodwill in accordance with God's good pleasure."

He went on to wish them all well in their own dioceses, to dwell on the silent work necessary before the next, and, as he hoped, final session, with a word of praise for the modern communications which made this so easy.

"In this hour of heartfelt joy, it is as if the heavens are opened above our heads and the splendor of the heavenly court shines out upon us, filling us with superhuman certainty and a supernatural spirit of faith, joy and profound peace. In this light, as we look forward to your return, we salute all of you, Venerable Brothers, 'with a holy kiss,' while at the same time we call down upon you the most abundant blessings of our Lord, of which the apostolic blessing is the pledge and promise."

And so, moved by the sense of the occasion, he gave them his blessing, stepped down from the platform and walked quietly out through a side door of the great basilica.

20   Apostolic Death

Pope John did not really expect to be there for the end of the Council, but he continued to work toward its realization as if he would be. The next few months saw an extraordinarily active program for a man of eighty-one, already attacked by a fatal disease; it culminated at Easter 1963 with the publication of the encyclical *Pacem in Terris*, prepared, with collaborators, during these last months of his life.

The very day after the Council session ended there was a canonization ceremony; special audiences began again; there was the Christmas message to broadcast: *Ut unum sint, ut unum sint!*—that they may be one: the prayer of Christ before his death. On the morning of Christmas Day he went once more to the children in the hospital of Gesù Bambino; on the last day of the year he was present at a Christmas concert given by the boys of the pontifical chapel in the Clementine Hall of the Vatican, for polio victims and crippled children. In January he went out into Rome again, and received many visitors; among them British Prime Minister Harold Macmillan, and British cabinet member Edward Heath, on February 2; six days later, Dr. Leslie Davison, president of the Methodist Conference of Great Britain; on February 25, Roger Schutz, Prior of the Protestant monastic community of Taizé, in France.

In December 1962 negotiations were begun which led to the release of Monsignor Josef Slipyi, Archbishop of Lvov in the Ukraine, after seventeen years in prison. Norman Cousins has told the story in the *Saturday Review* for November 7, 1964. After the solution of the Cuba crisis the negotiations for a test ban on atomic bombs were in progress and Cousins visited Khrushchev to try to smooth out some difficulties. Before he went, he suggested to the Vatican that he might take up the case of the imprisoned Bishops; since Moscow had allowed two Russian Orthodox prelates to attend the Council as observers, official relations were improving. Pope John suggested that Cousins should try to secure Monsignor Slipyi's release from prison.

Curiously enough, Khrushchev had been in the Ukraine for the funeral of Monsignor Slipyi's predecessor, and even admitted that his death might have been "accelerated." He said he did not know if Slipyi were alive or dead and was at first reluctant to go further; there would be headlines in the world press: "Bishop tortured by Reds." Norman Cousins assured him that the Vatican would not make capital out of the Archbishop's past; all that was wanted was to let him live his last years in peace—he was in his seventies. Khrushchev said he would look into the matter. He opened a drawer and took out two letters which he had already written with Christmas greeting to President Kennedy and Pope John. Yet Cousins was quite surprised when, some weeks later, he received the news from the Soviet Ambassador in Washington that Slipyi was to be unconditionally released—and what was to be done with him? Cousins contacted Father Felix Marlion, president of the Pro Deo University in Rome, who was then in the States and he telephoned the Vatican with the news.

Pope John was having his supper, necessarily frugal as he was on a diet, when he was told of the release. He was so delighted that he called for a bottle of wine, so that his entourage could drink the health of Monsignor Slipyi.

To collect the Archbishop was quite a problem, as his health was not good enough for him to fly. In the end Monsignor Willebrands of the Unity Secretariat was sent to fetch him; since he had already been to Moscow his presence would cause no comment. For it was important to preserve secrecy, so as to avoid those headlines. Monsignor Slipyi was met at a small station outside Rome and taken first to the Greek Basilian Fathers at Grottaferrata; afterward he was moved to Rome. Pope John received him on February 10. Photographs of Pope John embracing him appeared in the papers, and even those inevitable headlines BISHOP TORTURED BY REDS, in an American newspaper. The Russian government complained; the Osservatore Romano repudiated such an irresponsible report; equilibrium was maintained. And after seventeen years this Catholic Archbishop of the Byzantine rite was free.

Another extraordinary event of these last months was the award to Pope John of the Balzan Peace Prize, announced on March 1, 1963 and presented on May 10, only ten days before his terminal illness began. Eugen Balzan, "a humble son of the world of workers," as Pope John called him, including himself too in this category, had risen to riches and used them to endow prizes, in the Nobel tradition, for "Peace, Humanity and the Fraternity of Peoples." Signor Gronchi, the honorary president of the awards committee, called on the Pope to tell him. Pope John expressed his happiness at the honor accorded him and renewed his appeal for peace among the nations.

Before he received the prize Lent and Easter, the last of Pope John's life, had come and gone. Incredible as it may seem, he began his Lenten visits once more, going first to the stational church of Santa Sabina, the Dominicans' ancient and beautiful basilica on the Aventine hill. This was on February 27, and in the evening the Pope broadcast a special message for Lent. On March 3 he was in the new parish of the Ascension at the Quarticciolo for a penitential service; on March 10 at another church, in the Laurentino quarter. Mid-March was full of audiences: for the congress of the Food and Agricultural Organization; for American pilgrims at the beatification of Elizabeth Bayley Seton, the first American *beata*: and (which he must have specially enjoyed) for pilgrims from Bergamo for the beatification of Luigi Palazzolo, a Bergamasque priest whose sanctity Pope John remembered hearing of from his parish priest, as a little boy in Sotto il Monte. And his little village was honored when on March 18, 1963, in the Clementine Hall, he blessed the first stone of the John XXIII missionary college built behind the house where he was born.

So it went on, Lenten visits alternating with Council commissions and audiences all through March. On March 29 the Pope instituted the commission for the revision of Canon Law, an essential operation if the Council's measures are to achieve practical and permanent embodiment.

On March 24 Pope John visited the parish church at the

Lido of Ostia, in ancient times the port of Rome; the road there was crowded with people who had come out to see him. On March 31 it was another parish church in the village of San Basilio and he returned by a circuitous route. It is a very human touch that Pope John took care that there should be a seat for his secretary in the special car in which he made these tours. He joked about his days with Radini-Tedeschi, when the secretary (himself) had "to run behind his master's carriage." On Palm Sunday, April 7, there was the blessing of palms in St. Peter's; in the afternoon he went out to the parish church of St. Tarcisius (an early boy martyr, murdered as he carried the Sacrament home) and made "a festive return" through eighteen parishes. Though he loved these informal tours, they must have been tiring.

Two days later, on Tuesday of Holy Week, he signed the encyclical *Pacem in Terris*, dating it to Holy Thursday, April 11, and explained it in a radio message. On that last Holy Thursday of his life Pope John celebrated the Mass of the *Coena Domini* (the Lord's supper) at 5 P.M. in the Sistine Chapel, for the diplomatic corps, with a special address, relevant to the encyclical. In one thing it was without precedent: instead of being addressed to the Bishops and faithful of the Church, it was sent out to all men of goodwill. Peace was an interest common to all and Pope John felt that he must address his words to all.

On Good Friday, again at 5 P.M. he presided at the liturgy in the Vatican basilica. On Easter Day he gave his blessing and greetings to all nations from the balcony overlooking St. Peter's Square. He was very much moved by the great reception his encyclical enjoyed all over the world, as he often said during subsequent general audiences.

Yet it would be a mistake to regard these as weeks of unshadowed triumph, even apart from the trials and fatigue of his illness. There was a section of Italian opinion, conservative and Catholic and quite influential, which deplored Pope John's "opening to the left." This had become more noticeable since the publication of *Mater et Magistra*. All that John XXIII tried to do was to break with that tradition of papal and episcopal direction to Italian Catholics in political matters and the rigidity which had hitherto included all forms of *new approach to Socialism + Communism*

Socialism in the prohibition against joining or voting for Communists. He believed it possible for Catholics and Socialists to work together in Italy. It would be interesting to know more of his personal opinions on the subject, but his very mild exhortations to cooperation with men of goodwill roused a bitter opposition in some quarters. Italian elections were due in May and it was freely said that *Pacem in Terris* gave thousands of votes to the Communists. Visitors to Italy were surprised at the sharpness of the comment. Pope John was very much hurt by it.

Pacem in Terris was quoted because in this encyclical Pope John sponsored a new approach to Communist countries. While the Church could not of course accept the official atheist philosophy of Communism, *Pacem in Terris* suggested that it was possible to find ways of cooperating with the peoples of Communist nations in the common tasks of building up a peaceful and just world society. With his sense of history Pope John pointed out that societies and situations change and that men could learn to live and work together, even when they were in disagreement on the ultimate meaning of life. *Convivenza*, not simply coexistence, was the ideal, as Pope John said so often in his last years. The Pope's meeting with Khrushchev's son-in-law, Aleksei Adzhubei, then editor of *Izvestia*, and his wife, was resented in some circles, whose criticism was quite vocal. It was only a small gesture beside the new policy announced in *Pacem in Terris*, but it was significant of Pope John's approach. In this respect Pope Paul has followed him very closely, willing to go anywhere and meet anyone, risking humiliation and failure, in the cause of peace.

It is not surprising that Pope John's extraordinarily active program and the pictures of his smiling face on his journeys about Rome, deceived people in other parts of the world into thinking he had got over his illness; in spite of rumors its nature was not generally known. To one visitor to Rome just after Easter, the first impression at a general audience in St. Peter's was one of shock: Pope John's extreme pallor instantly suggested that he was a dying man. But still his eyes, deep brown and clear, were alive and alert, looking round with interest as he blessed everyone; his voice, after a slight initial hoarseness, was resonant and firm. He seemed to overcome his fatigue as he talked, making vigorous gestures, so that once he hit the microphone. He was full of Easter joy and hope, telling the thousands of pilgrims of all nations that they must be makers of peace, in their homes, at work, in their countries and in the world.

By the time he received the Balzan Prize, on May 10, his weakness was visible even in press photographs and in spite of his smile. He was presented with his own prize in the Vatican, but the next day he went to the Quirinal to see the other awards made. It was the first time a Pope had visited the Quirinal since it was taken from the Papacy and made the seat of the government of united Italy. On this historic occasion Pope John said: "Peace is a house, a house for everyone. It is the arc which unites earth and heaven, but to rise so high it has to rise on four solid pillars . . ." These pillars are truth, justice, charity and freedom.

Pope John was acting against the advice of his doctors in speaking in public. He could not altogether hide his exhaustion. He even referred to this, saying philosophically: "When the body is afflicted, the soul has to adjust itself."

Privately, he could joke about it. His secretary, Monsignor Capovilla, who was half his age, has recorded that once, overcome by a spell of faintness, he found himself being helped to an armchair by the Pope. "So you want to go before your boss, do you?" Pope John teased him. Another time when he was looking very pale, Monsignor Capovilla asked him how he was feeling. "Like St. Laurence on his gridiron!"

Pope John said his last Mass on May 17. After that he attended his secretary's Mass in the study next door to his bedroom, at 6:30 A.M. and received Holy Communion from him.

On May 20 he was due to receive Stefan Cardinal Wyszynski, Primate of Poland, and three Polish Bishops. Monsignor Capovilla suggested that he receive them in his bedroom but he insisted on descending to his library. "We haven't come to that yet," he said. "In any case, if I were to die during an audience, oh, what a splendid death that would be!" It was his hope to die in harness, to work to the last. So he went downstairs—for the last time, as it proved.

At the end of the interview Cardinal Wyszynski said, "Until September, Holy Father!" Pope John replied: "In September you'll either find me here, or another. You know, in one month they can do it all—the funeral of one Pope, the election of another." He said it with a smile—the smile that for months had deceived people into thinking him less ill than he was.

On the night of May 20 he had a severe hemorrhage. Two days later there was an official announcement of the suspension of general audiences and some, but not much, information was given on the Pope's illness. The next day, May 23, was Ascension Day that year. To the delight of the crowds Pope John appeared again at the window of his room, at noon, to recite with the people the *Regina Coeli*, the Easter antiphon for the Angelus. It was the last time.

He had been given a blood transfusion and seemed better for a few days. By this time the news of his illness and its nature had flown all over the world. The spontaneous reaction of millions of people is still astonishing to remember. They followed the course of his illness day by day, participating at a distance as if they were all members of his family, stricken at the thought of losing him. It was not because he was Pope, but because he was loved. The extent of that love had not been fully realized till his death agony made it manifest.

Cardinal Cicognani, the Secretary of State, brought him the news of all these people in so many countries who were praying for him. Pope John said, "As the whole world is praying, we must get the intention right." There were two alternatives, each with its appropriate intention. "If God wants the sacrifice of the life of the Pope—that it may bring grace in plenty to the Ecumenical Council, to Holy Church, and to mankind which desires peace. If instead it pleases God to prolong this pontifical service—that it may be for the sanctification of the Pope's soul and of those who work and suffer with him to extend the kingdom of our Lord in Christian communities old and new, and in all the world." The official *Acta* quote in Latin some further words of the Pope's, that he was "as a victim on the altar, for the Church, for the Ecumenical Council, and for the preservation of peace."

Some may not be familiar with this idea of a Christian's offering of his life for particular objects. It would be wrong to think of God as one who demanded victims, though there have been forms of piety with a morbid inclination to look at redemption in this way. The true basis of this self-offering is Christ's willing acceptance of death for love of men. In uniting himself to Christ the Christian can transform an apparently negative event, such as pain or death, into a positive and personal action. Instead of merely enduring it he enters it willingly, for the sake of others. The stronger the faith and love of the voluntary victim, the more clearly this mystery of action-in-passion is expressed. Pope John's death at Pentecost was such an action.

On May 29 he was surprisingly better and the next day the hemorrhage stopped. He expressed his gratitude for all the messages of love. "Oh, how grateful I am! I am moved to be the object of such delicate attention, but it leaves me perfectly calm in my habitual simplicity, as I feel more than ever united to the many, many people who are suffering in hospitals or in their homes, and who are afflicted in various ways." He hoped that this interest in him would help people to realize "that in life what matters is always to be found in the message of the Gospel: that is: gentleness, goodness, love." He wanted them all to know of his gratitude, so that they could find, united to him, the motive power for brotherly love of each other.

That night, near midnight, he had another attack so violent that he was not expected to survive for long. At 6:30 A.M. on May 31 he heard Mass and received Holy Communion and was told the end was near. At 10:30 he received Cardinal Cicognani, the Secretary of State, for the last time and then, quoting the psalm "I was glad when they said unto me, let us go into the house of the Lord," he made a last confession and received Extreme Unction and Viaticum. Then he spoke to all present, giving blessings and thanks to them all, mentioning Bergamo and Sotto il Monte especially; he asked pardon of everyone and said he loved them all and wished them all good. The refrain was: *"Ut unum sint! Ut unum sint!"* ("That they may be one.")

Worse in the afternoon, he heard a second Mass, "for the sick," said by his secretary. His mind was clear till about 7:30 P.M. when he lapsed into a coma. Now everyone thought the end had come. But Pope John's constitution was so robust that he revived once more and was able to speak to the members of his family, flown from Milan by Cardinal Montini, and bless them. It was the first of June and the next day was the Sunday of Pentecost, the great feast of the Spirit, which he had loved so much, always choosing that time for his movements toward the renewal he prayed that the Council would bring.

In his revivals of consciousness Pope John was quite himself, speaking to everyone about him quite naturally, talking to his brothers in Bergamasque dialect. "I'm ready to go; my baggage is packed," he said. Once he was able to take a cup of coffee. To Monsignor Taccoli he said, "I've been able to follow my own death step by step, and now I'm going gently towards the end."

Lying in bed next morning Pope John was able to follow the Mass of Pentecost, said by Cardinal Cicognani in the adjoining room. The epistle reminded him of Turkey, because of the mention of places there, in the description of the great crowd who heard the message of Christ's resurrection from the apostles, each in his own language. He joined in with various prayers said for him and was heard to whisper: "I want to be with Christ . . . I want to return to my God."

For him the day was full of pain; only partially alleviated by drugs. His attendants were in tears, but he said: "Don't cry. Pentecost is a day of joy." Late at night, he kept saying to himself, "That they may be one." This was his intention, offering the pain of his death for the unity of mankind.

He was still alive on Whit Monday, June 3. The day was one of alternating periods of lucidity and unconsciousness. But when he was conscious, he was always himself. He thought of all those about him, each for himself, so that afterward they felt he had not forgotten anyone. So, all that bright holiday he was painfully but calmly enduring the conflict between the disease and his body, still so strong even in age, awaiting the mysterious separation of flesh and spirit.

Outside in St. Peter's Square, Luigi Cardinal Traglia, said an evening Mass in the open air for the vast crowd assembled there, all praying and many weeping. As he said the final words of blessing and dismissal: *"Ite, missa est"* . . . ("Go forth, the mass is done,") at ten minutes to eight, Pope John died.

"There was a man sent from God, whose name was John."

Ut Unum Sint

BIBLIOGRAPHY

POPE JOHN'S OWN WORKS

Il Cardinale Cesare Baronio. A. G. Roncalli. Edizione di storia e letteratura. Roma, 1961. Don Giuseppe de Luca's edition, with preface and notes, of Roncalli's lecture published in Bergamo 1907 on the tercentenary of Baronius' death.

Mons. Giacomo Maria Radini-Tedeschi. A. G. Roncalli. Edizione storia e letteratura. Roma, 1963. Third edition, with articles etc., reprinted from *La Vita Diocesana* and notes by Monsignor Loris Capovilla.

La Propagazione della Fede. Pontificia Unione Missionaria del Clero Roma, 1958. Roncalli's missionary articles 1922–55, together with addresses on the subject given as Cardinal Patriarch of Venice; in press at time of his election as Pope.

Souvenirs d'un Nonce. A. G. Roncalli. Edizione storia e letteratura. Roma, 1963. (English edition: *Mission to France* [trs. Dorothy White] McGraw-Hill, New York, 1966). Collection of official speeches, addresses and some letters; in press when Pope John died; detailed chronology of engagements for 1945–53. Italian edition used.

Giovanni XXIII in alcuni scritti di Don Giuseppe de Luca. Casa editrice Morcelliana. Brescia, 1963. Letters between De Luca and Roncalli 1955–58, between De Luca and Capovilla till 1962; edited with notes by Monsignor Loris Capovilla.

Journal of a Soul. John XXIII (trs. Dorothy White). McGraw-Hill, New York, 1965. (Italian edition: *Giornale dell'Anima:* Edizione storia e letteratura. Roma, 1964.) Angelo Roncalli's retreat notes from the age of fourteen to his death, with prayers, spiritual testament, biographical notes, etc. Annotated by Monsignor Loris Capovilla.

OFFICIAL PUBLICATIONS

Acta Apostolicae Sedis. Vatican: 1958–63. Official volumes containing encyclicals (Latin) allocutions, etc., curial documents.

English versions of Pope John's encyclicals. Catholic Truth Society.

The Documents of Vatican II. ed. Abbott & Gallagher (USA) Guild Press, New York, 1966. Texts of all decrees with introductions by Catholic experts and comments by Christians of other communions.

BOOKS ON POPE JOHN

The Heart and Mind of John XXIII. Loris Capovilla (trs. Patrick Riley). Hawthorn Books Inc., New York, 1964. (Italian edition: *Giovanni XXIII.* Libreria editrice Vaticana, 1963). Seven talks on Pope John by his secretary with detailed chronology of his life. Quotations from English version.

Pope John and his Revolution. E. E. Y. Hales. Doubleday & Company, Inc., Garden City, N.Y., 1965. Excellent study by historian of nineteenth century papacy of Pope John's character and policies, drawn mainly from official documents.

John, The Transitional Pope. Ernesto Balducci (trs. Dorothy White). McGraw-Hill, New York, 1965. (Italian edition: *Papa Giovanni.* Vallecchi editors, Florence, 1964.) Study of Pope John by liberal Italian priest, with extracts from speeches and writings.

John XXIII. Leone Algisi (trs. Peter Ryde). Newman Press, Westminster, Maryland, 1963. (Italian edition: Marietti editori. French edition, from which English is taken: P. Lethielleux, Paris.) Facts checked and material supplied by Pope John himself, because the inaccuracy of popular *Lives* annoyed him; but he found the style of this too flattering. Written soon after the election, a chapter added later: pre-conciliar. Author was once priest in Bergamo seminary.

John XXIII, Pope of the Council. Zsolt Aradi with Michael Derrick and Douglas Woodruff. Burns, Oates. London, 1961. One of the better popular accounts, written soon after election with later but pre-conciliar chapter by Derrick, preface by Woodruff. Contains newspaper extracts, etc. Some inaccuracies.

Portrait de Jean XXIII. Louis Chaigne. Mame. Paris, 1964. Short popular life in French, completed just after Pope John's death.

Papa Giovanni, nei suoi primi passi a Sotto il Monte. Davide Cugini. Istituto Italiano d'arte grafiche. Bergamo, 1965. Notes and anecdotes carefully collected from surviving contemporaries and relatives, with short extracts from letters, of Roncalli's childhood and his interest in his native village, with a few stories of his years in Venice, compiled by lawyer from Bergamo who knew him personally. Cugini was a boy at the college at Celana when Roncalli was secretary to the bishop.

Wit and Wisdom of Good Pope John. Henri Fesquet (trs. Salvator Attanasio). Kenedy, New York, 1964. (French edition: *Les fioretti du bon Pape Jean*: Librairie Arthème Fayard, 1964). Best collection of sayings and anecdotes by top journalist (of *Le Monde*) with foreword by the Abbot of Downside.

GENERAL (Selection only: works in English except where none available.)

POPES

Leo XIII. E. Soderini (trs. Barbara Carter) 2 vols. Burns, Oates, London, 1934.

Benedict XV. Walter H. Peters, Bruce, Milwaukee, 1959.

Pope Pius XI. Philip Hughes, Sheed and Ward, New York, 1937.

Pope Pius XI. R. Fontenelle, (trs. M. Fowler), Sherwood, Cleveland, 1939.

Pius XII. Oscar Halecki, and James F. Murray, Jr., Farrar, New York, 1954.

MODERNISM

Le Modernisme dans l'Eglise. Jean Rivière, Paris, 1929.

Histoire du Dogme et Critique dans la crise Moderniste. Emile Poulat.

Blondel-Vallensin Correspondance. 2 vols.

Religious History of Modern France. Adrien Dansette (trs. from French edition of 1948). 2 vols., (trs. John Dingle), Herder, New York, 1961.

Maurice Blondel. Ed. Alexander Dru and Dom Illtyd Trethowan, London. (Contains introductions on historical situation and philosophical problems of Modernism.)

Modernism and the Present Position of the Church. Alexander Dru, (*Downside Review:* April 1964)

From the *Action Française* to the Second Vatican Council. Alexander Dru, (*Downside Review:* July 1963)

ITALY: CHURCH AND STATE

Church and State in Fascist Italy. D. A. Binchy, Cambridge University Press, London, 1941.

Italy and the New World Order. Luigi Sturzo, (trs. Barbara Carter), MacDonald and Co., London, 1943.

Christian Democracy in Western Europe 1820–1953. Michael Fogarty, Notre Dame Press, Notre Dame, Indiana, 1957.

Christian Democracy in Italy 1860–1960. R. Webster, Hollis and Carter, London, 1961.

A Short History of Italy. H. Hearder and D. Waley, Cambridge University Press, London, 1963.

Italy. Gerardo Zampaglione, Praeger, New York, 1956.

BULGARIA, TURKEY, GREECE

History of Bulgaria 1393–1885. Mercia MacDermott, Allen and Unwin, London, 1962.

The Emergence of Modern Turkey. Bernard Lewis, Cambridge University Press, London, 1961.

A Short History of Modern Greece 1821–1936. E. S. Forster, (3rd. ed., revised and extended by D. Dakin), Methuen, London, 1958.

Memoirs. Franz von Papen (trs. Brian O'Connell), Deutsch, London, 1952.

FRANCE: POSTWAR CHURCH

Destin du Catholicisme Français 1926–1956. Adrien Dansette, Paris, 1957.

The Church and Industrial Society. Gregor Siefer (trs. Isabel and Florence McHugh), with detailed bibliography, French, German, and English. Darton, Longman and Todd, London, 1964. (German edition: 1960).

France, Pagan? (*Le France, pays de mission?*) H. Godin and Y. Daniel (trs. M. Ward), Sheed and Ward, London, 1949. (French ed.: 1943).

Revolution in a City Parish (*Paroisse, communauté missionaire*). Chéry and Michonneau, Newman Press, Westminster, Maryland, 1949. (French edition: 1946).

Mission to the Poorest. (*En mission proletarienne*). Jacques Lowe, Sheed and Ward, London, 1950. (French edition: 1946).

Priest-workman in Germany. (*Journal d'un Prêtre-ouvrier en Allemagne*). Henri Perrin (tr. Rosemary Sheed), Sheed and Ward, London, 1947. (French edition: 1945).

Priest and Worker—Autobiography of Henri Perrin. (*Itineraire de Henri Perrin, prêtre-ouvrier, 1914–1954*). Holt, Rinehart & Winston, New York, 1964. (French edition: 1958).

Dom Lambert Beauduin, un homme d'Eglise. Louis Bouyer, Paris, 1964.

Quai d'Orsay 1945–1951. Jacques Dumaine, London, 1958.

VATICAN COUNCIL, ETC.

Vatican Assignment. Sir Alec Randall, Heinemann, London, 1956.

The Vatican from Within. Corrado Pallenburg, Harrap, London, 1961.

The Church on the Move. W. A. Purdy, Hollis and Carter, London, 1966.

Letters from Vatican City. Xavier Rynne, Farrar, New York, 1963.

Report from Rome. Yves Congar, Chapman, London, 1963.

Pope John and His Council. C. Falconi (trs. Muriel Grindrod), Ryerson Press, London, 1964.

The Council, Reform and Reunion. Hans Küng (trs. Cecily Hastings), Sheed and Ward, New York, 1961.

The Living Church. Hans Küng (trs. Cecily Hastings and N. Smith), Sheed and Ward, London, 1963.

Image Books

... MAKING THE WORLD'S FINEST CATHOLIC LITERATURE AVAILABLE TO ALL

I 6

Image Books

... MAKING THE WORLD'S FINEST CATHOLIC LITERATURE AVAILABLE TO ALL

ON THE TRUTH OF THE CATHOLIC FAITH
Summa Contra Gentiles Book II: Creation. Newly translated, with an Introduction and notes by James F. Anderson
D27—95¢

ON THE TRUTH OF THE CATHOLIC FAITH
Summa Contra Gentiles Book III: Providence. Newly translated, with an Introduction and notes by Vernon J. Bourke
D28a Book III, Part 1—95¢
D28b Book III, Part 2—95¢

ON THE TRUTH OF THE CATHOLIC FAITH
Summa Contra Gentiles Book IV: Salvation. Newly translated, with an Introduction and notes, by Charles J. O'Neil
D29—95¢

THE WORLD'S FIRST LOVE
By Fulton J. Sheen D30—85¢

THE SIGN OF JONAS
By Thomas Merton D31—95¢

PARENTS, CHILDREN AND THE FACTS OF LIFE *By Henry V. Sattler, C.SS.R.* D32—75¢

LIGHT ON THE MOUNTAIN:
The Story of La Salette By John S. Kennedy D33—75¢

EDMUND CAMPION
By Evelyn Waugh D34—75¢

HUMBLE POWERS
By Paul Horgan D35—75¢

SAINT THOMAS AQUINAS
By G. K. Chesterton D36—75¢

APOLOGIA PRO VITA SUA
By John Henry Cardinal Newman Introduction by Philip Hughes D37—95¢

A HANDBOOK OF THE CATHOLIC FAITH
By Dr. N. G. M. Van Doornik, Rev. S. Jelsma, Rev. A. Van De Lisdonk. Ed. Rev. John Greenwood D38—$1.45

THE NEW TESTAMENT
Official Catholic edition
D39—95¢

MARIA CHAPDELAINE
By Louis Hémon D40—65¢

SAINT AMONG THE HURONS
By Francis X. Talbot, S.J.
D41—95¢

THE PATH TO ROME
By Hilaire Belloc D42—85¢

SORROW BUILT A BRIDGE
By Katherine Burton D43—85¢

THE WISE MAN FROM THE WEST
By Vincent Cronin D44—85¢

EXISTENCE AND THE EXISTENT
By Jacques Maritain D45—75¢

THE STORY OF THE TRAPP FAMILY SINGERS
By Maria Augusta Trapp
D46—95¢

THE WORLD, THE FLESH AND FATHER SMITH
By Bruce Marshall D47—75¢

THE CHRIST OF CATHOLICISM
By Dom Aelred Graham
D48—95¢

SAINT FRANCIS XAVIER
By James Brodrick, S.J.
D49—95¢

SAINT FRANCIS OF ASSISI
By G. K. Chesterton D50—75¢

I 11

Ludovic Kennedy is the author of the bestseller, *Pursuit: The Sinking of the Bismarck*, *The Trial of Stephen Ward*, *Menace*, and two books on famous cases of miscarried justice: *10 Rillington Place* and *A Presumption of Innocence*. These were about Timothy Evans and Patrick Meehan respectively, both of whom were subsequently granted free pardons. The latter book, also published by Granada Paperbacks, tells the full story of the Ayr murder. In that brilliant work Ludovic Kennedy reconstructed the amazing case of this Glasgow safe-blower sentenced to life imprisonment for a murder he did not commit. Ludovic Kennedy's astonishing account was instrumental in preparing the ground for Meehan's eventual release.

Ludovic Kennedy is also extremely well known for his numerous television appearances in current affairs programmes and, more recently, 'A Life With Crime', 'Change of Direction' and 'The Obituary of Lord Mountbatten'.

What the press said about
A Presumption of Innocence
The Full Story of the Ayr Murder

'Written with much narrative skill and barely concealed passion'
C. P. Snow, *Financial Times*

'The truth about the affair is now absolutely certain . . . and it is set out by Mr Kennedy with clarity and confidence'
New Statesman

'It is a very convincing demonstration of the ease with which a presumption of guilt, supported by a few fragments of circumstantial evidence and a coincidence or two, can entirely displace the supposed safeguard of the much acclaimed presumption of innocence, in determining the outcome of a criminal trial'
New Society

Edited by
Ludovic Kennedy

Wicked Beyond Belief
The Luton Murder Case

Research by John Harrison

A PANTHER BOOK

GRANADA
London Toronto Sydney New York

Published by Granada Publishing Limited in 1980

ISBN 0 586 05172 4

A Granada Paperback Original
Introduction, compilation and editorial matter
Copyright © Ludovic Kennedy 1980
Copyright © Patrick Devlin 1980
Copyright © Bryan Magee 1980
Copyright © William John Thomson 1980
Copyright © Tom Sargant 1980
Copyright © Mrs Gareth Peirce 1980
Copyright © Dr Oonagh Macdonald 1980
Copyright © Wendy Mantle 1980

Granada Publishing Limited
Frogmore, St Albans, Herts AL2 2NF
and
3 Upper James Street, London W1R 4BP
866 United Nations Plaza, New York, NY 10017, USA
117 York Street, Sydney, NSW 2000, Australia
100 Skyway Avenue, Rexdale, Ontario, M9W 3A6, Canada
PO Box 84165, Greenside, 2034 Johannesburg, South Africa
61 Beach Road, Auckland, New Zealand

Set, printed and bound in Great Britain by
Cox & Wyman Ltd, Reading
Set in Intertype Times

Granada ®
Granada Publishing ®

CONTENTS

ILLUSTRATIONS

Ex-commander Kenneth Drury
Morris Lerman
Alfred Mathews
Patrick Colin Murphy
Michael Graham McMahon
David Cooper
The Hon Mr Justice Cusack
Lord Chief Justice Widgery
Rt Hon Lord Justice Lawton
Rt Hon Lord Justice Roskill

The photographs of Cooper and McMahon are both more than eleven years old and bear little resemblance to them as they are to-day. At my suggestion, and for use in this book, they put in requests to the Home Office for head and shoulders pictures to be taken, such as are permitted for prisoners whose near relations have been posted abroad. Astonishingly the Home Office informed me that they were unable to meet these simple requests.

Introduction

Early in 1979 my literary agent Michael Sissons sent me a
hand-written manuscript of some 100,000 words which had
recently come his way. It was an unusual manuscript in
that it had been written in prison by David Cooper, who
had been sentenced to life imprisonment in 1970 for the
Luton post office murder. At this time I knew no more
about the Luton murder than what I had read in articles
and seen on television programmes over the years.

On making further inquiries I found that Cooper's co-
accused, Michael McMahon, who was also serving life
imprisonment for the same offence, had also written a
100,000-word manuscript, and this was sent to me by his
solicitors. Although McMahon's manuscript was better
organized than Cooper's, neither was quite publishable as
it stood. But was the case for their innocence, which was
the theme of both books, sufficiently strong for extracts to
be used within the framework of a composite book, which
would seek to tell the whole story?

Having read both books twice and acquainted myself
with the background to the case, I had no doubts whatever
that what Cooper and McMahon had to say should be
presented to the public as soon as possible. I had written
earlier books about miscarriages of justice, and had not
intended to write any more; but if ever there was a case that
cried out for a further hearing and further action, this was it.
In all the cases of alleged injustice that have come my way
during the past twenty years, I have never read one that
was so riddled with corruption and incompetence from end
to end, which should never have been brought in the first
place, and which should have been rectified years ago.

Others more cautious than I have said forcefully that,
while it cannot be proved that Cooper and McMahon are
innocent, there must now be the gravest doubts, in the light

of the evidence that has emerged since their trial, about their guilt. I have no hesitation in going beyond that and saying that I am as certain as I am of tomorrow's sunrise that both Cooper and McMahon are wholly innocent, and that on the day of the murder were nowhere near Luton at all. They, and their fellow-accused, Patrick Murphy, whose conviction was later quashed, were, in criminal parlance, 'fitted-up'.

Reasons for this belief will be found in the pages that follow. They are concerned in part with the law, but they also go beyond the law. It has been my experience that men who are truly guilty of crimes for which they have been convicted, may continue to protest their innocence for a few weeks or even months after sentence. But it is a very rare thing for a guilty man to go on protesting his innocence, go on badgering authority with chapter and verse to back him up, year after year after year. (This is not only my opinion, but that of Tom Sargant, the Secretary of JUSTICE – the organization for legal reform – who has probably had more experience of miscarriages of justice than anyone else in Britain.) And it must be rarer still – indeed the odds must be astronomical – that two men like Cooper and McMahon, who both left school at fifteen and have never written a word for publication before, should *if guilty* set themselves separately the daunting task of writing book-length manuscripts in order to prove their innocence.

Moreover it is not the continued protests of innocence in themselves which are persuasive but the nature and quality of those protests. If McMahon and Cooper were guilty, if they were present at the killing of the Luton postmaster, it would in my view have been impossible for them to sustain over a period of eleven years attitudes, views, expressions of opinion, that are wholly inconsistent with guilt. I defy anyone to read their two manuscripts – even the extracts from them that appear in these pages – and say that both these men are brilliant purveyors of fiction, that the experiences they relate and the views they express are wholly false. Read their separate accounts on pages 1–2 of their thoughts when meeting each other in Brixton prison for the first time since before their arrest. Could these accounts have been written by guilty men? If so, they would need to be tale-spinners of genius, and certainly neither is that. There are many such examples throughout the book, which the reader will note for himself. From start to finish (and it is not finished yet) the attitudes of both men have been consistent.

It may be asked, indeed in certain quarters it *will* be asked (it is *always* asked) why one should bother about the fate of two petty thieves who were a thorough nuisance to society when they were at large, and are probably best out of the way anyway. There are two answers to that. The first is that, as is often the case with young long-term prisoners, and as is evidenced by their writings, both men have matured greatly during their time in prison: the Cooper and McMahon who are still behind bars today are not the Cooper and McMahon of 1969.

And the second answer is that once we start *selecting* those whom we think worthy or unworthy of justice, we shall all in the end be diminished; for even if justice is sometimes rough in practice, it must in theory be indivisible. For all their ten years of wrongful imprisonment, it is not for Cooper and McMahon alone that this book has been assembled; but for all those who, if justice is allowed to go by default, may come to suffer in their time.

This is the third book I have written about a major miscarriage of justice – the other two* concerned Timothy John Evans and Patrick Connolly Meehan, both of whom were subsequently granted free pardons. In all three cases justice miscarried because of the over-zealousness of CID officers who had persuaded themselves into believing (with greater or lesser justification) that the suspects they had apprehended were guilty, and who, by deliberate omission and/ or fabrication of evidence, took steps to ensure that their beliefs would be confirmed by the jury.

What can be done to prevent this sort of malpractice

---

* *Ten Rillington Place* and *A Presumption of Innocence.*

from occurring again? Fabrication of evidence (as in the Meehan case) is hard to prevent, for it depends entirely on the integrity, or lack of it, of the investigating officers. But omission of evidence is easier to remedy. At present the prosecution are only obliged to give to the defence the names and addresses of witnesses they do not intend to call. Why should it not also be obligatory for the prosecution to supply the defence with copies of all statements these witnesses have made, *whether favourable to the prosecution or not*?

This is a reform that JUSTICE, so far without success, has been advocating for years. In the case of Timothy Evans, statements by three workmen highly favourable to him (and three further contradictory statements which the CID browbeat them into making) never came to the notice of the defence at all. In the Luton case similar statements favourable to the accused by two witnesses named Seal and McNair were also unknown to the defence. Had the statements in both cases been made available, it is possible that one innocent man would not have been hanged, and two others would not have already spent more than ten years of their lives in prison. If such a reform were brought in, a *quid pro quo* might be repeal of the accused's traditional, and now outmoded, right to silence.*

I am grateful to many people who have helped me in the preparation of this book. Firstly, to the present Lobby Correspondent of the *Daily Mail*, John Harrison, who at one time spent more than three months investigating the Luton case, and very generously put all his notes and back-

---

* A more radical reform, which many lawyers think long overdue, would be the introduction of some independent authority, such as the *juge d'instruction* in France, to act as a buffer between the police and the accused. It is extraordinary that alone among civilized countries, England maintains a system where the police are both investigators and prosecutors of the same cause; and thus, to justify their detective work, have a very real interest in seeing the accused convicted. Opponents of such a reform say the present system is satisfactory. This book, and the others referred to above, show that it isn't.

ground material at my disposal, as well as shortening my task in supplying me with names, addresses and telephone numbers, and in providing me with several of the illustrations.

Secondly, for the immense help given to me by the solicitors of the two prisoners, Wendy Mantle of Bindman and Partners for McMahon, and Gareth Peirce of Benedict Birnberg, for Cooper. Both Mrs Mantle and Mrs Peirce have been representing the two men now for several years, for most of the time without fee or likelihood of any, so great is their belief in their innocence. Their own views on the case will be found in Appendix II together with those of Dr Oonagh Macdonald, MP, and Tom Sargant of JUSTICE, who have also both devoted considerable time and effort to the case. Mr Sargant's papers and advice have been of great assistance.

Lastly, my most grateful thanks to a distinguished former judge, Lord Devlin, and an eminent Parliamentarian, Bryan Magee, for their own original and valuable contributions.

Ludovic Kennedy
August 1979

Foreword

On 10 September 1969 the sub-postmaster of Luton Post Office was murdered by a gang of robbers. Two men, said to have been members of the gang, have now been in prison for ten years. They are the first men since criminal appeals were instituted in 1907 to be held in prison without a new trial after it had been discovered that the jury which convicted them had not heard all the evidence which obviously should have affected the verdict. They may indeed be the first men in the long history of trial by jury to be so held; if there were any such cases before 1907, they have not been publicized. Cooper and McMahon are in prison today because in 1976 three judges, who had not heard their evidence, heard and believed the evidence of their accuser.

It was this and other oddities in the appeals which followed the trial – for unprecedentedly the case has been five times before the Court of Appeal, three times at the behest of the Home Secretary – which drew my attention to the case. What interests me about this book is that it is not simply the story of the crime from the viewpoint of the accused. It examines the way in which the police conduct an inquiry into crime and present the material for the prosecution. In so doing it highlights the power, far greater than under any other comparable system, of the officer in charge; a corrupt officer has a far greater potential for injustice than a corrupt prosecutor or a corrupt judge. The book shows what undoubtedly could be thought to have happened when the officer is not above suspicion of malpractice; whether in fact it did happen the reader must judge for himself – unless the Home Office agrees to hold an inquiry. Finally, the book follows the creaking and cumbersome process of our criminal appeal.

Four men were originally charged with the murder; they were Mathews, Murphy, Cooper and McMahon. Mathews was the first to be arrested. In his statement to the police, while eventually admitting his presence at Luton at the time of the crime, he denied any part in the robbery. He incriminated the other three and in due course became the chief witness in the prosecution against them. These three denied that they were in Luton; their case was that Mathews in incriminating them was lying so as to shield the true criminals and conceal the part that he had himself played in the murder. No circumstantial evidence was produced to connect any of the three with the crime. The only other evidence of any sort against them was not weighty; it has been variously assessed as somewhere between negligible and slight. At the trial the only substantial question was whether Mathews's word was to be taken.

Mathews had led a life of crime. So had the other three, though none of the four had any record of violence. The Crown had to accept that Mathews was the sort of person who would lie whenever he found it convenient to do so. The Crown accepted also that a great deal of the evidence he gave at the trial was not merely untrue but incredible. But the Crown insisted that in his incrimination of the three he was telling the truth. The three had only family alibis to support their denials. The jury believed Mathews and consequently the three were convicted. They were sentenced to life imprisonment with a recommendation that they should not be allowed out on licence until after at least twenty years. At the time of the crime they were young men in their twenties.

After the convictions the families of the three men sought to strengthen their alibis. There has been produced a mass of new evidence. In 1973, in the Second Appeal, Murphy presented a Mr Edwards, a witness of good character, whom the Court found to be honest and impressive and who testified that at the material time Murphy was in London, where he lived, and not in Luton. Consequently Murphy's conviction was quashed. The other two have not been similarly blessed. The appellate process came to the end of the road with an adverse decision from the Fifth Court on 26 July 1976. The Home Secretary has wearied of well doing. Cooper and McMahon, however, will not give in. They have convinced enough people of their innocence to make this, their last appeal to the public.

Such an appeal is open to every man in a free country. But in my opinion it is likely to be a futile exercise unless he can show some irregularity in the process that convicted him. This is not an idea that will please those who believe that justice can be perceived in the light of nature and that forms and processes only hamper the discernment of it. But it is an idea that is necessary to society. The law settles the ways in which guilt is to be found and declared and, if they are not observed, there is anarchy. There cannot be a conviction by popular acclamation; neither can there be an acquittal: there must be due process. But where the process is not followed judges and juries lose the power of office. They join the men in the street whose opinions are open to debate.

If I thought that due process had been observed in this case, I should not be writing this foreword and commending this book to the public. In a lecture which I gave at All Souls College at Oxford on 2 May 1978 I reached the conclusion that the processes in the Third and Fourth Courts of Appeal in this case were seriously flawed. Since I have held high judicial office, I have had to consider carefully whether I ought to go any further. There is a sound convention, which applies in all walks of life and should apply especially in the judiciary, that the retired should not set up as public fault-finders. This has never been taken to ban discussion of trends in the law with those who are professionally and academically interested. Such discussion is indeed highy desirable and would be valueless if it included no criticism.

But it is quite a different matter to enter into a controversy which is likely to follow an appeal to the public against the decision of the Courts. The temptation to refrain would be irresistible were it not tempered by the conviction that in this case a failure of justice has gone unperceived with catastrophic consequences to two young men. I may wish, as selfishly I do, that I had never taken this particular path or met with this situation; but meeting with it, I cannot cross to the other side of the road. If there are any whom I have thereby offended, I express my regret.

While I started out with an interest only in the development of the law and in particular with what seemed to me a judicial encroachment upon the province of the jury, I have by now formed an opinion about the merits of the case which it would be pointless to conceal. All men are innocent in the eyes of the law until they are proved guilty by convincing evidence. The evidence of guilt in this case seems to me to fall short by a very large margin indeed of what could reasonably be called convincing. I think that if the natural and regular appellate process had been followed, Cooper and McMahon would inevitably have been acquitted at the same time as Murphy.

This brings me to the end of what is appropriate to a Foreword. But I think it would be unsatisfactory if I did not set out as shortly and as untechnically as I can, what I consider to be the irregularities in the appellate process. These cannot easily be described to a person who is unfamiliar with the course of events. So I invite the reader to turn to the main narrative and, when he has read it, to come back to me if he is so inclined.

Devlin
August 1979

Chapter One

On the afternoon of 10 September 1969, a warm, sunny day with the temperature in the mid-sixties,[1] a fifty-three-year-old villain of the deepest dye by the name of Alfred Mathews set off from the east of London with three other villains to rob a post office at Luton, Bedfordshire, 40 miles away. Mathews, who also went by the name of Elliott, was a slimly-built man, with sharp, foxy features, hollow cheeks and thinning grey hair. By trade he was a builder; but he had had convictions for stealing, housebreaking, assault and using explosives, going back to before World War II, and had spent almost as much of his life inside prison as out of it. He had robbed a post office before; and he had the reputation in the underworld of being a good getaway driver.[2]

There is evidence that the four men were seen to leave Mathews's flat at 4 Clarion House, Roman Road, E.3, at about 3.30 p.m., by his neighbour and distant relative, Ruth Brooks:

I was standing in the entrance-hall outside my street door, and I saw three men . . . and Mr Mathews* coming down the stairs and approach the exit. They went through the swing doors to the street, and I saw Mathews was carrying a brown hold-all. Of the three men with Mathews I would describe two in their early thirties; one was tall with dark hair with long sideburns, one was short, very thick-set and fair hair; the other man was possibly in his forties, short and tubby, dark hair growing at the sides.

All four crossed the road to Vivian Road. Mathews and the fat man walked to Mathews's Vauxhall car. I saw him put the hold-all in the boot of his car, then him and the fat man got into the Vauxhall, the tall dark man got into a green van, and the short, thick-set fair-haired man got into a red sports car, and all three motors drove away.[3]

Inside the brown hold-all was a sawn-off Italian-made shotgun. This had originally belonged to a criminal and police informer named Michael Good, but after his arrest for armed robbery, his wife had taken it round to her brother, another criminal, named Terence Langston.

At first Langston denied any knowledge of the gun, but later he admitted Mathews and another man had collected the gun from him.[4]

The idea of robbing the post office at Luton would seem to have been in Mathews's mind for some time. There is evidence that during the previous year he had approached two hardened criminals named Terence Leonard and Frederick Stephens and invited them to join him in the venture. The three had met in a pub in Roman Road called the Rising Sun, and later journeyed to Luton together to inspect the post office in High Town Road. Both Leonard and Stephens had been under the impression that it was a question of breaking into the post office and robbing the safe which, Mathews said, contained between £12,000 and £19,000. But now, sitting in the car and discussing the details, Mathews revealed his intention of holding up the postmaster with a gun, and then tying him up. On hearing this, said Stephens, he had said to Mathews, 'Leave me out. I don't know what Terry wants to do.' Terry, who didn't fancy the use of guns either, said he wanted to be left out too. All the way back to London, said Stephens, Mathews tried to persuade them to change their minds, 'but we wouldn't wear it, we wouldn't have it, and that was it'. The following year, Stephens met Mathews in prison when both were on remand, and asked him how the Luton job had gone. According to Stephens, Mathews said, 'Nothing's happened about it yet, but I'm still looking for another film.'[5]

Now Mathews was on his way at last, bowling along the M1 motorway in his Vauxhall, index number 5075 MV, together with the green van which had been stolen the day before and had been fitted up with false number plates, and the red sports car. On arrival at Luton between 5.15 and 5.30 p.m. the red sports car and the Vauxhall parked in the station car park. The car which the Vauxhall parked alongside was occupied by a Mr Kenneth Isaac, a sales representative of a confectionery firm, who was writing out orders to catch the evening post. Mr Isaac noticed the Vauxhall, because when the driver got out, the door of the Vauxhall touched the side of Mr Isaac's car. He observed the driver to be 'in his late forties or early fifties with greying hair', which was an accurate description of Mathews. The passenger he described as wearing 'a darkish blue overall or mackintosh type of thing'.[6]

One of the gang, possibly Mathews, now removed the hold-all from the boot of the Vauxhall and put it in the back of the green van. He and his passenger and the two men from the red sports car then entered the van, and with Mathews almost certainly at the wheel they drove to Barclays Bank car park in Welbeck Road, a quarter of a mile away. It was here that Mr Reginald Stevens, the postmaster of the High Town Road post office, some two hundred yards away, parked his car on arrival each morning, and drove away in it each evening after he had shut up shop at 6 p.m.

Mathews and his accomplices knew that Mr Stevens's routine was as regular as clockwork, and this warm late summer evening was no exception. They observed Mr Stevens locking up the post office, buying an evening paper at the corner newsagent's and, at about six minutes past six, approaching his blue Sunbeam Rapier car. The three younger members of the gang, one of them carrying the concealed shotgun, waited until he had climbed into the driving seat of his car, and then closed in on him. They intended to persuade him to enter the green van and there hand over the post-office keys. Later, presumably having collected their loot, they would dump Mr Stevens in the van somewhere before returning to London in Mathews's Vauxhall and the red sports car.

Exactly what happened next, whether there was resistance by Mr Stevens, or panic by the man holding the gun, is not known. What is known is that the shotgun went off at point-blank range, the pellets boring a large hole in Mr Stevens's abdomen, killing him instantly and splattering his murderer with blood.

The noise was heard by two people, Mrs Margaret Crawley and Mrs Peggy Calvert, who were chatting over a garden fence in nearby Brunswick Street, some sixty-five yards away. Mrs Crawley told the police later that evening:

> We had been there about five minutes when I heard a bang – like a tyre exploding. I looked towards Welbeck Road and saw somebody run from a blue car to get in a green van in the Barclays Bank car park. The van was already moving towards High Town Road, and I saw the man jump in the back . . .
> The man I saw running seemed lean, perhaps in his late teens, dark-haired. He appeared to be in dirty working-clothes, and I don't think he had a jacket. I wouldn't recognize him again.

This assertion by Mrs Crawley, made within an hour or two of the crime, that she wouldn't recognize the man she saw again, is interesting in the light of what subsequently transpired.[7]

Two other people observed the van on its journey back from Barclays Bank car park to the station car park. Mr John McNair, a motor dealer, told the police later that evening that he was driving up Welbeck Road towards its junction with High Town Road when he saw the green van coming out of Barclays Bank car park, not by the normal exit but across the pavement. He saw two men inside the van and a third clinging on to it in the doorway on the driver's side. The van drew in behind him, and when they reached High Town Road and Mr McNair had to stop because of passing traffic, his attention was again drawn to the van by the driver revving its engine – an understandable reaction of someone wanting to get away as fast as possible from the scene of his crime. When the road was clear, Mr McNair turned right into High Town Road, and he saw the van turn left.[8]

Mr McNair had a good view of both the driver and the man clinging to the side. He described the driver as 'of slim build, thin faced and wearing a light-coloured trilby-type hat', and a few days later enlarged on this by calling him 'a slim-featured man, English looking and with a tired-looking face and very pale complexion'.[9]

The man clinging to the side of the van he described as 'dressed in a dark blue three-quarter-length raincoat which was of a shiny type of material', and in his second statement that 'his clothing was so blue that it stood out'. This tallied with the description by Mr Isaac of the passenger in Mathews's car – 'what sticks in my mind is a blue garment'.[10]

When the van turned left into High Town Road, it mounted the pavement briefly, then nearly collided with a car being driven in the opposite direction by a man named Edward Seal. Mr Seal had only a glimpse of the driver of the van as he passed by and shouted at him, but described him as 'between forty and forty-five years, wearing a brown and green check cap and a brown jacket, had a weather-beaten complexion, thin face tapering towards his chin, clean shaven, dark-coloured hair'. In a later statement Mr Seal said that the driver's hair wasn't long, and he was not wearing sideboards.[11] Apart from the discrepancy between the trilby hat and the check cap, and Mathews having grey not dark hair, this description tallies in part with what Mr McNair saw, and what in fact Mathews looked like.

The van reached the station car park without further mishap. Its arrival was witnessed by a Mr Herbert Andrews, a clerk in a London shipping company, who had just arrived back at Luton after his day's work. He was walking down the station approaches beside the car park when he observed the van drive over the footpath and come abruptly to a halt.[12]

Mr Andrews saw four men get out. The first was in his mid-twenties and wearing a navy-blue boiler suit. He was carrying a brown briefcase which he threw over the fence on to the grassy railway embankment, saying to one of his accomplices, 'Well, that's that'. The second man was aged about thirty, neatly dressed and with fair hair, the third man Mr Andrews was unable to describe, and the fourth man was clearly Mathews – 'in his late forties, and obviously the eldest of the four, 5 feet 9 or 10, tall, well built, grey or greying hair in a straight swept-back style . . . either dark-jowled or unshaven'. He thought he would be able to recognize him if he saw him again.[13]

Mr Andrews observed Mathews and the man in the blue clothing get into the Vauxhall, and Mr Isaac, who was still busy with his paperwork, observed them too: they were the same two he had seen arriving there three-quarters of an hour before. The other two men, said Mr Andrews, got into the red sports car, which he thought carried a Mercedes badge on the boot. Both cars then drove away.[14]

Because his suspicions had been aroused by the men's behaviour, Mr Andrews decided to take a note of the registration numbers of the Vauxhall and the red sports car. He wrote down on his evening paper '5075 MW' as the number of the Vauxhall (the actual number was '5075 MV'), and although he was unable to read the sports car's full number, he thought it had an 'E' registration letter, and among its numbers were either '51' or '15'.[15]

When Mathews arrived back at Roman Road that night there is some evidence that he told his wife, Florence, the full story of what had happened, and that the shooting of the postmaster had been an accident.[16] What is certain is that he took the Vauxhall to Ottaway Street, E.5, some distance away, and, having wiped it clean of fingerprints, abandoned it. He then told his wife to fill in what he called a change of ownership card for the Vauxhall, give an invented name and address of the new 'owner' (S. Kendall, 117 Evening Road, Stoke Newington), backdate the change of ownership to the day before the murder, and send off the card to the local authority.[17] But as the Vauxhall was

24

actually the property of his brother Reg, he made his way to Reg's house in Dagenham, told him he had sold the car and gave him £37, being the price he claimed to have been paid – £55 – less tax and insurance.[18]

After this Mathews cleared out, first to the house of a friend, then to Eastbourne with his wife, and later to the house of his other brother, Albert, in Ilford, where he went to ground.[19]

Chapter Two

The Luton crime was the latest in a series of post-office robberies that had taken place during the past two years — there had been one at Newington Green Road on 20 May, and a similar one at Middleton Road in east London on 7 July — and the murder of the hapless Mr Stevens caused a wave of outrage and disgust throughout the country. The Post Office, too, were deeply concerned and five days after the murder the Postmaster-General, Mr John Stonehouse (later to fall a victim to his own criminal activities), announced a reward of £5,000 for information leading to the apprehension of those involved.

The officer placed in charge of the inquiries was the head of Scotland Yard's Flying Squad, Detective Chief Superintendent Kenneth Drury. A large, burly, dominant man of fifty-three, he was a highly successful detective who had chalked up no less than twenty-three recommendations for his work in solving crimes. But he was also knee-deep in a bribery racket with Soho pornographers, and in a few years' time would be joining Mr Stonehouse as a guest of Her Majesty's prisons.

Thanks to the hawk-eyed Mr Andrews, Drury had several clues to work on. Firstly, the index number of Mathews's Vauxhall, which soon led to its ownership being traced, first to his brother Reg, and then to him. Several visits were made to the flat in Roman Road, but his wife, when at home, was unable to say where he had gone. His brothers could not help either. Mr McNair was shown a number of police photographs, and as second choice he picked out one of Mathews as being the driver of the green getaway van.[1]

The brown hold-all was retrieved from the railway embankment. Inside was found the shotgun, with Mr Stevens's blood at the end of both barrels. This was eventually traced to Michael Good, whose wife said she had given it to her brother Terence Langston, after Good's arrest for armed robbery.[2] When Langston arrived home one evening, the police were waiting for him.

He was taken to the police station and interviewed by Drury:

It was put to me that I knew what the questioning was about – murder. I was told that I was up to my neck in it, and that I was going to be charged with it. I had heard a lot of gossip about the Luton murder, but I knew of no connection between the gun and the murder . . .

I was then shown the gun. It was newish and had markings on the firing part. I had seen it in Good's flat when it had been in pieces and he had been cleaning it. When Drury showed it to me, the gun had blood on it.

But Langston denied any knowledge of handling the gun.[3]

Also found near the abandoned green van were a dark, trilby hat, and a pair of horn-rimmed spectacles – both almost certainly those of Mathews.

The only other clue was that of the red sports car. Mr Andrews was not altogether sure about what he had seen, so he was taken to see other sports cars, and as a result concluded that it was not a Mercedes he had seen but a red MG with a hard top; and the police now set in motion widespread inquiries for such a car with an 'E' registration letter, and including the figures '15' or '51'.[4]

From all this information Drury was able to deduce one thing: that the crime was not the work of a local gang but of criminals from the East End of London, from where Mathews, Good and Langston all came – criminals moreover who had probably committed or been suspected of committing post-office robberies in the past; criminals who included a man who owned, or had used, a red MG sports car with a hard top.

It was to this area that Drury now directed his attentions; and it is time to consider the three men on whom his suspicions eventually fell: John Disher or, as he later called himself, and is now know as, David Cooper; Michael McMahon, and Patrick Murphy.

They were all East End lads, McMahon 25, Murphy 26, Cooper 27; and their photographs can be seen in the illustrated section. All three attended school until fifteen, all three seem to have drifted into petty crime from an early age, all three were friends, and their stories all begin long before the Luton murder.

Murphy was an upholsterer by trade. He had married young and had a child by a wife from whom he was now separated. He had a girlfriend called Marlene Baker, and at the time of the Luton murder had been living for some time in her parents' flat, in a block called Haggerston House. Murphy drove a red Triumph sports car, and enjoyed playing football. He had already had eleven previous convictions, including stealing, receiving, housebreaking with intent, assaulting the police and dangerous driving.

But in the summer of 1969 he found himself in deeper trouble. It has been mentioned that there had been two other post-office robberies, one at Newington Green Road on 20 May and a similar one at Middleton Road on 7 July. Although Murphy was not involved in the July raid, his Triumph car was, and he himself was observed in the company of two of those subsequently convicted only two hours after the crime. The next day the police searched his room at the Bakers', and found over £300 in cash, which he said he had recently received from an uncle for the sale of a car. The day after this he was arrested and charged with taking part in the Middleton Road robbery. Eventually this charge was dropped, but on 17 July he was put on an identification parade at Wood Green police station, and was picked out as one of those who had taken part in the Newington Green Road robbery on 20 May. A week later he was charged with that offence, and released on bail.[5]

McMahon, when not thieving, was a painter and decorator and lived in Islington. He had a girlfriend called Susan Cochrane, a copy-typist, and he divided his time between her flat and his parents' home. The most intelligent of the three men, he had convictions for stealing, housebreaking, conspiracy to rob, possessing an offensive weapon, obtaining goods by deception, and driving while disqualified.

His friend John Disher (or David Cooper) was a window-cleaner. He had had an unhappy childhood because of poor relations with his father, but was devoted to his two brothers, Terry and Tony. He owned a red Mercedes sports car, index number DAH 996B, and a brown Labrador dog, but unlike McMahon and Murphy seems to have had no regular girlfriend. Among his convictions were stealing, assault, theft, office-breaking, and receiving stolen detonators. ·

A more serious conviction against him had been recorded in the summer of 1968. This was being in possession of a shortened shotgun, explosives, firearms and ammunition, which had been found in the boot of his car. His story at his trial was that a woman friend had been looking after these things for her boyfriend who had recently been remanded in Brixton prison, and she had asked Cooper to get rid of them in case her house was searched. He told the police he was on his way to dump them in a canal. The judge did an unusual thing in ordering the woman friend to be brought to court at once. She corroborated Cooper's story in every detail and, as a result, he was given the comparatively light sentence of twelve months' imprisonment.[6]

Cooper was the only one of the three to know Mathews. In 1969 he had been introduced to him by a friend of Mathews's named David Waitson. The three had discussed a plan to go out to Hatfield to rob the home of 'a successful authoress' (presumably Barbara Cartland). This scheme had come to nothing, but on another occasion, he, Waitson and Mathews had carried out a successful robbery on a costume jeweller who ran a stall at an East End market. They had followed the jeweller's car as he drove home, and when he stopped at a newsagent's to buy papers, had opened the boot of his car with duplicate keys and removed a bag of jewels. They took the jewels to Cooper's flat and shared them out equally; later Cooper sold his to a dealer in Brighton.[7]

Cooper says that during the early part of 1969 Mathews came to his house on several occasions, sometimes with Waitson, sometimes on his own. 'Apart from the jewel robbery, when he was in my front room for several hours, I don't think he came into my house. We would talk at the door for a few minutes or sit in the car to plan future robberies.' On other occasions Cooper visited Mathews at his flat in Roman Road. 'His wife was always very reticent and consequently hard to get to know. She was always very polite and whenever I was in the flat would make me a cup of tea. When Mathews and I had something to discuss, she invariably left the room.' Another time Mathews took Waitson and Cooper over to his brother's house at Dagenham for Reg, who was a mechanic, to repair the gear lever of Cooper's Vauxhall car.[8]

Cooper says that the jewel robbery was the only successful one in which he and Mathews took part. 'We did carry out two others, but these were completely unsuccessful.'[9]

Like Murphy, Cooper and McMahon were now to be caught up in the extensive police inquiries into the Newington Green Road and Middleton Road post-office robberies. On 9 July, two days after the Middleton Road robbery, McMahon returned to his parents' house, having spent the night at the flat of his girlfriend Sue. His mother told him that the police had called earlier that morning, searched his bedroom and left word for him to ring Wood Green police station. He did this, and was told that the officer who had left his name was out.

Hardly had he put the telephone down when a fellow criminal by the name of George Murray rang up. He told McMahon that he had just spent two hours at Wood Green being interviewed about the Middleton Road robbery. The police, said Murray, were very keen to talk to McMahon about the robbery too.

'My initial reaction,' wrote McMahon, 'was to get in touch with a solicitor, simply because I had no intention of walking into a police station alone. Past experience had shown me that some police officers were not slow in "verballing up" a suspect when they had him on his own.'

McMahon's solicitor agreed to accompany him to the police station the next day, and then, to avoid further police visits that day, he went to a flat he had recently bought in Leytonstone, and which was still only partly furnished. He was joined there by his girlfriend Sue, and by Cooper and one of his brothers.

Unfortunately for McMahon the police had discovered the address of this flat while searching his bedroom that morning, and at 9.30 p.m. they arrived in force:

> There was a knock at the door and I looked out of the window to find the place surrounded by police. Sue opened the door and they came charging in like men possessed. One of them pointed a revolver at me and shouted, 'If you so much as move an inch, I'll blow your fucking head off.' I was terrified and, needless to say, stood riveted to the spot.
>
> Cooper and his brother (who had never been in trouble with the police in his life) were handcuffed together and made to sit on the settee. I was bundled out of the room by two officers and taken into the bathroom, where they started their 'heavy tactics'; they wanted to know where a certain lock-up garage was.
>
> I had no idea what they were talking about, but the strange thing was they never once asked me a question about the post-office robbery, which ostensibly was their reason for charging into my flat with guns drawn.

On the pretext that some of the furniture in the flat was stolen (which McMahon admitted), the police took him to Wood Green police station. Later he was joined by Cooper, other officers having visited his flat and found a stolen washing-machine.

Before the two men spent the night in the cells they raised with the detective in charge the question of bail when they came before the magistrates in the morning. The detective, said McMahon, 'wanted to know how much we would be prepared to pay him and his colleague if they were to support our application for bail . . . after some haggling we settled on £100 each to be handed over in a public house the following evening'. He added, 'These kind of deals between criminals and police were a regular occurrence, and most criminals expected such "expenses" when they discussed the question of bail.'

In the morning the detective told Cooper that while there was no objection to his having bail, McMahon was to be remanded in custody. 'The Post Office,' he told McMahon, 'have taken an interest in you. They have got it into their heads that you fit the description of one of a little firm who have been robbing post offices during the past year.' And McMahon was remanded in custody in Brixton for seven days.

A few days later McMahon was taken to Wood Green police station for an identification parade. His solicitor, Miss Laville, of the firm of James Morton and Co. (who were also Cooper's solicitors), asked the officer in charge how many alleged offences McMahon was being put up for. 'Ten post-office robberies,' was the reply, 'and it's hoped that thirty witnesses will turn up, otherwise there may have to be a second parade later.'

McMahon was dumbfounded. 'What if one of the thirty picked me out by mistake? With thirty it was possible. This was the first identification parade I had been on, and even though I knew I was innocent of any post-office robbery, I was absolutely terrified of what might happen on the parade.'

He need have had no fears. There were twenty men on the parade – himself, another suspect and eighteen employees from a local factory. Between them the thirty witnesses picked out twelve of the factory workers (one of them twice, so that the officer in charge said, 'If you're picked out again, we'll have to charge you'). McMahon was not picked out, though he admitted 'my knees never ceased to tremble throughout'. He was released on bail, and a few days later paid the detective who had arrested him the £100 agreed.

During August McMahon was again in trouble with the police for dishonestly handling stolen goods, and was summonsed to appear at Thames Magistrates' Court on the afternoon of 10 September, the day of the Luton murder. He had understood originally that there would be a full hearing of his case for committal to a higher court, but the evening before Miss Laville had told him that the prosecution were not yet ready and there would be another remand.

McMahon and his two bail sureties, his father and a friend called Frederick Lawrence, arrived at the court at a little before 2 p.m. on 10 September. His case came on early. The prosecution asked for a remand, which was granted, and bail was renewed with the same sureties.

On leaving the court buildings at about 2.30 p.m., McMahon ran into Cooper, who had come to listen to the hearing.

He had with him his car, a red Mercedes sports convertible, and we gratefully accepted his offer of a lift home. When we arrived at my parents' house in New North Road, my father got out and went directly into the flat, while Lawrence went off down the road to his house which was only about 100 yards away. Cooper and I chatted for a few minutes before we departed, and I walked into the flat to join my parents.[10]

McMahon spent the rest of the afternoon watching the racing on television (it was the day of the St Leger). His father, a bus conductor, left soon after 4 p.m. to go on the late shift, and an hour later his mother went out shopping. At about 5.30 he made his way to his girlfriend Sue's flat, and let himself in with his own key. She arrived soon after. They cooked a meal, and stayed in the flat until about 9.30 when they went for a drink at a pub called the Queen's Head.[11]

Cooper meanwhile, having dropped off McMahon and his two sureties, drove to see George Murray who, like Murphy, lived in Haggerston House, and who owed him

£50. On the way, at about 4 p.m., he telephoned his solicitor, Miss Laville, about a court appearance he was scheduled to make the following day in connection with the stolen washing-machine.

George Murray wasn't in, so Cooper drove to his tailor, Morris Lerman, about a fitting for a new suit. He asked Mr Lerman when the suit would be ready, and Mr Lerman said not until the following week, as they were coming up to the Jewish holiday. He told Mr Lerman of his having to appear in court next day, and Mr Lerman wished him luck.[12]

According to Cooper he arrived home around 5.30 (at which time Mathews and his accomplices were arriving at Luton station) and found his brother Terry having a bath. At about 6 p.m. a friend called Raymond Dreezer called briefly to ask about borrowing the Mercedes. At 6.30 he and Terry went to a public house in Hackney where they had arranged to meet two girls. The girls didn't show up, so after spending some time in an amusement arcade and looking (unsuccessfully) for some nurses near Whipps Cross Hospital, they returned home.[13]

Next day, while Mathews was going to ground, and the papers were full of the Luton murder, Cooper drove his red Mercedes to Thames Magistrates' Court to answer the charge of the stolen washing-machine. He was remanded on bail for a probation report, and when the case came up again three weeks later, was given a six months' suspended sentence.

Now for Murphy's movements on the day of the murder. He had spent the night before at the Baker's flat, and stayed in bed until mid-morning. About noon Marlene's brother-in-law and Murphy's closest friend, Martin Edwards (who had already been charged with the Middleton Road robbery), came round to borrow Murphy's red Triumph sports car. He returned with it in the early afternoon, and at 3.40 Murphy, Edwards, Marlene and Mr Baker all watched the St Leger on television.[14]

At about 4.30 Murphy drove to his father's house at Ilford to see about borrowing some money. On the way he was seen – but unfortunately did not see – a Mr Terence

Edwards (no relation to Martin) who knew the Murphy family through his work as a sewing-machine mechanic. He arrived at his father's house soon after 5 p.m. No one was in, but five or ten minutes later his stepmother arrived, and then his father. They all had tea. At about 6 a plumber called Turner arrived to fix the kitchen sink. At about 7.30 Murphy returned in the Triumph to Haggerston House, and a little later went out with Marlene to look at some furniture shops, as they were intending to be married in January.[15]

The first inkling Murphy had that he was being considered as a suspect in the Luton murder came some ten days later. He had gone with his father to Tottenham Magistrates' Court for another remand on the Newington Green Road post-office robbery charge. In the entrance to the court, according to Stephen Murphy, a plain clothes officer approached him and told him that his son and Martin Edwards were both suspects in the Luton case. Stephen Murphy knew this could not be true, as his son had been with him when the crime was taking place.[16]

The first news Cooper had that he was suspected came a few days later. He returned home one evening to find a message asking him to meet two detectives of the Regional Crime Squad at a pub in Leytonstone. 'They started off by telling me they were assigned to the Luton murder case, and were making inquiries in the East End, from where it was thought the gang emanated.'[17]

One of the detectives, by name Laver, reminded Cooper that the Post Office had offered £5,000 reward money, and that if he could give information about the gang, 'there were ways of paying reward money in a very discreet manner'. Cooper replied that he had no idea who was involved in the Luton murder, and in any case wasn't an informer. The detectives asked Cooper if he still had his Vauxhall car. He replied that he had sold it. He did not add, because he was not asked, that he had since bought another car, a red sports Mercedes. To the detectives, who knew what Mr Andrews claimed to have seen, this was an interesting omission.[18]

It was also one they followed up; for a little later, being short of funds, Cooper asked the garage from which he had bought it, to put it in their forecourt for sale. Soon after it arrived there, the proprietor telephoned to say that two detectives had just called to look at the Mercedes, and had examined it closely. From what the proprietor said, it was clear to Cooper that these were the same two detectives who had interviewed him in the public house. The proprietor asked Cooper if he still wanted to sell the Mercedes, and Cooper said he did. Later he changed his mind, and took it back into his own possession.[19]

McMahon meanwhile was having the same sort of treatment. While attending Tottenham Magistrates' Court for another appearance on the charge of dishonestly handling stolen goods, he was approached by three detectives who asked him, as they had asked Cooper, if he knew anything about the Luton murder. They added, as they had done to Cooper, that there was £5,000 reward money, and suggested that McMahon should keep his ear to the ground. 'I resented that sort of inducement,' wrote McMahon, 'but all I said was that it was unlikely I would ever hear anything, because robbing post offices was not my scene.'

Not long after, McMahon received a surprise visit from Michael Good, the man who had once owned the gun that killed Mr Stevens. McMahon knew Good as a criminal, and used to see him occasionally in pubs with mutual friends. 'I thought him a bit of a nutcase and generally gave him a wide berth. He had never visited me before, and so far as I knew, didn't even know my address.'

Good's story was that he had spent the night in Ponders End police station being questioned by Drury about the Luton murder. In the course of the interview, he said, Drury had mentioned the names of other men who he thought were involved in the crime. 'Your name is on the list,' he told McMahon, 'and Murphy, Cooper and others.' And Drury had added, 'You can tell that lot I'll wrap this case up in the end.'

As Good was a police informer and had never visited

McMahon before, it seems reasonable to suppose that Drury had sent him along to test McMahon's reactions.

When Good had gone, McMahon confessed to a feeling of shock and incredulity:

> Coming so close on the Wood Green identification parade, I began to wonder if something dirty was afoot. I was completely baffled as to why my name was being stuck up in this manner, for I hadn't even contemplated joining the 'big league', i.e. robbing banks and post offices, much less participating in them. It seemed that the fact that I hadn't been picked out at Wood Green had done little to convince the police of my non-involvement in this level of crime. There was no reason at all for my name being on the suspect list for any post-office robbery, and this was the really puzzling factor. As a man who operated on the lower rung of the criminal ladder, I could have understood being suspected of crimes within my sphere, but it was not so in this case. It simply didn't make sense.[20]

McMahon telephoned Cooper to tell him of Good's visit. Cooper, too, had heard from several sources that he, Murphy and McMahon were among those suspected of the Luton murder. Other incidents occurred to confirm this belief. McMahon was convinced that he was being followed by a plain clothes officer, and one evening when Cooper and McMahon were driving in Cooper's Mercedes to meet friends at a pub, they were flagged down by detectives. McMahon was taken aside and when he came back, said Cooper, declared that one detective had told him that he was on the Luton short list. Another local criminal said to Cooper that Drury had told him the same thing.[21]

Murphy also was becoming increasingly worried. In the middle of October his friend Martin Edwards was taken to Ponders End police station to be interviewed by Drury about the Luton murder. Afterwards, he told Murphy that Drury regarded both of them as suspects. They were sufficiently troubled by this to contact their joint solicitor, Mr W. J. Bridges, of the firm of Montague, Gardner, and made an appointment to see him on 27 October.[22]

That the concern of Cooper, McMahon and Murphy at being suspects in the Luton murder was real and not imaginary is proved by an event that took place at Luton police station on 14 October. Detective Constable Peter Ames showed Mrs Crawley and Mrs Calvert a set of seventeen photographs to see if they could identify any of the men who had been seen running away from Barclays Bank car park. Both Mrs Crawley and Mrs Calvert separately picked out the photograph of a man called Carroll who had nothing to do with the Luton murder.[23] *But among the other sixteen photographs were those of Cooper, McMahon and Murphy,* none of which Mrs Crawley or Mrs Calvert picked out.

Chapter Three

It is now time to ask ourselves why Drury should have become so suspicious of Murphy, McMahon and Cooper when, in fact, they had nothing to do with the Luton murder. The first answer is that with Mathews still at large, time going by without further developments and the press calling for results, Drury had to focus his attentions *somewhere*.

Why Murphy, Cooper and McMahon? Any answer must be speculative, but in seeking for Mathews's criminal associates, Drury would have learnt, first, that Cooper was one of them; second, that he was the owner of a red sports car; third, that Cooper was also friendly with Murphy and McMahon; fourth, that Murphy, who also owned a red sports car, had already been arrested and charged with one post-office robbery; and, finally, that McMahon was on a list of suspects for another.

This was not just circumstantial evidence, it was in no sense of the word evidence at all. As a likely scenario it was pure fantasy; but in the continued absence of Mathews, and without a morsel of hard evidence beyond what he already had, it was a fantasy that Drury was loath to let go.

Whatever the cause, McMahon and Cooper were now as worried as Murphy, and made an urgent appointment to see their joint solicitor, Miss Laville. As it was a weekend, they met her at Kensington tube station and walked into the park. They suggested she should accompany them to the police station where they would make a statement to Drury. But her advice, said Cooper, 'was that since we had not been approached directly by the police, there was very little she could do, and we could do nothing either'. He continued, 'My fears were somewhat allayed when Miss Laville said there was no need to worry if we had nothing to do with the murder. I could see the logic of what she said, and

39

realized I was getting worried about the situation when I really had no need to.'[1]

McMahon was less sanguine. 'The thought of being on a short list of suspects for murder was disturbing not only for myself but also for my parents and Sue. I told Miss Laville that unless I phoned her every day before 11 a.m., she should assume I had been taken into police custody, and should come to see me as soon as possible. This arrangement may seem strange, but I considered it to be vital because of my fear and distrust of the police – I had first-hand experience of their skulduggery and corruption.'[2]

But it was for Cooper rather than McMahon that the sands began running out first. Five weeks had now gone by since the murder, the press were keeping the case alive, and there was increasing pressure on Drury and his colleagues to show results. 'It seemed to me,' wrote Cooper, 'that the police were running around in circles, not knowing who they were looking for.'

On 21 October Detective Constable Laver arrived at Cooper's house to say that Detective Chief Superintendent Drury wanted to interview him at Ponders End police station about the Luton murder. They drove there in the red Mercedes, and on the way, said Cooper, Laver asked him if the car had ever been fitted with a hard top. Cooper said no, it had only ever had a soft canvas top. Not knowing of Mr Andrews's statement that the car he had seen had a hard top, Cooper saw nothing strange in Laver's question.

At Ponders End, Cooper was taken upstairs to a large room. A detective came in to say that Drury was on his way from Luton, but it was another hour before he arrived. 'It seemed that everybody was in awe of him before he made his entrance,' wrote Cooper. 'There was a flurry of people who came in and said he'd arrived, whereupon I was quickly hurried out of the room and into a much smaller one.'

Then Drury came in, 'a fairly big, rotund, grey-haired man, with long bushy sideburns and balding in front. His lips were thin and he gave the appearance of a hard mouth.

He had puffy eyes and a prominent jowl, and he looked tired.'

Drury began by telling Cooper that he had received a telephone call that Cooper was involved in the Luton murder, and what did Cooper have to say to that? 'I told him first of all I had nothing to do with the murder, and could not understand why anyone should tell him I had.' Drury asked Cooper for a written account of his movements that day, which Cooper gave him and signed. Drury then mentioned the names of other suspects, including McMahon and Murphy, and said that he would solve the case if it took him a year.

'For my part,' wrote Cooper, 'I told him I had nothing whatever to do with the Luton murder, and that if I had, I was sure I should not be sitting across a desk discussing it with him of my own free will – he would have had to find me. I said that although I was a thief, shotgun robberies were hardly the sort of thing I went in for. He must have known this was true . . . in fact he told me he did not think I was involved in the Luton murder.'

After looking at Cooper's car, Drury asked him if he had any objection to attending an identification parade. 'I said I would not object, but emphasized he should have something more than a phone call to go on before thinking about IDs. He promised me that any ID parade would be scrupulously fair, and I was naïve enough to believe him.'[3]

But now, at long last, came a break for Drury. Repeated promises to Albert Elliott that he would share in the reward money for information that would lead to the whereabouts of Mathews, plus the accumulative strain of harbouring Mathews, had their effect. Albert telephoned Drury to say where Mathews was. The day after the interview with Cooper, Drury's men surrounded Albert's house. They knocked and had no reply. Then they caught Mathews coming out of the back door, like a fox slinking out of the coverts.[4]

Mathews was taken straight to Luton and there interviewed by Drury. The notes of this interview have only come to light in recent years. Had they been available to the defence at the subsequent trial, at which Mathews was chief prosecution witness, they would have gone far to destroy his credibility. From beginning to end Mathews's answers are a catalogue of the most outrageous lies.

On the day before the murder, said Mathews, a man had knocked at his door in Roman Road, and asked if his Vauxhall was for sale. ('How did he know it was for sale?' asked Drury, and Mathews, thinking quickly, said, 'I stuck a notice on it.') Mathews replied that the Vauxhall was for sale, and that he wanted £55 for it. The man agreed. 'I wouldn't accept a cheque, so he said he would come back. About 2 or 3 this chap came back, he came in. My wife wrote him a receipt. He said not to worry about his address, he gave me the money and I gave him the log-book and keys.'

On the Wednesday of the murder, said Mathews, he was ill in bed with dysentery and never left the house. In the evening at about 5 or 5.30 p.m., his brother Reggie came over, and as he was the owner of the car, he gave him the £55, less £20 which Reggie owed him. The next day he went to his doctor about his dysentery. 'Then my wife and I decided we'd have a holiday. On Saturday we went horse-racing, and on Sunday we went to Eastbourne. There I was ill for two days with dysentery and 'flu. We came back on a Monday, and I went to where you found me.'

On arrival at Albert's house, said Mathews, his brother had told him that Drury had been inquiring for him. 'He said it was about a murder. I said to my wife, I didn't fancy this with my record, so naturally I said I'd wait until you captured the people. My brother said you knew who they were. It was the best thing to do. I kept going to come to see you, but the last time the police lied and cheated, and my wife was charged with obstructing the police. Anyway, I decided I was going to keep out of the way.'

Drury said, 'The person you are supposed to have sold the car to does not exist at that address. Do you always tell the council when you sell a car?'

'Yes,' said Mathews, 'my wife wrote it out and I signed it. I left it up to her because I felt dodgy.'

42

Then Drury asked Mathews the crucial questions. If the car had been sold on the day *before* the murder, why had the card to the council been posted the day *after* the murder?

Mathews was ready for this. Unbelievably, he was going to try and convince Drury that the fictitious man who had bought the car had done so to use in the Luton robbery.

'Oh,' he said, 'after I sold the car, my wife was approached, and a woman said if anyone asks who I sold the car to, I wasn't to remember, otherwise there would be trouble. I was approached, too, by a man who said if I didn't want to get hurt, I'd better forget who I sold the car to . . .'

Well, said Drury, if Mathews had nothing to do with the job, why hadn't he come to see him?

Mathews's reply was typical of the incoherent, evasive answers he invariably gave to any awkward questions.

'I don't go about with these hounds. It's a dead loss to me. I was going to see my probation officer. They were trying to push it off on me. I even asked where Scotland Yard was. What if I picked the man out, and his associates came around?'

Drury asked Mathews to describe the man he had sold the car to, and the man who had threatened him. His replies were pure Joe Orton. Of the man who had bought the car, 'He was dark. He'd done a lot of sunbathing. Looked as if he'd lived off the fat of the land' (here Mathews may well have been describing one of his accomplices, one of whom was said by some witnesses to be of 'Italian appearance'). Of the man who had threatened him, 'Short. Lots of black hair going back. Longish face, about twenty-five. I'd know him again. He was hard. Doesn't give 2d for no one.'

'I am putting you up for identity,' said Drury.

'I wouldn't entertain anything like this,' said Mathews. 'I wouldn't even go with them.'

'If you knew it was going to be a murder?'

'I tell you straight, I wouldn't even kill a bird. This isn't my game.'

'As far as I am concerned, you were asked to be the driver.'

'No.'

'I will put you up for identity and see if the witnesses pick you out. You resemble the Identikit picture.'

'So did the bloke I sold the car to. He looked a bit like me. My wife can tell you.' (Mathews had quite a nerve telling Drury this, having said a moment before that the man was dark, had done a lot of sunbathing and looked like he lived off the fat of the land – the very opposite to Mathews's own appearance.)

'I am going to put you up for identity,' said Drury, 'and if you are picked out, I shall charge you with murder.'

'I've never had anything to do with murder or guns,' said Mathews. 'When I read about it, I thought, "Lunatics". I thought it was one of those vengeance things.'

'All I'm suggesting is you drove one of the motors?'

'I wish I was fit enough to go on a job like this.'

On conclusion of this interview, Drury's men saw both Mrs Mathews and his brother, and both made statements. The following evening (23 October) Drury approached Mathews again: 'I have made inquiries yesterday and today. I have a statement from your wife. Your story is lies in the main. Read your wife's statement.'*

Mathews read it, and was then allowed by Drury to telephone his wife. A note was taken of what Mathews said:

Alf here. I have had your statement read. What has Albert done? Do you realize what you've done? Can you come down and see me? I'm in Luton police station, in the court part. Can't you get him to bring you down? We can square it up. Stop crying, you've made yourself upset. Aren't you coming to see me? Hire a car. Why can't he do it?

Who's that? Is Albert there? No, I don't want to speak to him. That you, Reg? Can you bring her down, it don't take long on the M1. I don't know what's happened, they have read her statement. Can't you bring her down here?

---

* This statement has never been made public.

All right, Reg. Can't you bring her down tonight, it's not all that long . . . Do you realize what's happened? He's just read a statement Florrie wrote.

Drury then had a second interview with Mathews. His object now was to make things easy for Mathews in order to persuade him to confess. When Mathews asked why his wife had made her statement, Drury said, 'Because she wanted the truth to come out. She asked me to treat you fairly, and that's what I'm doing.'

Tea was brought in and, in a more relaxed frame of mind, Mathews volunteered: 'I know that if a man goes with some others, and they murder someone, they're all murderers.'

'That would depend on the circumstances,' said Drury helpfully, and then seeing the opening Mathews had given him, 'What did you have in mind?'

'I wouldn't entertain violence,' replied Mathews. 'You know my record. I've never carried a gun. When I was a kid I used to do a lot of shooting, and one day I heard a hare scream. Since then, I couldn't kill a bird.'

'No one is suggesting you shot anybody,' said Drury patiently. 'Nobody is suggesting you knew a gun was going to be used. Your wife says you didn't know. I am prepared to believe her.' (This seems to confirm that he had already confessed to his wife his part in the crime.)

'When I was caught on the hospital job and got five years,' continued Mathews, 'they wanted to tie up all the cleaners. I said I didn't want to know that, and we didn't tie up the cleaners. But when I pleaded guilty, they didn't take any notice of that – I still got the same as the others.'

'Nobody,' said Drury, 'is suggesting you used any violence. I'm quite prepared to believe that this was a blagging that went wrong, and you had no part in the actual shooting – but I don't know. The only people that know the full story are those that took part, and from my inquiries I think you are one of those people. What part you took, I don't know. The story you told yesterday was entirely false, as your wife says.'

'Have you taken a statement from my brother Reg?' asked Mathews anxiously.

'We have taken one,' said Drury, 'and we will be taking another. You have spoken on the phone to him, and you know he's not going to alibi you now. You know your wife isn't going to alibi you either. Do you now want to tell me the truth?'

The last seven exchanges between Drury and Mathews were recorded as having started at 8.02 p.m. The notes then say, 'Pause. 8 minutes.' But the whole interview did not end until 11.15 p.m., and the record says, 'No further notes taken.' What happened during the remaining two and a half hours of the interview when no notes were taken, and what happened during the next two days when Mathews remained in custody at Luton police station, is the key to the Luton murder case.

And what did happen? Suggestions have been made as to the possibility of collusion and in view of the astonishing statement that Mathews was allowed to make in the early hours of 25 October, and which Drury must have known was untrue, collusion cannot be ruled out.[5] Indeed Drury himself was later to admit that Mathews had been 'leaned on a bit'.[6] Let us now look at that statement.

On Wednesday, 10 September 1969, I was at my home when a knock came at the door, when a chap named John knocked at my door and told me Dave sent him, and would I like to go to Luton with him, using my car to carry something back. It would be worth my while. I said, 'Is it anything dodgy or any villainy?' He said, 'Not anything you would have to worry about.' I said, 'So, it must be then.' He then said, 'I've got a cover to bring it back, so you've got no worry.' I understood it to mean that he had an order to bring whatever it was back. In fact John had called the previous day with the same proposition, except that on this day he said it was villainy, and I told him I wasn't interested as I was earning a fair wage working hard as a builder.[7]

To continue with the Wednesday, when he told me

about the order, I decided to go with him to make up my day's pay as I had been off sick. I left with him and drove in my Vauxhall, Index no. 5075 MV, to Forest Gate. [*Ed.: This is where Cooper lived.*] He went in his own car. When we arrived at a road in Forest Gate, he stopped at a house and I waited outside just past it. Two men came out with him and walked off up the road. One of them was carrying a large hold-all, I think brown in colour. John came over to me and said, 'Follow us, we are going to Luton.'

One of the men went to a green van, the other got in John's car with him. I followed them in my car all the way to Luton. On the way I realized what a fool I was being, as I felt everything wasn't legal. I was deciding whether to make out I had broken down and to stop my car on the motorway, but I knew if I did this, they would come back and try the car and then find it was all right. Foolishly and against my better judgment, I carried on. We arrived at Luton at somewhere about five to six.

I followed the car into the station car park but the van went on, where to I did not know. One man who was in the other car must have left, as I did not see him go as I was parking the car, but he must have gone through the station which led on to another road. John came up to me and said, 'Hang on for a few minutes. Have you unlocked the boot?' He then walked off in the direction of the station. I thought I wouldn't stand about there, so I walked up to the station, through the station and stood on the bridge watching the trains, thinking they'd got to come back that way. It must have been after a few minutes went past. By the way, the bag which I saw at Forest Gate which the man was carrying went into the van at Forest Gate.

After the few minutes had passed, John came back on his own rather hurriedly and said, 'Come with me quick.' We walked on the other side of the bridge and along the road where we came to a turning on the right. He said, 'Wait here,' and pointed out a shop, and asked me to watch if anyone leaves after a man does. John left me, and went down a turning.

I stood on the corner and as my eyes didn't allow me to see without glasses, which I did not have with me, I then walked a few yards in the direction of the shop and noticed a man come out and pass me. I then stopped and looked at the shop to see if anyone came out, as I had been asked to do. I did not see the man after that. I did not see the van again after I turned into the station car park. After the man left the shop and walked up the road, I saw two of the men who had come to Luton standing on the corner of another turning further up the road. I took my eyes off them, and when I looked back, they had gone.

A few minutes went by, when I heard a van pull round the corner into the main road I was in. It drove up to where I was, and someone said, 'Get in quick.' I got in as the van was half-moving, and I heard the three men arguing and shouting at each other. One said, 'Get going, you have shot him.' I tried to ask what had happened, but could get no sense out of any of them. They were all in a state of panic. Realizing that something bad had happened, I asked them to stop and let me off, as I wanted nothing to do with it. One said, 'You stay where you are,' and stopped me from getting out of the van. I had no chance to get out of the van, as it was being driven too fast and too erratically.

We got to the station car park and I got out, intending to leave on my own and not drive my car, but two of them rushed and got in the red car, and the other shouted, 'Wait for me.' The red car drove off. The other man who had shouted 'Wait for me' went to my car which was locked and said, 'Hurry, get it open.' I said, 'Look, you can't come with me as I haven't taken part in any villainy.' He said, 'You get in if you know what's good for you, as you're in it, you mug.' I opened the door of the car intending to drive off on my own, but I did open the other door, and he got in.

I drove out of the station car park and went down the

road. After I had travelled about half a mile, I stopped the car and told the chap I didn't intend to go any further. I got out of the car. He then got out of the car and walked down a side road. I then got back into the car and drove it home. I still did not know what had happened, but gathered from their conversation that something had gone wrong with whatever they had done.

I got home about 7.30 p.m. to 8 p.m. and explained to my wife how these men had tricked me. I was sitting at home with my wife that evening, and when the ten-o' clock news came on the television, it was said that a man had been shot in Luton. You can imagine how I felt, and I said to my wife, 'Good God, look what they've done.' I couldn't really believe it, as I did not see any guns but they must have had one in the bag I saw them carrying at Forest Gate when they first went to the green van.

I was panicstricken on hearing this on the television and foolishly, instead of going to the police right away as my wife advised me to, I took the car to Stoke Newington where I knew, from what John had told me, these men associated, and parked it in a side turning – hoping it would lead the police to these men, as I had no time for what they had done and was disgusted with them for doing this sort of thing. In my state of panic, and I was absolutely panicstricken, I asked my wife to get a change of ownership card, and on my instructions she filled it in at my dictation, and at my request she posted it.

I discussed with my wife what I should do, and we agreed I should go to the police. In fact I went up to Scotland Yard to see you on about three occasions, but for some reason I cannot explain – I think it was because I was so worried and felt so sick for this poor man and his wife – that I couldn't bring myself to go to you.

Over the last weeks I have been to work as usual, which I felt would help to take my mind off it, but this was impossible. I could not sleep at night, and even had nightmares. I have made myself ill at the very thought of it. At no time did I ever see the gun nor did I know they had a gun. I did not see or hear the occurrence, but if I had been there, I would have stopped this. I did not take any part in the murder of this man. I did not know it was going to happen, and was not anywhere near where it occurred. In fact I did not know where it occurred.[8]

The statement was recorded as having started at 1.25 a.m. and ended at 3.15 a.m.

Underneath Mathews's signature there is an addendum by him to say that the statement is true and made of his own free will (the first a lie, the second of dubious truth), and a typical Mathews postscript:

In addition to what I have said, I want to say that I feared these men would come to me, and do the same to me as they had done to the postmaster, as they must have known I was innocent, and could tell the police what happened. I feared this, and this was the reason I went to work from early in the morning till late at night [*another lie – he was skulking in Albert's basement to avoid the police*].

Chapter Four

It would be difficult to think of a statement that contained so many palpable untruths, such feigned moral outrage and such snivelling self-pity. Yet unbelievably this was the statement which, together with a later and even more shocking one, was the basis on which the Director of Public Prosecutions allowed Mathews to turn Queen's evidence. In the light of the interview between Drury and Mathews, his decision was, and remains, incomprehensible.

Now the first thing that Drury should have done after his interview with Mathews was what he told Mathews he was going to do – put him up on identification parade and, if he was picked out, charge him with murder. Why did he not do this? After all, McNair, Seal, Isaac and Andrews had all had a glimpse of him, and there was a good chance that one if not more of them (and particularly McNair) would have picked him out.[1] Drury's subsequent explanation was that if nobody did pick Mathews out, he might renege on his statement – but as there was already massive evidence against Mathews as a member of the gang, this was quite unconvincing.

But worse was to follow. For not only did Drury fail to put Mathews on an identification parade, but within hours of Mathews making his statement, he obtained a further statement from McNair – the witness most likely to identify Mathews – *in which McNair omitted any mention of the driver of the getaway van at all.*[2] McNair – and Seal too – could now drop out of the picture.

Next Drury showed Mathews a rogue's gallery of some fifty photographs and from these Mathews 'picked out' (to use a euphemism) those of Cooper, whom he already knew, and Murphy and McMahon, whom he didn't.[3] Drury also interviewed Mrs Mathews. Having shown her also a set of photographs which included that of Cooper, he obtained from her a lying statement which not only directly contradicted the statement she had already given the police, but in describing Cooper as the man who had left the house with her husband on the afternoon of the murder, dovetailed with her husband's description of 'John' in his statement.[4]

Next it was the turn of Mrs Crawley who, it will be remembered, was chatting with her neighbour Mrs Calvert at the back of some houses facing Barclays Bank car park at the time of the murder. All she was able to tell the police on the evening of the crime was that after hearing the bang, she had observed one man running from Mr Stevens's car to a van which was already moving off in the direction of High Town Road. Her description of the man was 'lean, perhaps in his late teens, dark-haired ... in dirty working-clothes, and I don't think he had a jacket', and she added positively, *'I wouldn't recognize him again'* (my italics).[5] Two days later Mrs Crawley made a second statement in which she again stated that she had seen only one man.[6]

But as the days went by, Mrs Crawley was persuaded to make further statements, and her story of originally having seen only one man running from the postmaster's car now took a step back in time to having first seen *two* men running to the van ('I have no idea what they looked like'), and hearing them shouting to the original man, who was still standing by the car and who subsequently ran after them. She elaborated too on the description of the original man, 'probably a teenager, about 5' 10", slim build, dark hair, and he reminded me of the singer, Engelbert Humperdinck'.[7]

Six weeks later, wonderful things had happened to Mrs Crawley's memory. The woman who had twice said she had seen only one man, whom she wouldn't recognize again, who four days later said she saw two other men but didn't know what they looked like, now gave a further detailed description, not only of the original man but of the other two. One of the latter she described as '35 to 36 years of age, 5' 6" to 5' 8", medium build, fair hair, no part-

ing, brushed back at the sides with a small quiff at the front'
(all this of a running man glimpsed for a few seconds from
sixty-five yards away!). And the original man who in her
last statement had been a teenager of 5′ 10″ of slim build
was now transformed into a man 'between 19 and 25,
nearly 6 ft and swarthy-looking with sideburns'. Such is
the power of suggestibility.[8]

The above statement was made on 25 October, the
same day as Mathews made his preposterous 'parcels
story' statement. At 6.30 p.m. on the same day Drury
formally charged Mathews with murder. But in view of
the other events that had taken place that day it was a
charge, even at that stage, that he was not likely to have to
answer.

The next day, a Sunday, McMahon was spending a
leisurely morning in his parents' flat. 'My mother pointed
out an item in the *Sunday Mirror*. It reported that a man
named Alfred Mathews had been charged in connection
with the murder of the Luton postmaster. It is not in my
nature to be happy at a man's arrest for any crime, but
I had to admit to a feeling of great relief when reading
of his arrest. I did not know anyone by the name of
Mathews, and I naturally thought this would be the end
of the matter so far as I was concerned.'[9]

Unfortunately for McMahon, it was only the beginning.
Four officers arrived at his parents' flat with a search
warrant, and removed a shirt and a pair of overalls. Before
leaving, one of the officers asked him where he would be
if Drury wanted to talk to him about the Luton case. 'I
told him I could always be reached at this address or Sue's
flat. I added that I had had enough of my name being
bandied about all over the place, and that I knew Drury
was behind it. The detective's reply will always stick in
my mind. "Well, it's a very unusual case, Mick." '[10]

Murphy's reaction to the charge against Mathews was
much the same. He had never heard of Mathews in his
life, and hoped that the police would now no longer
trouble him about the Luton murder. But having been
fitted-up, he believed, for one post-office robbery, he was

taking no risks. The next day, the 27th, he and Edwards kept the appointment with their solicitor, Mr Bridges, and at his suggestion Murphy dictated a statement about his movements on the day of the murder. A copy of this statement was found in his pocket when, two days later, the police arrested him and took him to Luton.[11]

The evening after that, the 30th, McMahon took Sue out for a drink. She was five months pregnant, and they discussed their forthcoming wedding, planned to take place in a Registry Office within three weeks. But there was to be no wedding. At 8 a.m. the next morning, Drury's men came for him. 'The governor would like to have a chat with you about the Luton murder.'

They took him first to Ponders End police station, then up the M1 motorway to Luton. Before leaving Ponders End one of the officers said to him, 'Alfie [Mathews] and Patsy [Murphy] have both made statements, Mick. We now know everything.' McMahon commented, 'This is a very old and worn ploy used by the police when they attempt to play one person off against another. Even though I had nothing to be evasive about, I was under no illusions about my detention and so decided to steer clear of futile conversations.' Later, one of the officers tried again: 'We know it was an accident, Mick.' McMahon replied that he knew nothing about it.

On arrival at Luton police station, McMahon's head was covered with a raincoat, and he was taken to an upstairs room. Drury and another officer came in. 'This was the first time I'd set eyes on Drury,' wrote McMahon. 'He was a large grey-haired man with a round pugnacious face and a nose that one would normally associate with the first floor of the Thomas à Becket pub in the Old Kent Road.'

McMahon had been expecting a lengthy interview, but it was quite brief. 'If would appear,' said McMahon, 'that he had already made his mind up about me, and was not going to waste time asking too many questions.'

'I am investigating the murder of Reginald Stevens,' said Drury, 'who was murdered in Luton on 10 September.

From evidence in my possession I believe you may have been concerned.'

'I was told by my solicitor,' replied McMahon, 'that she had been given an assurance that this was just an interview. If I'm a suspect, I can't help you, and I want my solicitor present.'

'That's all right. I shall be putting you up on identity parade, and if you are picked out, I will charge you.'

'I don't know anything about it.'

'Two men have already been charged.'

'So I've been told.'

'Where were you on September 10th?'

McMahon told him, and Drury must have been relieved to hear (if he hadn't heard it already from Michael Good) that at the time of the murder McMahon was claiming to have been with his parents or girlfriend. No jury would expect them to contradict his story.

'OK,' said Drury, 'you will be on ID later today.'[12]

That afternoon McMahon was taken to the room where the identification parade was to be held. He took his place among a row of other men, and presently Mrs Crawley came in. He did not know that she had recently been shown a photograph of him (nor that on 14 October she had failed to pick him out from a series of photographs then shown to her). She walked up and down the line, then tapped McMahon on the shoulder. 'To the best of my knowledge,' she said to Inspector Lett, in charge of the parade, 'I would say this is the man.'

McMahon was taken downstairs to a cell. 'I was in a state of shock, and couldn't help thinking that had I known when sitting at Ponders End police station that a few hours later I would be charged with murder, I would have walked straight out of the station and disappeared as quickly as possible.'

How was it, he asked himself, that the woman had picked him out? 'Had she just made a mistake? Had she been briefed by the police before entering the room? Something of the sort must have happened because I was never in Luton on September 10th.' He was taken before

Drury and charged. Asked if he had anything to say, he replied, 'Only that I am completely innocent.'[13]

Murphy meanwhile had also been put on identification parade. Mrs Crawley had failed to pick him out, though Mrs Calvert subsequently made a statement which could have meant that she had identified him or another man.

On 1 November McMahon was taken before the magistrates for remand, and then to Leicester prison. During his first few days there,

> I gave my position a great deal of thought, and although I was naturally bemused at finding myself sitting in a prison hospital on a charge of murder, my mind started to function again. I reasoned that it was highly unlikely that the magistrate would commit me for trial at a higher court on such flimsy evidence as Mrs Crawley's identification. When Sue visited me on the Monday, her attitude was one of disbelief that I should be accused of a crime which had taken place at a time when we were together. My optimism placated her, and we both concluded that it was only a matter of time before the whole ridiculous affair was sorted out.[14]

The time had now come for Drury to pull the third man in, and on 4 November Cooper was arrested and taken to Luton. Drury told him he would be put on ID parade and, if picked out, would be charged with murder. Cooper replied, 'I wasn't there, Mr Drury.' The next day he appeared on ID parades before Mathews and Mrs Mathews. Mrs Mathews picked him out as the man who had called at her flat on the afternoons of 9 and 10 September, and Mathews as the man who had driven in a red Mercedes sports car to Luton. Then Drury charged him with murder and Cooper said, 'I am completely innocent of this charge.'[15]

Two days later it was Murphy's turn. He also was identified by Mathews who said to Inspector Lett, 'That is one of them.' Whereupon Murphy said to Lett, 'I don't know this man at all, sir.'[16]

Finally on 10 November, McMahon was brought from Leicester prison to undergo the same treatment:

A middle-aged, grey-haired and bespectacled man walked into the room. As he neared the line-up, I became aware that I knew him by sight. I had met him once with Cooper when we visited the flat of a friend of his named Dave Waitson. Mathews was sitting in the front room of the flat and Cooper seemed to know him quite well.

Inspector Lett said to Mathews: 'On September 10th you witnessed a certain incident. Will you look along this line, and see if any of the men you saw at the incident are here today?' Mathews walked past me to the end of the line, then turned and advanced towards me again. He stopped directly in front of me and, tapping me on the shoulder, said to Lett, 'It's that man.'

As Mathews was making his identification, I said to him, 'That's right. I know you.' The police later tried to construe the remark as being something sinister and threatening, but I had uttered it spontaneously because I had recognized Mathews from our former meeting.[17]

McMahon returned to Leicester prison, as baffled and worried as the other two.

The optimism I had expressed to Sue on her first visit was now evaporating, and I was becoming convinced that the police were involved in some sort of conspiracy against me. I had no idea what Mathews had been identifying me for, but I realized it was obviously connected with the murder. All that Inspector Lett had asked him during the parade was about an incident he had witnessed on September 10th. He had not specified whether the incident was in London or in Luton.

What exactly was Mathews's involvement in the

murder? Had I known, I might have been in a better position to work out just what he was up to. As it was, I went back to Leicester that day a very worried and confused man.[18]

Chapter Five

Drury's case against the three accused men was now beginning to take shape. But there were still one or two difficulties to be overcome.

The first concerned Cooper's alibi for the late afternoon of the murder. It will be recalled that when he gave an account of his movements to Drury on 21 October, he had said that at around 5 p.m., he was at the shop of his tailor, Mr Morris Lerman, fitting a suit. If Cooper's defence solicitors contacted Mr Lerman and obtained a statement from him that Cooper was there at the time, this would seriously undermine the case against Cooper. But was it not possible that Mr Lerman had made a mistake? If so, and he, Drury, was able to obtain a statement from Lerman first, then the defence would be prevented, by the rules governing potential witnesses, from contacting Lerman themselves.

It was therefore vital for Drury to act quickly, and *on the very same day, 5 November,* as he charged Cooper with murder, he sent Detective Constable Beck and another officer to interview Lerman at his shop in Mare Street, Hackney. Lerman told Beck that he knew Cooper had been in his shop on 10 September because Cooper had mentioned that on the following day he had to attend court in connection with a stolen washing-machine. The next day the two officers came back, and Beck opened the conversation by saying, 'I am not satisfied with your story yesterday. Is there anything else you want to say about it?'[1] But Lerman stuck to his guns. He knew it was 10 September, because it was the weekend before the Jewish holiday. The officers, said Lerman, 'nagged at me, saying I must be mistaken . . . They tried to turn me against him. They asked me how I would like it if one of my relatives had been shot in the guts.'[2]

Beck and his colleague having failed to shake Lerman, Drury decided to visit him. When his car arrived in Mare Street, he didn't go to the shop himself, but sent an officer to fetch Mr Lerman and bring him to the car; if you are going to try and bring your influence to bear on somebody, you have a better chance of succeeding if you do it on your territory rather than his.[3]

Drury had one court card up his sleeve in that Cooper had made a second court appearance in connection with the stolen washing-machine on 2 October, also a Wednesday. Could not this have been the day that Cooper had come? No, said Lerman, he knew it must have been 10 September because in addition to Cooper mentioning his court appearance next day, he remembered saying he could not finish the suit quickly because of the Jewish holiday ahead. Drury told Mr Lerman he was wrong, and Mr Lerman told Drury he was mistaken. According to Mr Lerman, Drury said he was never mistaken. 'He was very dogmatic,' said Lerman, 'and left in something of a huff when I stuck to my story.'[4] But though Drury had not obtained what he had hoped to obtain, he could still technically enter Lerman as a prosecution witness and so prevent the defence from contacting him themselves. Thus Cooper's strongest alibi witness was cut from under him.

Another matter that concerned Drury was what had happened to the shotgun after Good's wife had given it to her brother Terence Langston, but which Langston denied having seen. According to Langston, Drury visited him in Ford open prison.

Drury told me that he had caught the three men who had done the murder. I knew only their names. Drury again showed me the gun, and said he wanted a watertight case, and that there was £5,000 reward money which could be paid to me and my wife if I was prepared to say the gun went to Murphy. I asked him why, and he said there were people who said I had given the gun to Murphy. He said, showing me the gun and pleading, 'This was a married man who had his head blown off.'[5]

But once again Langston, who was in enough trouble already, denied ever having seen the gun.

The time had now come for Mathews to prepare the final scenario, to fill in the names that had been deliberately left blank in the first statement, and to cast the helpless Cooper, McMahon and Murphy in the roles that were to be allotted to them. Cooper was to be the driver of the red sports car, Murphy was to be the driver of the getaway van, McMahon was to be the one who carried the gun and fired the fatal shot.

If the statement was to stick, there were certain things that needed emphasizing:

(1) In his first statement Mathews had not stated the make of the red sports car. Now, to incriminate Cooper, he must emphasize that it was a Mercedes wherever possible.

(2) Murphy also had a red sports car, a Triumph Spitfire. It might be profitable to introduce that.

(3) He had noticed that Cooper was wearing a sheepskin-lined jacket when they had appeared on remand together on a cold day in mid-November. Why not say that Cooper was wearing this jacket on the day of the murder? There were objections to this in that the day of the murder was very warm, and nobody in their senses would go on a job like that wearing a sheepskin jacket. But it might stick none the less.

(4) A trilby hat and a pair of spectacles had been found on the ground near the abandoned getaway van in the station car park. Both almost certainly belonged to Mathews. McNair had seen the driver of the van wearing a trilby hat, and Mathews's wife had stated that her husband owned 'an Anthony Eden' hat. Mathews wore spectacles, and Murphy, McMahon and Cooper didn't. As Murphy was to fill the role of the driver of the van, he would attribute these two articles to him. (The idea of Murphy, a cockney of twenty-six, going on a raid in an Anthony Eden hat, was perhaps stretching it a bit, but with any luck, that too would stick.)

(5) One witness had seen one of the gang wearing a navy-blue boiler-type suit, which Mathews as one of the gang

knew to be true. He would assign this suit to McMahon. (6) As regards the conversation that had taken place in the van after the shooting, he would say just what he had heard at the time: that would make it sound authentic.

And so the final statement was written down, the damning document that at the end of the day was to send Cooper, McMahon and Murphy to prison for life.

In essence it was an enlarged version of the first statement, but with several incriminating additions (author's italics throughout).

On the day before the murder, said Mathews, after Cooper had left his flat, 'I went outside with him to the communal balcony. He went downstairs and I remained at the balcony window, from where I saw John enter a *red Mercedes sports car* . . .'

On waiting for the three to emerge from the house in Forest Gate, 'I sat in my car for about 5 to 10 minutes. I did see another sports car there, a *red Triumph Spitfire* . . . what attracted my attention was seeing the two cars, the *Spitfire* and John's *Mercedes* together. After 5 or 10 minutes John came out of the house. He now had on a *sheepskin-lined jacket,* and with him were two other men that I had never seen before . . . One, a dark-haired man [McMahon] . . . carrying a brown hold-all . . . went over to the van, opened the driving door, put the hold-all inside . . . The man, with the lighter hair of the two [Murphy] . . . got into John's car.'

The description of the journey to Luton, parking the cars, hanging about at the station, and going to watch the post office were much the same. But after being picked up by the van after the murder, the story is subtly enlarged:

The van drove off at a fast speed, and I noticed John was wearing dark, tinted glasses. Another man [Murphy] had on a *pair of dark-horn-rimmed glasses similar to what Mr Drury has shown me.* He was the driver. *He also had a hat on, and it was similar in every respect to the one shown me by Mr Drury.* There was another man, the dark-haired one who I now know is

McMahon and who was the man who drove the green van from Forest Gate to Luton, in the back of the van hurriedly putting on *a boiler suit, dark navy blue in colour.*

There was a lot of shouting and hollering between them and one, I think it was the driver, who said to McMahon, 'You've killed him.' McMahon said, 'I didn't, he grabbed the gun and pulled the trigger.' I then asked what all this was about, and asked them to stop the van and let me out. One, I think it was McMahon, said, 'Shut up, you mug.' I did try to get out of the van, but it was going too fast . . . As we were travelling from where the van picked me up to the car park, and as McMahon was putting on the overalls, I noticed what looked like bloodstains down the front of his shirt, and at some stage he said, 'I've got blood all over me.'

On arrival at the car park the van pulled in between two parked cars, and they all scrambled to get out of the van by the two front doors, pushing me aside. I noticed *the dark trilby hat the driver was wearing* was flung past me on to the ground . . . I then left the van and walked towards my car. McMahon and the man with the lighter hair I now know to be Murphy came from the direction of the grassy bank which separates the car park from the railway line, and came near my car.

At that moment *the red Mercedes,* with John driving, pulled up. Murphy ran to the *Mercedes,* jumped in the passenger seat. McMahon started to run to the *Mercedes* and shouted, 'Wait for me.' He was still trying to button up the front of the boiler suit. The *Mercedes* pulled off violently in the direction from which we had come into the car park earlier on. I noticed this while I was getting into my car.

McMahon then came back to my car and said, 'I'm coming back with you.' I told him I did not want him with me as, whatever they had done, I had taken no part in it and wanted no part of it. He said, 'Open that door, you mug, if you know what's good for you. You're in it, you mug.'

I did open the door and he got in beside me. It was then I noticed blood over the back of his hands, and he was wiping it off with a handkerchief. The front of the boiler suit was open and I noticed blood on the front of the shirt . . . *It was then I realized more so that these men had done something bad.*

Mathews's account of driving off with his passenger, stopping the car and both of them getting out, is much the same as in the first statement, as is the account of his return to London. Then comes a real gem:

On my return home, I conversed with my wife about what had happened, and was very worried trying to puzzle out what these men had done. At ten-o'clock I was looking at the television and the news came on, and I noticed there had been a postmaster shot in Luton. *I did wonder whether this was the incident, comparing the blood I had seen on McMahon's hands and shirt.*

Finally, there is an account of a late-night imaginary visit by Cooper, invented to explain why Mathews had not gone to the police (in addition to incriminating all three further):

At about twenty past ten John came to my flat and seemed in a panic. He looked nervous and said, 'Let me come in quick.' I took him into my lounge as he half pushed past me. I said to him, 'Surely you haven't killed this postmaster I've just seen on television?' I was annoyed, and he said to me, 'Be patient a minute and I'll explain it.' He went on to say, 'You've got nothing to worry about as you weren't there and knew nothing about it. McMahon lost his head and shot the man, but he didn't mean to do it, as the man grabbed the gun and pulled the trigger. I had nothing to do with it really. I was at the back. It was McMahon and Murphy who were struggling with him.'

I asked him what it was all about, and what they were

going to do, and he said, 'All we intended to do was get him in the van, take his keys and empty the post office.' He then said, 'What I've come to tell you is to keep quiet about this as Murphy and McMahon are bad people and have plenty of friends, and they have told me to tell you to keep your trap shut, and you know nothing of this as you have yourself and your wife to consider.' He said, 'I'm not threatening you myself, Alf, it's the other two who have given me this message to give to you.'

He told me, 'I've been running around all evening fixing up with friends an alibi over this, and could I borrow your car as I daren't use mine.' I said, 'No.' He also said, 'This job's been a bock to me. We've been up there many times. The last time the wheel came off the van on the motorway.' He then left . . . I was really worried now. I decided, as my wife and I had been threatened, I would take the car, the Vauxhall, and leave it in a position the police could find it.'[6]

This appalling piece of fiction was made on 3 December 1969. Now one further nail was needed to clamp down Cooper's coffin. It will be recalled that Mr Andrews had stated on the evening of the murder that he thought that the red sports car he had seen had a Mercedes badge on the boot, but in every relevant statement since had affirmed that the car was an MG.[7] He was now shown Cooper's Mercedes, and a photograph of it, and *the very next day* after Mathews's final statement, i.e. on 4 December, he made a further statement in which he claimed that the car he had seen at the station did have a Mercedes badge on the boot, and that the Mercedes sports car and photograph of it that he had recently been shown were similar to the car he had seen at the railway station. He still insisted however that it had a hard, red top (Cooper's had a soft beige one), an 'E' registration number (Cooper's had a 'B' registration number) and that, included in its numbers were '15' or '51' (Cooper's numbers were '996').[8]

Twelve days later all four men appeared at Luton for

committal proceedings, and on Drury's recommendation to the Director of Public Prosecutions, no charges were preferred against Mathews, who it was announced would now appear as a prosecution witness. And so Mathews, the only one of the four to have taken part in the Luton murder, walked from the court a free man.

Chapter Six

The defence, in preparing their case for the three accused, were thwarted in a number of ways. In accordance with practice the prosecution supplied the defence with the names of witnesses whom they did not propose to call, and these included Seal and McNair. But when Murphy's lawyers wrote to them, they received from one a dusty answer and from the other no answer at all.

When McNair received their letter, he telephoned Luton police station, and was told that 'everything was in order', and that he could reply if he so desired. Not knowing that what he had seen (Mathews driving the van) could be of immense help to them, 'I got my wife to reply and say that I had no information that could be of value.' Seal also informed the police of the letter he had received and was told, 'Ignore it, and do nothing about it at all.' When the trial was over, Seal was shown a photograph of Murphy and said that definitely he was not the driver of the van; and later he went one better and identified a photograph of Mathews as the driver of the van.[1]

Cooper's lawyers were also hindered in discovering, thanks to Drury's nimbleness, that Lerman, their strongest alibi witness, was now being called for the prosecution and so was beyond their reach. But McMahon's lawyers found a wholly new problem facing them.

On his return to Leicester prison on 10 November, McMahon found that he had been moved from the hospital wing to the remand wing, which he said was most unusual, as all prisoners on a murder charge always stayed in the hospital wing during the period of their remand. Here he became friendly with two prisoners called Derek Jackson who was in for buggery, and Thomas Weyers who was in for burglary, and both of whom had a long string of convictions. 'These two often walked with me on our daily exercise period, and the conversation we had on exercise naturally included the charges we were facing respectively. Although both of them admitted their guilt, I discussed my case from the point of view of my innocence.

On 20 November Jackson was sentenced to seven years' imprisonment, and instead of being allocated to the main wing of the prison or, as a homosexual, to the segregation unit, he was given a cell next to McMahon. On the other side of Jackson was Weyers, and there was a pipe running through all three cells with enough space round it for them to talk through, and partially see one another. As the date of the trial approached, McMahon was horrified to hear from Miss Laville that Jackson had been interviewed by the police and made a statement alleging that McMahon, far from protesting his innocence to him, had admitted his guilt.

This had happened on several occasions, said Jackson, first when they were both on remand, when McMahon admitted to having accidentally shot the postmaster, and later, after Jackson had been convicted of buggery, when they were sitting in adjoining cells and conversing through the pipe hole. Here, like Pyramus and Thisbe, they had sat on the floor on either side of the wall while McMahon gave Jackson a blow-by-blow account of his movements on the day of the murder and Jackson, with pen and paper in hand, solemnly recorded them.

Here is an extract from Jackson's allegedly contemporary notes of what McMahon said:

Left court at 2.30 p.m. ARR Home at 2.50 p.m. had cup of tea. Left home at 3.10 p.m. went out to meet mates for the job. Started for Luton at about 3.30 p.m. arr in Luton at about 5.10 p.m.

It was obvious to McMahon, as it must be to the smallest intelligence, that this was a 'plant'. Although prisoners often discuss their cases in a general way, it would be astonishing for a *guilty* man to communicate to a fellow prisoner the sort of boring details about times and places that one normally associates with the taking of a police statement. It would be even odder for the fellow prisoner to go to the bother of recording it all on paper unless he had something to gain from it. And in Jackson's case there was something to be gained from it, in the shape of reward money. It is difficult to resist the conclusion that Jackson, having been fed details of the crime, had been given the opportunity to incriminate McMahon further.[2]

When McMahon heard this, he told Miss Laville that there was only one way of counteracting it, which was to get in touch with Weyers, who had since left the prison. He had proclaimed his innocence several times to Weyers, and had no doubt Weyers would support him. But when Miss Laville finally tracked down Weyers, she discovered that the police were calling him as a prosecution witness as well. Once again Drury, or one of his men, had got in first.

Weyers's statement and subsequent evidence was even more bizarre than Jackson's and indeed contradicted Jackson's in some respects:

He [McMahon] said that a team of four of them had gone to a car park in Luton. They had gone down in a van which was parked in a road near the car park. They had gone with the intention of blagging the keys of the post office off the postmaster. As they had approached the postmaster, he had turned towards them and swung at them with a bag or briefcase. In the bit of a struggle that followed the gun had gone off, and the postmaster turned and fell forward into the car . . . [McMahon] said there was £26,000 in the post office.

McMahon comments on this:

There are three things wrong with that. Firstly, the van was seen to be parked in Barclays Bank car park and not in any road nearby. Secondly, the postmaster could not possibly have swung a bag or briefcase at the robbers because he had no bag and his briefcase was found locked in the boot of his car. As for the £26,000, I discovered later that the exact figure was £25,960, and that this was made up of National Insurance stamps to the value of £17,000, postal orders worth £1,600, and £900 in postage stamps. It is inconceivable that any robber could have known of this figure, and, in view of all the skulduggery which had taken place, I think that Weyers was given it by police officers involved in the case.

In one part of his statement Weyers said that McMahon 'began to boast about the post offices he had done'. McMahon had never robbed a post office in his life. In another part, Weyers had clearly confused his information. The red Mercedes was evidence implicating Cooper, but Weyers seemed to think it concerned McMahon, and he ought to say something about that. So he said that McMahon had told him that he had paid £800 for a red sports car, *and was very worried about where the car had got to.* McMahon had never owned a red sports car.
Why had Weyers made this statement, McMahon wanted to know. He had his own ideas:

The prison authorities must have been well aware from letters sent by me to Miss Laville that my solicitors were trying to contact Weyers with a view to calling him in my defence. And as they had clearly shown by placing Jackson in the cell next to me, they were willing to work hand in glove with the police . . .
I believe the prison authorities informed the police of our attempts to contact Weyers by passing on copies of my personal correspondence, and once the police knew of this, they decided to interview Weyers. He was finally arrested in Nottingham for the very minor offence of stealing some car keys, but instead of being remanded to prison, the police kept him in the police

station for ten days which is virtually unheard of in such a petty case. I have no doubts that certain officers involved in the murder investigation spent many an hour briefing Weyers on what they wanted him to say. The fact that he eventually bungled part of his evidence only means he was not as good a liar as they would have wanted him to be.[3]

But there was an even more convincing explanation. Weyers, like Jackson, was in for a slice of the reward money. And both, according to Drury, had part of their sentences remitted.[4]

* * *

At the end of the year all three men, having been carefully kept in separate prisons, were transferred to Brixton in London, prior to an Old Bailey trial. Cooper recorded his reactions:

It was with great relief I entered Brixton prison for two reasons; firstly it was a great burden on my family to travel every week to Birmingham, and secondly I was anxious to speak with McMahon and Murphy to discuss just where they stood in this affair. I wanted to give them both a chance to see what they had to say, but because of anxieties I felt about my own predicament, I did not give much thought to the possibility of their innocence, and in fact while at Winson Green, thought that they were both involved with Mathews in the crime. This, of course, was a quite natural reaction, and perhaps subconsciously I was hoping they were guilty, in which case they could vindicate me.

Soon after speaking to McMahon and Murphy, it became clear that they were as bewildered and anxious as I was. Unless they were very good actors, they sounded very convincing to me when they said they were innocent.[5]

And this was McMahon's reaction:

Now that the three of us were together, we had at last the opportunity to discover where each one of us stood regarding the Luton murder. True, we had discussed the matter prior to our arrest when our names were being bandied about, but so much had happened in the last couple of months that it was only natural that each of us, segregated and perplexed, should start to wonder about the other.

If the air needed clearing, then our first conversation did exactly that, for it saw each man strongly protesting his innocence and strenuously denying any involvement in the murder. Given my own predicament, I was left in no doubt that Cooper and Murphy had also been fitted up. Cooper was in a state of disbelief, tempered only by his reluctance to believe he could possibly be convicted.[6]

At Brixton McMahon, like the others, had regular visits from his family:

I saw my mother for the first time since my arrest, and I knew the visits were heartbreaking for her. I think every mother has a favourite child, and I know I was my mother's favourite. I was the only member of my family who had ever been in trouble with the police; whether this had anything to do with it, I don't know. The most heartbreaking aspect of this for her was the fact that she knew I was innocent and yet was powerless to do anything about it.[7]

The trial was scheduled to take place at the Old Bailey on 26 February 1970, before Mr Justice Cusack.

Before it opened, however, there was one interesting development. Because of the weakness of the prosecution case on the murder charge (it was generally accepted that the shooting of Mr Stevens had been an accident) the Crown invited the three accused through their counsel to consider pleading guilty to reduced charges – in the cases of Cooper and McMahon a charge of conspiracy to rob, which carried a maximum of five years' imprisonment, in the case of Murphy, a charge of manslaughter. All three men, never having been near Luton on the day of the murder, rejected the offer out of hand. 'I am innocent,' McMahon told his counsel, Mr William Hudson, QC, 'and I have no intention of doing any deals with the prosecution.' Yet had they been guilty, it is inconceivable that they would not at least have carefully considered the opportunity given them of serving sentences that would be far less than that of life imprisonment.[8]

Chapter Seven

On the morning of the opening day of the trial, wrote McMahon,

Cooper, Murphy and myself were led out of the security wing of Brixton prison and escorted to a waiting prison van to be taken to the Old Bailey. Outside the prison gates we were greeted by a convoy of police vehicles. Moving ahead of us were two motor-cycle outriders followed by a siren-blaring squad car, while behind was a car load of plain clothes policemen.

As we sped through Brixton, the tremendous noise being created by the sirens and the unnecessary sensationalism of holding up traffic to enable us to break red lights, all ensured maximum attention. I couldn't help but feel that this exhibition was a contradiction of the fundamental principle of British justice whereby a person is supposedly innocent until proved guilty. For it is highly unlikely that anyone witnessing the sight of such a convoy, jurors included, would conceive that the persons concerned were innocent.[1]

The chief prosecution witness was, of course, Alfred Mathews. Mr Victor Durand, QC, for the Crown, steered him through his incredible statements. He said he had never met Murphy or McMahon before in his life, and had met Cooper only once or twice. As Cooper was to remark later, it would surely have improved Mathews's chances of being believed if he had said that he did know him. Then it was the turn of the three defence lawyers. They did what they could to shake him, but he had learnt his brief too well (his survival as a free man depended on it); and when he found himself in a tight corner, he fell back on rambling, evasive answers. Sometimes he cracked.

Mr Eric Myers, QC, for Murphy, was trying to ridicule Mathews's story of being asked to go to Luton to fetch parcels when two other cars were going anyway. Mathews agreed, he couldn't really understand it himself. Then Mr Myers suggested his story simply wasn't true.

'Do you want me to say it isn't true?' Mathews shouted at him. 'Do you want me to tell lies? I am telling you the truth. If you want me to tell lies, I will tell lies, but I daren't tell lies. I won't tell lies.'

And what about when they reached Luton, and Cooper was taking him to look at a shop? Didn't he ask then what was happening about the parcels? Mathews's reply was typical of his evasiveness.

'It was a mild conversation. I said, "How long are we going to be? What's all this about parcels?" He said, "I have got to see somebody down there." That is the words that were said. I don't know if it makes any difference. We still went down this road.'

There was one moment when Mathews nearly gave himself away altogether. Mr Hudson, cross-examining for McMahon, read out from Mathews's first statement of 25 October that as he had got into the van, one of the men in the back had said, 'Get going, you have shot him.' This couldn't have been addressed to McMahon, suggested Mr Hudson, as Mathews had already said McMahon was in the back – it must have been addressed to the driver.

For a minute Mathews forgot his story of not being at the scene of the crime, and remembered the truth of the matter, that he himself was the driver.

'Are you trying to say I shot him?' he yelled.

'No, no, no,' said Mr Hudson.

'This is ridiculous, what you are saying,' shouted Mathews. 'You are trying to put a false impression into my mind and other people's mind.'

Asked by Mr Myers why, if he was as innocent as he claimed, he had not gone straight to the police to report what had happened, he gave a particularly nauseating reply:

I stood in this court last week and all my particulars,

the whole of my previous convictions and my past was read out. I stood here, disgusted and ashamed of myself, because there is nothing for me to be brutal. A man with a record in anything like that, if he becomes involved with the police or anything like that, well, naturally he fears that it will be put down to him. I feared that. Now you see why I never went to the police immediately, and why I feared going to the police. But the police in this case realized that I had no part in this, and they done justice, as they usually do. That is my answer to the question.

Equally repulsive was his answer to a suggestion by Mr William Hemming, QC, appearing for Cooper, that he was framing Cooper just to get himself out of trouble: 'Utterly ridiculous. As I have explained before, never would I do such a thing. What sort of man would he be? He would be the scum of the earth to put a man innocently and tell lies in a case like that, and never could anyone do that, and surely you can see no one would do such a thing.'[2] Yet the jury must have found it quite plausible.

Jackson and Weyers told their damaging stories, Mr Andrews said the sports car he had seen was similar to the red Mercedes (Cooper's) he had been shown (though still insisting that it had a hard top, an 'E' registration letter and the numbers '51' or '15'), Mrs Crawley spoke of identifying McMahon, and Mrs Calvert of possibly identifying Murphy.

It is not suggested for a moment that these last three testified to anything they did not believe to be true; but in the hands of over zealous police officers, potential witnesses are highly suggestible. Because they know the police know more than they do, because as good citizens they want to help bring criminals to justice, because they are flattered in being told their opinion is of moment, they become disposed to say and do what the police want them to. In the case of these three, there was also the question of reward money. Whether this was mentioned or not we do not know; what we do know is that at the end of the day they all were given their cut.

For the defence there were two unexpected bonuses. First, although the prosecution expected Mr Lerman to say that it might have been 1 October that Cooper visited his shop, he insisted – despite Drury's intimidation – that it was 10 September. And a prisoner called Sewell who had known Mathews in Parkhurst testified that he had met him again in the London Hospital in February and said to him, 'There's a whisper going about that you've stuck some people up for a shooting,' and that Mathews had replied, 'Well, it was the only way I could get out of it.'[8]

At this time the defence were unaware of the existence of either Mrs Brooks, or Leonard and Stephens; but for all three defendants, their families and friends came forward to support their alibis. And they themselves all went into the witness-box and, despite lengthy cross-examination by the Crown, maintained throughout their evidence that they were wholly innocent of the charge.

For Murphy, his girlfriend Marlene, her father Mr Baker and her brother-in-law Martin Edwards, all testified that he had been with them watching the St Leger in the early afternoon; and his father, his stepmother and the plumber, Mr Turner, all gave evidence that he had been with them at Ilford at the time of the murder in Luton.

For McMahon, his father testified that he too was watching the St Leger with him in the early afternoon, and his girlfriend Sue that he had been with her thereafter.

For Cooper, his mother, brother and Raymond Dreezer gave evidence supporting his alibi. And his solicitor, Miss Laville, gave evidence that at about 4 p.m. on the day of the murder – a time when, according to Mathews, he and Cooper were *en route* to Luton – Cooper had telephoned her *at her request* in connection with his court appearance the following day.[4]

In numbers it was a formidable list of witnesses. Unfortunately for the accused, juries always view the supporting evidence of close friends and relatives with some scepticism. Would they be likely to say anything else?

In his summing-up Mr Justice Cusack said two important things. The first was that the case really turned on Mathews, who was obviously far more involved than he let on in his evidence. But even if he was lying about that, was he also lying about the participation of the three defendants? 'To involve three innocent men in this way would surely be wicked *beyond belief*' (my italics).[5] In other words he was inviting the jury to consider that the framing of the accused by Mathews was not credible. Clearly the old adage about the bigger the lie, the more chance of being believed, had not occurred to him; and yet that was, and is, the core of the Luton case.

On the morning of the last day of the trial, the judge finished his summing-up, and invited the jury to retire. McMahon watched them file into the jury-room.

During the next two and a half traumatic hours I was to experience a sense of tension which was to become all too familiar in later years, as my case was dragged through the Courts of Appeal. Thoughts raced through my head, but I found it impossible to concentrate on any one aspect. Although I felt the judge had summed up against me, I still clung to a shred of hope that the jury would see through Mathews's incredible parcel story, and declare me innocent.

However the realities of the situation pointed to a verdict of guilty, for if such men as Durand and Drury were both saying that Mathews was telling the truth, what jury would go against them? I was confused and frustrated because I found myself trapped in a situation that should never have come about if British justice is all it is made out to be. They had put two and two together, and come up with five.[6]

At 2.15 the jury returned to court, and the three accused were brought up from the cells. In turn the clerk of the court asked the foreman of the jury how they found, and in turn the foreman said they found all three men guilty.

Then the judge addressed them.

Patrick Colin Murphy, Michael Graham McMahon,

and David Cooper, you have all been convicted of murder ... The offence you committed was one which must have been carefully planned because that was essential in carrying it out. It was a brutal offence in which an unfortunate man in a moment of time was dispatched out of life. It is also to be noted that the weapon used was a sawn-off shotgun, a deadly weapon, as indeed it proved to be in this case.

I think it necessary that this matter should be dealt with in a way which will bring home to those who are disposed to carry firearms, that they must receive such sentences as will express the strongest possible public disapproval and horror, and may serve to deter other people ... On each one of you I pass the sentence which is prescribed by law, that each one of you shall be imprisoned for life, and I shall recommend to the Secretary of State that each one of you, before you are released on licence, shall serve in prison a minimum period of twenty years.[7]

All three were shattered. McMahon wrote: 'Although the verdict had not been entirely unexpected, actually hearing it numbed me. My mouth and throat were bone-dry, and even if I had been able to think of something constructive to say, the vocal cords would not have obliged.'

With the others he was taken back to the cells.

I was completely drained, mentally and physically. It seemed as if I was entering a tunnel of darkness, where not even the faintest glimmer of light existed. Sitting down on the wooden stool, I tried to focus my mind on what had just happened, but it was no use as the shock waves swept over every effort to concentrate. For what must have been an hour I sat listlessly with head in hands, feeling too hot and too cold at once. I certainly did not fit the popular notion of the innocent and wrongly incarcerated, undeterred by sentence and adamantly proclaiming that in the end justice would be done. No, I was bloody shattered. The unacceptable face of British justice had just given me an enormous kick in the balls.

He was told that his father and Sue had come to see him, and was taken upstairs to the visiting-room. They sat down on either side of a glass screen.

During their visit, I was unable to lift my head, and kept my eyes firmly fixed to the iron grille, through which you spoke at the bottom of the glass screen. In the one glimpse that I'd had, I'd seen the pain and heart-break on their faces, and felt it impossible to look at them again without showing my feelings, and thus upset-ting them even more. Listening to their brave attempts at consolation was like having a knife twisted inside me. Seeing those closest to you suffer is not easily forgotten, and the memory of that visit is as vivid today as it was then.

Later that afternoon the three men were taken to the prison van that was to convey them to Wandsworth. On the way, McMahon thought back to the trial:

I had sat in the dock, listening to the big words and complex arguments without understanding them, or realizing my life was being taken away from me. The sheer enormity of the occasion, and the atmosphere of the quaint courtroom and the polite mannerisms and gentlemanly conduct of all concerned, had completely disguised the savage climax to come.

Mathews, Jackson and Weyers had blatantly lied in the witness-box, and yet they couldn't have done that without the assistance or prompting of the police. I was fully convinced that some extraordinary acts of skul-duggery had taken place, but without proof I was totally helpless. Looking out of the van window at the people going home, I couldn't help but feel that somebody up there didn't love me.[8]

At Wandsworth, Cooper, who all along had never doubted that he would be acquitted, was taken to the prison hospital in a state of shock:

I was there for about three days, and was glad of the

night sleeping-draught given me each evening. During the day I sat in the chair which was by my bed, and just stared at the wall for the whole day . . .

It was during this period that my thoughts turned for the first time to suicide . . . the only avenue left to me in putting a quick end to my misery and morbid self-pity. I suppose it is true when this is said to be cowardly and selfish, but unless one experiences deep depression and the breaking to pieces of one's life, it cannot in any sense be understood. It was only the thought of what such irrevocable action would do to my family that in the end deterred me.[9]

In a few days, they were all put on the traditional prison pastime of sewing mailbags. McMahon wrote:

The monotony of this soul-destroying job seemed to compound the sense of bitterness that was now upon me. It was no use telling myself that they couldn't do this, because they had. It was no use telling myself that a terrible mistake had been made, because it hadn't. It had been a cold, deliberate fit-up from the start, but how could I prove it? Who was going to believe me? Who would be prepared to accept the word of Mick McMahon, a small-time thief from the East End, against one of the most esteemed police officers in Scotland Yard?[10]

Yet if the three men inside could do little to remedy their situation, the same could not be said of their families and lawyers. It is not exaggerating to say that Murphy's girlfriend and her father, his own father and stepmother, Cooper's mother and brother, McMahon's father and girlfriend, all felt personally insulted by the verdict of the jury; for not only had the accused not been believed when giving their alibis, but they, who had spoken the truth when supporting the alibis, had not been believed either. All three families, therefore, as well as the defence lawyers, were extremely active in seeking fresh evidence, as well as taking other steps to prove that justice had miscarried.

Chapter Eight

Before any of this could take effect, however, the long-promised £5,000 Post Office reward money was paid out; paid out on Drury's recommendations and paid out in secret. And paid to the wrong people for wrong reasons. This was the shocking list:

Mathews	£2,000
Albert Elliott	£500
M. Good	£500
D. Jackson	£500
T. Weyers	£500
H. Andrews	£400
K. Isaac	£200
Mrs Crawley	£200
Mrs Calvert	£200

All the people in that list had, either deliberately or inadvertently, provided information that had led to the conviction of three innocent men. Mathews was rewarded for lying about his own part in the crime and for falsely incriminating Cooper, McMahon and Murphy. His brother Albert was rewarded for shopping Mathews, who had got off scot-free. Weyers and Jackson were rewarded for falsely incriminating McMahon, Mr Isaac for providing information that Mathews was able to slot into his lying statement, Mrs Crawley for wrongly identifying McMahon, and Mrs Calvert for wrongly identifying Murphy.

Now one of the most curious aspects of the disposal of the reward money was this. Six of those in the list had cheques sent to them directly. But Mathews, his brother Albert Elliott and Michael Good had their cheques sent care of Drury, and moreover this was at Drury's request.[1] Why? The question has never been answered. But it must still be asked. Was it because these three had made a deal with Drury to share with him whatever sum he was recommending them to be given? Did any such arrangement also extend to Jackson and Weyers? Let us examine that suggestion.

There is evidence from three sources that Drury shared Mathews's reward money. In 1971, when the allocation of the reward money was still a secret, a journalist named William Thomson interviewed Mathews.* During the conversation, says Thomson, *Mathews admitted that Drury had got half of what was due to him, Mathews, and that he, Mathews, got £1,000; and Drury had also told him that he, Drury, had taken a cut of some of the other payments.*[2] Thomson also interviewed Albert Elliott 'who told me on at least three occasions that Drury got half of the reward money the Post Office paid to his brother'.[3] In 1972, in an article in the *Sunday Mirror* that carried his byline and which he corrected before publication, Mathews again stated that he had received £1,000.[4]

This assertion is supported in general terms from another source, that of the Soho pornographer, James Humphreys, whose bribes to Drury not to take action against him subsequently led to Drury's conviction and imprisonment. In a statement made in Gartree prison in 1975 Humphreys said that Drury had told him that he had had 'a good drink' from the informants' money.[5] There is also the undeniable fact that *on the same day as Mathews was handed the £2,000 cheque from Drury and paid it into his bank, he drew out £700 in cash.*[6] What did he need this money for? Did he in fact take this £700, together with another £300 which he already had (he always carried large sums on him and had £500 when arrested), and give £1,000 to Drury?

Supporting evidence that Drury was taking cuts from

---

* Thomson's account of his dealings with Mathews which not only throw further light on the disposal of the reward money, but give a sharp insight into Mathews's character, will be found in Appendix 1.

other informants' money comes not only from Mathews but also Michael Good. Now there was no explicable reason why Good should have received *any* of the reward money. He had made no statement or given any evidence in court that had led in any way to the apprehension or conviction of the accused. Why then should Drury have recommended him as someone worthy of a very substantial reward?

Any answers to that question must be entirely speculative, but perhaps a clue is to be found in the fact that Good was, in addition to his criminal activities, a paid police informer. It will be recalled (page 35) that McMahon received a surprise visit from Good, whom he hardly knew and what he did know disliked, during Drury's investigations into the murder. It has already been suggested that this visit was made on Drury's instructions. Did Good sound out McMahon as to his movements at the time of the murder, and did he subsequently report to Drury that McMahon's only alibi at the material time was his girlfriend Sue? We do not know, but if that was the case, it could well qualify Good for a recommendation for part of the reward, and moreover one from which Drury might benefit.

At all events, Good was interviewed by the police in 1976 and made a lengthy statement.[7] He begins by saying that before the Luton murder, he knew a Detective Sergeant 'X'* (for whom he had done 'work' about which he did not wish to give details at this stage). After the murder, 'X', and later Drury, had interviewed him about the gun used in the murder, and which he admitted he had once owned.

After the conviction of the three accused,

'X' picked me up at home, and told me that Drury wanted to see me at Scotland Yard. I went with him to Scotland Yard where he took me to an office where

---

* Pseudonym for an officer who has since resigned from the force.

I saw Drury. I knew before I saw Drury that day that he wanted to see me about reward money paid out in that case by the Post Office. I had been told this by 'X' before I got to Scotland Yard ...

When I got into Drury's office, Drury said very little to me as I remember it. He asked me to sign a receipt and a cheque, and I did so ... while I was in Drury's office with Drury and 'X', 'X' asked me to step out of the office with him, and go with him to the gentlemen's lavatory on the same floor. I did so, and in the lavatory 'X' said to me, 'Do you want any of it, Mick?' (meaning the Post Office money). I can't remember his exact words, but what he then said was, did I want to give Drury all of it, or take some of it myself and give the rest to Drury, or what? I think, at one stage, he suggested I take two hundred pounds and give the rest to Drury. He said, 'Drury wasn't bothered one way or the other.'

I told 'X' Drury could have the lot. At the time I half suspected that what 'X' was really doing was acting for himself rather than Drury, and that what he was really after was the money for himself. I had only his word that the money would go to Drury, because Drury himself never made any sort of suggestion about the money to me at any time.

After the conversation with 'X' in the lavatory, we went back into Drury's office. Nothing was said about the conversation I had had with 'X' in the lavatory. Drury just wished me good-bye, and I left his office with 'X' who was holding the cheque.

'X' then took me to a bank, the National Westminster, just across the road from Scotland Yard, and handed the cheque in. The cashier was a woman. I remember now I probably signed the back of the cheque in the bank at 'X's request and not, as I said previously, in Drury's office, although I did sign the receipt in Drury's office.

'X' then drew some money out of the bank himself, I think by writing out a cheque himself. I didn't watch him carefully as to what he was doing, but I was in the bank with him. We then left the bank together, and 'X' went back into Scotland Yard, and he asked me to wait outside the building whilst he did so. I thought at the time that he was taking the money to Drury.

I waited for at most ten minutes for 'X', then he joined me with the driver who had taken us to Scotland Yard in the first place. I was then driven back home, where they left me . . .

I have never received any part of that £500 from the Post Office, and at no time did I expect to, although 'X' did suggest that I have some of it, as I have explained . . . I have only 'X's word that Drury had that money himself, because it was all arranged through 'X', and all the discussion I had with Drury about it in his office on that one occasion was formal and quite proper as though, on the face of it, it was a proper and legitimate transaction so far as Drury was concerned. My opinion however is that Drury did have the money.[8]

The reader will have noticed that Good says that he 'did not expect' to receive any of the reward money, and may wonder why. The short answer, as has already been stated, is that Good never said or did anything publicly that led to the conviction of the accused. His activities on behalf of the police were covert, and for these he would have been recompensed in the usual way. Indeed there are some people who believe that Good, as the one-time owner of the gun that killed Mr Stevens, and also as a man who was on friendly terms with Mathews, may well know much more about the Luton case than he has ever let on.

Jackson and Weyers both received their cheques in prison (Drury would hardly have been able to accept cheques on their behalf there), and these were paid into their respective accounts. But when McMahon's and Cooper's solicitors came to visit Weyers in prison in 1975, he claimed during the conversation that he had received only *£250 reward money*.[9] What had he done with the remaining £250 of the £500 which it is known that he received?

From all of this there does emerge *prima facie* evidence to suggest that Drury, or others acting on his behalf, either intended to receive or did receive part of the reward money. Through his solicitor he has denied this,[10] but when one remembers that he was later to deny his corrupt dealings with the Soho pornographer James Humphreys, for which he was eventually convicted and sentenced, his denials regarding the reward money cannot be accepted as proof positive. And if he did receive, or intended to receive, any part of the reward money, there arises an added motive for Mathews's false incrimination of Cooper, McMahon and Murphy.

Chapter Nine

It wasn't until nearly a year after the trial – in February 1971 – that the Court of Appeal was ready to hear the prisoners' application for leave to appeal. During this time the defence lawyers had succeeded in unearthing two things: the statements of Seal and McNair which Drury had suppressed, and which was strong evidence that they had seen Mathews driving the getaway van; and the claim of Mrs Brooks that on the afternoon of the murder she had seen Mathews leave the flat with three other men, and put a brown hold-all which she had often seen him carry, into the boot of the Vauxhall.

Seal and McNair made further statements, both of which described the driver of the van as 'hollow-cheeked' and somewhere between thirty-five and forty-five (Seal) and 'well into his forties' (McNair) which was far nearer to Mathews than any of the three convicted;[1] and although Mrs Brooks told Cooper's solicitors that she did not want to get involved, she did make a statement to the indefatigable Stephen Murphy, who *knew* his son was innocent.[2] And all three agreed to attend the hearing in case they might be called to give evidence.

But they, and even more the three appellants, were to be disappointed. The judges first rejected the statement of Mrs Brooks on the grounds that 'the circumstances in which it was taken and the length of time afterwards' made it not likely to be credible. Then, of the statements of Seal and McNair they said this:

> In our view it really would not afford any ground for allowing the appeal once one assumes, as we all do, that the jury clearly must have reckoned that Mathews was very much more deeply in this than he said, and whether he was the actual driver of the van, or exactly what part

he was playing, perhaps does not matter. The vital matter on which clearly the jury believed him and rejected the applicants was that they were the three men who were with him making up this party.[3]

McMahon's comments on this are worth recording:

According to the judges it did not matter that Mathews was lying about the extent of his own involvement in the crime. But when one considers the fact that if Mathews *was* the driver of the van, he had then clearly lied to the jury and substituted Murphy in place of himself in the role of the getaway driver. If that were the case, then the judges were clearly wrong to dismiss the evidence of Seal and McNair in the way they did. If Mathews was prepared to lie to that extent, then who was to say he wasn't lying when implicating the three of us in the murder instead of naming the real culprits?[4]

In other words, if Mathews had wrongly cast Murphy in the role of the getaway driver, what reasons were there to suppose that he had not cast McMahon and Cooper in false roles too? McMahon continued:

It was also quite wrong for the judges to state that the jury must clearly have reckoned that Mathews must have been very much more involved in the crime than he said. How could they put themselves in the minds of the jury? The prosecution had put Mathews forward as an innocent man, cunningly tricked by Cooper into going to Luton to pick up some non-existent parcels. Who could say that even if the jury had had the benefit of hearing the evidence of Seal and McNair, they would still have returned verdicts of guilty?[5]

Cooper's comments were similar:

It is difficult to understand why it did not matter that Mathews may have been the driver of the van. Did it not

matter that it might have been someone else? The judges'
words seemed to imply that Murphy may have been convicted on evidence which was inaccurate in detail, but
that this was irrelevant.[6]

McMahon says that when he heard that the application
for leave to appeal had failed, he had half been expecting
it. But Cooper was incredulous. 'I had really built my hopes
on the appeal . . . my family had told me that the solicitor
had felt confident that the conviction would be quashed. It
took me quite some time to overcome the defeat.'[7]

As the months went by without any further opportunities
for redress, continued imprisonment affected Cooper and
McMahon in different ways. Cooper, less resilient, began
to have nightmares:

I was plagued by them for about two weeks, and in
that time I never went to bed. This is quite literally true.
I either sat up reading or studied a little. And if I was
not doing either of these things, it was because I
attempted to take a chance on some sleep, and only found
that another seizure had gripped me.

I began to employ all sorts of diversionary tactics. I
would leave my radio on one of the music stations, turned
down very low, but that did not help. I would leave my
light on in the hope that it would relax me. But this did
not help either.

Quite obviously I could not continue like this, but I
was reluctant to go and see someone in authority about
them. Apart from having no faith in any remedies they
might prescribe, I was anyway embarrassed about them.

Sometimes when I had these attacks I would attempt
to cry out or move a limb in the hope that it would break
the seizure . . . sometimes moving one of my feet ever so
slightly would help to bring me out of it.

One day, after a bad night, my next-door neighbour
asked me what was the matter. He had heard some of the
noises I had made in trying to pull myself out of the
seizure, and he said they were quite weird. He said I was

making gurgling noises with my throat, which built up into a scream.

I told him a little about the problem, but kept details to a minimum, because it was something I felt unable to completely come out with.

After two weeks of absolute hell, the seizures subsided, and I was able to resume a natural pattern of sleep.[8]

McMahon's reaction to the prospect of spending another nineteen years in prison was more positive. He made two attempts to escape, first from Parkhurst prison in the Isle of Wight, and later from Hull prison, to which he was transferred at the end of 1970. Both failed, and after the second attempt he was sentenced to two months' solitary confinement as well as wearing the compulsory trousers with yellow stripes to foil any future attempts.

During the first couple of weeks in the block, I went into a state of deep depression and consequently lost over a stone in weight. I drifted through the days apathetically, staring at the bare walls and engulfing myself in pathos to such an extent that I came close to developing a persecution complex. After about three weeks, and in spite of an unwillingness to pull myself out of this mental trough, a series of questions popped up in my mind demanding answers. Was I really sure that my 'Fuck their justice' attitude was correct? Wasn't it possible that there were people out there who, if my case was explained to them in detail, would actually have faith in me? Was I going to let Drury and company off the hook?

Gradually I began to respond to these questions. Starting from the fact that I was an innocent man, I reviewed my attitude towards the whole case and concluded that, whether I liked it or not, I was going to have to vigorously renew the fight through legal channels. My reluctance to admit that I was once more turning to legality, having held it to ridicule for so long, was more than countered by a new rock-solid determination to clear my name of the Luton murder.[9]

During 1971 the first break for one of the accused men came. The magazine *Private Eye* had been running articles on the Luton case, and now a man called Terence Edwards came forward to say that he had seen Murphy on the afternoon of the murder at a time when it would have been impossible for him to have been travelling down the M1 with Mathews. Edwards knew the Murphy family slightly through his work as a sewing-machine mechanic, and he remembered 10 September well, as it was his brother's birthday. At about 4.30 p.m. he had just come out of a shop where he had bought a sewing-machine (which the shop's records confirmed) and was about to cross the road to buy his brother a birthday card when he saw Murphy driving his red sports car. The time and place of his seeing Murphy fitted in with Murphy's own evidence of driving from the Bakers' flat after the St Leger to visit his father at Ilford. Edwards had waved to Murphy, but Murphy had not seen him, and did not wave back.[10]

Two other people also came forward as a result of the article in *Private Eye*. These were Terence Leonard and Frederick Stephens who, it will be recalled (page 18), claimed that some eighteen months before the Luton murder Mathews had proposed to them a plan he had to rob that very same post office. Neither of these two men knew the accused or their families.

Early in 1972 a further possible break came for the convicted men when the Sunday newspaper, the *People*, published a story that Drury and the Soho pornographer and former criminal James Humphreys, together with their wives, had been on holiday in Cyprus.[11] Following on this Drury was suspended from duty and later, realizing that his dealing with Humphreys were likely to be exposed, resigned.

Later Drury sold his memoirs to the *News of the World*, in which he claimed, in a statement that rivalled that of Mathews in its mendacity, that he had not gone to Cyprus for a holiday with Humphreys, he had gone there to look for the escaped train robber, Ronald Biggs. Humphreys, he said, was a police informant and had given him the tip-off that Biggs was hiding in Cyprus.[12] Subsequently Humphreys denied being a police informant, said that the Biggs story was quite untrue, and that he had paid for the holidays both of Drury and his wife.

Chapter Ten

All through 1972 pressure by MPs and others, including Tom Sargant, the Secretary of JUSTICE, who had now taken an active interest in the case, was exerted on the Home Secretary to send the case back to the Court of Appeal. But in spite of their repeated requests, the answer was always the same: the Home Secretary was considering the matter.

In October of that year the BBC current affairs programme *Midweek* devoted the whole of its forty minutes to an examination of the case by one of its most experienced reporters, Tom Mangold. In essence the programme set out to show the guilt of Mathews and the innocence of Murphy. For Murphy, Mr Edwards recounted how he had seen him in his sports car on the day of the murder, and why he happened to remember it. Mr Turner, the plumber, gave a convincing account of seeing Murphy having dinner at his father's house at the time of the murder ('I know definitely without any doubt that Patrick was there, because I saw him at least twice'). But perhaps the most convincing answer as to why he thought Murphy innocent came from Murphy's father, when interviewed in his house by Mangold.

My son was sitting there – right there, at that spot. I am as certain of it as you are certain you are speaking to me now. He was there. This is why I know he is innocent. I absolutely *know* it. I don't need proof or anything. I've got my own eyes. I know he was there, sitting at that spot.

For the case against Mathews, his brother Reg appeared, and after describing how Mathews had arrived at his house on the night of the murder saying he was in trouble and in need of help, he was asked by Mangold if he thought Mathews had actually been at the scene of the murder.

'Having listened carefully to this brother of mine,' he replied, 'I felt convinced he was. Yes, I do really.'

Then Frederick Stephens was wheeled on, and Mangold referred to the meeting that he and Terence Leonard had had with Mathews in 1968.

'What did he want with you?'

'He wanted me and a friend of mine to go with him on a job . . . to Luton. We went down – on the Saturday or Sunday – and we went to Luton, parked the car by the station and walked down to the post office.'

'This was which Post Office?'

'This was in Luton High Road, I believe . . . in the main road.'

'High Town Road?'

'Yes. We walked down there. Looked in through the windows, then walked away. There was no mention of what we were supposed to do by him, but by the conversation I thought it was going to be just a normal break-in job. So when we went back to the motor, there was a mention of a gun, and we'd got to get the keys off someone to get into the post office.'

'Who mentioned that?'

'This was Elliott [Mathews]. So anyway as soon as he mentioned a gun, I quickly said, "Well, leave me out," and the friend that I was with said, "You can leave me out also." And he kept trying to convince us it was a good thing and the best way was to use the gun. So we left Luton and all the way going back to London, he kept trying to talk us into it, and we dropped him off at Whitechapel.'

'What is being said in your circles now about Alfred Mathews?'

'Well, they've fitted some people up. What they are saying is that it's diabolical – that he got away with it.'

Then Mangold spoke to Terence Langston, the brother-in-law of Michael Good:

'Back in the summer of 1969, you were asked to look

after a gun by a friend; and that gun, I believe, was collected from your house. Can you tell me how it was collected?'

'Yes. It was collected by two men, and they came up to my house, knocked at the door, asked for me – and I handed it over. He thanked me and they both left.'

Mangold showed Langston a number of photographs, and Langston pointed to one as that of one of the men to whom he had given the gun. The photograph was of Alfred Mathews.[1]

Later, after this interview, Langston made a further statement, already referred to (see page 60), that Drury had tried to get him to say that Murphy was one of the two men to whom he had given the gun; and that he had refused to do so.

In December 1972, as a result of representations made about Murphy's alibi, the Home Secretary at last decided to refer Murphy's case back to the Court of Appeal.[2]

When McMahon heard this, he wrote, 'I was overjoyed at this news, for if Murphy's appeal was successful, it would obviously cast considerable doubts on my own conviction. If Mathews's evidence against Murphy was proved to have been false, then the whole prosecution case would be seriously undermined.' In anticipation of the appeal, he was moved to Wandsworth, which meant more family visits:

During this period I was receiving frequent visits from my parents and Sue, which helped brighten my drab existence. They had become euphoric with the recent turn of events, and although I myself was hopeful, the cynical streak was still there. I tried to temper their optimism with realism, but this was to no avail, as they were already convinced that the truth was about to surface. While I was pleased with the progress being made, the mere fact that I was in prison at all was a constant reminder of how the mechanism of British justice can go wrong.[3]

In the event, Murphy's appeal was postponed because

his lawyers considered that the Home Secretary's terms of reference to the Court of Appeal were too restrictive. They wanted not only the new witness, Edwards, called, but also Seal, McNair and Mrs Brooks. The Home Office took a long time considering this request, but in the end decreed that the basis of the appeal should be the new evidence of Edwards. The Appeal Court judges – Lord Widgery, the Lord Chief Justice, sitting with Lord Justice Stephenson and Mr Justice Browne – decided they would hear Edwards first, and then consider whether or not to hear the other witnesses.

In the event, they had no need to go further than Edwards. In November 1973 – more than three years after the murder – Lord Widgery gave the court's decision:

One may say at once that if Mr Edwards had made a bad impression, if he had given us the impression that he was shifty, not particular about the truth, embarrassed, contradicting himself, if he had exhibited any of those features, there is little doubt but that we should have given this case very short shrift, and said there is really no reason whatever to think that the contribution made by Edwards had really significantly affected the matter at all.

But Edwards did not appear to us like that at all. He is a man of good character: he is a man who, as I have already shown, was not intimately connected with the Murphys, and knew them quite distantly, and his demeanour in the witness-box and the way in which he gave evidence was impressive. He certainly did not contradict himself except to the extent an honest man might do so. He seemed to answer frankly, and his answers seemed to be convincing and fit the general pattern of what he had to say.

It is because of the favourable impression that Edwards made upon us that we find it necessary to abandon our somewhat cynical original view of this story, and to recognize that unlikely though the story may be, we have had it put before us honestly on his oath by a man who is on the face of it capable of belief, and in the result because Edwards' evidence has made us feel that the identification of Murphy by Mathews was unsafe, we have decided that this appeal must be allowed, and that the conviction must be quashed.[4]

This decision did not mean that Murphy was now a free man, for after the Luton case, he had been tried and convicted for the Newington Green Road post-office robbery, and he still had to serve the remainder of the twelve-year sentence imposed on him for that.

Any hopes that McMahon and Cooper had of their own identification by Mathews being called into question were at once quashed by what Lord Widgery had to say at the end of his judgment.

The other and last thing that the court wishes to say is that it has been concentrating entirely on the case of Murphy. It has not had before it the case of Cooper and McMahon, and it expresses no view about those cases except to say that it should not be assumed that the Court's view expressed today necessarily means that Cooper's and McMahon's convictions are in any way rendered unsafe. What we have said is that we have doubts about Mathews's identification of Murphy. That is all we have said, and that is the basis of our decision.[5]

Nevertheless both Cooper and McMahon were euphoric at the Court's decision. Cooper wrote:

It was wonderful news when I heard it on the radio, and a result that nobody expected. I immediately sent Stephen Murphy a telegram of congratulations; he had worked hard for something like three years, and had spent a considerable amount of money in that time to vindicate his son.

My feelings of elation were not confined to Murphy winning his appeal. This put me in a much better position in my fight to prove my innocence because Mathews had, unequivocally, been discredited in the case against Murphy . . . my hopes for a new hearing of my case were now greatly increased.[6]

McMahon was equally overjoyed. 'The quashing of Murphy's conviction was a great boost, and Widgery's cautious reference to the cases of Cooper and myself did nothing to diminish the feeling of elation . . . I was hopeful that the Home Secretary would now refer my case back to the Court of Appeal.[7]

Early in 1974 Tom Sargant, the Secretary of JUSTICE, wrote to the Home Secretary, Robert Carr:

I do not know how you have interpreted the result of Patrick Murphy's appeal apart from the obvious inference that, by the judgment of the court, Mathews was proved to have been a false witness who committed perjury in respect of all that he said at the trial about the involvement of Murphy. It is therefore a justifiable inference that he also gave false evidence about Cooper and McMahon, and without this evidence the case against them would never have got off its feet. This was plainly the opinion of the trial judge.[8]

The next month there was a general election, and Labour came into power. The new Home Secretary was Roy Jenkins, a man noted for his liberal views and who had not hesitated to recommend a posthumous free pardon for Timothy Evans a decade earlier. Four months later, in May 1974, he again referred the case of Cooper and McMahon back to the Court of Criminal Appeal. In his letter to the Court he took up Tom Sargant's point: 'While recognizing that the new evidence adduced in Mr Murphy's case was immediately material only to that case, the Secretary of State has come to the conclusion that the decision to allow Mr Murphy's appeal raises an issue about the credibility of Mr Mathews's evidence against Mr Cooper and Mr McMahon which makes it desirable that the Court of Appeal should also be asked to reconsider their cases.'[9]

Some people read into this a hint that the Court of Appeal should in fact have reconsidered the cases of McMahon and Cooper at the same time as, and in the light of, their quashing of Murphy's conviction.

McMahon heard the news from the assistant governor with unconcealed joy. 'Although I had been praying for this to happen, now that it had been confirmed, I was too stunned to reply. I left the office walking on air, feeling that at last the tide had turned in my favour; that the world wasn't such a bad place after all.'[10]

When Cooper heard the news, his health was not of the best. In March 1974 he had gone on hunger strike for twenty-five days as one of the few protests left to him (he felt then that nothing more could be done) and afterwards, instead of remaining within the prison community, opted for solitary confinement in the segregation block. It was from here that he was fetched by a prison officer to see his assistant governor.

As he sat down behind the table, I felt instinctively that he was going to tell me something very important; there were no outward signs from him to indicate this, and when he read from the piece of paper in his hand that the Secretary of State had referred my case back to the Court of Criminal Appeal and that I was now an appellant, one would think he was reading the latest bulletin on the weather forecast.

I remember the A.G. asking me if I would now go back to the main wing in view of the news he had just given me, but I could hardly talk. So long had I been waiting and hoping to hear that my case was to be looked at again by the Court of Appeal that I was completely robbed of my equilibrium. I just turned, walked out of the office and back to my cell, and such was the exhilaration I felt that a profound euphoric feeling went through my whole body. There was a tingling in my fingers so powerful that it caused me to look at them and rub them together . . . I thought of my family and in particular my younger brother Terry, who had given so much of himself over the years in trying to establish my innocence, and wondered how they must be feeling on hearing the news.[11]

Chapter Eleven

The wheels of the law, if not of justice, grind exceeding slow, and it wasn't until February 1975, or five years after the original trial, that the Court of Appeal assembled to hear the case for the third time. McMahon was delighted with the new legal team that were to represent him: Wendy Mantle, his solicitor, of the firm of Bindman and Partners, and his two counsel, David McNeill, QC, and Peter Susman. Cooper, too, was pleased with his new representatives, Gareth Peirce, of the firm of Benedict Birnberg, and his counsel, Bryan Anns, QC, and Julian Gibson-Watt. Statements had been taken from the journalist William Thomson (see page 83), Seal and McNair, and Leonard and Stephens. In addition Mr Anns applied to the Court for Mathews to be cross-examined on his evidence, and he was summoned to appear in case the application was successful.

'Only someone who had not worn his own clothes for five years', wrote McMahon, 'could understand how I felt that Monday morning when I was handed my own attire.' His girlfriend Sue, still faithful after five years of waiting, had sent him a kipper-style tie for the occasion, which was not in fashion at the time of his conviction. 'I had never worn one of these before, so I struggled for an embarrassing five minutes to produce what I considered to be a reasonable knot.'[1]

On arrival at the Law Courts the two appellants conferred with their defence team separately, then, for the first time in a year, met each other briefly before being hand-cuffed and taken up to the Court to await the arrival of the Lord Chief Justice, Lord Widgery, together with Lord Justice James and Mr Justice Ashworth. Mr Victor Durand, QC, counsel for the prosecution at the original trial, had again been briefed for the Crown.

Before being taken up, both men were handcuffed together. 'This,' wrote Cooper, 'was absolutely ludicrous, as it would inevitably restrict me in the notes I wanted to make. An application was made to Lord Widgery by Mr Anns that the cuffs be removed, but after consultations with the other judges, he refused. I could not understand the logic of our being shackled: a psychological reminder perhaps that as close to our freedom as we might appear to be, we were still convicted murderers. However I did manage with extreme difficulty to make notes to pass to my counsel.'[2]

It had been agreed that Cooper's case should be heard first, and on the first day Mr Anns applied for Mathews to be called for cross-examination. 'It was obvious from the very outset,' wrote McMahon, 'that the judges did not want to allow the application. Widgery said he could not remember any case where a witness at the original trial had been called back for cross-examination.'[3] Anns said that if the new material that had come to light had been available at the original trial, questioning Mathews would have been a cross-examiner's dream. He also argued that the whole basis of the appeal related to Mathews's credibility, and the only logical way to test a witness's credibility was to put him in the witness-box.

Astonishingly, the judges rejected the application on the grounds that this could only be considered in an exceptional case, and that this one was not it. It was a strange decision, for there could be no denying that the case was about to come before the Court of Appeal for an exceptional, and unprecedented, third time.

Application was made and granted for Frederick Stephens and Terence Leonard to tell their story of how Mathews had invited them to join him in a raid on the Luton post office eighteen months before the murder. 'Durand,' said McMahon, 'took the opportunity to cross-examine both men, but he failed to discredit their story in any way.'[4]

Then Mr Anns read out William Thomson's statement that Mathews had told him that he had split the £2,000 reward money with Drury, and that Drury had also taken a cut from other participants in the reward. To this Lord Widgery said, 'We're not investigating Superintendent

Drury's credibility, are we? How does this relate to Mr Mathews?'

'If,' replied Anns, 'it's true that Mathews split the reward money with Drury, that in itself casts a shadow over the whole prosecution case.' From the beginning, he said, Drury knew that Mathews was involved in the murder, but had never put him on an identification parade. 'The inference I ask the Court to draw,' he continued, 'is that if this evidence is true, Drury and Mathews conspired together to put false evidence before the Court. I go on to say there is a considerable amount of evidence from which that can be inferred.'

'This is all highly uncomplimentary of Mr Drury,'* said Lord Widgery. 'What evidence is there to suggest a conspiracy?' Anns referred not only to Drury's failure to put Mathews on an identification parade, despite John McNair having picked him out from a photograph album, but also to the fact that part of the reward money had gone to Mathews's brother. This cut at the very credibility of Mathews. 'It showed,' said Anns, 'that he was a liar without scruples prepared to blacken anybody.' The three judges conferred, then said they were not prepared to receive Thomson's statement on the grounds that 'it cannot on a fair reading be evidence of any prior conspiracy between Mr Mathews and Mr Drury'.

'By this stage,' wrote McMahon, 'I was becoming increasingly pessimistic about the outcome and on entering the Solicitors Room below the Court that evening Peter Susman asked me how I thought it was going. 'I think we have lost it already,' I replied. Susman tried to assure me that everything was going okay, and that I should not be disheartened by the way the judges constantly interrupted during the course of the argument.'[5]

The next day McMahon's counsel, David McNeill, addressed the court. 'He concentrated,' wrote McMahon, 'on

---

* Drury's relationship with the pornographer James Humphreys was at this time still being investigated.

the narrow argument that was the hub of the case, that the quashing of Murphy's conviction had impugned Mathews's credibility to such a degree that the convictions of Cooper and myself were unsafe and unsatisfactory.' At the beginning of his address McNeill referred to Mrs Crawley's first statement in which she said that there was only one man in the car park and she would not be able to recognize him again. 'Perhaps,' rejoined Lord Widgery, *she was only being modest* when she first stated she wouldn't be able to identify him.'[6] A strange remark from a Lord Chief Justice.

The judges then indicated that it would be a waste of time proffering evidence that supported Mathews, for the case stood or fell on the evidence of Mathews alone. If counsel could persuade them that Mathews was *lying* in his identification of Murphy, then the other two convictions would have to be quashed. This, said Mr McNeill, was just what he was arguing. On Mathews's evidence alone, he had been sitting next to Murphy in the van: he had described in detail his hat, his glasses, his coat – both as to colour and length – as well as giving graphic descriptions of his shouting and vaulting into a car. A mistake was out of the question. 'Are you saying', asked Lord Widgery, 'that this Court cannot come to the conclusion that Mathews may have been *mistaken* about Murphy?' And McNeill replied, 'With respect, I am saying it would be wrong for the Court to come to that conclusion.'

Mr Victor Durand rose for the Crown, and submitted that the arguments and evidence put forward on behalf of the appellants did not justify the quashing of their convictions. Had the original jury heard the evidence of Terence Edwards, they could have found that Mathews had made a mistake about Murphy, yet would still have found Cooper and McMahon guilty. Then for the appellants came a ray of hope. 'If Mathews *was* lying about Murphy,' asked Widgery, 'then doesn't the prosecution case against Mr Cooper and Mr McMahon collapse like a pack of cards?' At this McMahon turned excitedly to Cooper and said, 'I think we've won it.'

The judges left the courtroom to confer, and McMahon

wrote: 'I really believed I would be going home with my parents and Sue, who had tensely sat the proceedings out in the public gallery.' But Cooper was less sanguine:

The waiting seemed interminable, and not unnaturally I was very tense. McMahon spoke to me, but what he said I do not know. He, like myself, was feeling the strain of the past weeks, and although I did not look at him, I could feel that he was tense and nervous.

I looked across the courtroom, and there in the same seats they had occupied for the last three days, sat my mother and two brothers, Tony and Terry. I had nodded and smiled to them every day on entering and leaving the court. I had looked at them at odd times and smiled wryly, but now it was so incredibly painful. I was sickened by the misery being meted out to these people I loved; a love so absolute, it was strangling up my insides to see how they were suffering now. I felt the tears well up behind my eyes, as I looked at them and thought of the past years they had fought to prove my innocence, and knew there was no way in which I could comfort them.[7]

After only fifteen minutes, the judges came back into court. What they had to say took a few seconds. 'Both appeals are dismissed. Reasons will be given later.'

'I felt,' wrote McMahon, 'as though I had been struck by a sledgehammer. Sick and speechless, Cooper and I were led from the dock like zombies. Once back in our cell below the court we sat opposite each other in silence, completely shattered physically and emotionally.'

He was taken to the solicitors room to meet his lawyers.

McNeill, who I feel sure did not comprehend just what I was going through at this moment, said, 'Well, we put up a good fight. I thought for one moment we were going to win.' I was certainly in no mood to be consoled by the fact that we had put up a good fight. I was an innocent man, and this shattering defeat had sunk me to the depths of despair. 'I have never witnessed such legal manoeuvring

106

as took place up there,' I replied. 'Those bastards have bent over backwards to uphold my conviction.' McNeill was too close to the bench to agree with me, but tactful enough not to disagree. After a few more minutes Wendy Mantle, looking very disturbed with the outcome, promised me that the campaign to establish my innocence would continue.

He was allowed briefly to see his mother and Sue. 'They were both visibly stunned, and the sight of my mother in tears was enough to put my own sorrow aside, while attempting to assure her I was temporarily okay, and that this was not the final decision.' Back in the cells with Cooper, who had been through the same painful experience with his family, McMahon said,

John, we've only got a few minutes. We're going to have to fight harder than ever. I feel as gutted as you, but if we let ourselves drift into apathy, we're never going to beat these crooked bastards. But all Cooper could say was, 'Mick, my brain is so fucked up I just can't think straight at the moment.'

After a few more minutes in which bitterness towards Mathews, Drury and the judiciary was expressed, the cell door swung open. As I was led to the waiting van, I knew I was going to have to call on all my inner resources to pull myself through the depressing days ahead. As we moved out of the Law Courts it was raining heavily. Observing people huddled under umbrellas, it was excruciating to think that by rights I should be out there among them.

In half an hour McMahon was back in Wandsworth. At reception his civilian clothes were taken away from him and packed into a cardboard box. 'I wondered how long it would be before I saw them again.' He believed that after five years in prison he had become immune to utter despair, but that night, he wrote, was the most despondent of his life.

'In the darkness of my punishment cell block* I lay listlessly on the wooden plank bed. Above the patter of the rain was the voice of the man in the next cell, shouting to a prisoner a few cells away that he had only two days left to serve. So I was forced to listen to this gate-happy creature portraying how he was going to have his first woman in two years, take a drink, become a human being again. It was to this background of driving rain, accompanied by the voice of a man on the verge of emancipation, that for the first time since childhood, tears ran down my cheeks.'[8]

On 22 February 1975 the Court of Appeal published its reasons for not granting the appeals. As regards their refusal to receive the statement of the journalist William Thomson, they said that it referred more to the credit of Drury rather than the credibility of Mathews.[9] On a strict interpretation of the laws of evidence, this was probably correct. But had evidence been proved to show that Mathews *had* split his reward money with Drury, the door would then have been opened for inquiring as to when this arrangement had been made and why. It went to the very heart of the matter. For what other possible reason would Mathews give Drury part of his reward money, if indeed he did, than because of a previous arrangement between them which, by the incrimination of Cooper, McMahon and Murphy would enable Mathews to get off the hook, Drury to clear up the case, and both of them to share in the profits. Admittedly the reward money had not been paid out until after the trial was over, but that £5,000 was on offer was known five days after the murder.

As regards the refusal of the court to accept the evidence of Leonard and Stephens, the judgment declared:

We find it incredible that twenty-one months or so before the event, Mathews could have nominated as the

---

* Just before the appeal he had been awarded seven days' solitary confinement for a minor offence.

place which the sub-postmaster would be held up, the car park in which he was shot.[10]

But why, asked McMahon, was it so incredible?

The evidence at the original trial showed that the post-master had been a man of settled habits. If he parked his car in the same car park every day and returned to it at about the same time every evening, it is hardly incredible that someone planning to rob him would choose the car park in which to do so; or that having put his plan to potential accomplices who rejected it, that he should put the identical plan into operation with other accomplices some time later.[11]

In regard to the evidence of McNair the Court found that although he was a credible witness, 'the maximum effect his evidence would have had on the jury is that they would have believed that Mathews played a part in the offence as the driver of the van on its journey from the bank car park, and that Mathews's evidence as to the part he played was false'. The judgment admits that it must have been clear to the jury that Mathews 'was far more involved than he was prepared to admit in his evidence . . . and this fresh evidence does not touch the crucial question of the reliability of Mathews in respect of his evidence as to who were the members of the team who went to Luton'.[12]

The dottiness of this reasoning becomes apparent when we consider the final reasons of the court for rejecting the appeal, and which they called 'the nub of the appeal'. This was that Mathews, in identifying Murphy whose appeal they had allowed, did not have to be lying, but *could have been mistaken*. This really takes the breath away. For if one accepts the court's arguments that Mathews was far more involved than he was prepared to admit and indeed, if McNair was right, was the driver of the getaway van, how could Mathews *possibly* have been mistaken?[13] And how could any jury possibly believe that Mathews, as one of the central figures in what the judges admitted was a *carefully planned robbery*, was ferrying to and from the scene of the crime three accomplices, *two of whom he didn't know*? How can you carefully plan a robbery without knowing who you are carefully planning it with? Either Mathews was in Luton to collect parcels, in which case he *might* have been mistaken about who was with him, or he was one of the gang, in which case he knew who was with him. You couldn't have it both ways. The court, without realizing it, had been hoist with its own petard.

No wonder that on reading the judgment, Cooper wrote as he did: 'Such was the humiliation, anger and frustration I felt on reading it, that I could not contemplate the idea of trying to understand or find the logic behind the court's reasons. The judgment was quite ludicrous.'[14]

But this was not the end of the matter. Both Mrs Mantle and Mrs Peirce, for whom both McMahon and Cooper had nothing but feelings of the deepest gratitude and highest praise, and who were convinced of their clients' innocence, determined to fight on, whatever the cost. During the coming weeks and months there was a spate of articles, editorials and television programmes deploring the court's decision, and in particular their refusal to allow Mathews to be called as a witness, which the Home Secretary's reference back had clearly anticipated. The *Sun* and the *News of the World* had leading articles, David Napley, then Chairman of the Law Society, appeared with Tom Sargant and Bryan Magee in the BBC's *Panorama*, and in *The Times* Bryan Magee wrote:

> It is contrary to common sense to suppose that if the jury had known Mr Mathews's evidence against one of the men they were convicting to be unreliable, they would still have regarded his evidence against the other two men as beyond reasonable doubt. Yet this is what the appeal court judges then explicitly asked us to believe in their final judgment, and I sat in the courtroom scarcely able to believe my ears.[15]

McMahon himself managed to smuggle out a letter to *The Times*:

I have fought and overcome many obstacles during the past five years to prove my innocence, and I felt confident of being allowed to do so when my appeal was heard in February. The decision by the appeal judges completely shattered me ... The only hope I and the other convicted men have of getting a fair and impartial hearing is if the Home Secretary orders an independent inquiry.[16]

Both McMahon and Cooper were active in writing to anyone – MPs, trade unionists, journalists, churchmen – who they thought might be able to help. Often their letters were blocked by the authorities on the grounds that the addressees were not personally known to them. One of McMahon's addressees was the Archbishop of Canterbury:

I am not a religious person, but as my whole life was at stake, I was prepared to write to anybody. I set out my case in detail, and virtually begged the Archbishop for assistance. When my letter was stopped on the grounds that I did not know him, I petitioned the Home Office that as I had been born and raised in East London, and did not mix in the same circles as the Archbishop, I had never had the opportunity of getting to know him personally.

I argued that I should be permitted to write to the Head of my Church whenever I felt the need to do so. The Home Office decided to back down on this one by replying that as the Archbishop was a member of the House of Lords – a fact they had overlooked – they had now decided to post my letter.

The reply of the Archbishop, when it finally arrived just before Christmas, is worth quoting in full:

Dear Mr McMahon,
In the last few months about twenty-six thousand people have written to me, and you will understand that I cannot physically answer all the letters myself.
But I am writing to you personally, and I want you to realize that although I cannot take up your case in the

111

way you ask, I want you to know that God Almighty still cares for and loves you. I know you find this hard to take, but I should not be writing personally if I did not believe that this is the Christmas message for you.

McMahon's reply is worth quoting too.

In my worst moments I tell myself there are many people in this world suffering a far worse fate than I am. There are some who have to spend their lives hanging from baskets on hospital walls, having neither arms nor legs, and being unable to speak. I do this in order to remind myself that, even though I am the victim of a terrible miscarriage of justice, I still have everything to live for. But no matter what frame of mind I am in, a certain quotation remains with me. 'I rage, I melt, I burn. The feeble God has stabbed me to the heart.'[17]

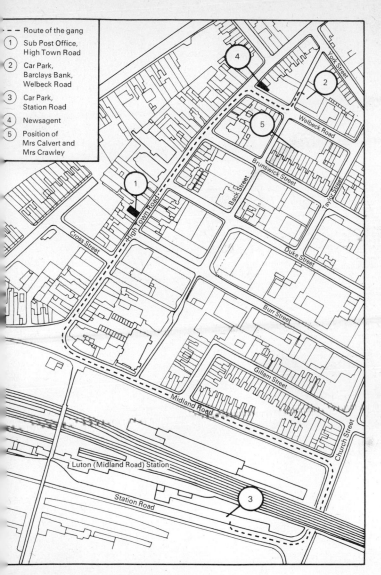

Map to show scene of crime and the route the gang took.

Ex-Commander Kenneth Drury
Daily Mail

Morris Lerman, Tailor
Daily Mail

Alfred Mathews
Daily Mail

Patrick Colin Murphy
Topix

Michael Graham
McMahon
Daily Mail

David Cooper – happier
times on holiday
Daily Mail

The Hon Mr Justice
Cusack
Camera Press

Lord Chief Justice Widgery
Popperphoto

Rt Hon Lord Justice Lawton
Keystone Press

Rt Hon Lord Justice Roskill
Keystone Press

Chapter Twelve

Later in 1975 there were further setbacks for the two men in that the Court of Appeal refused their application for leave to appeal to the House of Lords, and for McMahon in that the Law Society had turned down his request for legal aid to bring an action against Mathews for perjury.

However there were always fresh surprises in this most surprising of cases, and now another one came. Drury was arrested and charged with corruption in relation to his dealings with the pornographer Humphreys. He was taken to court with his head covered, as he himself had taken so many criminals in the past – a situation which McMahon saw as nothing less than 'poetic justice'. On a subsequent court appearance, Cooper's brother Terry attended the hearing, vaulted over the public gallery and began abusing Drury as he stood in the dock. Cooper was much moved by this, 'as Terry was normally a shy, placid sort of person', yet also saddened, 'as it reminded me in a poignant way of how far-reaching had been the effect of this case on the family'.[1]

In May 1975 Humphreys, then serving a prison sentence himself for wounding his wife's lover, made the statement already referred to (see page 84) in which he declared that Drury had told him that he had had 'a good drink' from the informants' money. Later he swore an affidavit saying that over lunch with Drury at the Grange restaurant in 1972,

Drury went on to tell me that Mathews named some men who had accompanied him to Luton. Murphy, he said, was framed because he was an alibi witness for the other men named. When I asked Dury why he had done this, he said that Murphy was 'a little bugger'. He had to be charged to prevent him from giving evidence for the robbers. I suggested that it was a bit hard for Murphy to get a life sentence. Drury's reply was that it served Murphy right, because of all the post office robberies he had done.[2]

Now came what appeared to be a new break for Cooper. His brothers Tony and Terry had been having a drink in a pub one evening when they ran into a man called Slade. His father, William Slade, had once been an associate in Cooper's father's window-cleaning business, but since had retired and bought himself a hotel in Margate. As a result of this conversation, the father was interviewed, and it transpired that he had seen Cooper on the day of the murder, not just once but twice. On the first occasion he had had a cup of tea with him in a café after the St Leger, and then later that evening he had seen, but not spoken to, Cooper in the amusement arcade with his brother Terry. A statement was taken from Slade by Cooper's solicitors, and later by the police.[3]

Cooper was well aware that coming so long after the murder, many people would assume that Slade's evidence must be a fabrication. But if this was so, what was the explanation for the fact that, as he and his family never knew Slade well, by agreeing to come forward, Slade 'had nothing to gain except a great deal of worry and harassment. He was then, I believe, sixty-nine years old and sick. He would have been aware of all the inconvenience his evidence was going to cause him, and yet would a man of untainted character like him come forward to tell a pack of lies to try to get someone out of a murder conviction?'

Slade's statement was sent to the Home Office, and in due course he was interviewed by the police to whom he confirmed what he had said. Armed with this new information, Mrs Mantle and Mrs Peirce, supported by Bryan Magee, Tom Sargant and others, now put great pressure on the Home Office to have the case sent back to the Court of Appeal for a second time – indeed for the case or a part of it, to be considered by the Court an unprecedented fourth time.

In April 1976 the Home Secretary acted. In referring the case to the Court a fourth time he asked for three things. First, that the court should evaluate the evidence of the new witness Slade. Second, in view of the previous application of the Court to hear the evidence of the journalist William Thomson, that the recent statement by James Humphreys should be made available to them. And third, and in the most tactful language, the Home Secretary made it plain that even if the court had not seen fit to call Mathews as a witness the last time, there was every reason for doing so now:

> The Court will be aware that in the judgment delivered on 21 February 1975, it was said that while it might be that the Court had power under the statute to order the attendance of a witness for this purpose, the case in which the use of that power would be appropriate would be a wholly exceptional one; the appeals of Cooper and McMahon were not considered to be such a case at that time. It may be that the Court will wish to reconsider this matter in the light of the further evidence.[4]

On 8 April the two prisoners were given the good news by their respective governors. McMahon wrote: 'I felt better on leaving the governor's office than I had done on the previous occasion at Hull. They might as well have told me I was going to be released, such was my immediate sense of confidence and joy.' When Mrs Mantle came to see him, 'she was naturally delighted with the latest turn of events. Her "cushion caution" fell on deaf ears, as I told her there was absolutely no way in which I could envisage us losing it now'. Cooper confessed to being 'quite overwhelmed by the news, so much so that I felt a momentary lack of support in my legs'.[5]

On 14 May McMahon was transferred to Wandsworth to allow him to be nearer his solicitors, and here came fresh news to bolster his spirits. A prisoner called James Wilkinson told him he knew Mathews, and that Mathews had possessed a cannibalized red MG midget sports car – what criminals call 'a ringer' – in the summer of 1969. He himself had connected Mathews with the Luton crime 'because of an earlier conversation about it'. Mathews had visited him five days after the murder, had appeared agitated, and told him to 'forget' he had ever laid eyes on the red MG. McMahon informed Mrs Mantle, and a statement was taken from Wilkinson.[6]

The appeal was set for 12 July and Cooper, now at Wormwood Scrubs, was finding the waiting almost unbearable. 'I was feeling absolutely wretched, and what made it worse was that I was keeping my emotions bottled up inside me during the day, so that no one could see how I was truly feeling.' At night he was plagued again by nightmares:

They were nothing like nightmares as is generally understood. Everybody at some time experiences nightmares. I think we all know what they are, but what I had to endure was no ordinary nightmare. As the welcoming drifts of sleep began to take me into that nebulous world of dreams, I would suddenly be seized by some horrific power. I couldn't move or have any control over my body. This sounds quite absurd, I know, but it was as though something or somebody had taken complete possession of me.

When Bryan Magee came to visit him, he was told by the assistant governor that the visit would have to be supervised. 'I exploded, saying he couldn't do such a thing, and stormed from his office. After leaving his office, I was close to a nervous breakdown, and went back to my cell, feeling as a wounded, caged animal might feel at the zoo after having been incessantly prodded with sticks . . . Apart from my own feelings of humiliation, I considered it beneath contempt that such disrespect should be shown to my MP.'

At first Cooper said that if the visit was to be supervised, he wouldn't see Magee, but later a sympathetic assistant governor persuaded him to change his mind.

Cooper told Magee that if the appeal failed again, he was going into solitary confinement, and didn't want Magee to do anything more for him. 'He must have wondered if I was quite sane. My feelings were, to put it bluntly, that I was losing touch with reality. I had had unaccountable bouts of crying, my nightmares were getting worse, and my explosions with the screws were quite often as the result of some trivial confrontation. I could not remember afterwards what fully transpired.'

Magee succeeded in calming him to some extent, and told Cooper that even if the appeal did fail, he would not allow things to rest as they were. 'At the conclusion of the visit he said that he would attend the appeal for its duration, which gave me a lift. I couldn't help feeling immense gratitude to this man, who had already given so much of his time and energy to the case.'

In contrast to McMahon's continued optimism, Cooper rose at 7 a.m. on the day of the appeal with mixed feelings. 'On the one hand I was feeling quite relieved that the day had arrived, on the other apprehension. I had a real fear that something was wrong.' The early part of the day had a familiar air to it. 'The memory of having prepared to depart from the prison to the Appeal Court eighteen months earlier was disturbingly vivid; the gathering together of documents I thought I might need, the passing through reception where I would change my lifeless prison garb for civilian clothes, the snapping on and aggressive inspection of the weighty hand-cuffs, and the familiar short walk to the heavily caged, glisteningly clean van all had a sense of unreality about it. And the eighteen months' gap might have been eighteen weeks, the memory was so vivid.'[7]

On his entering the van, however, there was a difference. McMahon was already there, having been picked up first at Wandsworth. They exchanged greetings, but afterwards spoke little as the five prison officers in the van 'had an inhibiting effect on conversation'. At the Law Courts, they were taken down to the same cell where they had waited for the last appeal eighteen months earlier.

At 10.30 a.m. they were brought up to the court, and presently appeared the three judges who were to hear the appeal – Lord Justice Roskill, Lord Justice Lawton and Mr Justice Wien. The two appellants had the same defence team as on the previous occasion, with the exception of Mr Anns, who had been drowned in a swimming accident, and whose place had been taken by Mr Brian Capstick, QC. Mr Victor Durand, QC, again appeared for the Crown.

On the first day William Slade was called, and told his story about seeing Cooper twice on the day of the murder. McMahon was not much impressed by Slade as a witness (who it was clear had been somewhat influenced by the over-zealousness of Cooper's brothers) and felt that his evidence wasn't going to win the appeal. Nor was anyone much impressed by the evidence of Wilkinson, which, the court said later, 'bore the hallmark of recent prison manufacture designed to help a fellow prisoner in trouble'. 'But', wrote McMahon, 'it was unlikely the Court would refuse the application to have Mathews recalled, and I felt confident that with all the evidence that had come to light since the trial, we would destroy his credibility once and for all.'[8]

At the lunch interval, said McMahon, 'Cooper told me he was feeling so strung up that he could not bear to sit through the rest of the hearing, and decided to remain in the cell below the court. I fully understood how he felt. The strain of sitting in the dock was almost unbearable. Whenever I left the courtroom, I found my shirt drenched with sweat, and this had nothing to do with the heat.'

Cooper had only agreed to attend the hearing because his family and supporters wanted him to. He remained below for the rest of the hearing, 'an excellent arrangement for me', as he put it, 'as I didn't have to sit and listen to the three judges putting on a superb performance of impartiality'.[9]

On the morning of the second day, David McNeill rose to submit that Mathews be recalled. Mr Durand opposed the submission on the grounds that the previous appeal had ruled that such an application should only be granted 'in a wholly exceptional case'. McMahon's spirits rose when Lord Justice Lawton asked, 'This is the first time that this court has twice had a case referred back to it, and you say these appeals are not wholly exceptional?' And the application was granted.

'Call Alfred Mathews,' shouted the court usher.

'Mathews [said McMahon] entered almost immediately. As he made his way into the witness-box, I noticed he had not altered at all in appearance since the trial over six years earlier. When the usher called his name, I became extremely tense, but the tension turned to nausea as he took his place in the witness-box directly opposite to where I was seated.'

Here was the man who had robbed me of seven years of life. If I live to be a hundred, I will never hate anyone or anything as much as I hated Mathews at that moment – this parasite, who with help from people in high places, had been allowed to get away with the most notorious piece of substitution in criminal history. He was to spend the next two days in the witness-box, but never once met my eyes which, considering we were only a few feet apart, was a remarkable feat on his part.[10]

Almost from the start of his evidence Mathews lied. He lied about his original interview with Drury, he denied that Drury had ever suggested to him that he was the driver of the getaway van, he lied about the reward money, he continued to lie about Murphy's involvement, he continued to deny his own involvement, he denied ever having known Wilkinson until Wilkinson was brought into court to confront him, there was rarely a word of truth in anything he said. And not only did he lie, but sometimes his answers were evasive to the point of incoherence. Asked by David McNeill if he did not think it odd to have been asked to accompany two strangers in two other cars to fetch parcels from Luton, he said:

The only answer I can give to that is I did think it out, and when I did think it was something illegal, I thought to myself, 'Why was I involved?' with the van and the car. This was when we were in Luton, just entering Luton. My mind was carrying away through the streets I did not know, trying to memorize the way back. I could only say that I, being an elderly person compared with these other three, it could be something illegal that they could put in my car. I did not know what, and most likely the police seeing a person of my description, would stop me if it was illegal. I did have that in mind.[11]

When Brian Capstick asked him if he was not afraid that he might be arrested after the crime, he said:

In a sense, no. I reasoned myself. I knew I had not been near the scene of where the crime had been committed. I could not really believe it had been committed. No one could say they had seen me, so why shouldn't I walk back? But at the same time under the circumstances one's mind can be in a turmoil, and, well, anyone can reason how one feels under the circumstances. Under the panic and one thing and another, something must have happened drastically for me, and I saw this. I must have seen it had happened. One would not be a fool, and people don't joke over things like that.[12]

To Mr Capstick's suggestion that he brought the gun with him in the hold-all, he replied:

Now you are being a comedian. I am sorry to say it like this, because it is funny to me. You are saying such a ridiculous thing to me. In my life I have done a lot of things, and I thank God I have left it all behind me now, anything like that. I live quite a reasonable and good life as the next. But never in my life have I ever had to use a gun, and would never use one. I see no reason for it, and it wasn't fair. We all had the greed for money. It is ridiculous to insinuate such a thing to me.[13]

And when David McNeill was questioning him about

Wilkinson's evidence concerning the stolen red sports car and his being careful not to leave fingerprints in it, he said:

This is still making me laugh. It is all so ridiculous. You see, you get these on the films when you read like that, because I mean to say foolishly I have done a lot of silly things in my life that had caused me to do a lot of punishment in prison, and I have come to the conclusion that I don't want no more of it, but during my experience I have proved that what you are saying is the amateur who first starts off. He goes and buys himself a load of rubber gloves and things like that, which is all unnecessary. If anyone is going to steal a car or make a ringer, as you say, it is so ridiculous what you are trying to say that I had a red ringer, and you are trying to ring it round. But anyway you carry on, if it makes you happy, to say such stupid things.[14]

Because of the court's later remarks about the credibility of Mathews, these samples of his gibberish have been given at length. One observer at the trial thought him 'demented', and McMahon wrote, 'As I sat in the dock watching him ramble on incoherently, it would have come as no surprise to me if the men in white had entered, and carried Mathews off to the funny farm.'[15]

Down below, Cooper was becoming increasingly apprehensive as to the outcome:

My QC came down to the cells to see me on a few occasions, and on about the fourth day he came and told me that things were not going at all well. I was quite numb with fatigue and shock. I had the strange sensation that my brain was beginning to operate in slow motion. I was not really listening to what my lawyer was saying, but absorbed with this sensation of everything slowing down. It was quite strange.[16]

After having heard the evidence of Drury and Wilkinson (but not that of Humphreys, as the appellants had agreed to base their case on Mathews's credibility alone) the court adjourned for the weekend. Back in Wormwood Scrubs, Cooper had one of his worst nightmares yet:

It must have been about one-o'clock in the the morning. There was no nightmarish dream – I was in fact awake. My whole body had a complete seizure. Even now, in trying to relate this incident, my heart quickens and I feel a slight panic.

I could see the room around me, familiar objects in the darkened room. I was desperate to get to the light-switch, and saw myself moving from the bed towards it. Then I came out of the nightmare, gasping, with my heart pounding fiercely. I was saturated in sweat which had soaked through the sheets of the bed. I realized very quickly that the light-switch I was moving towards was in my imagination, which frightened me. It seemed to me incredible that I had only imagined that I had risen from the bed towards the light-switch.

I had encountered this sort of experience at least once before . . . this was the fiendish nightmare at its most extreme, and I don't think I could have withstood any more at such intense level without going mad.[17]

For McMahon, not knowing whether he and Cooper would be free men in forty-eight hours, the weekend was agonizing too:

The tension gradually built up within me over the weekend, and by Monday I was a good advert for tranquillizers. As a result I was unable to grasp a single sentence of the legal arguments put forward in the court that morning. My mind was firmly focused on the announcement of the verdict, as I impatiently awaited freedom. When the occasional doubt presented itself, I would dismiss it in the same manner as one who is about to be married dismisses last-minute doubts.

Despite my confidence, I was still extremely nervous,

and it didn't help matters when at about 3.30 on the Monday the day ended in anti-climax. The arguments had been completed, and only the judges' verdict was required to bring the appeal to a close. But instead of retiring, they announced that judgment was to be deferred for a few days. So, having geared myself up over the weekend for the big moment, I now had to attempt to unwind for two or three days; to move down the mountain face, having almost reached the peak. I found it impossible to relax, and the more I tried the more confused I became until in the end my nerves were in shreds.[18]

He and Cooper were taken from their cells to a prison van. Cooper wrote:

I told Mick on the way back to our respective prisons that I would not attend when judgment was given. He understood this but was, I think, disappointed that he would be there on his own. We had always been very good friends, and there is no doubt that the case had drawn us closer together.

It was a poignant moment for me as I said good-bye to him at Wormwood Scrubs. I was very sad because I felt in myself that we had lost again, and because all the frustrations, pains and depressions I had felt, I now saw mirrored in Mick's own face as I turned to him before getting out of the van. We shook hands, then I left him . . .[19]

On the morning of 26 July McMahon was taken back to the court to hear the judges' decision:

At about 11.30 I was led into the dock. As the judges took their seats at the bench, I scanned their faces for an indication of what was to come, but they looked as devoid of feeling as ever. I didn't have to wait long, for Roskill's first words caused my head to slump forward and my heart to drop. 'Both these appeals have

123

failed,' he told the packed courtroom. 'Copies of the judgment will be supplied to counsel.' He then proceeded to read the court's judgment.

As he rambled on with the reasons for dismissing the appeals, I sat in the dock with my head in my hands, in utter despair. What have I got to do to win this case, I asked myself? What kind of crooked, twisted men* are these judges. They have sat there listening to Mathews's evidence, one of them, Lawton, even going so far as to call part of it 'a cock and bull story', and yet they are prepared to condemn me for life on that bastard's word.

Then came a dramatic moment:

This mental onslaught continued for a few minutes until I finally snapped. One moment I was sitting bent over in the dock, the next I was on my feet with arms outstretched, screaming at the judges, 'I AM FUCKING INNOCENT – *INNOCENT*. CAN'T YOU UNDERSTAND THAT?' Lawton, who was sitting only a few yards away, rapidly shifted towards the edge of his seat in readiness for a quick getaway. He need not have worried, as I was immediately dragged from the dock by the screws and led to the cell downstairs.[20]

And what did the judgment say? Having rejected the evidence of Slade and Wilkinson, accepted that Drury had not omitted to put Mathews up for identification before Seal and McNair for any sinister reasons, and explained that the quashing of Murphy's conviction as a result of Edwards's alibi evidence did not mean that Murphy was necessarily innocent, it came to Mathews. 'Our decision', said Lord Roskill who was reading the judgment, 'must depend upon the view we take of the veracity of Mathews's incrimination of the appellants and Murphy.'[21]

---

* They were not crooked or twisted, but one can well understand McMahon's reasons for thinking them so.

Having admitted that Mathews had lied 'in a large number of respects' both at his original trial and at the appeal, the judgment went on:

Each of us watched him closely while he was giving his evidence. The conclusion which each of us independently has reached in this court on the vital part of his story is that he was clearly telling the truth . . . we see no justification for disturbing the verdicts which in our view were entirely correct.[22]

Chapter Thirteen

There are many aspects of the Luton murder case that are deeply shocking. The incrimination by Mathews of Cooper, McMahon and Murphy is one of them. The disposal of the reward money is another. The judgment quoted in the last chapter, though in a different category, is no less so. Cooper described it as 'an insult to me, to common sense and to natural justice'. McMahon wrote: 'Their Lordships alone were able to decipher some esoteric signals from Mathews's gibberish, implying veracity ... they had drawn a hypothetical line across a quagmire and told us the smaller section was arable because nobody there had yet slipped in ... they were saying that Mathews had lied where he was proved to have lied, and telling the truth where he wasn't proved to be lying.'[1]

There have been criticisms of this judgment (in this book and elsewhere) of various kinds: that if the conclusion of the court was to depend on a subjective view of Mathews's veracity, it should also have taken into consideration the veracity of the appellants; that in any case it was not for the judges to reach a conclusion on what *they* believed, but on what the original jury might have believed in the light of the further evidence.

But there is another way of looking at it, and that is this: in saying that they believed Mathews to be telling the truth in inculpating Cooper and McMahon, they were not in fact revealing anything about Mathews but something about themselves. And what they were revealing was that they could not bring themselves to believe, any more than Mr Justice Cusack could bring himself to believe, that Mathews could have, as it were, plucked the names of three men out of thin air; that the calculated framing of completely innocent men was simply not

126

credible – it would have been, as Mr Justice Cusack had put it, wicked *beyond belief*.

What the judges did not consider – and as no evidence was led to support it, one can hardly blame them – was the alternative: that it was not Mathews on his own who had drafted the false scenario for the trial, but Mathews with the assistance of Drury;* that it was Drury who had been focusing his attentions on Cooper, Mc-Mahon and Murphy long before Mathews was arrested, and had come to believe – though God knows with little enough evidence to support it – that they were the guilty parties; and that when Mathews refused, as he must have done, to reveal the names of his real accomplices, Drury already had at hand three ready-made suspects.

The extreme gullibility of the three judges was again evidenced in their comments on Mathews's attitude towards the reward money. Ever since this had become public, Mathews had insisted that the money he had received was not reward money as such, but compensation for the loss of work and inconvenience he had suffered after turning Queen's evidence. The judges put this down to Mathews's 'vanity' – 'a marked reluctance to admit that he could have received £2,000 for "grassing" on those who were involved in the crime with him'.[2] In fact it was the opposite that was true, that not even that deep-dyed villain could bring himself to admit that he had received £2,000 for 'incriminating' three men who were *not* involved in the crime with him.

Once again there was widespread criticism of the judgment, epitomized by a leading article in *The Times*:

> The function of the Appeal Court in such cases is to decide whether the verdict of the jury at the trial was unsafe or unsatisfactory. It is not for the appellant

---

* In an article in the *News of the World* of 28 May 1972 Drury admitted that Mathews had been 'leaned on a bit'. Despite this the judges said they 'had no hesitation in rejecting the allegation that Drury leaned on Mathews . . . There is no evidence whatsoever to support it.'

to prove his innocence to the appeal court. A lurking doubt as to the safety of the conviction is enough to justify its quashing even where a strong suspicion of guilt may still remain. These principles are well known to all judges of appeal, and were indeed referred to at some length by the court in the Cooper–McMahon appeal. Its decision, however, appeared to be completely contrary to the application of those principles. The court held that the jury's verdict was not unsafe or unsatisfactory, indeed that it was 'entirely correct'. It defies logic and common sense to have come to that conclusion in the circumstances of the case . . .

In saying that they believed Mathews's evidence that Cooper and McMahon were involved in the killing, and pointing out that the jury must have believed it too, the judges were applying the wrong criteria. The question was whether the conviction was 'safe'. Whether or not they believed Mathews is only part of the answer to that. To most sensible, rational people a verdict which depends on the evidence of a man like Mathews, in the circumstances in which he gave that evidence, cannot be safe.[3]

The two appellants reacted to the judgment differently. Cooper by now had more or less given up the ghost. He had said before the appeal that if it failed, he would go into voluntary solitary confinement, though less as a protests against his continued wrongful imprisonment, than as a desire to withdraw from the world completely. 'I was desperate for some solitude.'

He was taken to the punishment block and changed his ordinary prison uniform for the special drab, navy-blue clothes worn only by those in segregation. 'They have the effect,' wrote Cooper, 'of enhancing one's feelings of humiliation and degradation. They do not fit one, and neither are they meant to. One is made to look a complete clown, without the face make-up.'

The first few days, he said, passed in a haze. 'There were several visits from various people, but I can't remember anything of significance happening. For the most part I just lay in bed, going over various aspects of the case from the very time I was caught in its inexorably weaving plot. It was very uncomfortable when thinking deeply about this . . . I began to wonder whether some inexplicable, immutable force outside my control had a devilish hand in the direction of my life.'

Cooper remained in solitary confinement for four months, a time of both renewed hope and bottomless despair. At one moment he could write that, painful and traumatic though his years in prison had been, one good thing had come out of them – his thinking, his perceptions, his psyche, had all been altered. 'Paradoxically, though it has given me side effects I would much sooner not have, yet at the same time doors have been forced open into my inner self and barriers broken down, giving me a vision of life, and myself, that I would not before have thought possible.'

Such valuable insights were too often clouded by other thoughts. 'I began to feel that my reserves of energy, all the resources I had called on in the past to pull me through extremely difficult periods, were slowly leaving me, and I felt that there was nothing which might motivate me or pull me out of my depression. I felt no pity for myself, or indeed my family, whose suffering had most deeply wounded me in the past.'

His sleeplessness returned too. 'It was sheer hell at times, with some of the nights spent just looking at the ceiling. Quite often I lay awake all night with only the birds at dawn breaking the many hours' silence through the night. I would look forward to their singing at four and five in the morning . . . it was a wonderful and most comforting sound to hear after a black sleepless night.'

He was well aware of his schizophrenic state of mind. 'I was in a perpetual state of anxiety. On the one hand I wanted to stay there, at other times I determined to ask for a move to another prison. Many times I thought of asking to be moved to Long Lartin prison, where McMahon was.

129

In the end I just made no firm decisions, but lived from one day to the next.'

Despite his withdrawal from the world, he was still sensitive to kindness. One day a prison officer came in with a cardboard box containing biscuits, cigarettes, squash, and toilet articles. 'He explained that some of my friends in D wing had made a collection to buy a few comforts for me. I was quite overwhelmed with emotion, and my eyes filled with water. The prison officer said he had been in the service a long time, and said he had not seen anything like the concern being expressed for me. That my defeat should have touched other prisoners in this way affected me very deeply.'[4]

McMahon, on the other hand, bounced back quickly. 'Considering how committed I was to winning the case on this occasion, I managed to pick myself off the ground much easier than on previous occasions. Perhaps I had become punch-drunk with all those judicial blows.'[5]

His solicitors and Cooper's now petitioned the Home Secretary to recommend the grant of the Royal Pregorative of Mercy. There seemed a reasonable chance of this succeeding for, as the *Guardian* said, 'That Mr Jenkins is deeply concerned that Mr David Cooper and Mr Michael McMahon are serving life sentences is beyond doubt . . . it is understood that Mr Jenkins assumed that after the last referral back, Mr Cooper and Mr McMahon would be freed.' But the Home Secretary felt unable either to recommend the Royal Pregorative or to order an independent inquiry into the case. Such an inquiry would be 'wholly exceptional', and would not be justified in this case. But, pointed out McMahon, 'wholly exceptional was how the Appeal Court had described the case when it was referred back to them a second time. So much for bureaucratic clichés! '[6]

McMahon himself applied to the Appeal Court to argue in person an application to appeal to the House of Lords. His request to appear in person was refused (because, McMahon thought, of his outburst to the judges during the last appeal); but when counsel argued it instead, it was dismissed in less than a minute because there was no point of law.

Next he applied to the Home Secretary to be given a lie-detector test, which his family would pay for, but this was refused on the grounds that 'the reliability of lie-detector tests has not been established'. As a result of approaches by his brother, another MP, Dr Oonagh Mac-donald, took up the case and pressed for further consideration of it in the House of Commons. In February 1977 McMahon again petitioned the Home Secretary in a long letter arising from the Court of Appeal's last decision. All in all, he was determined never to give up.

Indeed the only news that afforded him a grain of satisfaction at this time was that of the trial and conviction of Drury who was sentenced to eight years' imprisonment, later reduced to five, for corruption in the Soho pornography case:

> After spending so many years in prison, feeling sorry for those just sentenced comes naturally to me. But I would be a liar if I said I felt any sympathy for Drury. When the news of his conviction was broadcast on the radio, my reaction was a simple, 'I told you so.' I had always believed that the man was basically corrupt and totally unscrupulous: otherwise the trumped-up charge would never have been brought against me, much less made to stick.[7]

After his conviction and sentence Drury was sent to Wormwood Scrubs, which, said Cooper, did nothing for his peace of mind. 'Although he was on the other side of the prison to me, I did catch sight of him one Sunday morning while I was on my way to have a game of badminton. He was in the exercise yard, walking round with one of his companions. I rather lost my head a little and shouted some abuse at him before my path was blocked. It quite upset my morning, but thankfully I never saw him again.'[8]

Chapter Fourteen

One would have thought that so far as the law was concerned, that was the end of the case, but incredibly one more twist in it was yet to come. In March 1977, seven years after the original trial, another alibi witness raised his head. His name was Richard Hurn.

It will be recalled (see page 33) that on the day of the murder Cooper had turned up at Thames Magistrates' Court to attend the hearing of McMahon on a charge of dishonestly handling stolen goods, and that afterwards he had driven McMahon and his two sureties, his father and a man named Lawrence, to McMahon's home in New North Road. McMahon had gone inside to watch the racing on television, and at about 5.30 p.m. had walked to the flat of his girlfriend Sue, where he had remained until about 9.30 p.m. Lawrence meanwhile had bumped into his friend Hurn after leaving Cooper in the red Mercedes. Lawrence had told Hurn that the Mercedes was for sale, and this interested Hurn, as he was looking for a replacement for his Volvo.

Lawrence and Hurn did not meet again until 1977, as Lawrence himself had gone to prison in December 1969 for two years, and Hurn had moved out of the district. They recalled the last time they had met, which Hurn remembered well. He also remembered that 'about a couple of hours' after this, he had spotted McMahon on the corner of Kingsland Road, Shoreditch, while he (Hurn) was waiting at a bus-stop – a place which was on the route that McMahon would have taken in walking from New North Road to his girlfriend's flat. Hurn had thought of speaking to McMahon, but didn't, as McMahon was clearly on his way somewhere, and the bus was approaching.

So long after the event, this information did not at first make any impression on Lawrence. But when he began to think about it, he realized that here was a possible new alibi for McMahon. He contacted McMahon's parents and informed McMahon's solicitors, who took a statement from him. There was some difficulty in finding Hurn, as all he had told Lawrence was that he lived in Harlow. He was eventually traced through the electoral roll.

The question that McMahon's solicitors wanted to know was why this information had not emerged years earlier. But Hurn had a perfectly good explanation. He knew nothing about the Luton murder case, as he never read the papers, and even if he had, he would not have associated McMahon with it, as he knew him only by the name of 'Mackie'. A full statement was taken from Hurn and, together with two statements by Lawrence (one taken by the police), forwarded to the Home Office.[1] There they remained for several months, but eventually on 15 December 1977 the Home Secretary asked the Court of Appeal whether they would be prepared to receive them in private as evidence. This was now the fifth time that the case, or a part of it, was to be considered by the Court of Appeal.

On 11 April 1978 the Court rejected them, and on grounds which McMahon found highly unsatisfactory. First, they suggested that even if Hurn had sighted McMahon at the time stated, McMahon was not then at an 'inhibiting distance from Luton'.[2] Possibly not, but if Hurn's sighting was true, it completely destroyed Mathews's story of McMahon leaving Forest Gate at around 3.30 p.m.

Second, the court stated that Lawrence had been cited as an alibi witness for McMahon at the original trial, and though summoned to the court, he was not in fact called.[3] Here the court was making an appalling factual mistake, for Lawrence had *not* been cited as a witness for McMahon *but for Cooper*. 'This blunder', said McMahon, 'was an extraordinary one for such an eminent body to make.' Nor, he goes on to point out, even if his solicitors had cited Lawrence, would it have been of the slightest help, as Lawrence *did not know* of Hurn's subsequent sighting of McMahon two hours later.

Finally the Court did not find that Hurn's sighting of

McMahon necessarily took place on the day of the murder.[4] This was because when interviewed by the police in 1977 Lawrence had said that he had travelled to the court only once, on the day of the murder, in Cooper's red Mercedes; but in his original statement in 1969, he had said that he had gone to the court with McMahon's father on *three* separate occasions and that on the day of the murder he had travelled there with McMahon and his father in a mini-cab. Therefore Hurn could have sighted McMahon on any of these three occasions.

McMahon comments on this as follows:

> After eight years, it was not to be wondered at that Lawrence's second statement showed some inconsistency with his first one. In some respects these sort of elementary mistakes give the ring of truth to his evidence. If he was colluding with me or my sympathizers, it is precisely the sort of mistake which would not be present. Nevertheless, after his interview with the police, Lawrence corrected his mistakes in a perfectly natural way.

But this was not all. What was incontrovertible was that although all three of McMahon's hearings had been attended by Lawrence, two of them had taken place in the morning and only one – that on the day of the murder, in the afternoon. 'This fact', said McMahon, 'is a matter of public record, not the partisan memory of sympathetic witnesses.' And it was in the afternoon and not the morning that Hurn's sighting took place. This vital piece of information never came to the court's notice because, as the hearing was in private, McMahon was not represented. Had he been, the matter could have been pointed out.

McMahon concluded his critique of the Court's rejection of the new evidence: 'I do not, nor have I ever, considered the fresh evidence of Hurn and Lawrence as conclusive proof of my innocence. A fairer court than the one that judged this evidence could have found it not credible, but *never* for the reasons adduced by the Court of Criminal Appeal . . .' and he ended:

I sit here in my cell writing this, having served almost nine years of a life sentence for a murder I did not commit. In some respects fighting my case has given me some respite from the great bitterness I felt in the early years. Over the years I have seen the evidence on which I was convicted just crumble away and collapse like a dynamited chimney stack. This has given me no mean satisfaction, despite the fact that I remain a prisoner. I also know that I sit in this cell now, not because of any evidence against me, but because of the legal establishment's concern for its own pretensions to infallibility. Is this the statement of an embittered, biased man? I do not think so.[5]

Before concluding this book, there is one further important event to record. Lord Devlin, a former Lord Justice of Appeal and one of the most eminent judges of our time, was persuaded to take an interest in the legal aspects of the case; and in May 1978, in a lecture at All Souls College, Oxford, he delivered a scathing attack on the manner in which the Court of Appeal had exercised its functions. What he had to say will be found in his own chapter in this book. Although his comments as yet have had no practical effect, they are yet another contribution, and a powerful one, to a case which, until justice is finally done, will never go away.

Chapter Fifteen

We have reached the end of the two manuscripts written by Cooper and McMahon during their long years in prison. So let them have the last word. First Cooper:

Many years have passed now since my trial in 1970, and I have much to reflect on since that time. Days pass into months, months into years, years into . . . what? How does one cope with imprisonment for life, and a recommendation to the Secretary of State that I should not be released for at least twenty years? It would be difficult enough for any man to contemplate this and come to terms with such a future, but what is his situation when he is not guilty of the murder for which he has been convicted?

Who can feel the intolerable sense of outrage, of indignation, of pain, depression and loss which overwhelms my whole being? Who can know my grief? And who or what can encourage my heart to hope that the bitterness which has encrusted me will be removed?

Nothing is more demoralizing or soul-destroying than anxiety without an end or a focusing-point. Anxiety and waiting, waiting for something to happen in putting right what is so obviously wrong, and which affects the mental stability of a man becomes, in the end, a real suffering. A physicial pain is more endurable than the mental torture of suffering. The quality of pain is to bind one to the instant, while suffering binds one to time. Pain is a wound, a blow, a toothache, it touches only the periphery of one's being. Suffering penetrates all the defences and takes its seat in one's heart. There is no question of rejecting it. One must analyse it, penetrate it, be penetrated by it. It obliges us to examine ourselves thoroughly.

On that fateful morning of the 10th September, 1969,

as people went about their daily business with a purpose, I too planned the events of the day ahead, but in an abstract way, having no definite ideas of what I was going to do. I did not know then that my mental stability was going to be pushed to its very limits; nor did I know that the recurring bouts of depression I was going to experience would have to be fought with a sustained will that at one stage was to have me on the borders of madness.

I have spent much time in segregation, especially at Wormwood Scrubs, where in my solitude, I had much time to reflect and take stock of myself. I found this both enriching and rewarding. I read a lot of different books that I thought would give me more insight into life, more knowledge and wisdom in trying to keep the pernicious environment of prison life from touching me.

One of the books I read was the brilliant and moving novel by Alexander Solzhenitsyn, 'The First Circle', which says much more effectively things about life in prison than anything I could say:

Descriptions of prison life tend to overdo the horror of it. Surely it is more frightening when there are no actual horrors; what is terrifying is the unchanging routine year after year. The horror is in forgetting that your life – the only life you have – is destroyed . . . This is something that cannot be imagined; it has to be experienced. All the poems and ballads about prison are sheer romanticism . . . The feel of prison only comes from having been inside for long years on end.

The difficulties I have had to meet as a result of the Luton murder have had the effect of bringing a vast change over me. My failure to surmount these difficulties has caused me to grow proportionately to their size, and instead of succumbing to madness, as I am sure I very nearly did, I have instead grown stronger. I can look at all my manic depressions with dispassion . . . and I can see how prison has helped me to mature and understand the problems of others better.

I have learned not to think too deeply about Mathews,

137

his wife, Drury, etc., at night, because the questions which these people raise are not conducive to a good night's sleep. The pain and suffering these people have caused me has been hard enough to bear, but to have witnessed over the years to what extent their mendacity has affected my mother and two brothers has been a burden I find impossible to express in words. When I explain to my brothers that they should try and lead their own lives, and not devote so much of it to a cause that seems hopeless, they will not listen. My younger brother Terry, when I once explained this to him, said, 'Is that what you would do, John, if our positions were reversed?'

I always think of Disraeli when I get depressed and am thwarted by the courts to prove my innocence. In his maiden speech in the House of Commons in 1837, he said, 'Though I sit down now, the time will come when you will hear me.'

I shall be vindicated. I am more certain of that than I am of anything in my life, and although it is a slow and at times agonizing road I tread, the time will come when I shall be heard and cleared of the indictment held against me.[1]

And now McMahon:

At the time of writing I am in my ninth traumatic year in prison. Under any circumstances the enormity of such an ordeal would take its toll, and my own case has been no different. My bitterness directed at our so-called British justice is so ingrained as to be permanent, and I believe I will carry this to the grave with me.

Nothing can ever compensate for the extreme suffering and anguish caused not only to myself but to my family and those close to me. Even the combined total of my criminal escapades is superficial stuff when compared to the unfathomable depths to which the judiciary sank in order to uphold my conviction; for in the final analysis it was they, through the Court of Appeal, who had the opportunity to make partial amends for my wrongful conviction. I say 'partial' because there is no way in which I can regain the years lost in a prison cell.

Some friends outside have expressed surprise that I haven't vegetated or deteriorated in the manner expected of a man who has spent so long in prison. They seem to think that, as an innocent man, my plight should be worse than that of the guilty, and that the prison monster should by now have devoured my mind.

Here however is the paradox. True, my plight is worse, far worse, than that of a guilty man in so far as I am going through hell for a crime I did not commit. But this is the sustaining factor. The fact that a massive injustice has been perpetrated against me will not allow me to rest until my name is finally cleared.

For the past ten years I have been keeping vigil in a nocturnal maze, and will continue to do so until daybreak. I am sometimes weary, sometimes depressed, sometimes afraid of being struck down by illness, but throughout even these moments, the driving force created by the injustice never deserts me.

Have the Home Office the courage to take the required, positive action on the case? Only the Home Secretary and his immediate advisers can answer this question. But one thing they can be sure of. I will not conveniently go away. In or out of prison I will relentlessly fight my case until my conviction for the murder of Reginald Stevens is finally quashed.[2]

Can any reasonable person, and particularly the Home Secretary, continue to maintain, after reading this account, that the convictions of Cooper and McMahon for murder are still 'safe and satisfactory'? And if the Home Secretary cannot so maintain, will he take immediate steps to recommend the Royal Prerogative of Mercy, award suitable compensation to the two men for more than ten years' loss of liberty, and set up a full and impartial inquiry into the whole sorry affair?

Afterword

The English process requires, first, that guilt should be proved to the satisfaction of a jury, which thereupon convicts; and, second, that the conviction, if challenged on appeal, should be found by the appellate court to be safe and satisfactory. The appellate court does not try the case over again. It examines it on paper and this enables it to take a detached view. For example, the First Court of Appeal* in this case could have held that, although Mr Mathews had obviously given his evidence in a way that persuaded the jury that in essentials it was true, it was just not safe to act upon evidence from so tainted a source, however persuasive it sounded. With evidence of that character, it could be argued, there must always be 'a lurking doubt' about the safety of relying only on the physical image of truth or deceit to be obtained from the manner in which the story is told. But this is the sort of issue that must be left to the determination of the judges who are appointed to settle it. The First Court rejected the appeal.

The ordinary process of appeal becomes complicated when after the trial new evidence is discovered. The key question used to be whether the new evidence could have made any difference to the verdict. If it could not, the answer was easy. If it could, then manifestly the verdict was useless; the judges could say whether the new evidence *could* have made a difference, but only the jury itself could say whether in fact the new evidence did make a difference. It was not thought practicable to re-assemble the old jury and submit the matter to it.

The next best solution is to have a new trial with a new jury; but since traditionally the English dislike second

---

* See pages 88–90.

trials, this solution was not made available until 1964. Before then, the accused was given the benefit of the doubt; it was assumed that if the new evidence could have made a difference, it would have, and he was acquitted. The dislike of the second trial has persisted even after 1964. This is to the advantage of the accused, provided the old test is strictly applied; for then he is acquitted, as Murphy was, without the matter being put to the hazard of a new trial.

A change was made in the process by the Criminal Appeal Act 1968. It is more correct to say that the change was made in 1966, since the later Act re-enacted a provision made in the former. The year is unimportant: the change does not appear conspicuously in the text of either Act and so had to wait for its effect until it was revealed by the decision of the House of Lords in Stafford v. D.P.P. in 1974. The House then declared that, when new evidence was received, the duty of a court of appeal was to consider it in conjunction with the old and decide whether or not it made the conviction unsafe, and to quash or uphold the conviction accordingly. The change was made too late to affect the proceedings in the Second Court. I shall consider it again when I come to the proceedings in the Fourth Court.

The turning point in the process in this case lies in the decision of the Second Court.* Two things about that decision seem to me to be obvious. The first is that it was manifestly right whatever standard is applied. A case that is based on a single dubious witness is too weak to sustain a fresh wound. The second thing is that, although the Second Court postponed the issue, the acquittal of Murphy was bound to make a heavy impact on the case against the other two. The defence argued that Mathews's opportunities of seeing Murphy were so good that, if he was shown to be wrong in his identification, he must be lying; no one would then try to argue that the conviction of McMahon and Cooper could be any safer than that of

---

* See pages 96-99.

Murphy. If however he was mistaken about Murphy, the matter would depend upon the possibility of a similar mistake about the other two. Mathews was in the company of all three for about the same period of time; McMahon and Murphy were both strangers to him and he had, he said, seen Cooper only once before.

So the next step plainly was to ask Mathews whether he was still confident about the other two and, if so, what made him feel that, while possibly mistaken about Murphy, he could still be sure about the other two. In other words, what as a matter of identification distinguished the three cases?

If it had been a police investigation, the officer in charge would have had the answer within an hour. The courts move at a more majestic pace. It was not until after a further two years and eight months of imprisonment for two maybe innocent men that the answer was obtained by the Fourth Court.* Mr Mathews then refused to admit the possibility that he was wrong about Murphy. Thus by implication he said that there was nothing to distinguish the three cases. Unless the Fourth Court was ready to repudiate the conclusion of the Second, there would seem to be no alternative to the acquittal of Cooper and Mc-Mahon.

May I illustrate this by directing attention to the way in which the Fourth Court dealt with the evidence of Mr Slade. His evidence related directly only to Cooper's alibi; it would have been, if established, of no greater, and no less service to McMahon than Edwards's evidence in the case of Murphy. After a thorough analysis of Mr Slade's evidence the court rejected it. But at the beginning of its examination of the evidence the court said of it: 'If it is, or may be true, Mathews's credibility is obviously gravely shaken as regards Cooper, and if false as regards Cooper clearly cannot safely be relied upon as against Mc-Mahon.'

It is necessary only to change the names. Edwards's

---

* See pages 115-128.

evidence had been established as evidence that 'is or may be true': Mathews's evidence had been so gravely shaken as regards Murphy that Murphy had been acquitted: so Mathews's evidence clearly could not safely be relied upon against Cooper and McMahon. Surely this must be correct. But when the Fourth Court came to consider the conclusion of the Second Court it reasoned quite differently. It stated its reasoning in four points.

The first point was that the Second Court had not said it believed Edwards's evidence, only that it was capable of belief. What it said was as much as it had any power to say and was quite enough. 'Is *or may be* true' is the way in which the Fourth Court correctly phrased the requirement in the case of Slade.

The second point was that Edwards's identification evidence was of the kind now known as 'a fleeting glance' unsupported by any other evidence and that a prosecution based on such evidence would have failed. It is not, I think, correct to say that Edwards's evidence was of the kind usually typified as the 'fleeting glance'. This description is given to witnesses who have only a fleeting glimpse of a stranger; quite a different weight is to be attached to a fleeting glimpse which is a recognition of a known face. In any event, that such a prosecution would have failed is irrelevant. Cooper and McMahon, like Murphy and unlike any prosecutor, can rely on evidence that 'may be true'.

The third point was that Mr Edwards, though to be accepted as honest and impressive, might be mistaken. So of course might Mathews. And if the possibilities of both sides are equal, the defence wins. The job left to the Fourth Court was to find out whether the possibilities were equal. This was the exercise which was frustrated by Mathews's refusal to admit the possibility of any mistake at all.

The fourth point was that the Second Court had only a transcript of Mathews's evidence while the Fourth Court was 'more advantageously placed'. This is true, but so is the converse; the Fourth Court had only the transcript of Edwards's evidence while the Second Court saw him in the witness-box. Where two honest witnesses conflict (the Fourth Court unreservedly accepted that Edwards was an impressive and honest witness and affirmed that Mathews was) the only explanation is mistake. This takes one straight back to the third point.

On the strength of these four points the Fourth Court expressed its conclusion that 'the quashing of that conviction (i.e. Murphy's) cannot of itself now avail the appellants in very different circumstances'. It was not the quashing of the conviction as such that the accused wanted to avail themselves of. What the accused are relying upon is the evidence of Edwards accepted as credible; the quashing of the conviction is relevant only as putting the seal on that. If Edwards had been called at the trial, would any judge have directed the jury that in considering whether or not Cooper and McMahon were correctly identified, they must disregard Edwards's evidence? What then are the different circumstances that are to prevail when the same question is being considered by an appellate court?

The emergence of Mr Edwards was not the only factor making it questionable whether Mr Mathews as sole incriminator was still to be relied on. There was a good deal else, and all of it was carefully considered by the Fourth Court. Stafford *v.* D.P.P. requires, as I have said, that the Court should assess the new material in conjunction with the old and itself decide, without a new jury, whether or not the conviction is still safe. Certainly this is now the law if the assessment does not, as it did not in Stafford *v.* D.P.P., involve any question of truthfulness. But the better opinion – and the one which was in fact adopted by the Fourth Court – is, I think, that truthfulness remains, as it always has been, a jury question.

The division of function between judge and jury on 'credit', as it is called, is the division between what is believable and what is true. A judge decides whether the evidence is believable; only a jury can decide whether it is true. The Second Court decided that the evidence of Edwards was believable. The natural step would then be to order a new trial so that a jury could decide whether it was 'true'. Since the Second Court was unwilling to do that, it had to assume that the evidence was 'true'.

Why have I put 'true' in inverted commas? Because, since the burden of proof is always on the prosecution, the vital question is not whether the evidence for the defence is true, but whether it is such as to create a reasonable doubt about the truth of the evidence for the prosecution. There may be members of the public who think that the hub of this case is simply that Murphy 'proved' an alibi and the other two did not. The defence never has to prove an alibi or anything else. The prosecution has to prove beyond reasonable doubt that the accused was on the spot. If the accused produce a credible witness who says he was somewhere else, the evidence creates a reasonable doubt about whether he was on the spot. This is what Murphy did. He established that Mathews's identification of him was unreliable, which means no more than insufficiently convincing. By so doing he instilled a doubt about the safety of Mathews's other identifications.

With the exception of the last sentence, all that I have just written has already been lucidly expressed by the Fourth Court. The Court referred to Stafford v. D.P.P. as deciding that the Act of 1968 had freed the Court from some of its shackles and widened its powers of review. The Court continued:

> But it must not be forgotten that constitutionally the tribunal to whom falls the duty of determining issues of fact upon which . . . verdicts of guilty or not guilty depend, is the jury.

Later the Court said:

> Where fresh evidence is adduced, this Court is not, at least in the majority of cases, concerned to cast upon appellants the burden of proving that that which the

new evidence asserts is true. It is concerned, so far as is presently relevant, that that new evidence is credible as opposed to incredible, that is, that it is capable of belief and if placed before a jury might be believed by them as opposed to something which it is impossible to believe. Once that evidence is shown to be credible, that is capable of belief, a conviction arrived at in the absence of that evidence is likely to be unsafe or unsatisfactory unless and until the truth or untruth of the facts which that new evidence asserts is determined one way or the other. The constitutional tribunal for the determination of that issue is, as we have already said, a jury. Hence the power under section 7 of the 1968 Act to order a new trial in the appropriate case where credible new evidence is adduced and certain other conditions are satisfied. But the ordering of a new trial by this court is not always possible, especially after a long lapse of time. In such a case it is the plain duty of this court to quash the conviction not because it is necessarily accepting the truth of what the new evidence has asserted, but because until that truth has been tested, any conviction reached in the absence of that testing is likely to be unsafe or unsatisfactory.

But as the judgment proceeds, the signposts pointing to the conclusion are altered. The first new indication comes when the judgment proposes to consider 'how, in the light of the totality of the evidence now before us, we should regard Mathews's evidence'. Next, the judgment states baldly: 'our decision must depend upon the view we take of the veracity of Mathews's incrimination of the appellants and of Murphy'. Note, the view we take not of his credibility, but of his veracity. Then, a little later, 'we come back to the need to assess Mathews's veracity in the essential respect upon the basis of our impression of him in the witness box'. Then comes the conclusion: 'The conclusion which each of us independently has reached in this Court on the vital part of his story is that he was clearly telling the truth.'

Thus we find the judges deciding the very thing which they have earlier said could constitutionally be decided only by a jury. It is true that that statement of principle related to the case against Murphy. But there is not one constitutional principle for Murphy and another for Cooper and McMahon any more than there is one principle for the evidence of Slade and another for the evidence of Edwards. The contrast between the beginning and the end of the judgment is so vivid as to create a wild surmise that some explanatory paragraphs have been lost. So far as I know there is no case in which a court of appeal has examined again a witness at the trial and taken it upon itself to say whether or not he was speaking the truth. The novelty of the thing is so striking that an explanation is indispensable.

It is unusual, but not at all improper, for a witness at the trial to give oral evidence before the Court of Appeal. If new evidence has created a new situation for him to explain, an explanation given in the witness-box and upon which the witness can be questioned may be the most businesslike way of dealing with this new situation. If the Fourth Court had thought that the new evidence could have made no difference to the trial jury's estimate of Mathews's credit, they could have so found and such a finding would, as a matter of form, have disposed of the appeal. As a matter of substance such a finding would have attracted powerful criticism. To consider only one item of the new evidence, many lawyers as well as laymen would have agreed with Bryan Magee when he wrote in *The Times* that 'it is contrary to common sense to suppose that if the jury had known Mr Mathews's evidence against one of the men they were convicting to be unreliable, they would still have regarded his evidence against the other two men as beyond reasonable doubt'.

This criticism is diverted by the Fourth Court's decision, if it be within their power to give it. If under the constitution the Court had the right and duty to determine whether or not Mathews was telling the truth and they validly determined that he was, that is an end of the matter. But if they had not, it does not remedy the deficiency to say that the trial jury 'took the same view' or that they were taking the same view as the trial jury. The same view of what? Not of Mr Edwards's evidence because the jury did not hear it. Not of whether or not Mr Mathews was telling the truth, because that is not a question which can be answered solely by observing a man when he speaks and without considering how his evidence fits into the frame of the whole. The jury were seeing it in one frame and the Fourth Court in another. With the change of frame, with the completing of a case that was before incomplete, the verdict given on incomplete evidence becomes obsolete. If that were not so, then the form which a new trial would take would be that of an inquiry into whether the old verdict should be confirmed. But it is a statutory precondition to a new trial that the obsolete verdict is quashed.

In my opinion the judgment of the Fourth Court is defective in the respects given below.

First, the Court's decision was a usurpation of the function that constitutionally belongs to the jury. No doubt the decision, unless it can be reopened, closes as a matter of form the legal process. But it is not a decision which can demand the respect belonging to the decisions of a properly constituted authority, whether they are welcome or not. The decision cannot end debate.

Second, the Court forgot the requirements of natural justice. If the judges are going to decide the case on their impression of the way in which a witness gave his evidence they ought to offer the same opportunity to the defence as to the prosecution. It is true that Cooper and McMahon were disbelieved by the trial jury, but, if a new trial had been ordered, the slate would have been wiped clean. The two accused would have had the chance of persuading a fresh jury in circumstances much more favourable to them than those which existed at the trial. Who can say how they would have acquitted themselves? What is certain is that if the Fourth Court had ordered a new trial, it could not have limited it to the issue of whether or not Mr Mathews was to be believed, nor could it have directed that on that issue Mathews alone was to be heard.

Third, the decision of the Fourth Court is inconsistent with that of the Second. In the passage from the judgment which I have already quoted, the Fourth Court said that their decision must depend upon the view they took 'of the veracity of Mathews's incrimination of the appellants and of Murphy'. They were right to look upon the incrimination as indivisible. The decision was that 'on the vital part of his story Mathews was clearly telling the truth'. Among the truths which he reiterated as beyond possibility of mistake, there was his identification of Murphy. The Fourth Court was thus saying, almost as forcefully as if it had said it expressly, that the decision of the Second Court was wrong. It is not possible to exact public respect for a system of justice which allows life sentences to depend on accidents of this sort. The Fourth Court should have accepted the decision of the Second Court whether it thought it to be right or wrong (if they had not been travelling outside their province, they would not have been tempted to think it wrong) and drawn the logical consequences.

Fourth, the Court, pursuing their self-appointed task of assessing the truthfulness of Mathews, thereby disqualified themselves for the job they should really have been doing. The verdict of the trial jury established that to all appearances Mr Mathews was telling the truth. The task of a court of review was to determine whether in all the circumstances, including the new circumstances, it was safe to go by appearances. The question for the Fourth Court was whether, however convincing Mathews might sound, it was safe to act upon the evidence of an habitual liar, who even at the trial had not come clean, who was an accomplice almost uncorroborated, and who had turned Queen's evidence in the hands of a police officer who was not above suspicion. This question they neither formulated nor answered. Instead, they said that they agreed with the jury about appearances. It would indeed be difficult, if not impossible, for a court to say, 'We observed him to be truthful but it is unsafe for us to act upon the truth.'

I know the three judges who sat in the Fourth Court personally or by repute. I have not the slightest doubt in the world about their anxiety to do justice. Justice requires the conviction of the guilty as well as the acquittal of the innocent; though the safeguarding of innocence is their first charge, judges cannot ignore the danger to society if too scrupulously they shrink from the conviction of those guilty of brutal crime. To my mind the text of the Court's judgment displays convincingly their anxiety to put aside technicalities and to get at the real truth. They started out with an impeccable statement of the principles to apply; yet somehow or other they lost the way.

I think, with deep respect, that they lost it for the simple reason that they did not follow the beaten track. At the outset of the judgment they referred to 'the 1968 Act' as freeing the Court from some of the shackles previously imposed. I think, again with deep respect, that this is a delusion. No one who reads the Parliamentary debates which led to the 1966 Act (which the 1968 Act on this point merely repeated) can suppose that the legislators saw themselves as striking off shackles. No one began to talk of shackles until a decade later.

The safe road to conviction, at any rate where conviction depends upon truthfulness, is still the same, as the Fourth Court itself affirmed, as it always was. The temptation of the short cut has still to be resisted. If, the tempter says, judges are now free to decide whether or not convictions are unsafe and unsatisfactory, why should they not proceed swiftly to the crucial question? Let them summon the vital witnesses and decide for themselves whether they are telling the truth. Proceeding swiftly, the tempted overlook that what they are doing is something that can be done only by a jury after a new trial.

To return to the terms of the judgment. The points on procedure which I have noted above are of public importance and will have to be settled by the House of Lords. Sooner or later in the course of some future appeal one or more of them is likely to be raised. The trouble is that it may be later. Years from now two men, whose lives have been broken on the wheel of a twenty-year sentence, may learn that their guilt was never proved according to due process of law. This is not a pleasant thought.

Alternatively, the House may hold that where new evidence changes the picture and necessitates the reconsideration of the credit of a prosecution witness, this is a task that can properly be performed by judges without a jury. This would be a new doctrine which would come as a surprise and as a shock to many. If the law is to be settled that way, it is imperative in the interests of justice generally that it should be done speedily. The House would then be able to specify how the judges should discharge their new responsibilities, whether by a new trial before themselves alone or whether by simply sending for the witness and saying what they think of him.

It is too much to expect the Home Secretary to refer the case for a fourth time back to the Court of Appeal with a view to a further appeal to the House of Lords. The practical course is for the Lord Chancellor to appoint a committee to report and recommend. If the committee recommends a clarification of the law, it can be done by an amendment of the 1968 Act. This will remove the present uncertainties and make the law shipshape for criminals to come.

And what about Cooper and McMahon? For them there would remain only the plenitude of the power to pardon or remit. As a general rule the Home Secretary is surely right to leave all justiciable questions to the courts. But there are exceptions, however rare, to every rule. There are occasions, however rare, in all our affairs, legal, political or domestic, when things get into such a tangle, when the disentangling would take so long and cause such additional misery that the only decent and humane thing to do is to cut the knot. We have here a prosecution which has been dogged by misfortune – a witness upon whom almost all depends and whom no court can feel to be generally reliable, a police officer who turns out to be a lamentable exception to his calling, an unprecedented series of references by the Home Secretary. Doubts do not just lurk: from the first they have flown about the case like bats in a belfry. Ten years have been spent in trying to find out whether all the doubts are unreasonable and we do not yet know the answer. Even if the judgment of the Fourth Court is accepted as impeccable, we still do not know what damage to the safety of the conviction an unscrupulous officer might have caused. How much longer?

The law is marked out in black and white: men must be guilty or innocent. For the prerogative of mercy, which is above the law, there are no such markings. These men have now served more than half of the exemplary sentences passed upon them. It is less than their full deserts if they are guilty, but yet by any standard a drastic punishment. If they are innocent the thought of another ten years out of their lives is not tolerable. If the Home Secretary now cuts the knot, I do not believe that there is a voice in England that would be raised in protest.

Devlin
August 1979

An MP Takes Up the Case

One constantly hears of this or that MP taking up an injustice against some individual constituent and fighting the case, but I suspect that few members of the public have much idea of what actually goes on when this happens. So I hope that this account of my involvement in David Cooper's case will give an answer to this wider question, well as adding an extra facet to a particularly fascinating story. But the very fact of setting out to describe my own involvement means that I shall be writing a lot of 'I did this' and 'then I did that', so I should warn the reader in advance not to let this distort his perspective: I was never more than a peripheral character in the story, and my frustrations and disappointments were as nothing compared to those of the imprisoned men.

Becoming an MP for the first time involves, among so much else, inheriting a constituency as a large and complicated going concern in which, overnight, one has to take on responsibility for all kinds of things one knew nothing about before. These include a host of unconnected private problems concerning individuals, families, firms and institutions of every kind, and each problem has its own back history. This is how I first became involved in David Cooper's case: I 'inherited' it as a result of the General Election of February 1974 from Patrick Gordon Walker, my predecessor as MP for Leyton. The constituency simply happened to include Leytonstone, where David Cooper and his family live.

This aspect of an MP's experience is quickly enlarged by the fact that most of those of his constituents who lay claim to grievances and have failed to get them rectified by his predecessor have another try with the new man, so to the running cases are immediately added a whole lot of old cases which return from the past: closed files reopen, and cases which had been pronounced dead rise from the dead. It is impossible for the new man to know in advance who among the people who thus come to him is genuinely hard done by and who is merely trying it on, so his only fair course is to review every case he is asked to review, and make a fresh judgment. This, of course, is what makes it worth everyone's while to try him out. But he quickly learns, if he did not know it before, that most of the prisoners who proclaim their innocence are only too obviously, on serious inquiry, guilty. He also learns that most of the good-hearted well-meaning people who take up such cases on behalf of others are deceived.

So I approached David Cooper's case with caution and scepticism. I decided that I would not visit him in Wormwood Scrubs until I had mastered the detail of the case, partly so as to view that detail with a more assured detachment and objectivity, partly because if I were to come to the conclusion that he was probably guilty I would want to keep my involvement with him limited. I read through the documents with a critical eye, and sought adverse as well as favourable comment from expert observers. But there was no doubt about the conclusion I was forced to. It was not so much that David Cooper was innocent as that the case against him was full of obvious and gaping holes. The prosecution had never come anywhere near to proving that he was even in Luton. And under British law a man is supposed to be innocent unless proved guilty. My constituent had manifestly not been proved guilty.

It was on this basis that I decided to take up his case. The implied distinction seemed to me essential as a matter of tactics as well as intellectual honesty. Because I could not demonstrate David Cooper's innocence I decided not to let it appear as if that were my aim, for if I did, people would see that I was not proving my case, and I should be courting failure. On the other hand it seemed to me that anyone with common sense could be got to see that the case against Cooper was shot through with corruption and lies, not to mention a plethora of implausibilities, self-contradictions, and doubts of every sort. Therefore my argument would be not that he was innocent but that the case against him had not been made out, and *therefore,* this being so, that he ought not to be in prison. I have stuck to this ever since.

The General Election that brought me into the House of Commons also brought the Labour Party back into power from opposition, and Roy Jenkins replaced Robert Carr as Home Secretary. Carr had already refused leave for Cooper and McMahon to make a fresh appeal, but Jenkins took a different view, on the following grounds. The case against the imprisoned men consisted almost entirely of Mathews's identification of them as the men with whom he went to Luton. Yet Patrick Murphy had now had his conviction quashed on fresh alibi evidence. However weakly this might be interpreted – even if it did not mean at all that the Court of Appeal was convinced that Murphy had not been at Luton, but only that they thought there was room for doubt in the matter – this could not do other than cast an equal doubt on Mathews's identification of the two other men. And, in a phrase which has become famous, it requires only a 'lurking doubt' for the court to be under an obligation to acquit. So in May 1974 Roy Jenkins wrote a letter to the Court of Appeal in which he said he had 'come to the conclusion that the decision to allow Mr Murphy's appeal raises an issue about the credibility of Mr Mathews's evidence against Mr Cooper and Mr McMahon which makes it desirable that the Court of Appeal should also be asked to consider their cases'.

Nine months went by after this letter before the appeal was heard – nine months during which two young men whose guilt the Home Secretary clearly thought was open to serious question simply sat in their prison cells and waited. This, it seems to me, is a barbarism for which no serious justification can possibly be provided. Much has been said and written, over hundreds of years, about the law's delays, and anything I say on the subject is likely to seem platitudinous; but a civilized country ought not to accept this sort of thing as a matter of course.

The appeal hearing began on 10 February 1975, and I

went along to observe. Mathews was summoned to the court, obviously with a view to his cross-examination, and was held outside the door until such time as he should be called. But then came an utterly unexpected bombshell. The defence asked leave to cross-examine Mathews – and was refused. I could scarcely believe my ears. Why had the judges summoned him, then? More to the point, the whole case hung on the credibility of his evidence, and in a British court of law the only way this could be tested was by cross-examination – so what the judges' decision meant in practice was that they had decided not to do what the Home Secretary had asked them to do. There was a serious confusion here, and it came as no surprise that some delay occurred before the judgment was read.

When the judgment came on 21 February it made the confusion worse. The Appeal Court judges announced that 'quite clearly the question which the Secretary of State desired the court to investigate was the credibility of Mathews's evidence'. They then recalled with much approval how the trial court judge had 'warned the jury, in the clearest and strongest terms, against the danger of relying upon the evidence of Mathews – whether or not they found him to be an accomplice – unless they found evidence which corroborated his', and then they themselves went on to describe the sum of such other evidence against Cooper as 'slender'. At this point in the argument a man of common sense might have been forgiven for supposing that the Court of Appeal was going to order the release of David Cooper. Not a bit of it. The judges went on to say that it did not fit in with the accustomed procedure of the Court of Appeal to allow cross-examination of witnesses. Anyway, they said, even if the jury had known that the verdict on Murphy was to be overthrown on the ground that Mathews's evidence against him was unsafe, it does not inevitably follow from this that they would have placed any the less confidence in his evidence against Cooper and McMahon. The convictions were upheld.

Even as a politician I have rarely heard such a bad argument put forward seriously in public by people who are supposed to be intelligent. They must have realized how lame some of it was. In reality, what they were doing boiled down to this: they were choosing to send two possibly innocent men back to prison for life rather than admit an unaccustomed process, namely cross-examination, into Appeal Court procedure. They thereby also opened up an important issue of public policy in that they uncovered a gap between the Home Secretary's power of referral and their own powers of review as they insisted on seeing them. Their combination of complacency, brutal indifference and lack of common sense was one I was unprepared to encounter in High Court judges. But I was to encounter it again before the story was out.

Perhaps I had been spoiled in my expectations of judges by the fact that the two most eminent to have emerged in Britain since World War II happened to be friends of mine, and it would have been impossible to imagine either of them talking, or thinking, the nonsense that had just emanated from the Court of Appeal. In my various attempts now to find a way forward I turned to one of these, Lord Devlin, for advice. Although retired, his eminence necessarily made him cautious, but fortunately the case caught his interest purely on grounds of its legal peculiarities, and so, without transgressing the bounds of what it was proper for someone in his position to do or say, he gave me invaluable advice from then on.

Before approaching Lord Devlin I stirred up as much fuss in the press as I could about the Court of Appeal's decision. I wrote an article in *The Times* on 7 March, and encouraged journalists on other newspapers to take up the story. I appeared on BBC television in a *Panorama* programme which was devoted wholly to the Luton murder case. And since, in the Appeal Court, the defence lawyer had mentioned the possibility of corruption on the part of Chief Detective Superintendent Drury, I put down a question in the House of Commons to the Attorney General asking him to request the Director of Public Prosecutions to launch an investigation into this aspect of the case. The trouble with all this publicity was that its practical outcome was zero. (The DPP's investigation which I had demanded did indeed take place, but its outcome was inconclusive.) I began to see that publicity, of itself, was not going to get us anywhere. The only people who could order David Cooper's release from prison were judges or the Home Secretary, and it was difficult to see them being materially influenced in such a decision by newspaper articles or television programmes – indeed, I myself would have had to admit that for them to be so influenced would be wrong.

So when David Cooper's application for leave to appeal to the House of Lords was turned down, I realized that the way forward as far as I was concerned was to address myself not to the media but to the Home Office, and I managed to secure a date for a private meeting there with the civil servants who had been seconded to the case. The Minister of State who was to preside at the meeting, Alex Lyon, wanted also to invite McMahon's MP, Michael Spicer, and to discuss the two cases together; but I refused to go along with that: I was not going to have my man's case lumped in together for consideration with what looked to me like a less good one. Whereas the *only* evidence against Cooper was the testimony of Mathews, in the case of McMahon there was a little other evidence besides. This was not to say that McMahon was guilty, but it questionably meant that the case against Cooper was weaker than the case against McMahon. As a matter of tactics, it seemed to me that the right approach was to concentrate on destroying the weaker case separately and letting the other man then benefit from this, as he was bound to do by this stage in the proceedings (and as indeed he did, eventually, do).

It so happened that by coincidence I had known Bryan Anns, the QC who had defended Cooper in the latest hearing, for some twenty years, so this emboldened me to enlist his help in briefing me for the legal aspects of the argument I was to have at the Home Office. He did so in a long, detailed and immensely helpful document which was almost the last thing he was ever to write. For before my meeting even took place he had to fly to Singapore to take part in some legal proceedings which involved the exposure

158

of public corruption there – and soon after his arrival he was found dead in his hotel swimming pool in circumstances that were never explained but aroused obvious suspicions of murder. Thus did one real-life tragedy possessing all the characteristics of a thriller link up fortuitously with another from opposite sides of the world.

Briefed with advice from Bryan Anns, who was now chillingly dead at the age of forty-six, and also from others, I went along to the Home Office meeting on 22 July 1975. What I was asking for was a special Home Office inquiry into the case of David Cooper. My submission rested on two basic arguments. The first was that Cooper had been the victim of a lacuna in our judicial system such that, although the Home Secretary had asked the Court of Appeal to re-examine the evidence against him, the Court had declared to do so, with the result that what were plainly the Home Secretary's intentions (and were declared by the judges to be his intentions) had been thwarted. In other words he was the accidental victim of procedural technicalities. My second basic argument was that there was a good deal of evidence in Cooper's favour which had never been put to the jury and which would have been elicited at the Court of Appeal by cross-examination of witnesses if only that had been allowed. The first of these points was so clear as not to be susceptible of very much discussion, so our meeting concentrated on the second. The upshot was that the Home Office officials asked me to assemble on paper the new evidence in Cooper's favour and present it to them as a single document. This was done for me by his solicitors, who had already made careful preparation for a detailed cross-examination which never took place. On receipt of it the people at the Home Office announced that it was going to take them a good long time to consider. And it did.

Months went by, during which David Cooper went into a decline – self-isolation within the prison, hunger strike, depression, nightmares. I started to badger the Home Office ministers for a decision: Alex Lyon had been put in charge of the matter, and I raised it with him every time I met him anywhere in the House of Commons. (On one occasion I pinned him down in a corridor and talked to him about it for three-quarters of an hour.) The reaction of the ministers was that they were being put in the position of judges: *they* were having to decide whether certain evidence would have impressed a jury, *they* were having to decide whether or not to overturn a conviction. Roy Jenkins in particular rebelled against this. He was of the opinion that it was essential to the character of our whole society that legal cases should be tried by judges and not by party politicians, and that politicians should not overthrow the decisions of judges except in the most plainly justifiable circumstances. My arguments failed to convince him that this was just such a justifiable case. The conclusion he came to was that he would be prepared to refer it back to the judges yet again if he could find grounds on which to do so, but was not prepared to override their ruling; nor would he institute a special inquiry. And since all the evidence I had brought to his attention had been in existence at the time of the latest appeal, he did not regard it as constituting grounds for a fresh appeal.

We were back at square one. Only this time there was no way forward at all, unless some genuinely new evidence were to turn up. It was difficult to see how this was going to happen five or six years after the crime. I began to fear that the case would languish and be forgotten. My policy became one of keeping it in the public mind by occasional references, and in officials' minds by letters to the Home Office whenever I could find a good excuse. But what I was really doing was marking time and hoping for something to turn up.

Then at last something did turn up – a new alibi witness in the form of Mr Slade, a former business partner of David Cooper's father. Mr Slade claimed to have seen David Cooper in East London not once but twice on the afternoon of the murder. There was a prodigious fluttering in the dovecots and all our hopes revived. But when the police were put on to Mr Slade to test his evidence, and there was another long and by this time familiar delay, it was borne in on me that one of the things that had gone wrong all along in this affair was that the evidence in Cooper's favour had been surfacing in dribs and drabs, and each new morsel had been evaluated separately on its appearance, so that at no point since the trial had his case really been viewed by officialdom *as a whole*. If only all the trial evidence, plus everything that had come to light since, including the imprisonment of Drury for corruption, were to be marshalled in an organized way and treated as a single case, it was inconceivable to me that any jury could find a man guilty on the basis of it, or any Home Office official imagine that they might.

With Slade as my excuse I secured another official meeting with Alex Lyon and his Home Office advisers on 15 March 1976. At this meeting I put forward the whole case for David Cooper as it now stood, pointing out one by one the gaps and holes and discrepancies and self-contradictions, the obvious lies and the hints of corruption, until it all stood before them as a single picture. Even so, so complex had the detail of the story become that after I had left the meeting I thought of all sorts of additional points I wished I had made, so I sent them to Alex Lyon next day in the form of a letter. On 8 April he wrote me a reply which began: 'I am writing to let you know that, after considering the matters you raised in our discussion on 15th March and in the letter you sent me on the following day, the Home Secretary has again referred the case of David Cooper (alias John Disher) to the Court of Appeal . . .' And thus it was that the case of David Cooper (and of McMahon, who at this point reaped the benefit of being connected with it) became the first in the history of British law to be referred back to the Court of Appeal twice by the Home Secretary.

This time the Court of Appeal had little choice but to permit cross-examination, for it was the only possible way they could even know what Mr Slade's evidence was. And to evaluate this evidence they would have to hear the evidence of others with which it conflicted – and since they were permitting Mr Slade's cross-examination they could not raise any objection in principle to the cross-examination of others. In short, they were in a position where they now had no choice but to permit exhaustive cross-examination of witnesses on both sides. In effect this would mean almost a retrial of the case. So it proved, and lasted six full days in court between 12 and 22 July 1976. Mathews's evidence alone occupied two days.

David Cooper had been so shattered psychologically and emotionally by the failure of his previous appeal that he feared for the effect on his mental stability if this one should go against him. He had even been through a stage with me in which he had insisted that he *did not want* another appeal. I had dissuaded him from this, but now that the rehearing was actually scheduled he was dreading the prospect. He determined that he was not going to endure the mental anguish of sitting in court throughout the proceedings; and most of all he was terrified of the possible traumatic effect on himself of another adverse decision, for by this time he had lost faith in the likelihood of receiving justice from the courts. I tried to persuade him to be there, but without success. After the first morning the whole rehearing took place with McMahon alone sitting in the dock.

I attended the court for every hour of the six-day hearing. The courtroom was so small that I was no more than a few paces from everyone else in it, including the judges; and I found myself so wrapt in watching and listening at these surprisingly close quarters that I disallowed myself the distraction of taking notes. I retain from the proceedings some of the most vivid impressions of my life. The faces of Mathews and Drury are engraved on my brain, the cunning positively gleaming out of them. Both men were highly experienced in courtroom proceedings, and were almost theatrical in their attempts to make the desired effects on their audience, though their eyes and tone of voice persistently betrayed them (or would have done to attentive observers). Their apparent self-confidence was in striking contrast to the pitiable nervousness of the non-criminal, man-in-the-street witnesses who were desperately at sea in these alien surroundings, almost crushed with intimidation by them, and obviously wishing to be somewhere else. But above all I remember the complacency of the three judges. Their general demeanour was like that of elderly clubmen determined that it should be clearly understood that they are men of the world, fully alive to all the tricks of your Tom, Dick and Harry; yet their actual questions and comments positively revealed that they had not the remotest notion what sort of a world it was that these East End people they were listening to actually lived in, or how to evaluate their characters and the plausibility of what they said. Lord Justice Lawton, for instance, was positively at pains throughout the trial to demonstrate what an old East End hand he was, yet nearly everything he said in order to do so was embarrassingly irrelevant, wrong, or out of date. The smug and self-amused way in which these men disposed of other people's lives would require the pen of a Swift or the brush of a Hogarth to do it justice.

They came to the quite incredible conclusion that although Mathews was a villain and a liar, and had lied extensively in the evidence he had given before them in this very trial (Lord Justice Lawton described Mathews's whole account of his personal involvement in the crime as 'a cock and bull story') there could be no doubt about the safety of two convictions which depended decisively on that evidence. The three crucial sentences in a judgment which runs to forty-four pages of foolscap are: 'Each of us watched him closely while he was giving his evidence. The conclusion which each of us independently has reached in this court on the vital part of his story is that he was clearly telling the truth. We do not therefore find it in the least surprising that the jury took the same view both swiftly and surely.'

This is, I'm afraid, simply not true, and I personally am an eye witness. The judges did not watch Mathews closely while he was giving evidence. I watched both them and Mathews closely throughout both days, while he was giving evidence, and for most of the time all three of the judges had their heads and eyes down on the notes they were keeping. Every now and then one of them would look up,

163

but then almost always quickly back again. Sometimes one of them would settle back in his seat and watch for a full minute or two before returning to his note-taking. But for most of the time all three of them had their heads down, writing. Over and again, when confronted with a crucial question, Mathews's face would be invaded by a shifty look, and he would turn his eyes away, and falter, and then visibly pull himself together and resume talking, but in a suddenly improvisatory tone of voice. Whenever this or anything like it happened I always shot an immediate glance at the judges to see how they were reacting, only to find at least four times out of five that not a single one of them was looking at him.

However, it is not necessary to have been an eye witness to perceive the folly of the judges' conclusion. On 2 August 1976 *The Times* devoted an editorial (in which I had no hand) to the case, in which it wrote: 'It defies logic and common sense to have come to that conclusion in the circumstances of the case'; and it concluded: 'To most sensible rational people a verdict which depends on the evidence of a man like Mathews, in the circumstances in which he gave that evidence, cannot be safe.'

What agonies the judgment put Cooper and McMahon to I hesitate to imagine, for even I was almost beside myself with frustration and rage. Every responsible person except for the judges now seemed to agree that the case against Cooper was riddled with unacceptabilities, and yet the judges imperviously upheld the Court's previous decision. I could see perfectly well that it was natural for the Court of Appeal not to want to overturn its own decisions, and to fear that if it did so there might be a general undermining of its position. By the same token I could see that an invitation from the Home Office to do this might be met with resentment and hostility – indeed, I was told by my lawyer friends that the Court of Appeal had come to regard itself as involved in something like a feud with the Home Office, for a number of reasons, of which this case was only one. But it seemed to me as plain as could be that the court was doing far more damage to its reputation by reading out judgments which affronted common sense and constituted a denial of natural justice. I myself had had my respect for it irreparably harmed. And this is not to mention the moral and human consideration due to the two imprisoned men.

Be all this as it may, we had reached the end of the road as far as the courts were concerned: if a second referral back by the Home Secretary had been unprecedented, a third was obviously out of the question. So the only hope left now was a personal intervention by the Home Secretary. I sent Roy Jenkins the following letter:

2 August 1976

Dear Roy:

In case it escaped your attention I enclose an article of mine from today's *Times* on the subject of the latest Appeal Court review of the Luton murder case. The Court's judgment was unsatisfactory, chiefly for the reason set out in my article. But there are further grounds for dissatisfaction, which I want to put to you in this letter. (I'll be as brief as I can, though I'm afraid a certain minimal length is unavoidable.)

All the judges at all the hearings have agreed that the conviction of Cooper depends almost entirely on Mathews's evidence. One of them described corroborating evidence as 'slender'. There are four points in the narrative put forward by Mathews at which his evidence implicates Cooper: —

1. Allegedly, Cooper made a total of three visits to Mathews's home on September 9th and 10th, 1969, to persuade him to collect some parcels from Luton. Mathews finally agreed.

Criticism: The Appeal Court has consistently rejected the parcels story and said that Mathews must have been much more deeply involved, clearly implying that he went to Luton as a fully informed member of a team to do a job. But if the parcels story is rejected, the Court should at least doubt Mathews's story about Cooper's visits, since the alleged purpose of those visits has then been demolished. (See under 4 below for other grounds for doubting these visits from Cooper.)

2. Allegedly, Cooper drove his own red Mercedes sports car to Luton, with the hood down.

Criticism: The witness Donald Leek, not called at the trial, says in an agreed statement that a convoy of three vehicles, like those used in the crime, pulled in at the K Garage where he worked – the garage given as the stopping place by Mathews. But Leek says (i) that the driver of the sports car was dark and of foreign appearance: this could not possibly be a description of Cooper, who is fair and balding; and (ii) that the red Mercedes had a hard top: this was corroborated by the witness Andrews, who was called at the trial. If accepted, this evidence would suggest that Mathews was lying (i) in saying that Cooper was the driver of the car, in which case doubt is then cast on whether Cooper was present at all; (ii) in saying that the red sports car was Cooper's; and (iii) in saying that Murphy made his escape by leaping into the 'open' sports car without opening the door.

Cooper was driving around in his car without concealment in the days immediately following the murder. It is scarcely credible that he would have done this had both he and the car been involved in the crime.

3. Allegedly, from Luton Station Cooper led Mathews to a shop and asked him to wait there and see if anyone came out. Mathews waited, until the van drove up and he was told to jump in. Mathews saw Cooper in the back of the van.

Criticism: Both McNair and Seal saw the driver of the van at or near the murder. Their descriptions fit Mathews exactly, but could not be of Murphy, McMahon or Cooper. If their evidence is accepted, then either Mathews was driving the van, in which case he was at the scene of the murder, or else he has lied about the identity of at least one of his confederates.

It is noteworthy that Mathews says nothing at all about what Cooper said or did in the van: he tells us what Murphy and McMahon said or did, but nothing about Cooper.

4. Allegedly, Mathews left Luton without knowing what had happened, and learnt of it only from the News at Ten on television that night, followed by a visit from Cooper.

Criticism: The witness Carole Ann Ellis saw a car on the outskirts of Luton which answered the description of Mathews's Vauxhall, and saw part of the registration, which was also consistent with his. The car, being driven at great speed, had a passenger – and this was within half an hour of the murder. If this evidence is accepted, and Mathews drove home with a passenger, it is not credible that he did not know about the murder. He would also have known about the murder if, in accordance with the evidence of McNair and Seal (see above), he was the driver of the van. In either case the story of the subsequent visit to his home by Cooper, and the content of their conversation, could not be true. There is yet another point here: in their first statements to the police both Mr and Mrs Mathews omitted to mention Cooper's visit to their home after the murder. It is not credible that both of them separately could have forgotten such a highly charged dramatic incident – if in fact it occurred.

Having drawn your attention to these points, let me remind you as forcefully as I can that in the case of Cooper, unlike McMahon, the only evidence that he had anything to do with the crime comes from Mathews. It is true that on the pillow in the hold-all in which the murder weapon was found abandoned there was the hair of a Labrador dog, and that Cooper had a Labrador of that colour – but so did one of Mathews's brothers (who even on Mathews's evidence play a role in the events succeeding the crime).

At the latest Court of Appeal hearing not only was the central narrative om Mathews's evidence described by one of the judges as a 'cock and bull story', but there were lies within his lies. His insistence under oath that he had not drawn out any of the £2,000 reward money from his bank account was nakedly exposed when he was ordered by the court to produce his bank statements and these showed that on the same day as he paid the money in he drew out £700. He gave two entirely different accounts of his movements in Luton after the crime: one how he made determined efforts to find his way back to the station so as to inform the police, but got lost; the other how he tried to get out of town as quickly as he could. He admitted having locked and abandoned his car after the murder, but when asked why he had wiped the interior clean of fingerprints he denied that he had, and said that this must have been done by someone else – a story described by the judges as an obvious lie. He even lied under cross-examination about matters unconnected with the crime – for instance he twice denied knowing what the word 'monkey' is slang for, when every East-Londoner knows (even I know) that it means £500. Perhaps there was a sum of £500 that he was over-anxious to deny knowledge of – see the point above about the big withdrawal from his bank account: there have been persistent rumours for years that he gave £500 of the reward money to someone else.

You may find it scarcely credible, as do I, that the judges gave it as their opinion that no serious doubt was cast on a conviction which rests almost solely on the evidence of which all these lies were part.

But such is the case.

May I appeal to you – as your parting shot as Home Secretary – to exercise the power of discretion vested in you, and take some initiative? I see two alternatives. One is to make a compassionate decision on grounds of Cooper's health. The other is to ask the Court of Appeal to consider the narrow point of whether Cooper's conviction for murder should not be reduced to manslaughter under section 17. 1. b of the 1968 Act (rather than 17. 1. a). As you know, the Lord Chief Justice thinks that the power to refer on a specific point is under-used. And even if Mathews's evidence is accepted in its entirety it not only clears Cooper of any active part in the killing but describes him as being immediately 'grieved' by it.

I know you have only a short time left in office, and many other things on your mind, but what is at stake for my constituent is another 14 years in prison for a murder he may have had nothing to do with, and I therefore beg you to give this matter the full and serious consideration it deserves.

With thanks.

Yours,

Bryan

This reference towards the end of the letter to the fact that Roy Jenkins was about to give up the Home Secretaryship was due to the fact that he had just accepted the Presidency of the European Commission, and was indeed about to leave British politics altogether. But he declined to leave with the parting gesture I proposed to him. He said it would make a mockery of his referral of the case back to the Court of Appeal if he himself then refused to accept its verdict; and indeed, for him to free the two men immediately after the court had re-affirmed their guilt would be an insulting and direct flouting of the court. I wondered aloud why the Home Secretary possessed his special powers at all if they were never to be used – and if they were to be used on occasion, why not here? But my wondering got me nowhere. Outwardly I refused to take No for an answer, but inwardly I was already beginning to console myself with the thought that there would soon be a new Home Secretary for me to make fresh approaches to. But here I was to be disappointed. The new Home Secretary, Merlyn Rees, (no doubt on official prompting) reacted quickly and negatively to my approaches, and sent me a letter whose obvious intention was to close the file on the case for good.

At just this time the *Daily Mail* took an initiative. My most recent *Times* article had given them the idea of of mounting a national campaign for the release of Cooper and McMahon. But before committing themselves to it they wanted to make as sure as they could that the two men were innocent. So they sent their chief crime reporter, John Harrison (since promoted Lobby Correspondent), to see me, and after our discussions he devoted three months of full-time work to investigating the case. With all the skill of a practised reporter he tracked down witnesses whom the police had been unable to trace, including some who were living in hiding,* secured photographs of sensitive meetings and tape recordings of secret discussions, and even some signed statements. And of course all this was evidence which had not been before any court.

Armed with this, I secured my first official meeting about the case with Merlyn Rees. However, although he was new as Home Secretary, the officials who flanked him on either side were the same. And it was obvious that they were by now thoroughly fed up with these endlessly repeated demands for review. Merlyn Rees said to me, not unreasonably, that he could not comment on this fresh evidence without first taking time to consider it. I was to find that this consideration took a very long time indeed. Once a month I wrote to the Home Secretary and asked for a progress report, but always the reply was that these were such extremely important matters that their consideration should not be hurried. The new evidence was submitted to a police inquiry, and this took a long time on its own account.

In the course of all these dealings I learned that Merlyn Rees, as befitted such a close personal as well as political associate of James Callaghan, was a man whose social instincts were conservative with a small 'c'. Not only would he never, it seemed to me, throw aside the rule book, but he was unlikely ever to depart from the advice of his

* For instance Michael Good, still living in hiding seven years after the murder. It is typical of the whole bizarre story that this man, a known criminal who admitted having supplied the murder weapon (which was stolen and for which there was no licence) was allotted £500 of the reward money, which he subsequently denied ever having received.

departmental officials. And by now I knew only too well how richly the Home Office officials deserved their own special reputation for small 'c' conservatism.

The decision, when finally it came, was negative and evasive, just as all the previous ones had been – hiding, as they had hidden, behind procedural considerations, and failing, as they had failed, to confront the central issues of the case. The worst aspect of it all was that we seemed now to have reached the end of the road with the Home Secretary, having already reached it with the courts. What to do next? As before when we had been becalmed, I went through a period of writing to the Home Secretary whenever I could find a good excuse – for instance whenever a particularly good article about the case appeared in the press I would send him a copy with an accompanying letter adding my own comments; or when Thames Television screened a documentary programme about the case I drew his attention to it in advance and suggested he watch it. The last in this particular series of letters was the following:

3 May 1978

Dear Merlyn:

Yesterday I attended a public lecture given at All Souls' College, Oxford, by Lord Devlin, in which he made extensive reference to the Cooper–McMahon case. The central thesis of his lecture, which was entitled 'Undermining the Jury', was that in recent years we have increasingly developed in this country something which he called 'trial by judge'. This, he averred, had gone beyond anything envisaged by Parliament or the Law Officers, had never been discussed by them, and would certainly not be approved by them.

Throughout his lecture Lord Devlin drew his main examples from the Cooper–McMahon case. He concluded that Cooper and McMahon had never received a proper trial by jury, in the traditional sense of appearing before a jury which heard all the relevant evidence, nor had they been allowed a proper appeal in the traditional sense either, in that the appeal courts (and he analysed this in detail) had persistently failed to perform the functions traditionally required of them.

It seems to me that things have reached a pretty pass when this case is being held up in one of the most prestigious colleges in the world as a paradigm example of bad judicial practice. The lecture was attended by many of the ablest professors at Oxford, and will in due course be published in full by the Oxford University Press. An account of it even appears in today's *Times,* which rates it as front page news. I enclose a photostat copy.

Does this not really bring home to us all the fact that it is high time that something more practical was done about this lamentable case? I spoke to Lord Devlin after his lecture, and he said he would be perfectly willing to send you a full text of it if you so request.

Yours sincerely,
Bryan

Merlyn Rees did indeed send for Devlin's lecture, but after a long period of 'reflection' he sent me another of his stonewalling and would-be final letters. To this I replied:

28 July 1978

Dear Merlyn:

Your letter to me of the 26th July concerning David Cooper is a matter for deep regret. The conclusion it comes to is so profoundly unreasonable, given all the considerations you should have taken into account before arriving at it. This being so, we seem to have reached a point at which the personality of the Home Secretary is decisive. I cannot resist the conviction that your predecessor would by this time have released David Cooper, and rightly so.

The unreasonableness of your position also makes it difficult to argue with. In any case it would obviously be fruitless at this moment to repeat arguments we have been through together before, in many cases more than once.

But the case will not lie down or go away, in fact I don't think it will stop being a focus of public attention until David Cooper is released. So I'm quite sure that your Department will hear a good deal more of it yet, and perhaps quite soon.

Yours sincerely,
Bryan

It was indeed soon after this that David Cooper's brother Terry turned up at one of my constituency surgeries in Leyton clutching an armful of manuscript paper. This was a book which, unknown to me, David Cooper had written in prison and smuggled out piecemeal via the members of his family who visited him. Now that it was completed it was being brought to me for advice and help about getting it published. When I read it I was forced to the conclusion that it was unpublishable as it stood: there was very little organization to the material; large parts of it were only marginally relevant, others were repetitive, and there were serious gaps in the treatment. The tone throughout was overwrought. And owing to the fact that Cooper had been under-educated for his intelligence, the writing itself was not of publishable standard. On the other hand the manuscript contained uniquely interesting material, and was likely to convince any fair-minded person who read it of Cooper's probable innocence. The question therefore was, could it be edited by someone else into something that would be publishable?

I handed the manuscript over to my literary agent, Michael Sissons, for an impartial judgment on this. Now it so happens that Michael Sissons also acts as agent for one of the best writers in the country of books about miscarriages of justice, Ludovic Kennedy, so he passed it along to him for an opinion. The outcome of it all — I need not recount each intervening step — is the volume which the reader now holds in his hands.

This brings my story not to an end but to the present —

the end lies in the future. What is the chief lesson to be learned from it up to now? It is, I think, the danger of becoming so entrenched in a position that, without meaning or wishing to distort the issue, one ceases to judge it on its merits because other considerations have assumed greater importance in one's mind. This happened in turn to the judges, to the civil servants, and to the Home Office ministers concerned with this case. We ought none of us to lose sight of the fact that human beings count for more than institutions or procedures or precedents, and we ought always to be willing, given justification, to sacrifice the latter to the former.

My own role in the case, I fear, shows merely how much an MP may do and yet accomplish so little – as I write this sentence, David Cooper is in prison just as he was when I first became involved. I provided a small element of personal support simply by being there and taking an interest, and that was obviously worth while. I did what little I could to counter David Cooper's despair by trying to get him to look forward rather than back, encouraging him to think in terms of what he will do when he comes out of prison, and to involve himself in practical measures towards that end, such as an A-level study course. My contribution here was slight, but it may have helped in a dark time. At any rate, I like to think so.

But what of him, Cooper, the human being at the centre of it all as far as I have been concerned? Perhaps the most disconcerting paradox in the whole case is that the experience of it, by maturing David Cooper almost out of recognition, has made him a superior human being to the one he was before. He has been through the fire – several years of it – and it has made him an altogether more reflective, deeper, wiser, more compassionate, more self-aware person. As the Victorians would have said, it has made a man of him. I have watched it happen over the years, and he is himself aware of the change. One consequence of it is that he now looks back with genuine disdain at the person he used to be, the small-minded petty crook showing off in a bright red car and pinching anything he could get away with from coins to refrigerators. But the brutal fact is that if it were not for his wrongful conviction that is the sort of person he would still be. So — incredible though it may sound — I can envisage that a time may one day come when, looking back with detachment over these tragic events which have caused such a deep change in his character and personality, he will not be able to find it in his heart to wish them otherwise.

Bryan Magee
August 1979

Appendix I

(see page 83)

Memorandum of William John Thomson, Freelance journalist

I first began to take an interest in the Luton case in May 1971. Stephen Murphy, the father of the convicted man Patrick Colin Murphy, came to see me at the *Ilford Recorder*, where I was a staff reporter.

In an effort to get a clear and balanced story relating to the case, I attempted to get in touch with Alfred Mathews (his real name being Alfred Vernon Mathew Elliott). I managed to do this through his brother, Albert Elliott, who lived at Caernarvon Avenue, Clayhall, Ilford. He told me he would try and get his brother to contact me. I told him I considered this fair because of certain allegations that were being made against him.

Albert Elliott telephoned me at my office at the *Ilford Recorder* on 30 September 1971. It was lunchtime and I could find no one to go with me to witness the conversation. However, I took the precaution of arranging with the editorial secretary to telephone me at Elliott's home thirty minutes after I had left the office.

When I arrived, Mathews was already there. He was sitting in a straight-back chair in front of the window, leaning on a dining table. He maintained this position throughout the interview which lasted one hour and twenty minutes.

He constantly looked out of the window, gazing up and down Caernarvon Avenue, presumably to see if anyone had followed me. He chainsmoked throughout the interview, rolling his own, the tobacco coming from a tin which he had placed on the table in front of him. The cigarettes were thin and badly made and constantly needed relighting. He did this from a lighter which he spent part of the time fumbling with. The remainder of the time he spent fiddling with a set of car keys and an empty match box, and by the time the interview had finished he had carved a hole in the box.

Throughout the interview he showed signs of severe nervousness. I found him talkative, at times excessively so. Occasionally he would fall back into a rambling type of talk that I had difficulty following. On other occasions, especially when I tried to question him too severely, he would enter into a long tirade of religious banter.

During the interview he accused me of being in Murphy's pay. He also claimed that other people, including the then MP for Ilford North, Tom Iremonger, was also being paid by Murphy to 'say the right things'. When I corrected him on this matter he entered into one of his religious rantings saying, 'I'm a God-fearing man', and, 'God guided me through all this'.

On one occasion I answered this type of ranting by saying: 'I'm sure our Lord would not approve of an innocent person being jailed for twenty years.' At this he became agitated and aggressive with me.

I found it very difficult to keep his mind on one line of thought; he would switch from one subject to another without stopping to think what he was talking about. On another occasion he said that Murphy senior had offered him £2,000 to say he had lied in Court. He kept on insisting that I was being paid to say lies about him. When I laughed at this suggestion he became angry and threatened to leave.

Throughout this interview his brother Albert was present, but took little part in the proceedings.

An interesting stage in the interview came when I asked him about the events leading up to the murder.

He said: 'You've read it all. I've said all I'm going to say, you can't trap me.' I then asked him to tell me what he had seen in Luton. Among the well-rehearsed phrases was the following: 'I heard Murphy shout, "Leave the old bastard alone, there's nothing we can do for him now." '

I later checked with the trial transcripts and Mathews's statements and could find no reference to such a statement. He claimed in court that he had heard someone shout in the getaway van, 'You've killed him.'

He said to me that he would not have gone on the job if

he had known what was going to happen. I then said that I knew that he had planned this particular robbery, for I knew that he had gone to Luton some eighteen months before the killing with two other men to plan the very robbery on which the postmaster had died. He seemed stunned by this, and he remained silent for a short period. He then shouted at me and said I was trying to trap him into saying something he might regret.

Shortly after this he said that he knew that Cooper and McMahon were going on the job before they had asked him to drive to Luton with his van (he did in fact go in his own car). I asked him if he knew this, why did he go on with the job. He started to give me an answer and I then accused him of trying to find a lie to fit the conversation. After a brief silence he looked dejected and said: 'I didn't know the old fella was going to die.'

From then on it became difficult to conduct the interview and he became increasingly haggard and worried looking. Several times he got up to leave, but remained, only to carry on his religious rantings.

It was during one of these rantings that I told him that two witnesses had identified him as the driver of the getaway van. He was startled at this and got up and went to leave. He said: 'I'm going to see Mr Drury and get this stopped'.

I asked him if he was still friendly with Mr Drury. He said: 'He looked after me before, he'll do it again. You people won't be able to touch me. If you want me to go to court, I'll refuse. Mr Drury will look after me.'

I then asked him if Patrick Murphy was involved in the Luton job. Without looking at me, and obviously without thinking he said: 'I might have made . . .' He never completed the sentence, but I was of the opinion he was going to say 'mistake'. Mathews then accused me of trying to trap him. He became angry and I decided to leave.

The next time I met Mathews was on a Sunday morning in November 1971. I cannot be precise about the date.

It was after the *Sunday Times* ran the story. Peter Steele of the London *Evening Standard* and I went to see Mathews at his home in Witham near Chelmsford. I can recall that it was a sunny day and Peter had met me from a station and we travelled to Witham by car.

As I recall, we did not see Mathews that day. I can remember that we went to his house which was on the right-hand side of a cul-de-sac and was about the third from the end. I think it was number seven, but I cannot be sure without going to the address. Mrs Mathews came to the door and told us her husband was not in. There was a rather large Alsatian in the house.

Peter and I returned to Mathews's house on the Sunday. We saw Mathews and he agreed to let us in the house. He sent his wife out of their lounge with the dog. She appeared to be nervous. Mathews himself was aggressive with us and said, if I can recall accurately, that he wanted nothing to do with the case. He said nothing of any significance and we left. I did not record the conversation in any way, mainly because it was short and sweet and secondly because there was no story value in his comments.

At the beginning of December 1971, I think it was 3 December, I telephoned Albert Elliott to see if he had heard from his brother. Alfred was there. He spoke to me and was brusque and short with me. He told me to leave him alone. He wanted to say nothing and nobody would get him to say anything. He said he had said all he was going to say at the trial.

It wasn't until nearly a year later that I made contact with Mathews again. He telephoned me on 3 November 1972, at my office in Romford. He seemed agitated. He said he had been thinking about the matter and wanted to talk to me. He said he wanted me to stop people annoying him. He said some people were harassing him – but never said in this telephone call who these people were.

By this time I had become interested in the allocation of the reward money. This was because of a couple of East End tip-offs that 'the cops had copped some of the money.'

I also knew at this stage that officially the Post Office had paid Mathews £2,000 on the recommendation of

Detective Chief Superintendent Ken Drury. Mathews's brother had already told me that Mathews had got £1,000; an East London contact also suggested that Mathews had only got half of the official figure. I considered that if this was true, and what is more important, if it could be proven without a shadow of doubt, it cast a different aspect on the whole case.

So in this conversation I made a point of asking Mathews if he had received any of the reward money. He confirmed that he did get some of the money, 'but not as much as people thought'. He would not under any circumstances expand along this line.

In the main the half-hour conversation was taken up listening to Mathews's complaints about his problems and the way his 'life had been interfered with.' He agreed to call me again but refused to give me his telephone number.

About midday on Saturday, 4 November, Mathews telephoned me again. He said he was interested in selling his life story to a newspaper if the money was right. I said I would be pleased to talk to him about this and would see if any news editor was interested. The conversation was very disjointed and most of the time he spent his time on the telephone telling me of the problems he had had since the murder. He briefly said that he had been attacked by people who were friendly with Murphy and the others.

My own opinion of the offer to write his story was that it was a significant step in the right direction, but it would only have been any good to Murphy and the other two if Mathews decided to give a different version of the events on the day of the killing. Even then he may still not have been telling the truth.

Mathews gave me his home telephone number, which I recall was a four-digit Rivenhall one. However I have since lost the number.

I made inquiries at a couple of papers about the possibility of selling Mathews's story to them. The *Sunday People* turned it down. The *Sunday Express* said they were not interested. However the *Sunday Mirror* said they were interested only if they knew what he was going to say: then a decision could be made.

I telephoned Mathews and told him this. He seemed pleased and was very talkative with me. During this conversation he said that he was angry with his brother over appearing in the television film. Mathews also said that his brother had received £500 for doing the deal with Drury and shopping him.

Throughout this interview he seemed preoccupied with what he was going to say in his life story.

On Sunday midday I telephoned him again and asked him how soon we could meet. He appeared worried that I might 'do the dirty on him' and take all the information and not pay him. I agreed that I would sign a letter stating that I agreed not to sell any of the material which he supplied me with until the financial position had been settled.

He appeared friendly and willing to talk. I said that one subject that interested many people was the question of the part played by Mr Drury in the case. He told me that if he was to say anything about him it would land him in jail. I asked him how much Mr Drury had recommended that he should be paid. He replied without hesitation, 'a grand'.

During this conversation he said that he didn't get all of what was due to him, 'I had to share it with someone else'. I asked him who this was, Was it the police. He answered, 'It could have been, you might be right.' I took this as in the affirmative. We agreed that we would meet the following day to begin the task of writing his story.

The following day, 6 November, Mathews came to my office at Ingrave Road, Romford. I took him into my private office. He seemed very nervous and said he was worried that I might be taping the conversation. He said he was also worried that I might 'turn him over'. I took this to mean that I might con him in some way.

We went over in general terms what he was going to say. I found that in the main this was nothing more than the ramblings of a small-time crook who wanted to act the big shot. He told me of the bomb attempts on his life and the

184

high-speed car chases – all from men who, he said, wanted to kill him because of the Luton case.

I said that I wanted to know for certain if Murphy was at the scene of the killing. He answered. 'Do you want me done for perjury. I've said all I'm going to say.' He neither confirmed nor denied that Murphy was involved in the killing.

During this two-hour interview I tried several times to get him to talk about the case and his involvement. He avoided any talk about this. He was more interested in me knowing some of the jobs he had pulled in the past and trying to convince me that he never used violence or anything like that. I told him that I knew that he was known as a 'gelly man': he said that this stuff was safe and that he could throw it on the fire and nothing would happen.

He returned to his religious theme during this interview, but when I told him that I was not interviewing him for *Stars on Sunday*, he kept quiet.

Towards the end of this interview I asked him: 'Did Mr Drury take any of the reward money?' He replied: 'I only got a grand for my troubles. Someone else got the rest and I paid it in cash.' I asked again if this someone was Drury. He said : 'It might have been. Why ask me? You know what sort of funny deals were done. I handed some to others, yes.' 'Was it Mr Drury?' I asked. He replied, somewhat agitated, 'I can't say that, you know what it's about, leave it out, I can't do that. You know what sort of things went on. I've got to think of myself.'

I let Mathews calm down and we discussed going to a Romford solicitor and drawing up an agreement. We did this and Mathews signed it in the name of A. Elliott (the original of this document is with David Cooper's solicitors, Birnberg and Co.).

I came back to my office with Mathews and we went over certain points again. I said it was important for me to know if anyone else received any of the reward money other than himself. He said something like, 'Of course they did, he got a cut.' I asked him who this was and he replied with something on the lines of 'Leave it out, you know whom I'm on about. Drury, that's who.' I said, 'Are you telling me for certain that it was Drury who shared the reward money with you? He said, 'Well I didn't get it all, did I. Some had to go in cash.'

I asked him how this was done. He said that Drury had recommended the amounts, and it had been agreed that he would get some if he, Mathews, was left alone. I asked him how this took place and he said, 'They paid me by cheque and I changed it, they wanted it in cash.' He did not say who collected it, or where.

He went on to say that he would deny that he had told me this and if I used it he would not do his story with me.

I deeply regretted that this interview was not either recorded or witnessed in any way.

William Thomson
March 1973

Appendix II

Three people who for several years have been working tirelessly on behalf of Cooper and McMahon are Tom Surgant, secretary of JUSTICE; McMahon's solicitor Wendy Mantle; and Cooper's solicitor Gareth Peirce. Their views on the case follow, together with those of Dr Oonagh Macdonald, the MP who has been campaigning on McMahon's behalf

Statement of Tom Sargant

I have closely followed all the developments in the Luton murder case ever since Patrick Murphy's father came and sought my help. This led me to investigate the case in depth and subsequently to assist in the presentation of the BBC documentary film which led to the first reference back to the Court of Appeal.

The aspect of the case which has worried me from the beginning was the effective suppression of evidence of two witnesses that clearly pointed to Mathews having been the driver of the getaway van and his presentation to the jury as a witness of truth to testify that Murphy was the driver. If this evidence had been produced as it should have been, the whole tragic charade of trial and successive appeals, with the mental torture they have inflicted on the two men still serving their sentences and the incalculable wastage of time and effort on the part of the lawyers involved, would not have been played and brought such discredit on our courts.

I have always been convinced that David Cooper was innocent because of the obvious genuineness of his alibi which was perverted by Drury at the first trial and suffered from being presented and considered piecemeal at the subsequent appeals. I was not so fully convinced about Michael McMahon because of the evidence of the two prisoners, Jackson and Weyers. I changed my mind, however, after I had had long talks with him and his father, and learned that the two prisoners had been given substantial rewards. The evidence of the new witness, Hurn, which was summarily rejected by the Court of Appeal without hearing argument, semed to me to be conclusive.

Tom Sargant
September 1979

Statement of Gareth Peirce, legal adviser to David Cooper

I came to David Cooper's case cold. I had no previous knowledge of the facts or the background. At my first meeting with him in Wormwood Scrubs, five years ago, he asked if I believed in his innocence. I could say truthfully that on a reading of the papers then in existence, that the prosecution case was flimsy in the extreme and that I *thought* that he was innocent.

After six months of working on his fresh appeal, that first response was changed into conviction. By then it was clear that the case presented at the original trial formed only the tip of the iceberg. The Post Office finally provided a breakdown of payment of reward monies; we discovered that the prosecution had failed to disclose the existence of over 800 statements taken within days of the murder, many of which suggested a very different course of events and cast of characters than that portrayed at the trial; other witnesses came forward to throw further doubt upon Mathews's story – Leonard, Stephens, Langston, and in particular Morris Lerman interviewed for the first time by anyone on Cooper's behalf, and who provided a revelation as to Drury's *modus operandi*. It was clear that Drury had been *determined* that Cooper was at Luton despite all the evidence which, had he been conducting an objective investigation, should have driven him to a contrary conclusion.

Cooper should not have been convicted at the original trial. Nor should his conviction have been upheld at his first appeal. The strongest criticisms, however, over and above those levelled at Mathews and Drury, must be reserved for the Court of Appeal and the way it dealt with Cooper's and McMahon's cases after Murphy's conviction was quashed.

In order to uphold their convictions three successive

Courts of Appeal (one sitting in camera) had to ignore, contradict, disbelieve or distort thirty-seven powerful new witnesses or pieces of evidence that had emerged since the trial. Cooper and McMahon, at the very least, deserved that all their new witnesses should have been heard, together with the prosecution witnesses as a whole, at a fresh trial.

Cooper has now been in prison for ten years. For the past five years I have anticipated his release each year. During that time I have come to know him well. I not only know that he is innocent of any part in the murder of Reginald Stevens, but to be a man of dignity and maturity, and with great reserves of strength and stoicism in the face of the repeated injustice meted out to him. I value him as a friend and will rejoice in his release. His continuing imprisonment can only be viewed as a disgraceful indictment of our whole system of justice.

Gareth Peirce
July 1979

Statement of Dr Oonagh MacDonald, MP

I first heard of Michael McMahon when his brother, John, came to my surgery the day after I won the by-election in Thurrock in 1976. I did not realize at the time that the McMahon case was a cause célèbre. But after studying the papers, I decided to visit McMahon to form my own judgment of him. I spent two hours in private conversation with him in Long Lartin prison. He presented a clear and honest picture of himself as a small-time crook, constantly at loggerheads with the police, but not a violent one. Even on the day on which he was supposed to have taken part in the allegedly carefully planned robbery at Luton, he appeared at Thames Magistrates' Court on a charge of dishonestly handling stolen goods. He could not have known the timing of his appearance before the magistrate – hardly the day to choose for a serious crime.

The whole case against McMahon struck me as pure fabrication. He was convicted on the evidence of Mathews, whom judge and jury agreed was a liar. Mathews's evidence at the first trial was corroborated by selected eye-witnesses. But nearly 800 statements were never revealed to the defence at the original trial. Even some who gave evidence at the trial – like Mrs Crawley – changed their descriptions and identifications in the course of making statements to the police. It took thirteen statements from Mrs Crawley for her description of the man she saw in the car park to fit McMahon. All that was concealed from the defence. Later alibi evidence – a man called Hurn saw McMahon entering Kingsland Road, Shoreditch at about 5.00 p.m. on the day of the murder – was dismissed by the Court of Appeal in March 1977. The court seems to be determined to believe Mathews's identification of his accomplices, despite the fact that he has lied about every other detail of the events at Luton.

Worse still, all charges were dropped against Mathews, and he received £2,000 reward money on Drury's recommendation, himself later found guilty of corruption. He got better treatment than any other supergrass since then. Others, like Bertie Smalls and Leroy Davis, have only been given relative immunity. Mathews got off scot free. Why?

That is why I raised the case in the House on 14 December 1977, For a newspaper report filled in a significant gap – the reason for Mathews's choice of McMahon and the others as his 'accomplices'. James Humphreys, the one-time 'porn-king' said that Mathews was 'instructed' to organize the raid. It was a put-up job which went badly wrong. Someone had to carry the can. McMahon was known to the police and an obvious choice. He could be quickly and easily located. On the basis of that speech, the case was referred to the Court of Appeal once again, but that too failed.

McMahon's conviction will remain as a festering sore, unless and until the Home Office is prepared to carry out a full public investigation of the original conviction and trial and the activities of the Flying Squad in the late 1960s.

Oonagh Macdonald
October 1979

Statement of Wendy Mantle, legal adviser to Michael McMahon

I first met Michael McMahon in June 1974 when he instructed me to represent him in connection with the Home Secretary's first referral of his conviction to the Court of Appeal.

My connection with the Luton case began three years earlier when I was consulted by Stephen Murphy, Patrick Murphy's father. It was then apparent that the three men, convicted of murder in March 1970 and sentenced to serve a minimum of twenty years in prison, had been convicted because Alfred Mathews was believed when he said that they were the three men who accompanied him on the robbery expedition to Luton.

After the Court of Appeal quashed Murphy's conviction in November 1973 I did not believe that it could be long before the conviction of McMahon and Cooper would be quashed, on the basis that since their convictions, too, rested on his evidence it would be unsafe and unsatisfactory to allow them to stand. I believed this notwithstanding the concluding words of the Lord Chief Justice's judgment.

The evidence which has accumulated in the nine years since the original trial is now a labyrinthine network which has been mastered by Ludovic Kennedy with consummate skill. Future historians of criminal case law will find this book the indispensable introduction to an examination of the Luton case. Contemporary citizens who do not accept that some wrong convictions are an inevitable casualty of any legal system will experience on reading it a keener sense of injustice than they may have hitherto imagined possible.

Those of us who have campaigned for the freeing of McMahon and Cooper, and the clearing of their names, will be encouraged by the publication of this book to fight on by all lawful means to achieve those goals. *Wicked Beyond Belief* cannot give back to two innocent men the years which prison has taken away but it must rekindle for them and us the hope that they may be released before another decade of their sentence has passed.

Wendy Mantle
June 1979

List of Sources

CHAPTER ONE

1 London Weather Centre.
2 Statement of Mathews to Luton Police, 25 Oct. 1969.
Article by Mathews in *Sunday Mirror* 12 Nov. 1972.
Memo of W. J. Thomson (see Appendix 1).
3 Statement of Ruth Emily Brooks to Stephen Murphy, 3 June 1970.
Affidavit of Ruth Emily Brooks to Voss and Co., Commissioners for Oaths, 9 Nov. 1973.
4 Statement of Terence Langston to Luton Police, Nov. 1971.
Statement of Terence Langston in Wandsworth Prison to Wendy Mantle, 25 Oct. 1973.
Statement of Patricia Joan Good to Luton Police, 27 Sept. 1969.
Trial. Evidence of Michael Good.
5 Affidavits of Terence Leonard and Frederick Stephens to Wendy Mantle, July 1971.
6 *Trial.* Evidence of Kenneth Isaac.
7 Statement of Margaret Irene Crawley to Luton Police, 10 Sept. 1969.
8 Statement of John McNair to Luton Police, 10 Sept. 1969.
9 *Ibid.*
10 *Ibid.*
Trial. Evidence of Isaac.
11 Statement of Edward Seal to Luton Police, 12 Sept. 1969.
Affidavit of Edward Seal to Mr W. J. Bridges of Montague, Gardner, Solicitors, 13 April 1970.
12 Statement of Herbert Andrews to Luton Police, 11 Sept. 1969.
13 *Ibid.*
14 *Ibid.*
Trial. Evidence of Isaac.
15 Statement of Andrews to Luton Police, 11 Sept. 1969.
16 Notes of interview of Mathews by Detective Chief Superintendent Kenneth Drury, 24 Oct. 1969.
17 *Ibid.*
Statement of Florence Mathews to Luton Police, 24 Oct. 1969.
Trial. Evidence of Mathews and Florence Mathews.
18 Statement of Reginald Elliott to Luton Police, 27 Oct. 1969.
19 Statement of Mathews, 25 Oct. 1969.
Statement of Mrs Mathews, 24 Oct. 1969.

CHAPTER TWO

1 Court of Criminal Appeal, 26 Feb. 1971. Judgment.
2 Statement of Patricia Joan Good to Luton Police, 27 Sept. 1969.
  Statement of Terence Langston to Wendy Mantle, Wandsworth
  Prison, 25 Oct. 1973.
3 Statement of Terence Langston to Luton Police, 30 Sept. 1969.
4 Statement of Herbert Andrews to Luton Police, 12 Sept. 1969.
5 Memorandum of Bindman and Partners.
  Trial of Patrick Murphy, June 1970. Summing-up.
6 *Trial*. Evidence of past convictions.
7 Cooper MS.
8 *Ibid.*
9 *Ibid.*
10 McMahon MS.
11 *Ibid.*
  Trial. Evidence of McMahon, Susan Cochrane, Elizabeth
  McMahon.
  Statement of Susan Cochrane to Luton Police, 5 Dec. 1969.
12 *Trial*. Evidence of Cooper, Margaret Laville, Morris Lerman.
  Statement of Cooper to Luton Police, 21 Oct. 1969.
13 *Trial*. Evidence of David Cooper, Raymond Dreezer, Terry
  Disher.
  Statement of Terry Disher to Luton Police, 3 Dec. 1969.
  Statement of Cooper to Luton Police, 21 Oct. 1969.
14 *Trial*. Evidence of Patrick Murphy, James Baker, Marlene
  Baker, Martin Edwards.
15 *Trial*. Evidence of Patrick Murphy, Stephen Murphy, Emily
  Murphy, Peter Turner.
  Statement of Terence John Edwards to Detective Chief Inspector
  J. McFadzean, 13 Apr. 1972.
  Affidavit of Patrick Murphy to W. J. Bridges, of Montague,
  Gardner & Co., 27 Oct. 1969.
16 *Trial*. Evidence of Stephen Murphy.
17 Cooper MS.
18 *Ibid.*
19 *Ibid.*
20 McMahon MS.
21 *Ibid.*
  Cooper MS.
22 *Trial*. Evidence of Patrick Murphy, W. J. Bridges, Martin
  Edwards.
23 Statement of Detective Constable Peter Ames, 11 Dec. 1969.

198

CHAPTER THREE

1 Cooper MS.
2 McMahon MS.
3 Cooper MS.
4 Statement of Detective Constable W. Laver, 19 Nov. 1969.
5 Notes of interview of Mathews by Drury, Luton Police Station. 22-24 Oct. 1969.
6 Article by Drury in *News of the World*, 28 May 1972.
7 This was not the first time that Mathews had put forward as a defence against charges of robbery a story that he had only been the driver of the gang. In a statement to Birnberg and Co., a criminal named George Madsden declared: 'In September 1953 I went down to Gillingham in Dorset with S.C. and W.C. and Alfred Elliott. We started off from my house with Elliott and me in my car and the other two in the other car. My car was a bit troublesome, so we left it at the Dome Garage in Western Avenue and joined the others in their car. When we got down there, we blew several safes at an egg-packing station, a grocer's, and a B.R.S. Depot, and stole in all about £300 to £400. Elliott was the man who blew the safes. We were all arrested on the way back to London.

'S.C. and W.C. pleaded Guilty to the offences and were sentenced to two and four years' respectively . . . I pleaded Not Guilty, but I was found guilty and sentenced to six years' imprisonment.

'Elliott pleaded Not Guilty and *his defence was that W.C. paid him £10 for his services driving us down to Gillingham. He denied he knew why we had gone to Dorset and tried to make the court believe he was only a driver* . . . He received a six months' prison sentence.

Madsden added of Mathews: 'In my opinion he is a rat, and will do anything to extract himself from trouble. He has no scruples at all in what he does. Some years ago we were both serving a sentence in Parkhurst prison, and he had to appear before the Parole Board. For months before this he had spent all his recreational time making a crucifix and jewel box. He smuggled these two objects into the room where the Board was sitting, and presented them to the padre in the presence of the Board, no doubt hoping to influence their decision. He also cried during the course of his interview, and pleaded with the Board to be given parole, saying he was now a reformed character.'
8 Statement of Mathews to Luton Police, 25 Oct. 1969.

CHAPTER FOUR

1 In a statement to Luton Police on 26 Oct. 1969, Mr Andrews said: 'The older man with the grey hair is the only one I could really identify again. His hair was most unusual, iron grey mop brushed backwards, a bit untidy, but it looked like it belonged to a much older man.'
2 Statement of John McNair to Luton Police, 25 Oct. 1969.
3 Statement of Drury to Luton Police, 11 Dec. 1969.
4 Statement of Florence Mathews to Luton Police, 24 Oct. 1969.
5 Statement of Margaret Crawley to Luton Police, 10 Sept. 1969.
6 Statement of Margaret Crawley to Luton Police, 12 Sept. 1969.
7 Statement of Margaret Crawley to Luton Police, 14 Sept. 1969.
8 Statement of Margaret Crawley to Luton Police, 25 Oct. 1969.
9 McMahon MS.
10 *Ibid.*
11 In this statement Murphy said: 'If the police wish to question me about this incident at Luton, I am willing to speak to them but know nothing about it.'
12 Notes of interview of McMahon by Drury, 31 Oct. 1969.
   Ibid.
13 McMahon MS.
14 McMahon MS.
15 Notes of interview of Cooper by Drury, 4 Nov. 1969.
   Statement of Mathews to Luton Police, 5 Nov. 1969.
16 *Trial.* Evidence of Inspector Lett.
17 *Ibid.*
   McMahon MS.
18 McMahon MS.

CHAPTER FIVE

1 Statement of Detective Constable Jack Beck on 12 Dec. 1969 of interview with Morris Lerman, 5 Nov. 1969.
2 Affidavit of Morris Lerman to Birnberg & Co. 1974.
3 Affidavit of Roderick Firmstone, 14 Dec. 1974.
4 Affidavit of Morris Lerman to Birnberg & Co., 1974.
5 Statement of Terence Langston to Wendy Mantle, Wandsworth Prison, 25 Oct. 1973.
6 Statement of Mathews to Luton Police, 3 Dec. 1969.
7 *Trial.* Evidence of Drury.
8 Statement of Andrews to Luton Police, 4 Dec. 1969.
   From the statements of various other witnesses interviewed by the Luton Police, and who were not called to give evidence at the trial, it would seem likely that the red sports car was what

criminals call a 'ringer', i.e. that it was probably an old cannibalized MG with a Mercedes badge fixed to the boot. (Statements of Daniel Line, 13 Sept. 1969, Edward Curd, 13 Sept. 1969, Tom Morris, 13 Sept. 1969, 15 Sept. 1969, 16 Sept. 1969, Frederick Mitchell, 25 Sept. 1969, Paul Lapihuska, 17 Sept. 1969, Derrick Barker, 18 Sept. 1969, Stanley Impey, 18 Sept. 1969, Ronald Green, 19 Sept. 1969.)

CHAPTER SIX

1 Affidavits of Edward Seal and John McNair to W. J. Bridges of Montague, Gardner, 13 Apr. 1970.
A photograph of Mathews was attached to these affidavits, and on the back of it Mr Seal wrote: 'I can positively identify the man on the reverse side of this photo as being the man I saw driving the green Transit van at approx. 6.10 p.m. on the 10th Sept. 1969 . . . I picked this photo out of several different ones shown to me by Mr Stephen Murphy.'
2 Statement of Derek Jackson to Luton Police, 15 Nov. 1969. McMahon MS.
Trial. Evidence of Jackson.
Notes taken by Jackson of alleged statements by McMahon (*Trial*, Exhibit 65).
William Thomson also interviewed Weyers at a later date, and stated: 'Weyers told me that Jackson had lied about his part in this so-called "confession". He said that McMahon would have nothing to do with Jackson because Jackson was a "queer".' (Memo of Bill Thomson to Laurie Manifold, assistant editor of *Sunday People*, 17 Jan. 1975).
3 Statement of Thomas Weyers to Luton Police, 13 Feb. 1976. McMahon MS.
Trial. Evidence of Weyers.
4 Article by Drury in *News of the World*, 28 May 1972.
'Weyers told me that he got the £500 because he had done a deal with Drury to say "the right things", and he, Drury, would see that he was let out early. Weyers was later convicted of housebreaking and got an early release' (memo of Bill Thomson to Laurie Manifold, assistant editor of *Sunday People*, 17 Jan. 1975).
5 Cooper MS.
6 McMahon MS.
7 *Ibid.*
8 *Ibid.*

CHAPTER SEVEN

CHAPTER EIGHT

1 Post Office (Mr P. E. Whetter) to Drury, 20 May 1970:
'Cheques are being sent direct to Mr Isaac, Mr Andrews, Mrs
Crawley and Mrs Calvert, and at your suggestion, are being
sent to Messrs Weyers and Jackson via their respective prison
governors.

'I would, however, like to take advantage of your kind offer
to co-operate in effecting payment to the Elliott brothers and
to Mr Good. I do not think I need trouble you and them to
attend at this office, but perhaps you would be good enough to
arrange to give each of them one of the enclosed envelopes
containing a letter of explanation and a cheque . . .

'I should not wish to let this opportunity pass without offering
you my personal thanks and congratuations on the successful
outcome of the murder inquiry.'

2 See Appendix 1.

3 Memo of Bill Thomson to Laurie Manifold, assistant editor of
Sunday People, 17 Feb. 1975.

4 Article by Mathews in *Sunday Mirror*, 12 Nov. 1972.

5 Statement of James Humphreys to Detective Sergeant Stagg,
Gartree Prison, 23 May 1975.

6 Court of Criminal Appeal, 22 July 1976. Judgment.

7 Statement of Michael Good to Detective Chief Superintendent
F. Cater, Brixton Prison, 23 June 1976.

8 Prior to the 1976 appeal the Crown had prepared evidence to
rebut this statement of Good. This consisted of
(a) Certain passages edited out of Good's statement.
(b) A statement of Detective Chief Superintendent Cater
relating to interviews with Good and 'X', dated 29 June 1976.
(c) A statement of 'X' and questionnaire answered by him,
dated 29 June 1976.

(d) An extract of the Bank Account of 'X' at the National Westminster Bank, Potters Bar.

As evidence relating to the disposal of the reward money was not introduced at the 1976 appeal the nature of these rebuttals is not known.

9 Interview of Thomas Weyers by Wendy Mantle and Gareth Peirce, Leicester Prison, 20 Jan. 1975.
10 Letter to the author from J. B. Wheatley and Co., Solictors, 8 Aug. 1979.

CHAPTER NINE

1 Affidavits of Edward Seal and John McNair to Mr W. J. Bridges of Montague, Gardner, 13 Apr. 1970.
2 Statement of Ruth Brooks to Stephen Murphy, 3 June 1970.
3 Court of Criminal Appeal, 26 Feb. 1971. Judgment.
4 McMahon MS.
5 *Ibid.*
6 Cooper MS.
7 *Ibid.*
8 *Ibid.*
9 McMahon MS.
10 Statement of Terence John Edwards to Detective Chief Inspector J. McFadzean, 13 Apr. 1972.
Statement of Alfred Diamond to Detective Chief Superintendent A. Dunlop 26 Apr. 1972.
11 The *People*, 5 Mar. 1972.
12 *News of the World*, 21 May 1972.

CHAPTER TEN

1 *Midweek*, 25 Oct. 1972, 10.45 p.m. (transcript of recording).
2 Home Office to Registrar of Criminal Appeals, 13 Dec. 1972.
3 McMahon MS.
4 Court of Criminal Appeal, 13 Nov. 1973. Judgment.
5 *Ibid.*
6 Cooper MS.
7 McMahon MS.
8 Tom Sargant to the Home Secretary, 14 Jan. 1974.
9 Home Office to Registrar of Criminal Appeals, 22 May 1974.
10 McMahon MS.
11 Cooper MS.

CHAPTER ELEVEN

1 McMahon MS.
2 Cooper MS.
3 McMahon MS.
4 *Ibid.*
5 *Ibid.*
6 *Ibid.*
7 Cooper MS.
8 McMahon MS.
9 Court of Criminal Appeal, 22 Feb. 1975. Judgment.
10 *Ibid.*
11 McMahon MS.
12 Court of Criminal Appeal, 22 Feb. 1975. Judgment.
13 'An analysis of the transcript of Vol. 1 of Mathews's evidence
[*at the trial*] showing a detailed sighting of Murphy over a
sustained period of time in which he could describe in precise
detail his glasses, his coat (both colour and length even though
Murphy was sitting down at the time) and graphic descriptions
of him shouting and vaulting into a car demonstrates the real
mendacity of this judgment' (Brief to Cooper's Counsel for
Appeal, 7 July 1976).
14 Cooper MS.
15 *The Times.* Article by Bryan Magee, 7 Mar. 1975.
16 McMahon MS.
17 *Ibid.*

CHAPTER TWELVE

1 Cooper MS.
2 Affidavit of James Humphreys, July 1976 to Bindman &
Partners.
3 Affidavit of William Slade, 8 Nov. 1975.
Statement of William Slade to Detective Sergeant P. McMaster,
1 Jan. 1976.
4 Home Office to Registrar of Criminal Appeals, 8 Apr. 1976.
5 McMahon MS.
Cooper MS.
6 Affidavit of James Stanley Wilkinson to Bindman & Partners,
2 July 1976.
7 Cooper MS.
8 McMahon MS.
9 *Ibid.*
Cooper MS.
10 McMahon MS.
11 Court of Criminal Appeal, July 1976. Evidence of Mathews.

12 *Ibid.*
13 *Ibid.*
14 *Ibid.*
15 McMahon MS.
16 Cooper MS.
17 *Ibid.*
18 McMahon MS.
19 Cooper MS.
20 McMahon MS.
21 Court of Criminal Appeal, 22 July 1976. Judgment.
22 *Ibid.*

CHAPTER THIRTEEN

1 McMahon MS.
2 Court of Criminal Appeal, 22 July 1976. Judgment.
3 *The Times*, 2 Aug. 1976.
4 Cooper MS.
5 McMahon MS.
6 *Ibid.*
7 *Ibid.*
8 Cooper MS.

CHAPTER FOURTEEN

1 Affidavit of Richard Hurn to Bindman & Partners, 26 Apr. 1977.
Affidavit of Frederick Lawrence to Bindman & Partners, 19 Mar. 1977.
Statement of Frederick Lawrence to Detective Chief Superintendent Ranson, 20 July 1977.
2 Court of Criminal Appeal, 11 Apr. 1978. Opinion.
3 *Ibid.*
4 *Ibid.*
5 *McMahon:* Memorandum on the evidence of Richard Hurn, July 1978.

CHAPTER FIFTEEN

1 Cooper MS.
2 McMahon MS.